THIS BOOK
was donated to
L.I.F.E. BIBLE COLLEGE LIBRARY
by

Centinella Foursquare
Church

church_____

UNITED FOURSQUARE WOMEN

DATE DUE

GAYLORD 234   PRINTED IN U.S.A.

PASTORAL PSYCHOLOGY

Other Books by Dr. William Goulooze

A Manual for Ministers, Elders and Deacons

Pastor's Personal Record Book

A Young People's Life of Christ

A Young People's Heidelberg Catechism

A Young People's Confession of Faith

Intermediate Doctrinal Stories from the Old Testament

Intermediate Doctrinal Stories from the Gospels

Intermediate Doctrinal Stories from the Acts and Epistles

The Sovereignty of God in History

Consider Christ Jesus — Radio Sermons

Victory Over Suffering

Blessings Of Suffering

Pastoral Psychology

Applied Psychology in Pastoral Theology
in America

by

WILLIAM GOULOOZE, Th. D., D. D.

Professor at Western Theological Seminary
Holland, Michigan

3237

BAKER BOOK HOUSE

Grand Rapids   1954   Michigan

258
G

Library of Congress Catalog Card Number 54-11386

DEDICATION

This volume is affectionately dedicated to the
EIGHTH REFORMED CHURCH OF
GRAND RAPIDS, MICHIGAN

For their prayers and their loyalty during my pleasant and busy pastorate, 1931-1939, when I served this large and growing congregation.

For their grant of a leave of absence for post graduate study at the Free University of Amsterdam, the Netherlands.

ACKNOWLEDGMENT

I desire to express my sincere appreciation to all those who have made it possible for me to carry on the study and research required for the writing of this book. Their number is so large that I dare not venture to individualize. My thanks is no less genuine and warm.

I do want to make a few exceptions. I cannot refrain from publicly acknowledging my indebtedness to Professor Doctor J. Waterink of the Free University of Amsterdam, the Netherlands. Without his active interest, encouragement, and guidance this study would not have been completed.

A special word of thanks is also due to Dr. and Mrs. C. Baumann of Amsterdam, for their warm welcome and congenial fellowship tendered us during our residence in their city. My appreciation must likewise be expressed to the members of my family for their encouragement and coöperation during my pursuit of this study and the preparation of the manuscript.

All thanks is due our sovereign God and Jesus Christ, His Son, our Savior, for a marvelous recovery of health and strength which made possible the completion of this work. To Him be all the glory.

WILLIAM GOULOOZE

INTRODUCTION

An introduction should properly consist of a moderate and scholarly analysis of an author's work. In this instance, however, I find it difficult to restrain enthusiasm for this extraordinarily comprehensive study of the unified working of pastoral theology and psychological understanding.

Here is a thorough, intelligently conceived, well-balanced outline of the developing skills employable in the treatment of human nature. The book is buttressed by sound scholarship, extensive research, genuine common sense, and an authentic personal spiritual experience. Never, even for an instant, is there any wavering in loyalty to Jesus Christ as Lord and Saviour. While scrupulously maintaining the supremacy of the Gospel, the author, with keen insight, convincingly presents the thesis that modern scientific knowledge of human nature and tested psychological techniques may be used by clergymen in their pastoral work with great success.

The rather general notion that pastoral theology has only recently tended to assume the characteristics of an exact science is shown to be inadequate by the author's interesting history of theory and practice in this field from the early nineteenth century to the present time. This study reveals that certain procedures and formulas currently employed by pastors trained in psychological methodology were used decades ago, although perhaps in a more simple pattern, as a therapy for mental and spiritual health.

The book also contains a unique laboratory demonstration in the field of sickness and mental suffering. This is perhaps more fully documented in the author's inspiring book, VICTORY OVER SUFFERING, but in this volume it is impressively shown that matters of a spiritual nature may be handled reverently and yet in a manner designed to produce facts through data scientifically utilized and compiled.

Coming from the mind and heart of a theologian of undisputed standing, a professor in one of our soundest seminaries, this book makes of no effect the superficial criticism about substituting psychology for Christianity, a criticism which we are pleased to note is decreasingly voiced.

The thesis of this book is reverently and securely based on Scripture. Indeed, the reader and student of this volume will inevitably develop new enthusiasm for the Bible, discovering in it hitherto unrealized sources of penetrating insights into human nature. The Bible will grow upon him as an astonishing textbook of mind, soul, and even body therapy.

The author has sifted an amazing bibliography in the field under consideration to bring to the reader a survey of an extraordinarily wide range of thought.
One of the chief contributions of this book to serious students is the author's
remarkable assembling of literature dealing with pastoral theology as it relates
to psychological knowledge.

As one who for years has had a deep interest in the assistance that the personal counsellor may receive from psychology, and as a pastor who works daily
in close coöperation with psychiatrists and psychologists in a Church counselling clinic, I deem it an honor to write this introduction and to say that I believe this book is a "must" for all who desire to understand and help present-
day people.

NORMAN VINCENT PEALE

Marble Collegiate Church
Fifth Avenue and 29th Street
New York City, New York

*Dr. Norman Vincent Peale is pastor of the large famous Marble Collegiate
Church of New York City; radio speaker of the program, "The Art of Living";
author of "A Guide to Confident Living" and of other books which reflect the
heart of a sympathetic pastor: an understanding insight into human nature,
and a triumphant faith for victorious living. Dr. Peale conducts a large and
effective church clinic for the mental and spiritual problems of people who flock
his church. He is in constant demand all over the nation for lectures, preaching
and clinical advice which come from his rich and vast experience with people.*

TABLE OF CONTENTS

Introduction by Dr. Norman Vincent Peale 9

PART I. HISTORICAL ANALYSIS
of Pastoral Theology in Relation to Our Time

CHAPTER I. OUR TIME OF CRISIS
A. The Psychological Crisis 17
B. The Crisis in Applied Psychology 17
C. The Social Crisis 18
D. The Nervous Tension Crisis 20
E. Pastoral Psychology for the Crisis 21

CHAPTER II. BEGINNINGS IN PASTORAL THEOLOGY, BEFORE 1850
A. The Person of the Pastor 26
B. Experience and Common Sense Method 28
C. Systematic Visitation 29
D. Individual Case Study 30
E. Pastoral Counseling 32
F. Biblical Application 33

CHAPTER III. DEVELOPMENT IN PASTORAL THEOLOGY, 1850-1900
A. The Person of the Pastor 35
  1. Personal Experience of the Pastor 35
  2. Personal Manners of the Pastor 35
  3. Personal Devotion of the Pastor 36
B. Organized Pastoral Theology 37
C. Pastoral Visiting 39
  1. Systematic Visitation 39
  2. Specified Visitation 39
  3. Sick Visitation 40
D. Individual Case Study 41
  1. Importance of Case Study 41
  2. Examples of Case Study 42
  3. Classifications of Individuals 42
E. Pastoral Counseling 43
  1. Counseling Opportunities 43
  2. Counseling Suggestions 44

F. Applied Scripture 45

G. Applied Psychology 45

   1. Psychological Understanding of Community 46

   2. Psychological Understanding of Human Nature 47

   3. Psychological Understanding of Individuals 47

CHAPTER IV. APPLICATION IN PASTORAL THEOLOGY, 1900 TO THE PRESENT

A. The Person of the Pastor 49

B. Knowledge of Human Nature 52

C. Individual Case Study 54

D. The Sociological Approach 57

E. Pastoral Counseling 60

PART II. RESEARCH ANALYSIS

Concerning Sickness, Suffering and Sorrow
in Relation to Pastoral Psychology

CHAPTER V. QUESTIONNAIRE INVESTIGATION OF SICKNESS, SUFFERING AND SORROW

A. The First Questionnaire 65

B. The Final Questionnaire 66

C. People Who Received the Questionnaire 69

CHAPTER VI. QUESTIONNAIRE RETURNS ON SICKNESS, SUFFERING AND SORROW

A. Experiences Reported 71

B. Lessons Learned from Afflictions 72

C. Choice Selections of Scriptural and Poetic Help for the Sick and
    Suffering 76

D. Recommendation of Other Afflicted People 77

PART III. CONSTRUCTIVE ANALYSIS

of Pastoral Psychology

CHAPTER VII. COORDINATION BETWEEN PASTORAL THEOLOGY AND PSYCHOLOGY

A. Our Times Require It 81

B. Pastoral Theology Needs Psychology 83

C. Obstacles in the Way of Proper Coördination between Pastoral
    Theology and Psychology 84

   1. Imperfect Definitions of Religion 84

   2. Imperfect Conception of God 86

D. Separation of Pastoral Theology and Psychology 91
E. Coördination between Pastoral Theology and Psychology 92

CHAPTER VIII. CONVERSION
A. The Biological Interpretation of Conversion 97
B. Interpretation of the Soul 100
C. Biological-Psychological-Spiritual Conversion 103

CHAPTER IX. SICKNESS, SUFFERING, AND SORROW
A. The Importance of sickness, Suffering, and Sorrow 108
B. Mental Illness Must Be Faced 110
C. The Reason for Illness 112
D. Attitudes of Afflicted People 113
E. Cultivation of Mental, Physical and Spiritual Hygiene 115

CHAPTER X. CHRISTIAN LIVING
A. The Meaning of Christian Living 120
B. The Place of the Pragmatic in Christian Living 123
C. The Importance of Sex in Christian Living 125
D. Complete Christian Living Through Personality Development 131

PART IV. TECHNIQUE ANALYSIS
of Pastoral Psychology

CHAPTER XI. QUALIFICATIONS OF THE PASTOR
A. The Minister Himself 141
B. Seminary Training 144
C. Ministerial Training 147

CHAPTER XII. KNOWING LIFE SITUATIONS
A. Emphasis in Pastoral Theology 150
B. Individual Life Situations 151
C. Group Study 154

CHAPTER XIII. SYSTEMATIC COUNSELING
A. Significance in Pastoral Theology 156
B. Benefits of Psychology for Pastoral Counseling 157
C. District Advantages of the Minister as Counselor 160
D. A Protestant Conference 161
E. Systematic Family Visitation 167
F. Systematic Use of Scripture 172

CHAPTER XIV. MINISTER AND DOCTOR

    A. Emphasis in Pastoral Theology 177

    B. Coöperation Between Doctor and Minister 179

    C. The Duty of the Physician in This Coöperation 181

    D. The Duty of the Pastor in This Coöperation 184

        1. He Must Develop the Proper Attitude..................... 184

        2. The Minister Must Overcome the Preaching Complex 187

        3. The Minister Must Not Pose as a Psychiatrist 189

        4. The Minister Must Have Proper Bearing 191

        5. The Minister Must Have Purposed Conversation 193

CHAPTER XV. COMMISSIONED SPIRITUAL AMBASSADORS

    A. The Minister Must Know God through Christ 195

    B. The Minister Must Know God Himself 198

    C. The Minister Must Know His Commission 202

SELECTED BIBLIOGRAPHY

    I. Our Psychological-Social Crisis 213

    II. Pastoral Theology 214

    III. Psychology 219

        A. Principles of Psychology 219

        B. Applied Psychology 223

        C. Psychoanalysis 224

        D. Freud 224

        E. Personality Development 225

    IV. Pastoral Psychology 226

        A. Principles 226

        B. Christian Life 228

        C. Sickness-Health 230

        D. Sex and Family Life 231

        E. Effects of War 231

        F. Physical, Mental and Spiritual Hygiene 232

        G. Counseling 233

    V. Articles 234

INDEX OF AUTHORS AND MATERIAL

    I. Bible References 239

    II. Author References and Material References 241

Part I
HISTORICAL ANALYSIS

CHAPTER I

Our Time of Crisis

IT HAS become trite for historians and psychologists to say that the age in which we live is the most crucial in the world's history. In every age there have been those who contended that their particular age was the most revolutionary the world had ever known. Even so, we believe that we may safely assert that we are now at the very turning point of history. The crisis touches every phase of life.

A. The Psychological Crisis

At the very center of life and at every point on the circumference of experience the crisis of our time is fused and focused with the prevalent psychological interpretations. In trying to understand human nature the science of psychology has brought about a crisis in the interpretation and experience of psychological influences. E. D. Martin described the issue, "The psychological point of view is today making changes in the world's thinking which are perhaps as great as were those which resulted from Darwin's work in the nineteenth century."[1] The very atmosphere of psychological investigation has made us psychology conscious. Our times have been particularly opportune for psychological investigation, and psychologists have been very aggressive to formulate and practice their theories.

In the process psychology has inflated its own technique and claims. Psychology has done this in a spirit of ridicule for traditional pastoral theology. "There is a glamour about psychology that tends to exaggerate its possibilities."[2] The spirit of exaggerations, without due regard for the findings and conclusions of writers in the field of pastoral theology, has brought about a spirit of resentment on the part of conservative scholars of human life and behavior.

B. The Crisis in Applied Psychology

We cannot pass the discussion of our crisis on to a few schoolmen or philosophers without feeling the very pull of the perplexing problems in everyday living. The field of psychology has reached into every part of our experience for the purpose of exploration and direction. This forces the crisis for every life, because applied psychology claims to study and solve the problems of every individual.

---

1. E. D. Martin, *Psychology*, Peoples Institute Publishing Co., New York, 1924, p. 1.
2. Eric S. Waterhouse, *Psychology and Pastoral Work*, Cokesbury Press, Nashville, 1940, p. 5.

Applied psychology reaches down into every phase of industrial, cultural, economic, emotional and spiritual living. While it was intended as an aid and asset, its dangers and extremes often precipitated a crisis. The problem is more serious than a mere surface disagreement, because the dispute has been with respect to fundamental aim and purpose.[3]

After reviewing the writings of ten psychologists and concluding that no three agreed as to religious consciousness, G. A. Coe[4] pointed to the fact that this disagreement ought not to be considered a weakness but rather a sign of vitality. While it is true that difference of opinion among interpreters of any given science may show vitality in disagreement, it is equally true that the extremes and extravagances in the study and application of psychology have continued until this day, thus giving as much evidence of weakness as vitality.

While we cannot expect psychologists to agree in detail, the proposed theories have been so varied that many have despaired of their usefulness. This divergence of thought and conviction in psychology has caused many writers on pastoral theology to steer clear of the views proposed. The findings and failures of psychology in the discovery and direction of interpreting religious impulses, emotions, reflexes and complexes have given cause for disturbance and distrust. The proponents and adherents of applied psychology have carried interpretations and applications farther than first intended. The advice of H. L. Hollingworth and A. T. Poffenberger is very much to the point:

> "One of the great dangers of applied psychology is that too much may be expected of it, and that it may be extended into fields where it is not prepared to go. In fact, its great popularity has led some venturous spirits to carry it quite beyond the zone of safety."[5]

C. The Social Crisis

The crisis of our times is aggravated and intensified because of the social structure and strife in modern life. Great social changes have taken place overnight. We have changed the very framework of life in the last decades. Before the turn of the century we thought of the Protestant Reformation and the French Revolution as great upheavals in the history of thought and life. In the last few years the sledge-hammer blows of modern life have changed the world with thought and actions so that our times seem more revolting than the Protestant Reformation and the French Revolution.

Discerning writers have evaluated the stage of our social crisis. P. A. Sorokin of Harvard stated, "We are seemingly between two epochs: the dying Sensate culture of our magnificent yesterday, and the coming Ideational culture of the creative tomorrow."[6]

---

3. Robert Sessions Woodworth, *Dynamic Psychology*, Columbia University Press, New York, 1918, p. 20.

4. George Albert Coe, *The Psychology of Religion*, University of Chicago Press, Chicago, 1916, p. ix.

5. Harvey Livi Hollingworth and A. T. Poffenberger, *Applied Psychology*, A. Appleton and Co., New York, 1920, pp. 18, 19.

6. P. A. Sorokin, *The Crisis of Our Age*, E. P. Dutton and Co., Inc., New York, 1942, p. 13.

E. S. Waterhouse[7] described our age as being different with respect to three aspects of life: (1) We have universal education, and still we should say that we are only half educated. (2) We now experience a tremendous industrial revolution which began two hundred years ago. Mass production, intensive advertising, and the increased tempo of life increase our difficulties. (3) A third feature of the present age is the post-war problem. This curse is typified by the sex-obsession of our modern novels.

> "The changes of the present century have made more difference to the social life of the land than those of the whole time since the Reformation. That is why this age is, much more than its predecessor, a new age. It is so new that it has not found itself."[8]

All that has happened since Waterhouse wrote his book in 1940 re-enforces his interpretation of our time. Social and psychological stimuli have been even more radical since that time. Today in many circles group interpretation has been substituted for individual volition. Crowd psychology has taken the place of personal conscience, and union bargaining has taken the place of private coöperation. Political machinery has been substituted for Americanism, while the sensational and sexual has been emphasized at the expense of the spiritual. In place of principles of conduct based on the Bible, the expedient and expressional have held sway. In short, we have substituted man in place of God. The trend is away from God. Psychologically this affects our outlook, prospect, and conduct.

The second World War increased the tempo and trial of our time. This war surpassed the first World War in intensity, cost, extensiveness and damage. It trampled upon the rights of the civilian and the lives of soldiers alike. All of us would like to forget this gigantic conflict, but we find it impossible. Highly mechanized combat, air bombings of soldiers and civilians, together with atomic bombs of shattering proportions, have made this war the most devastating in all history.

> "The logic of the situation which the atomic bomb symbolizes is as follows. Though the atomic bomb is the fruit of science, the solution of the problem is not a matter of science, since it is admitted that there is no technological defense. The only hope, therefore, lies in world organization . . . But since the world organization is dependent upon the trustworthiness of those concerned, the ultimate question is ethical rather than merely scientific or even political. The only answer to atomic power is more power."[9]

Not only has the atomic age produced devastation of property; it has also shattered nerves and ideals. E. Trueblood quoted a significant statement of Albert Schweitzer to this effect in another of his books, "We are living today

---

7. Waterhouse, op. cit., pp. 34-51.

8. Ibid., p. 40.

9. Elton Trueblood, *Foundations for Reconstruction*, Harper and Brothers, New York, 1946, p. 8.

under the sign of the collapse of civilization. The situation has not been produced by the war; the latter is only a manifestation of it."[10]

We must not make the mistake of "prolonging the war" by means of constant reference to it and the consequences which have come about by this horrible conflict. On the other hand we cannot escape the fact that this tremendous catastrophe has precipitated our present crisis. Its casualties linger in the hospitals and its mental cases crowd our institutions. The catastrophe continues to take its toll of lives by way of disappointment, mental derangement, physical disabilities, social maladjustment, and immorality. It has immeasurably accentuated the psychological, social, ethical, moral and spiritual perplexities of life. The war is over, but the net results of this mighty conflict will remain a part of our crisis for generations.

We cannot help knowing that this crisis exists — because it touches all of life. It has tensioned people in every phase of living. People live under tremendous pressure and their emotions are strung to a very high pitch. "Culturally we live in momentous times. We are the spectators in the closing scenes of a long and devastating war between science and religion."[11] The clash between science and religion has come to a head because of the war in Europe, since it has affected the entire world. And we are more than spectators; we are a part of this social and cultural structure now undergoing submarine changes of which we may not be fully aware. We are the actors as well as the observers of this undercurrent conflict. More than we realize, we are psychologically affected by the crisis of our time.

The needs of modern man in the present crisis are felt by a host of writers[12] and all of them are desperately aware of the fact that our social stimuli play a tremendous role in individual psychological reactions. All of them are deeply conscious of the multiple reactions of the individual in our so-called *streamlined society*.

D. *The Nervous Tension Crisis*

Our present crisis, stimulated by the psychological point of view and intensified by multiplied social changes, finds expression in a serious nervous tension. Living in our day, one cannot escape the nervous strain which is prevalent in modern society. We are influenced by the modern radio, newspaper, magazine,

10. Elton Trueblood, *The Predicament of Modern Man*, Second Edition, Harper & Brothers, New York, 1944, p. 1.
11. Raymond B. Cattell, *Psychology and the Religious Quest*, Nelson and Sons, Ltd., New York, 1938, p. 9.
12. Robert S. Carroll, *The Mastery of Nervousness*, The Macmillan Co., New York, 1917, p. 5.
S. H. Kraines and E. S. Thetford, *Managing Your Mind*, The Macmillan Co., New York, 1943, pp. 1-64.
Karl R. Stolz, *Pastoral Psychology*, Cokesbury Press, Nashville, 1932, pp. 15-24.
Carroll A. Wise, *Religion in Illness and Health*, Harper & Brothers, New York, 1942, pp. 3-12.
Gregory Zielboorg and G. W. Henry, *A History of Medical Psychology*, W. W. Horton & Co., Inc., 1941, p. 175.

and our rapid methods of transportation. Much of it is due to the weakness designated by Waterhouse as "headline mentality."[13] People are motivated by newspaper headlines. The newspaper molds their thinking, whips their nerves with epitomized sensational news interpretations, interprets life without proper evaluation, and increases the nervous tension of each day and every individual with a "stepped up" tempo.

The nervous tension of our time is very evident and no one aware of present day thinking and problems dares deny it. Says Preston Bradley:

> "The complexity of modern life makes ever increasing demands on the individual. The strain is evidenced not only in failures of confidence and courage for business and social life, but also, and most obviously, in the physical breakdown of man."[14]

Our nervous tension is the composite representation and conglomeration of the sexual, social, and psychological emphasis of our time. It finds expression in our complexes, and is explained in the common description, "high strung."

E. Pastoral Psychology for the Crisis

The crisis of our time touches the entire field of operation for the minister of the gospel. He cannot escape recognizing this problem and he should not avoid doing his part to solve it. The psychologist cannot present a balanced solution or contribution without due regard to the Bible. The minister has a special duty in this connection.

> "We are living in an age of peculiar psychical unrest, and the religious mind will not deem it apart from the providential ordering of God that important psychological discoveries should give the key to the allaying of that unrest."[15]

The Christian minister ought to believe this and as he proclaims the full counsel of God through the Bible, he ought to go all the way with a proper application of psychology for the satisfactory solution of our crisis. The minister must remember that psychology can teach him a great deal about human nature and about abnormal religious experience. It is true that applied psychology and psychoanalysis have been sadly overworked, but it is equally true that both have been overlooked by pastors.

The minister has a tremendous responsibility as a result of the findings of psychology. Revolutionary theories and applications have taken place since the average minister attended seminary. Most of his training in this area of investigation and service was very limited. The crisis for the minister increases year by year, and if he fails to utilize all his opportunities for study and investigation, he stands condemned for professional neglect. Pastoral psychology should engage his active interest if he wishes to minister properly to the complete personality development of his constituent members. The pastor should master the application of psychology for his field of activity.

---

13. Waterhouse, op. cit., p. 35.
14. Preston Bradley, *Mastering Fear*, The Bobbs-Merill Co., New York, 1935, p. 149.
15. W. Fearon Halliday, *Psychology and Religious Experience*, Hodder and Stoughton, London, 1929, p. 35.

> "Psychology, the science of human nature, has developed many vagaries, and has often been non-Christian and anti-Christian, but, aside from the study of the Scripture is perhaps the most important single subject which should be mastered by one who all his life must deal at first hand with people."[16]

In our revolutionary days, pastoral work is becoming increasingly important and difficult. Hyper-psychological stimuli, the tension of our times, and the nervous strain so prevalent in our day not only affect the parishioners in an average congregation; they also stimulate the minister in every experience of pastoral service. This presents increased difficulties.

> "The cure of souls is an ancient and honorable function of the Christian Church and the Christian minister. In our day, however, its practice is both peculiarly urgent and particularly difficult."[17]

Our times demand the best in knowledge and application. "It is not merely the standard of efficiency that needs to be raised to the level of that of other professions; the whole conception of pastoral theology needs to be lifted to a higher plane."[18] This level can be raised if we face psychology and all of its extremes with an open mind, founded on the Word of God. We may not condemn the writings and findings of psychology to the academic waste basket.

Christianity must minister to the total experience of life. It has often failed to do so. It is the task of the Christian minister to utilize all the powers of modern science in order to make Christianity the power of life it was intended to be by its founder, Jesus Christ. Psychology can help in this interpretation and application, according to E. M. Ligon.[19] We hasten to add that psychology can help to such a degree as God's true ministers of unadulterated Christianity seek to apply pastoral psychology to the life of the people. The connecting link for most people is the minister of the gospel who through the agency of pastoral psychology is interested in character building, personality development, and a Christian community consciousness, all of which is dominated by the Lord Jesus Christ, as Savior and Lord.

> "The world is sick and in need of a great physician, which waits only on the confession of our disability and our faith. The people of our day are bewildered, as sheep that have no shepherd, and the tragedy of it is that the Shepherd and the fold are there."[20]

This is a new day and a new crisis must be met. Old fashioned methods in the pastorate need the new application of modern findings. We cannot say that the old is good enough and new techniques are not necessary.

---

16. Gaines S. Dobbins, "Theological Education in a Changing Social Order," *The Review and Expositor*, Vol. XXXII, No. 2, April, 1935, pp. 193, 194.
17. Charles T. Holman, *The Cure of Souls — A Socio-Psychological Approach*, The University of Chicago Press, Chicago, 1932, p. ix.
18. Carl F. Rogers, *An Introduction to the Study of Pastoral Theology*, Clarendon Press, Oxford, 1912, p. 5.
19. Ernest M. Ligon, *The Psychology of Christian Personality*, The Macmillan Co., New York, 1935, p. vii.
20. Halliday, op. cit., p. 308.

"Many a minister of the Gospel who is able to preach effectively to an audience of five hundred persons is tragically impotent when face to face with one individual involved in a crisis. Although trained in the science and art of public ministrations, many have assumed the responsibilities of the pastoral relation without adequate preparation. Pastoral psychology was not taught in theological seminaries when the majority of pastors now in active service were students."[21]

And just because we have lacked this training in the past, we hesitate to welcome it now. Tragically enough, we meet with many individuals who need the kind of advice such training offers ministers. Too often we have taken what we thought would fit into our own merry way. Our crisis demands a new attitude on the part of the minister.

We must develop a Christian psychology and use all its contributions in the field of pastoral theology. The two must be made to work hand in hand for a Scriptural pastoral psychology. Our crisis spells unbounded opportunity because, more than we realize, we can be used of God to show the world the right way out of our prevalent complexes. In analysing this situation, F. Kunkel discussed the various psychologies and showed the predicament of modern man. One of his conclusions directs us to our specific responsibility.

"Finally it became clear, at least to some observers, that Christianity only was in possession of the key which would unlock the door to new life and culture, both for the individual and for nations. But the key did not yet work. The people to whom it was entrusted evidently did not know how to use it. They knew the key, but they did not know the lock and consequently were unable to enter the basement of the human mind where the powerful dynamos operated. Mankind was afraid of its own high voltage, and nobody knew how to deal with its power."[22]

When a medical doctor speaks in such a way, it is time for the minister to rise to the situation. Kunkel continued the challenge by stating that we need new faith for our modern predicament and a new application and collaboration between psychology and religion.[23] As ministers of the gospel we hold the key and through the work of the Holy Spirit we have some understanding of the lock of life. We face untold possibilities in the field of applied pastoral psychology.

This clarion call from the white harvest fields of burdened souls and bleeding hearts must be answered. The response through pastoral psychology may not be divorced from the gospel and the Biblical method of shepherding. It includes all of this, for only in this way can we really bring the Bible and Christ's salvation to a lost world and a dying civilization. This is our wonderful day of privilege.

"The opportunity of the clergyman has come. He can bring a divinely human Bible as the ground of his faith and appeal. He can bring the Lord the Healer; not a dumb and deaf and blind principle, but a loving Father to the help of his needy children. He can bring the real Christ of the New Testament — Emmanuel — God with us, to speak again the words, and give again the touch, and extend the hand to those possessed with the demons of unrest, disquiet, and bodily ills."[24]

---

21. Karl R. Stolz, *Pastoral Psychology*, Cokesbury Press, Nashville, 1932, p. 11.
22. Fritz Kunkel, *In Search of M..urity*, Charles Scribner's Sons, New York, 1943, p. 23.
23. Ibid., pp. 28, 29.
24. Samuel Fallows, *Health and Happiness, or Religious Therapeutics and Right Living*. Third edition, A. C. McClurg & Co., Chicago, 1909, pp. 87, 88.

Though these words were written back in 1909, their impact and appropriateness are very much to the point today. Ours is the task of bringing all the best influences of pastoral psychology to people who are blundering and broken in our generation.

The real essence of our crisis is a spiritual problem. At the heart of the difficulty is the spiritual relationship of man over against God. We contradict modern popular opinion when we make this assertion, but we agree with God's portrait of man recorded by Paul in Romans three and Romans seven. The very basis of pastoral theology means the total depravity of man and the need of divine redemption. And this must be the basis of a Scriptural scientific pastoral psychology. Therefore we have presented this urgent discussion on the crisis of our time. Without a real consideration for the full implications of this crisis, we cannot develop a genuine pastoral psychology for our day. We must be fully aware of the situation.

> "The sober truth is that, as a people, we do not believe we are engaged in a race with catastrophe. We are not aware of the dangers we face, and consequently we are doing relatively little to meet them. If we could put the same keen intelligence and careful judgment into the revival of faith and the discovery of the proper objects of faith that we now put into the production of magnificent machines, man's life on this earth might come to a new and glorious day. We fail to do this because we do not read the signs of the times or listen to our prophets."[25]

In this first chapter, we have tried to show the crisis of our time. Our psychological, social and nervous tension crisis demands a new pastoral psychology. By this we do not mean to say that true physicians of the soul have not appeared. A noble work has been done. One has but to read the grand story of noble spiritual physicians of the ongoing church through the centuries of time. C. F. Kemp in his book, *Physicians of the Soul*,[26] has given the romantic story about God's faithful pastors of bygone years. A noble work has been done by pastors and we set ourselves to review this in the historical section of this thesis — in order to demonstrate that much of the old, both in plan and practice, has been retained and modernized in our day. A study of this historical analysis follows the first chapter on the "Crisis of Our Time" and will evidence perspective, purpose and point for our study.

Part II of this study deals with the "Research Analysis" on the subject of sickness, suffering and sorrow. Research in this field is necessary, for our age is definitely an age of suffering and sorrow because of our fratricidal tendencies and our frustrating tensions. The purpose of Part II is to give first hand information of experience so that we may build a constructive analysis of our subject.

Part III is the "Constructive Analysis" of our project. Having studied the history of the original research in the area of experience it becomes necessary to set forth a constructive analysis as to basic principles, concepts and purpose.

---

25. Trueblood, *The Predicament of Modern Man*, op. cit., p. 19.
26. C. F. Kemp, *Physicians of the Soul*, The Macmillan Co., New York, 1947, pp. 3-66.

In Part III such relationships are determined, and the true theological Biblical basis is set forth as the only foundational ground on which to build a constructive plan and program for effective pastoral psychology.

Part IV completes this dissertation by dealing with the "Technique Analysis" necessary to bring into action and fruition the findings of history, the discoveries in the area of research, and the constructional framework and basis of our thinking on the subject of pastoral psychology. In Part IV the application, the *how to do it,* the methodology of actually accomplishing the work has been set forth. The four parts together demonstrate the wholeness of the treatise and the separate parts consecutively studied and analyzed. Only then can we meet the present "Crisis of Our Time" with an adequate pastoral psychology thoroughly based on the Word of God.

CHAPTER II

Beginnings in Pastoral Theology, Before 1850

WHEN pastoral theology came to the shores of America from Europe it was beyond its virgin state as a science. Its development in America has been particularly significant because of our American way of life. The American church has had a specific and peculiar development because of the European heritage and because of the unusual characteristics of American Christianity. This has also influenced the writers of pastoral theology because theological concepts and practices reflect themselves in the life and conduct of the pastor. The periods of pastoral theology in American history have each demonstrated specific characteristics — distinguished in trends and in variation of these trends. The three periods can be designated as (1) Beginnings, (2) Development and (3) Application — and in this and the following two chapters, these will be discussed.

In the period of beginnings in pastoral theology, the subject of this particular chapter, definite characteristics can be traced. The first of these is reflected in the person of the pastor.

A. The Person of the Pastor

The person of the pastor was strongly emphasized during the history of pastoral theology up to 1850, the year which marks the end of the period of beginnings. R. Baxter, in, *The Reformed Pastor*, set the pattern of this trend. The main part of Baxter's book was built on the text,

> "Take heed unto yourselves and to all the flock of God over which the Holy Ghost hath made you overseers, to feed the church of God which he hath purchased with is own blood."[1]

Part I of his book deals with, "The Oversight of Ourselves"[2] — the nature and the motives of this oversight. A few typical statements from Baxter demonstrate his emphasis on the person of the pastor:

> "Content not yourselves with being in a vigorous and lively exercise, and that you preach to yourselves the sermons which you study, before you preach them to others."[3]
> "Study and pray and confer and practice for in these four ways your abilities must be increased."[4]

---

1. Acts 20:28.
2. Richard Baxter, *The Reformed Pastor*, Revised Edition, The Westminster Press, Philadelphia, 1829, p. 89.
3. Ibid., p. 100.
4. Ibid., p. 114.

The context of these statements re-enforce his conviction about the person of the pastor. He warned to be very careful with respect to motives since the minister is always exposed to greater temptations than others and his sins have greater consideration because of the honor of Christ.

Other writers of this period also stressed the importance of the person of the pastor. The lectures of J. Smith[5] are largely a discussion of the manner of life of the pastor. E. Pond devoted the first lecture of his book to the piety, strong faith, love of Christ, love of souls, intellectual endowments and common sense.[6] The same evaluation was placed on the pastor by G. Herbert when he wrote, "The pastor is the deputy of Christ for the reducing of man to the obedience of God."[7]

Practical advice, bearing on the person of the pastor was also given in *The Pastor's Manual*. A few statements from one of the tracts, "Pastoral Cautions,"[8] illustrate the point. This particular tract was written by A. Booth, who indicated:

> "Take heed that your pastoral office prove not a snare to your own soul by lifting you up with pride and self importance."[9]
> "It is of such high importance that a pastor possess the government of his own temper, and a tolerable share of prudence, when presiding in the management of church affairs, that, without these, his general integrity, though undisputed, and his benevolence, though usually considered as exemplary, will be in danger of impeachment among his people."[10]
> "Hence, the ministers of Christ are commanded, in all things to show themselves a pattern of good works; to be examples to believers in word, in conversation, in charity, in spirit, in faith, in purity."[11]

A. Booth, the author of the tract just quoted, made the same emphasis in another tract by the same title, "Pastoral Cautions," printed in, *The Christian Pastor's Manual*.[12] He admonished the pastor to find religion in his own soul, to develop the gentleness and meekness of Christ, to take heed to temper, to beware of coveteousness, to remember his conscience and the necessity of giving account of stewardship.

Near the close of the period of beginnings, two men J. A. James and W. Meade reiterated the importance of the pastor as a person. The first mentioned, J. A. James, emphasized the viewpoint of sincerity and earnestness as a characterization which should dominate the entire ministry. His chapter on, "Examples of Earnestness,"[13] based on the examples of Jesus, Paul and later leaders

5. John Smith, *Lectures on the Nature and End of the Sacred Office and on the Dignity, Duty, Qualifications and Character of the Sacred Order*, A. Neal, Baltimore, 1800, 300 pp.
6. Enoch Pond, *The Young Pastor's Guide*, E. F. Duren, Bangor, William Hyde, Portland, Tappan and Dennett, Boston, Ezra Collier, New York, and A. H. Maltby, New Haven, 1844, pp. 2-26.
7. George Herbert, *Country Parson*, Henry Washbourne, London, 1832, p. 1.
8. A. Booth, "Pastoral Cautions," from *The Pastor's Manual, A Selection of Tracts on Pastoral Duty*, Sawyer, Ingersoll and Co., Hudson, Ohio, 1852, pp. 354-389.
9. Ibid., p. 357.
10. Ibid., p. 359.
11. Ibid., p. 361.
12. A. Booth, "Pastoral Cautions," from *The Christian Pastor's Manual*, edited by J. Brown, J. Whethram, Philadelphia, 1837, pp. 72-108, particularly pp. 73, 78, 80-83.
13. John Angel James, *An Earnest Ministry*, Dodd, New York, 1948, pp. 167-180.

of the church, gave proof of his Biblical foundation. W. Meade made his point clear by saying, "The minister's office is emphatically the pastoral office. He is a shepherd of souls."[14] These references and others teach us with clear language that there was a very definite trend in this period of beginnings to emphasize the importance of the person of the pastor.

SUMMARY

The person and position of the pastor as indicated in the Bible and experienced in the pastorate demands his complete dedication and unselfish service.

B. Experience and Common Sense Method

The idea that experience in the pastorate is the best teacher and that this experience must be applied with practical common sense is the second trend of this period we wish to discuss. C. Bridges in *The Christian Ministry*,[15] discussed pastoral work and claimed that experience is the main teacher. He said:

> "Medical skill is gained much more by practical experience, than by any system of abstract and well-directed course of reading, and the writer is far from depreciating its value, yet he is persuaded that the study of the human heart, of our own heart most especially, is far more important."[16]

Likewise, G. Herbert's *Country Parson* [17] revealed reliance on experience and common sense in the titles given to the thirty-seven articles which comprise the book. Experience in praying, preaching, visiting, charity, comforting, and other varied pastoral contacts serve to show the emphasis on common sense as a technique for service.

The approach of E. Pond can be epitomized in the following:

> "A good judgment, sound discretion, plain practical common sense, the whole being under the guidance of the word and Spirit of God will be a minister's best dictionary in regard to his intercourse with those various characters which go to constitute his flock."[18]

His statement reflects the attitude of many writers in this period, even though it is difficult to harmonize his assertion with the following expression in his book, "There is danger, that in our Theological Seminaries, both the study and the practice of pastoral duties will be comparatively neglected."[19]

Objection to experience and common sense as the only teacher for pastoral duties was raised by A. Gerard when he complained about the poor conception of the pastoral office in his day. He deplored the idea that ministers considered preaching, dispensing the sacraments and answering a few occasional calls as the sum total of their duties. He maintained that the minister should do more

14. William Meade, *Lectures on the Pastoral Office*, Stanford and Swords, New York, 1949, p. 180.
15. Charles Bridges, *The Christian Ministry*, Volume 1, Jonathan Leavitt, New York, 1846, pp. 93-241.
16. Ibid., p. 134.
17. Herbert, op. cit., p. 160.
18. Pond, op. cit., p. 77.
19. Ibid., p. v.

than follow his own inclination and the common manner of conversation like other men. He pled for a better training. He said:

> "To fit them for the more private labours in a parish no means are ordinarily used. Yet a very little reflection will convince you, that there are many private duties essential to the pastoral office."[20]

Since only a few writers of this period sensed the inadequacy of experience and the common sense technique, it must be set down as a characteristic of the early writers, that they relied too heavily on practical experience and acquired common sense.

SUMMARY

Practical experience and sanctified common sense, while not entirely adequate for pastoral work, assured the minister's accomplishment and success.

C. Systematic Visitation

While this period was only a time of beginnings, the endeavor to discover and advance systematic visitation in the pastorate was evident. The number who recommended systematic visitation presents an encouraging feature of pastoral work.

The urge for visiting by emphasizing the need of knowing the people of the parish was stressed by G. Herbert. He reminded ministers to go to the people in their needs, to prepare for such visits, and to develop an acquaintanceship of God's general providence in order to satisfy the desires of the flock.[21] The neglect of systematic visiting by young clergymen prompted P. Green to write, "Visiting is the only thing that will bring you into contact with those who do not come of their own accord, but may be induced to do so if rightly handled."[22] This is the thrust of his second chapter entitled, "Parochial Visiting,"[23] in which he urged sympathetic understanding, house to house visiting, and the making of notes concerning calls and special visits — such as those on the sick, those of long illness, and the chronic cases. He included concern for the unsaved of the community when he wrote, "Get from the day schools the names and address of all children who live in the parish."[24]

E. Pond devoted two lectures[25] to the matter of visiting so that the pastor might know the sheep and bring spiritual benefits to the flock. His list of the various kinds of visits included the usual variety. He suggested that there should be as much system as possible in making these calls.[26]

---

20. A. Gerard, *The Pastoral Care*, Long, printed for T. Cadell, Jr., W. Davies in the Strand: and A. Brown at Aberdeen, 1789, p. 97.
21. Herbert, op. cit., pp. 50, 51.
22. Peter Green, *The Town Parson*, Longmans, Green and Co., London, New York, 1814, p. 40.
23. Ibid., pp. 34-77.
24. Ibid., p. 76.
25. Pond, op. cit., pp. 53-56.
26. Ibid., p. 64.

Mason's, "Student and Pastor,"[27] the first treatise in *The Young Minister's Companion*, illustrated detailed rules for systematic visitation of the sick. He specified three things which ought to be done by every pastor:

> "1 — To lay down some general rules to be observed in order to secure a right execution of this part of your duty, 2 — To specify some particular cases, and 3 — To adapt yourself to his taste and understanding, as well as to the circumstances of his case, by making such observations and using such expressions as you know are most familiar and agreeable to him."[28]

And he also stressed the preparation that was necessary for such systematic visitation when he wrote:

> "A previous preparation for it is very proper; by considering what kind of address will be most necessary and suitable to the person you visit. It is sometimes strange that ministers who take so much pains to prepare for the work of the pulpit, should generally take so little to prepare for this which is one of the most difficult and most important offices in the ministry."[29]

While it is true that C. Bridges devoted only a few pages to systematic visiting,[30] and J. Smith failed to stress the importance of a concerted plan for such visiting,[31] yet we cannot escape the underlying tone of pastoral theology in this period in the attempt to achieve systematic visitation.

SUMMARY

Plans, preparation and execution of systematic visitation particularly of the sick, are part of a well ordered ministry.

D. Individual Case Study

This interesting trend, so important to the modern study of pastoral psychology, was part of Baxter's emphasis in Part II, "The Oversight of the Flock," of his book, *The Reformed Pastor.*

> "It is our duty to take heed to all the flock, we must pay special attention to some classes in particular."[32] "We must labor in special manner for the conversion of the unconverted."[33] "We must study to build up those who are already truly converted."[34] "We must be ready to give advice to inquirers who come to us with cases of conscience."[35] "We must have a special eye upon families to see if they are well ordered, and the duties of each relation performed."[36] "We must be diligent in visiting the sick, and assisting to prepare either for a fruitful life or a happy death."[37] "We must reprove and admonish those who live offensively and impenitently."[38]

27. Mason, "Student and Pastor," in *The Young Minister's Companion*, Samuel T. Armstrong, Boston, 1813, pp. 1-99.
28. Ibid., pp. 73, 74.
29. Ibid., p. 74.
30. Bridges, op. cit., pp. 172-178.
31. Smith, op. cit., p. 228.
32. Baxter, op. cit., p. 144.
33. Ibid.
34. Ibid., p. 152.
35. Ibid., p. 147.
36. Ibid., p. 156.
37. Ibid., p. 159.
38. Ibid., p. 162.

Similar emphasis on individual cases can be seen in the classifications of Bishop Burnett.[39] He wrote a tract and insisted on the special responsibility of the minister to the sick, the troubled in mind and the dissenters. Though this was only a tract, its influence in pastoral theology was noteworthy.

The same characteristic is found in the work of C. Bridges, *The Christian Ministry.* His list of proposed classifications for pastoral duty includes the ignorant, the self-righteous, the false professor, those who have natural and spiritual conviction, the young Christian, the backslider, the unestablished Christian, and the confirmed and established Christian. All of these classifications are related to the Bible and illustrated with Bible texts and incidents.[40]

It is refreshing to discover the approach of A. Gerard. The following statement gives evidence of his splendid appreciation of individual needs:

> "In order to perform this duty properly, it is first of all necessary that a minister discover the particular situations and character of the person to whom he addresses himself, and that he adapts his admonitions carefully to them, for the same sort of exhortation does not suit all, and that may be useless or hurtful to one which is profitable to another. As no two men are absolutely undistinguishable in their faces, though every face be composed of the same features; so, though the powers of human nature, which are the ingredients in character, be possessed in common by all men, yet by means of the different degrees in which they are possessed, or the different forms which they assume, and of the different way in which they are combined, they produce such an infinite variety of characters, that no two are perfectly alike."[41]

Other writers of this period gave evidence of understanding the importance of individual study of people. P. Green wrote, "Clearly methods must differ as the case differs."[42] E. Pond included eight classes of individuals who need special attention; the ignorant, the degraded, the heretic or infidel, those who have received personal injury, those who are inquirers, some cases of protracted melancholy, some who have less hope than they ought to have, and those who are comforted, elevated and rejoicing.[43] And W. W. Everts listed a number of Bible texts for the sick room with classifications according to individual needs.[44] More than might be expected in this period of beginnings, the writers understood the importance of knowing and ministering to the needs of individuals.

SUMMARY

Classification of various individuals leads to a better understanding and performance of pastoral work.

---

39. Bishop Burnett, "Discourse of the Pastoral Care," in *The Young Minister's Companion or a Valuable Collection of Scarce Treatises on the Pastoral Office*, Samuel T. Armstrong, Boston, 1813, pp. 196-202.
40. Bridges, op. cit., pp. 146-172.
41. Gerard, op. cit., pp. 138, 139.
42. Green, op. cit., p. 58.
43. Pond, op. cit., pp. 77-93.
44. W. W. Everts, *Pastor's Hand Book*, Lewis Colby and Co., New York, 1848, pp. 14-26.

E. Pastoral Counseling

Closely allied to the importance of individual case study is the modern urge for counseling. It is very interesting to note that already in this early period, pastoral counseling was part of the minister's task. The following statement from R. Baxter would make anyone unfamiliar with the time of his writing, think that it was written in the last decade:

> "A minister is not to be merely a public preacher but to be known as a counsellor for their souls as a physician is for their bodies and a lawyer for their estates so that each man who is in doubts and straits may bring his case to him for resolution, as Nicodemus came to Christ as it was usual with the people of old to go to the priest, 'whose lips must keep knowledge, and at whose mouth they must ask the law because he is the messenger of the Lord of Hosts.' "[45]

As an indication of Baxter's method, we take note of his directions for dealing with people. Some of his suggestions are just like the modern technique of pastoral psychology. He outlined the following:[46] (1) Set their minds at ease. (2) Deal with the people as individuals. (3) Begin your work by taking account of what they have learned. (4) When they do not understand draw out their experience with expository questions. (5) Give them personal instruction. (6) Enquire as to their religious state. (7) If the individual is unconverted use powers of heart and mind to bring light to enquirer. (8) Conclude the whole with a practical exhortation. (9) Mollify their minds by a few words, deprecating anything like offence. (10) Keep record of the necessities of your parishioners. (11) Deal with people according to their particular characteristics. (12) Extend charity to the poor if possible. One would think these rules had been written by some modern student of pastoral counseling.

Likewise, A. Gerard anticipated the so-called modern find of pastoral counseling when he said:

> "Another private duty of the pastoral office, which may indeed be regarded as a branch of the former, but at the same time so peculiar in its nature as to deserve a separate illustration, is counseling, or giving people advice in cases of conscience, which they may propose to their minister."[47]

He superseded modern counseling methods when he suggested that particular counseling should be given to those who felt the loss of assurance of salvation. W. Meade included some excellent advice and rules for religious conversation.[48]

SUMMARY

Private counseling and exhortation by the pastor must be studied, sought, and diligently applied in efficient pastoral work.

---

45. Baxter, op. cit., pp. 149-151.
46. Ibid., pp. 331-355.
47. Gerard, op. cit., p. 147.
48. William Meade, *Lectures on the Pastoral Office*, Stanford and Swords, New York, 1849, pp. 184, 185.

F. Biblical Application

The Biblical emphasis in pastoral work found expression in 1839 by A. Barrett in his *Essay on the Pastoral Office*.[49] The purpose of his book was to place into the hands of young Wesleyan Methodist ministers a hand book that would give them the Scriptural view of the pastoral office. Many references to Baxter's book, *The Reformed Pastor*, indicate that the Biblical basis inaugurated by Baxter infiltrated into other pastoral theology literature.

H. Thompson in *Pastoralia* recommended Scripture texts and passages which may be used with individuals for the purpose of correction, repentance, patience, confidence in God, thankfulness to God's fatherly visitation and submission to the will of God.[50] Recommended passages were also given for the ignorant, the unbelievers, the melancholy, for baptism and confirmation. In much the same way the book of W. W. Everts, *A Pastor's Hand Book*,[51] indicates selections of Scripture arranged for various occasions. Part II is exclusively devoted to texts for the sick room and deals with sympathy for the afflicted, the sanctified and the unsanctified. The afflictions of Job, Hezekiah and Manasseh were described in Scriptural language.

C. Bridges[52] in discussing the various classes of individuals devoted almost an equal amount of material to the characteristics of the cases and their importance in relation to the Bible. He illustrated with texts, Biblical incidents and the life of Christ. And J. Smith [53] made the point that the Bible is the sole comfort for the sick and therefore must be used by the minister.

SUMMARY

The Biblical basis for and the application of Bible truth and Bible passages are essential to a correct understanding of the pastoral office and work.

Summarizing the entire period of beginnings, we take note of the characteristics and progress in definite trends of thought and practice. The shepherd idea of pastoral care as outlined in the Bible gave background and purpose to all pastoral theology in this period. This crystalized in the conception of the person of the pastor and his method of experience in dealing with people. The importance of individual attention came out of the Biblical practice of Jesus and His followers. Its consideration received greater emphasis than might be expected by students of modern pastoral psychology.

The foundations for systematic pastoral theology and its requirements were laid in this early period. More than is usually considered, there was a search after system, technique, and improvement. The modern techniques of pastoral counseling, personal attention to individual cases, and the alertness of our responsibility for the age in which we live, were given by these early writers.

---

49. Alfred Barrett, *Essay on the Pastoral Office*, John Mason, London, 1839, 370 pp.
50. Henry Thompson, *Pastorialia*, Second Edition, C. J. G. and R. Rivington, London, 1832, 263 pp.
51. Everts, op. cit., 80 pp.
52. Bridges, op. cit., pp. 146-171.
53. Smith, op. cit., 30 pp.

In reality that was a period of BEGINNINGS. They began in the right way, and placed many foundation stones for pastoral psychology. We do well to remember the principles they enunciated and the practices they set forth to complete their ministry unto the glory of Christ Jesus the head of the church.

Reading this first period of pastoral theology literature brings one the realization that these noble beginnings needed development. Our second phase of this historical research brings us to the actual development which took place during the time of 1850-1900. It is the province of the next chapter to study these developments and see just how the beginnings made in the first period were developed and realized.

CHAPTER III

Development in Pastoral Theology, 1850-1900

THE second period of American pastoral theology should be dated from 1850 to 1900. Definite characteristics manifest themselves during this period. Many of the underlying trends of the period of beginnings continue to be marked during the new period now under discussion. Their continuation and amplification indicate development and progress. In addition other influences and trends demonstrate our characteristic of this period which we call development in pastoral theology.

A. The Person of the Pastor

1. Personal Experiences of the Pastor

In discussing the person of the pastor, several writers made mention of the personal experience of the pastor as part of the development of pastoral life and expression. In his book, *The Young Parson*,[1] P. S. Davis narrated the pastoral experiences of a young man to show how a young minister meets life. The book was written in a personal and intimate way. E. Spooner followed much the same pattern in his, *Parson and People*.[2] These books reveal incidents, names, places, characteristic of personal experiences as part of pastoral work.

H. W. Smith made the point that young men must study the experiences and conduct of other ministers as well as books,[3] and W. W. How stressed the factors of experience such as personal holiness, devotional reading, and careful Bible study.[4] These writers and others gave evidence of the great influence of personal experience upon the person of the pastor.

2. Personal Manners of the Pastor

Emphasis on this aspect is another characteristic of the basic trend concerning the person of the pastor. S. Miller demonstrated a specific interest in this

1. Peter Seibert Davis, *The Young Parson*, Smith, English and Co., Philadelphia, 1863, 384 pp.
2. Edward Spooner, *Parson and People*, Bunce and Huntington, and James Pott, New York, 1866, 260 pp.
3. Henry Wallis Smith, *The Pastor as Preacher*, William Blackwood and Sons, Edinburgh and London, 1882, p. 44.
4. W. Walsham How, *Lectures on Pastoral Work*, Wells Gardner, Darton and Co., London, 1883, pp. 3-52.

phase of the subject and dealt with dignity, gentleness, cleanliness, conduct and pastoral conversation.[5] W. G. T. Shedd dealt with the subject and included the religious, intellectual and social character of the clergyman.[6] Characteristics and rules for conduct were included in his material. A. P. Peabody said:

> "The best way of keeping clear of these and all other faults is the constructive method — the building up of our characters continually in the strength and beauty of evangelic holiness."[7]

3. *Personal Devotion of the Pastor*

Closely allied to pastoral experience and pastoral manners is the matter of personal devotion. This phase of the subject received attention in this period. H. Crosby expressed it this way:

> "The true preacher must be one who has an enthusiastic love for his Lord and Saviour. He is not so much to preach a proposition as a person, and the power of the presentation will be proportioned to his love of the person."[8]

W. M. Taylor stated it thus, "Let your sympathy be real. Do not say that which you do not feel. But that you may feel rightly, keep yourself in close fellowship with Christ."[9] In discussing the qualifications necessary for the care of souls, J. M. Hoppin included self-knowledge, an attractive and friendly manner, adaptation to time, place, and occasion, a true absorbing love of souls, and an earnest, hopeful, and courageous faith.[10]

D. D. Demarest summarized his viewpoint in the following statement:

> "The Christian character of the minister should be harmonious and well rounded, every grace existing in due proportion. Viewed from any point in any light, he should be seen and confessed to be a 'man of God.' "[11]

Confirming this viewpoint, J. Love, Jr., wrote the following:

> "After all, the world is very much like a mirror. It reflects back the face you present to it. There are some who are so richly endowed that they are uniformly buoyant, surcharged with good nature."[12]
> "The poverty of our resources matters nothing if the power of God be superadded. The question is not, 'How much talent have I for service?' but 'How much do I possess of the Holy Spirit?' "[13]

---

5. Samuel Miller, *Letters on Clerical Manners and Habits*, Revised Edition, Presbyterian Board of Publication, Philadelphia, 1852, pp. 27-71.
6. William G. T. Shedd, *Homilitics and Pastoral Theology*, Eighth Edition, Scribner, Armstrong and Co., New York, 1876, pp. 324-387.
7. P. Peabody, "The Importance of Personal Character in the Ministry," *The Homilitic Review*, Vol. XXV, March, 1893, p. 200.
8. Howard Crosby, *The Christian Preacher*, Anson D. F. Randolph and Co., New York, 1879, p. 121.
9. William M. Taylor, *The Ministry of the Word, Anson D. F. Randolph and Co.,* New York, 1876, p. 267.
10. James M. Hoppin, *The Office and Work of The Christian Ministry*, Sheldon and Co., New York, 1869, pp. 531-541.
11. David D. Demarest, *Pastoral Theology*, Press of J. Heidingsfeld, New Brunswick, 1897, p. 43.
12. John Love., Jr., "Ministerial Blues," *Baptist Quarterly Review*, Vol. 14, 1892, p. 152.
13. Ibid., p. 157.

We conclude our documentation with respect to the importance of personal devotion as envisioned by writers of this period with two statements from C. W. Heisler:

> "The pastor must be a man of heart, even though that be at the cost of a great vital force. The pastor's heart, if he have any, is a reservoir into which are poured streams of complaint, of want, of wretchedness, of sorrow and trouble from all parts of the parish."[14]
>
> "I am persuaded that this is precisely what many of us pastors need — just this spirit of deep love for our own people in particular, and for souls in general, to transfuse our being and to transform our pastoral service."[15]

SUMMARY

The person of the pastor in both experience and expression should manifest mannerly habits and a sincere devotion to God and to the people of his parish.

B. Organized Pastoral Theology

The second basic trend of this period to be analyzed is the attempt to present the principles and practice of pastoral theology in organized and systematic form. The first attempt was by J. S. Cannon. With thirty years of pastorate experience and a professorate at New Brunswick Theological Seminary, he was qualified to write on the subject. His book of six-hundred seventeen pages, including a fine analytical table of contents, furnished a real contribution to the literature of pastoral theology. His definition of pastoral theology set the organized purpose before his readers:

> "Pastoral Theology is that branch of the science of Christian Theology which treats of the qualifications, duties, trials, encouragements, and consolations of the Evangelical Pastor."[16]

This work included nine chapters on the qualifications and the art of composing sermons. Part II was devoted to "Pastoral Duties." Visitation was designated in two forms, the general and the occasional.

F. Wayland[17] presented his material in the form of letters and included the minister's call, manner of preaching, and pastoral visitation. His work was written from the viewpoint of the minister and his service. Blending theory and practice in one book, P. D. Kidder wrote, *The Christian Pastorate.*[18] He was a minister for thirty-five years and a professor for fifteen years. The author began this work of twenty-three chapters with a discussion of the ministry as instituted by Christ; then he outlined the ministerial call, and followed it with a consideration of the minister as pastor, leader, preacher and visitor.

J. M. Hoppin gave his book, *The Office and Work of the Christian Ministry,*[19]

---

14. C. W. Heisler, "The Pastor Among His People," *Lutheran Quarterly*, Vol. 24, New Series, 1894, p. 487.
15. Ibid., p. 495.
16. James Spencer Canon, *Lectures on Pastoral Theology*, Charles Scribner, New York, 1853, p. 1.
17. Francis Wayland, *Letters on the Ministry of the Gospel*, Gould and Lincoln, Boston, 1863, 210 pp.
18. David Parrish Kidder, *The Christian Pastorate*, Nelson and Phillips, New York, 1871, 564 pp.
19. Hoppin, op. cit., 620 pp.

to this field of literature in 1869. He described the pastoral office, the pastor as man, his relation to society, and his relation to the church.

W. G. Blaikie presented organized material but mainly for effective preaching, devoting twenty chapters to this phase, while he used only three chapters on the subject of pastoral work.[20] W. A. Plummer devoted three of his thirty-two chapters to the pastoral work of the minister.[21] P. Fairbairn was more complete in his book, *Pastoral Theology*.[22] He defined the office, the duties, the call and the preaching responsibility of the minister. W. G. T. Shedd in his book, *Homilitics and Pastoral Theology*,[23] devoted five chapters to the work of the pastor. The work of T. Murphy, *Pastoral Theology*,[24] dealt with the pastor in his closet, study, pulpit, parochial work, activities in the church, in the courts of the church and in other denominations.

Pastoral Theology of the New Testament,[25] by J. Beck is different. All three parts reflect the Biblical emphasis with respect to the conception of the pastoral office. Jesus is used as a pattern for individual work, and the Sermon of the Mount is made the standard of conduct. New Testament terms are used and the work of the Apostles is stressed. The emphasis is on soul winning instead of shepherding.

The influence of two foreign works translated for use in America must be considered. The first is A. Vinet's *Pastoral Theology*.[26] While this book was translated as early as 1752, its real contribution to American thinking came during the period of development. It was during this period that Vinet's book was quoted by many writers. Vinet emphasized the difference between pastoral work in the city and in the country. According to this author, the three phases of the duty of pastoral oversight are the material, the moral and spiritual. His classification of individuals was twofold, the external and internal groups.

The work of J. J. Van Oosterzee, *Practical Theology*,[27] was translated from the Holland language in 1895. This work represents an excellent attempt to present an organized treatment of pastoral theology. It includes a history, foundation, explanation, and application for homilitics, catechetics, and pastoral work.

In the attempt to present a comprehensive view of pastoral theology many writers made the common mistake of including the entire range of practical

---

20. William Garden Blaikie, *For the Work of the Ministry*, Strahan and Co., London, 1873, pp. 275-328.

21. William A. Plummer, *Hints and Helps in Pastoral Theology*, Harper and Brothers, New York, 1874, 377 pp.

22. Patrie Fairbairn, *Pastoral Theology*, T. and T. Clark, Edinburgh, 1875, 351 pp.

23. Shedd, op. cit., 429 pp.

24. Thomas Murphy, *Pastoral Theology*, Presbyterian Board of Publication, Philadelphia, 1877, 500 pp.

25. J. T. Beck, *Pastoral Theology of the New Testament*, Translated from the German by J. A. M'Clymont, and T. Nicol, Scribner and Welford, New York, 1885, 348 pp.

26. Alexander Vinet, *Pastoral Theology*, Translated from the French, T. and T. Clark, Edinburgh, 1752, 387, pp.

27. J. J. Van Oosterzee, *Practical Theology*, Translated from the Holland language, Kemink en Zoon, Utrecht, 1895, 396 pp.

theology instead of limiting the material to the requirement of the title, *pastoral theology*. Another weakness of the writers of this period was that they regarded a part of pastoral work as the entire service which a minister should render in the field. Often this material reflected the personal experience and viewpoint of the author writing the particular volume. Nevertheless, we should express appreciation for their excellent attempts at organizing pastoral theology.

SUMMARY

These writers sought for a systematized and organized presentation of the material for the purpose of an improved ministry.

C. Pastoral Visiting

This period reveals a serious attempt to meet the ever urgent problem of pastoral visitation. This attempt had some rather well-defined characteristics.

1. Systematic Visitation

The best expression of the concept of systematic visitation characteristic of this period is found in S. Miller's *Letters on Clerical Manners and Habits*. He made a plea for official systematic visitation of individuals and families.[28] The following statement from his book makes his position clear:

> "With a rigorous adherence to system in performing this duty, unite habitual, persevering faithfulness. Let it be your study, in the fear of God, to render your visit, however short, as useful as possible to the individual or the family of which it is the object."[29]

He also included a set of rules for pastoral visits, and a set of suggestions for social visits.[30] W. G. T. Shedd contended for systematic visitation and added the thought that our visiting should be professional.[31] And C. W. Heisler said:

> "We believe thoroughly in a regular old-fashioned pastoral visit, conducted of course without stiffness, formality and mannerisms, yet always partaking of a religious character."[32]

T. Murphy made the same claim for the purpose of getting acquainted, knowing spiritual needs, and improved preaching.[33] He included a set of rules to accomplish the task.

2. Specified Visitation

This phase of pastoral visiting was outlined in duties for specific occasions and particularized requirements. J. S. Cannon specified two kinds of visiting: the *general* to all the families of the congregation, and the occasional or *particular* visit on the sick, the awakened and the troubled.[34] G. T. Bedell indi-

---

28. Miller, op. cit., pp. 139, 140.
29. Ibid., p. 141.
30. Ibid., pp. 139-168.
31. Shedd, op. cit., p. 396.
32. Heisler, op. cit., p. 496.
33. Murphy, op. cit., pp. 224 ff.
34. Canon, op. cit., 539-568.

cated specific modes of visiting, and a practical technique for the accomplishment of the task.[35] W. W. How distinguished between the general and the specific visit,[36] reminding his readers of the difficulty of knowing the exact condition of the individual soul.[37]

Both W. P. Tilden,[38] and G. B. Willcox,[39] wrote concerning the danger of allowing the preaching interest to overshadow the importance and performance of specific pastoral visiting. Both recognized the danger and urgency of the increased pressure of the times in which ministers serve. T. L. Cuyler distinguished between two classes of people who needed treatment, those in the fold and those outside of Christ.[40] He also suggested that pastoral work is something to be learned by daily specified visiting.[41] In this connection we should mention the wholesome advice of T. Murphy in, *People and Pastor.* He instructed the congregation how to receive the minister's regular and specified visits.[42] He made the point that the advantage of a pastor's visits depended on the attitude and atmosphere of the family and the individual receiving the call.

3. *Sick Visitation*

One kind of specific visitation that was important to the writers of this period was visitation on the sick. In handling this problem, two writers gave a semi-theological discussion on the problems of illness. J. F. W. Ware included treatises[43] by various writers on the problems of sickness, and added selections from Scripture to solve such difficulties.[44] J. D. Wells introduced the distinction between the sick-bed and the death-bed,[45] specifying the proper treatment for both cases.[46]

The writers of this period stressed the importance of knowing the problems of the sick and preparing to meet the need even before the call is made. W. W. How reminded his readers of the importance of knowing how to deal with the sick and the dying in their special needs, since no general rules could be laid down for all.[47] J. M. Hoppin warned that there should be special preparation

35. Gregory Thurston Bedell, *The Pastor,* J. B. Lippincott and Co., Philadelphia, 1880, pp. 406-484.
36. How, op. cit., pp. 53-104.
37. Ibid., p. 68.
38. W. P. Tilden, *The Work of the Ministry,* Geo. H. Ellis, Boston, 1899, pp. 51-56.
39. G. B. Wilcox, *The Pastor Amidst His Flock,* The American Tract Society, New York, 1890, p. 144.
40. Theodore L. Cuyler, *How to be a Pastor,* The Baker and Taylor Co., New York, 1890, pp. 21-31.
41. Ibid.
42. Murphy, op. cit., pp. 51-59.
43. J. F. W. Ware, *The Silent Pastor, or Consolations for the Sick,* Third Edition, Walker, Wise and Co., Boston, 1864, pp. 1-60.
44. Ibid, pp. 85-108.
45. John D. Wells, *Pastor in the Sick-Room,* Presbyterian Board of Publication and Sabbath School Work, Philadelphia, 1892, pp. 1-90.
46. Ibid., pp. 90-128.
47. How, op. cit., p. 69.

for the actual remarks planned for the sick-room.[48] And F. R. Waynne characterized the importance of sick visitation by stating:

> "Whenever it is possible, give special study to the case of each patient.
> Think of the sufferer in your own chamber before you visit him in his.
> Settle in your mind beforehand what subject to suggest to him in conver-
> sation; not so as to bind yourself to that and that alone, but so as not to
> leave the subject to chance, and so as to bring the patient according to
> what seems to you his requirements, through an instructive series of definite
> lessons to his heart and conscience."[49]

SUMMARY

*Systematic visitation for specified needs and for calling on the sick constitutes
the emphasis for spiritual and efficient service in the pastorate.*

D. Individual Case Study

In the period of beginnings we noted the interest in individual case study.
In the period of development the interest was manifested along three lines,
namely, (1) its importance, (2) examples of case study, and (3) the classification of individuals.

1. Importance of Case Study

An increasing number of writers mentioned the importance of case study.
H. Latham pointed to the fact that our Lord used the method of individual
treatment and that His servants should also adopt it:

> "This individualizing in our Lord's treatment struck the disciples as
> something new; they do not indeed point it out as a novel feature, for they
> never remark upon our Lord's ways but the care of the evangelists in pre-
> serving the most striking instances of this diversity of treatment shows
> that it caught their notice. To our Lord's eye every human being had a
> moral and spiritual physiognomy of his own."[50]

C. C. Hall concluded the principle and technique of individual treatment
from the work of the physician when he wrote:

> "It will be found among the most eminent medical diagnosticians that the
> individuality of each case is grasped before any opinion of fact is given.
> Each detail of personality is noted with heroic care, each minute fact of
> morbid condition. The same principle of intense individualization governs
> the highest case of spiritual diagnosticians."[51]

A third representative statement to illustrate the importance of case study
is taken from G. T. Bedell's work:

> "He should discover the mental state of his patient; this in order to
> decide wisely as to the spiritual condition, for if the mind be unhealthily
> affected by disease, the spiritual symptoms must be interpreted accordingly.
> Lastly he should determine the condition of the soul. Then he is to deal
> with it faithfully. But great discretion is to be exercised."[52]

---

48. Hoppin, op. cit., p. 560.
49. F. R. Waynne, *Our Sacred Commission*, James Pott and Co., New York, 1891, p. 100.
50. Henry Latham, *Pastor Pastorum*, James Pott and Co., New York, 1891, pp. 374, 375.
51. Charles Cuthbert Hall, *Qualifications for Ministerial Power*, Hartford Seminary Press,
Hartford, 1895, p. 164.
52. Bedell, op. cit., pp. 414, 416.

This quotation reveals that he gave some very modern advice concerning the treatment of individual cases. He saw progression in the life of one individual and strongly urged the pastor to take note of individual ideas, purposes and actions.

The advice of F. R. Waynne serves as a summary of this emphasis:

> "One of the first lessons, that a pastor has to learn, and one that he has to keep learning always, is the separating of the flock into the living individuals which compose it. This has to be done in many ways. It has to be done in thought, in prayer, and in personal intercourse."[53]

This ought to be conclusive evidence of the intense interest on the part of writers of this period in the matter of individual treatment of persons in the parish. We could quote many other authors who gave the same emphasis.[54]

2. Examples of Case Study

We desire to call attention to three writers who made it a point to present examples in case study and application. Since the books have been discussed before, we only mention their characteristic treatment of case study at this point. I. S. Spencer's case records with related explanation and treatment, speak for themselves.[55] A. Bonar's contribution, *Visitor's Book of Texts*,[56] emphasized individual needs and specific texts to satisfy such needs. In the same way, the book by J. D. Wells, *Pastor in the Sick-Room*,[57] demonstrated the importance of distinguishing various cases of the sick and the dying.

3. Classifications of Individuals

It is very interesting to note the classifications of individuals as made by various authors during the period of development. Two writers, A. A. Bonar[58] and W. A. Plummer,[59] listed seven classifications of sick individuals. The two lists of characteristics are not identical although they are very similar. Bonar listed an additional classification for the sorrowful and indicated a sevenfold explanation with respect to kind and remedy.[60] A. Vinet[61] and J. J. Van Oosterzee[62] listed a double classification covering the external and internal states of individuals also. A. N. Littlejohn indicated five grounds on the basis of which

53. Waynne, op. cit., p. 45.
54. R. F. Weidner, *Practical Theology*, Fleming H. Revell, New York, 1891, p. 71.
   Heisler, op. cit., pp. 488, 489.
   Vinet, op. cit., p. 229.
   Miller, op. cit., p. 135.
55. Icabod S. Spencer, *Pastor's Sketches, or Conversations with Anxious Inquirers Respecting the Way of Salvation*, Two Volumes, 1850, 450 pp. and 1853, 430 pp. Dodd & Mead, New York.
56. Andrew Bonar, *The Visitor's Book of Texts of the Word Brought Nigh to the Sick and the Sorrowful*, Robert Carter and Brothers, New York, 1867, 230 pp.
57. Wells, op. cit., pp. 11-48.
58. Bonar, op. cit., 230 pp.
59. Plummer, op. cit., pp. 272-274.
60. Bonar, op. cit., pp. 102-166.
61. Vinet, op. cit., 229-347.
62. Van Oosterzee, op. cit., 297-347.

individuals seek counsel and direction.[63] W. W. How classified two kinds of sick individuals, the chronic and those having a sudden emergency. J. M. Hoppin[64] presented three classifications of individuals, the unbelievers and impenitent, the inquirer, and the young convert.

From this threefold phase of individual case study we have observed a persuasion of these writers which ties in well with modern recommendations on this important work. These writers developed the principles and techniques for their day.

SUMMARY

The growing importance of individual case interest reflected itself in the study and classifications of individuals.

E. Pastoral Counseling

This particular trend was also traced in previous period's findings and practices. The development during this period manifested itself along the two lines which are indicated in the discussion which follows.

1. Counseling Opportunities

A few representative statements will give point to the opportunities of pastoral counseling even as the writers of this period envisioned. C. C. Hall said it this way:

> "Transcending all that may be official and habitual in the discharge of pastoral duty, and opening a channel of ministerial power wider and deeper than any one life has yet been able to measure, a channel of power whose width and depth are limited only by the limits of personality, there rises that which is the supreme function of the pastorate, namely confidential intercourse with human lives."[65]

Hall was mindful of the tremendous opportunities open for the pastor in the field of pastoral counseling. J. Watson writing a year later felt likewise. "The pastor gives much of his time to consultation and it is likely he will have to give more and more every year."[66] The scope of counseling opportunity was stated by C. Geikie when he analyzed the ministry of Jesus.

> "The supreme passion revealed in our Lord's ministry was, as the gospels abundantly show a divine enthusiasm for humanity. Man as man was sacred in His eyes as the living temple of God in the new dispensation . . . Christ did not confine Himself to spiritual counsels, for while only one Gospel is mainly given to His words, three are devoted to His works."[67]

---

63. A. N. Littlejohn, *Conciones Ad Clerum*, T. Whittaker, place of publication not indicated, 1880, pp. 57-190.
64. Hoppin, op. cit., pp. 565-591.
65. Hall, op. cit., p. 158.
66. John Watson, *The Cure of Souls*, Dodd, Mead, New York, 1896, p. 235.
67. Cunningham Geikie, "The Preacher in Daily Life," *The Homiletic Review*, Vol. XXXV, Nov., 1898, No. 5, pp. 387, 388.

J. Love, Jr., felt that this opportunity spelled a responsibility, for he wrote:

> "From the very nature of his office he is expected to be a burden-bearer; whatever the pressure on himself, he must be the counselor of those in trouble, the servant of all, for Christ's sake."[68]

2. Counseling Suggestions

The writers of the period under discussion also presented suggestions for carrying out these counseling opportunities. P. D. Kidder emphasized the need for clear discernment in determining the character and moral states of individuals; the power of eliciting frank expressions of their feelings, fears and hopes; a tender and persuasiveness of manner; a capacity to remove from their minds any delusions; and a felicitous manner of presenting encouragements.[69] Warning was given by G. T. Bedell that pastors should offer advice slowly, know the peculiarities of the case, reflect on the issues involved, pray about the matter and then give counsel.[70] A suggestion often claimed as strictly modern in the field of counseling was expressed by W. P. Tilden during this period. He said, "One thing of almost supreme importance in making parish calls is the art of listening."[71] This practice is also amply illustrated in the books of I. S. Spencer,[72] because the very spirit of his volumes bespeaks careful listening, quiet contemplation and vitalized conversation.

A few statements from S. Miller's work, *Letters on Clerical Manners and Habits*, reveal the advice which he gave. One would think that he had written these words in the last few years, they are so much like the expressions of modern authors:

> "It is an error to imagine that the same methods of introducing and maintaining religious conversation are equally adapted to all persons and to all occasions."[73]
>
> "Let your conversation be adapted to the character of the company into which you happen to be thrown."[74]
>
> "Take pains to prepare yourself for conducting religious conversation in an easy and edifying manner."[75]

It is very evident that the writers of pastoral theology during this period understood something of the technique of pastoral counseling and brought to light many of the ideas which modern writers claim as original with the present generation.

SUMMARY

Pastoral counseling in both outreach and technique was developed in a marked way during this period.

---

68. Love, op. cit., p. 150.
69. Kidder, op. cit., pp. 474, 475.
70. Bedell, op. cit., p. 436.
71. Tilden, op. cit., p. 61.
72. Spencer, op. cit., 1850, 450 pp. and 1853, 430 pp.
73. Miller, op. cit., p. 109.
74. Ibid., p. 114.
75. Ibid., p. 135.

F. Applied Scripture

The use of the Bible in the application of the cure for individuals was outstandingly characteristic of the period of beginnings and it was continued and developed during the period now under discussion. In his book, *The Silent Pastor,*[76] J. F. Ware gave selections of Scripture to cover supplication, confession, pardon, assurance, divine protection, God's care, tribulation, patience, sufficient grace, gratitude for returning health, faith, hope and submission for support under severe sickness. The emphasis of the material is on the afflictions of life and fails to take into account the other side of Christian experience.

Believing that those who visit the sick should confine themselves to the use of Scripture passages, A. A. Bonar cited specific selections from the Bible together with statements of people who experienced the value of these quoted passages.[77] W. A. Plummer suggested that the minister should use Bible passages in visiting the sick, but he did not quote or refer to the actual passages which would be suitable for the sick.[78]

Suggesting the use of a visitor's book of texts, W. H. G. Thomas[79] claimed that the experience of the minister would be the best teacher as to which passages should be used for various individuals. A slightly different opinion came from W. P. Tilden,

> "In my own experiences with the sick, I have found remembered passages of Scripture, informally repeated, no matter how familiar, with a sweet hymn, far better than anything I could say out of my own thought."[80]

J. M. Hoppin believed that Scripture passages should be chosen and marked before the call was contemplated. W. M. Taylor said,

> "Consolation will be best imparted by you in the words of Scripture, for at such times there is no solace like that which is contained in the sayings of the Lord Jesus and His inspired servants. Search the Bible, therefore, for appropriate passages, and that you may have them constantly in readiness, lay them up in the memory of the heart."[81]

SUMMARY

The practice of applied Scripture, though mainly recommended for the sick and afflicted, manifested a direction and application in the use of the pastor's best tool in ministerial service.

G. Applied Psychology

The early manifestations of the application of psychology are easily discerned in much of the foregoing material. Unknown perhaps even to the writers themselves, they applied psychology in pastoral exhortation, in the study of individual cases, in the bearing of the pastor upon the flock, and in the wise

---

76. Ware, op. cit., pp. 85-108.
77. Bonar, op. cit., pp. 230.
78. Plummer, op. cit., pp. 272-274.
79. W. H. Griffith Thomas, *The Work of the Ministry,* Hodder and Stoughton, New York, 1910, p. 287.
80. Tilden, op. cit., p. 66.
81. Taylor, op. cit., p. 268.

use of Scripture for the cure of ills and troubles. In this section of our dissertation, we wish to study more specifically this trend of applied psychology as revealed in the writings of the period, and in doing so we discover three phases in the trend.

1. *Psychological Understanding of the Community*

In recent decades a great advance has been made in the correct understanding of the psychological and sociological characteristics of the community. It is very interesting to note that the writers during the period of development sensed the importance of such study for the success of the minister. A. Vinet's book introduced this thought:

> "The care of souls will not then be the same in town as in the country; in an agricultural country and manufacturing districts; in the midst of a people of simple manners, and among a refined and educated people. The pastor must take all these things into consideration, as also all geographic peculiarities, climatic, economic, dialectic and historic. He should know the habits, interests, wants, prejudices, and wishes of the people among whom he is located. He should not limit himself to some very obvious data, supplied by a few introductions, he should wish to study these as they are in themselves."[82]

In much the same way D. H. Greer wrote:

> "A parish in the city cannot be worked in the same way precisely that a parish in the country can, or a parish in one part of the city or country like a parish in another part of the city or country; or a weak parish like a strong parish, or a rich parish like a poor one."[83]

W. Gladden expressed his convictions on the matter by saying:

> "One reason for the apparent waste of ministerial power is that the real events of the special field are not known, and so are not ministered to. Each parish has its own peculiarities, and so has each person in it."[84]

These statements were likewise emphasized by C. Geikie,[85] and H. W. Warner, who said that the ministers must "study . . . business conditions"[86] because of the "secularizing influence in which men live."[87]

Not only did these men understand the importance of knowing the community into which they came and to which they should minister; they also felt the need of being sensitive to the impending changes which come in the average pastorate. E. D. Weigel warned the minister to be on constant guard with a positive gospel as the only remedy for the maladies which afflict chang-

82. Vinet, op. cit., p. 221.
83. David H. Greer, *The Preacher and His Place*, Edwin and Gorham, Church Missions House, New York, 1904, pp. 204, 205.
84. Washington Gladden, *Church and Parish Problems*, The Thwing Co., New York, 1911, p. 179.
85. Geikie, op. cit., p. 388.
86. Horace E. Warner, "The Pastor Among His People," *The Homiletical Review*, Vol. 34, July, 1897, p. 89.
87. Ibid., p. 88.

ing society[88] and G. B. Willcox pointed to the fact that "the parochial duties of the minister have gone through modifications."[89]

2. *Psychological Understanding of Human Nature*

According to G. T. Bedell the minister must not only know the spiritual and physical make-up of the individual,[90] he must also know human nature as it is in all people. A. N. Littlejohn explained it thus:

> "He who is charged with the cure of souls must know the sinfulness of sin not only as a general proposition, but the comparative guilt of particular kinds of sin and the peculiar guilt of this or that individual sin."[91]

E. Miller counseled his readers to know human nature in order to do effective work in the pastorate. He said:

> "A wide and profound acquaintance with human nature in general, as it is found among civilized and uncivilized people is needful, indeed; but the most needful of all is where the pastor is working. 'The field is the world,' but the soul and the climate are not the same in all parts of the world."[92]

Another writer, R. F. Weidner, expressed his views by saying:

> "The activity of the clergyman embraces in some shape all the relations of human life, from the cradle to the grave. Hence he must have an intelligent apprehension of these various spheres of life."[93]

These men understood the so-called modern interpretation of knowing the bare facts of human nature, and in addition they stressed what so many are missing today — the spiritual understanding of salvation for the curse of sin.

3. *Psychological Understanding of the Individual*

Much of what has been written on Individual Case Study earlier in this chapter has specific bearing on the *psychological* understanding of the individual. A brief documentation on the specific characteristic of psychological understanding will clarify and augment what has already been stated. We recall Spencer's advice — to know the case prior to the time of the visit and to study the case as thoroughly as possible. G. T. Bedell suggested to "draw out the whole of the parishioner's mind."[94] T. L. Cuyler also called attention to this in connection with the pastor's "friendly conversations."[95] And W. W. How anticipated the difficulty and urgency of the problem by writing:

> "It is often very hard at first to ascertain the state of the sick person's soul. You cannot ask searching questions all at once. You must at first be more or less general, except where previous intimacy gives you the requisite knowledge."[96]

88. E. D. Weigle, "The Ministry and Current Social Problems," *Lutheran Quarterly*, Vol. 24, New Series, Oct., 1894, pp. 467-476.
89. Willcox, op. cit., p. 144.
90. Bedell, op. cit., pp. 415, 416.
91. Littlejohn, op. cit., p. 58.
92. E. Miller, "The Pastor for Our Times," *Lutheran Quarterly*, Vol. 23, New Series, April 1893, p. 180.
93. R. F. Weidner, *Practical Theology*, Fleming H. Revell, New York, 1891, p. 71.
94. Bedell, op. cit., p. 436.
95. Cuyler, op. cit., p. 31.
96. How, op. cit., p. 68.

It was recognized that the condition of *spiritual life,* apart from life in general, could be ascertained only from an intimate knowledge of the individual. T. A. Bernard explained this relationship in the following manner:

> "The spiritual life on earth is by the will of God a part of a general life associated with the external scenes by which it is affected on all sides and in all ways. We cannot isolate the spiritual life, as if the soul were one being and the man were another."[97]

The writer showed the importance of the minister in relation to the individual, particularly the importance of understanding his psychological and spiritual life — which one author has called an "unfathomable infinite abyss of existence."[98]

The religious leaders in this period of development in pastoral theology came to emphasize a real applied psychology. Through a better understanding of the community, human nature, and the individual, they practiced many of the principles and techniques which modern leaders claim as original and singularly true of the science of psychology. Our interpretation reveals wisdom and application on the part of the writers during the period of development.

SUMMARY

Through study and practice the pastors of the period of development came to a better psychological understanding of the community, of human nature and of the individual.

Summarizing the entire period of development we come to evaluate the development so characteristic of this division of pastoral theology in the following sentences. Many of the underlying trends discovered in the period of beginnings were continued and developed in this period, in harmony with the times and the emergencies which arose. In each instance there was a deepening of insight and an improvement of technique. Writers during this period actually began to *develop* pastoral theology. This development was very evident in our discussion of the various subdivisions of thought.

There was also a marked refinement of organization in the material produced by the writers on pastoral theology. As a science, pastoral theology came to its own during this period of time. The aspect of applied psychology in pastoral theology, only faintly discernable in the period of beginnings, came to have a definite place in the interpretation and practice of pastoral theology during the period of development. Groundwork for further progress was clearly evident in the *growing, developing* and *unfolding* process which characterized this period as one of development.

The history of pastoral theology has unfolded itself progressively from a period of beginnings through a period of development, and has continued through a *period of application.* This last named period is dated from 1900 to the present time and is the subject of our next chapter.

---

97. T. A. Bernard, *Homiletical and Pastoral Lectures,* A. C. Armstrong and Son, New York, 1880, p. 306.
98. Ibid., p. 296.

CHAPTER IV

Application in Pastoral Theology, 1900 to the Present

BEGINNING with the twentieth century we find a new development in pastoral theology. Many of the trends found in previous periods were continued; but as these trends developed they came to be marked by a special application. In a sense the period now under discussion could be designated the period of specialization; yet, as we view the three periods together, the special interests of the twentieth century are not as readily distinguished as those in the others. The distinguishing feature is found in the manner and extent of application. For this reason the third period of pastoral theology, from nineteen hundred to the present time, can best be designated the *period of application.*

Not all writers within this period were consciously applying the technique of pastoral theology to individual needs; yet a distinct applicatory emphasis is evident in the literature. The first evidence of this distinct characterization can be discerned in the discussion about the *person of the pastor.* This phase of pastoral theology has been discussed in relation to both of the preceding periods in the foregoing chapters of this book. In the present chapter the emphasis is particularly strong.

A. The Person of The Pastor

At the very beginning of this period D. Bauslin wrote "A model pastor must have at least a fair capacity for leadership in the affairs of the church."[1] The pastor, according to Bauslin, has to be a man of good manners, patience and hopefulness to deal with men one by one in the care of souls. He prescribed spiritual leadership on the part of the pastor in the following words:

> "In the religious use of the word, a pastor is one who shepherds souls. His work is thus a distinctive spiritual work, a work that deals with motives, ideals, purposes and conduct of the people whom he tries to help."[2]

J. Sheepshanks stressed the importance of the pastor's personal life by saying:

> "We are to be wholly immersed in sacred things and give ourselves wholly to them. The account of the three who were willing to follow our Lord, but with reservation, Luke 9:57-62, is well worthy of our meditation."[3]

---

1. David H. Bauslin, "The Model Pastor," *The Lutheran Quarterly,* Vol. 36, New Series, July 1906, p. 393.
2. Ibid.
3. John Sheepshanks, *The Pastor and His Parish,* Hodder and Stoughton, London, 1908, p. 261.

Indicating the importance of personal conduct and consecration because of the high investment of the person of the pastor, F. W. Gunsaulus wrote:

> "There is no greater honor to be offered a human being in this world than to be chosen by God to this holy priesthood, and to be chosen by human beings to bear unto God the souls and destinies of those whom we love most when we try to help them. A man must live for such power as this, and he can afford to love everything and suffer everything for the spiritual life which gives and keeps for him this privilege."[4]

While T. W. Pym agreed with modern psychologists that the pastor must be a specialist in his field, he disagreed with them in the priorities of specialization. He said:

> "The first requirement in a shepherd of souls is that he should be a man of God. He cannot expect that knowledge of human nature or careful attention to technique are anything but second in importance to his own knowledge of God."[5]

He continued his plea for the spiritual importance of the pastor's life and conduct by depicting the times in which the pastor must apply himself.

> "The battle which Christianity will have to fight in the next fifty years will, in my opinion, be in the moral sphere as during the last fifty years it has been rather in the intellectual sphere. Christian standards or supposed standards of conduct will be more and more challenged not only in individuals but also in social ethics; the latter are of immense importance in the vocation of the Christian preacher and teacher."[6]

This spiritual note was also emphasized by F. J. B. Allnatt. He devoted over sixty pages of his book, *Studies in Soul Tending,*[7] to this thought, discussing meditation, intercession, and a plan for private devotions. He stated that one should feel the guilt of sin and have sufficient time for active spiritual living. Service to the living God should be rendered not merely with a better understanding of the mental life of the flock but with a greater appreciation of spiritual values. The double emphasis of his book is directed toward the pastor's care for his own soul and for the souls of those under his charge.

N. B. Harmon, Jr., spoke with confidence about a specialized application. He quoted a medical doctor, a Dr. Osler of Baltimore, as saying:

> "Imperturbality means coolness and presence of mind under all circumstances, calmness amid storm, clearness of judgment in moments of peril, immobility, impassiveness. . . . The physician who has the misfortune to be without it, who betrays indecision and worry, and who shows that he is flustered and flurried in ordinary emergencies, loses rapidly the confidence of his patients."[8]

Then Harmon added some sane advice, "If this be a good rule for the doctors medicae it applies equally well to doctors theologiae."[9]

---

4. Frank W. Gunsaulus, *The Minister and Spiritual Life*, Fleming H. Revell, New York, 1911, pp. 292, 293.
5. T. W. Pym, *Spiritual Direction*, Morehouse Publishing Co., Milwaukee, 1928, p. 41.
6. Ibid., pp. 211, 212.
7. F. J. B. Allnatt, *Studies in Soul Tending*, The Macmillan Co., New York, 1922, pp. 1-62.
8. Nolan B. Harmon, Jr., *Ministerial Ethics and Etiquette*, Cokesbury Press, Nashville, 1928, p. 93.
9. Ibid., p. 93.

In re-emphasizing the ideas of Baxter, G. S. Dobbins wrote:

> "Another question which the pastor should constantly raise with himself as he goes about this work of personal visitation is, what are my qualifications for this difficult task? Assuming his equipment of Bible knowledge and of the shepherd heart there are certain qualifications peculiarly necessary for success in personal pastoral counseling."[10]

Dobbins made even a stronger plea, and it is worthy of serious consideration:

> "More than every other demand and doubtless closer to the heart of Christ, is the supreme need that the minister be sent out into the field equipt with Christ mastered personality for the transforming of other personalities into Christ's likeness. What the preacher is, speaks more loudly than what he says. His religious life must be contagious if it is to be effective. He is to be far more concerned to bring to bear the saving power of Christ upon the lives of individuals than to preach eloquent sermons and raise church budgets. His success is to be measured far more in terms of intangible spiritual values than by statistics and standards."[11]

This applicatory tendency was carried to an extreme by F. A. Agar who saw the minister largely in the practical aspects of his work. He wrote:

> "This study of the minister and his opportunities is to be neither theological nor historical. It will concern itself largely with the practical aspects of a minister's varied work as it confronts him in the average church in the multitude of parishes around the world."[12]

Two books by A. W. Hewitt demonstrate his keen understanding of the rural pastorate. His first book, *Highland Shepherds*, depicted the person of the minister. Two of his chapters, "Qualities Essential to the Rural Pastor,"[13] and "Elements Fatal to the Rural Pastor,"[14] manifest the importance of the pastor in relation to the sheep of the fold. The logic of his position is clinched in his last chapter, "How To Be A Good Pastor."[15] In his second book, *God's Back Pasture*,[16] Hewitt demonstrated the possibilities of a rural pastor in the civil, social and community responsibilities which confront the minister. All of this, according to Hewitt, hinges upon the person of the pastor in relation to specified tasks.

H. W. Luccock, in his book, *In the Minister's Workshop*, made the following statement which characterized his book and the period in which he wrote:

> "The variety and magnitude of the demands on the minister's mind, heart, time and strength expose him to the danger of leading a minimum spiritual life himself in the time of maximum demand."[17]

---

10. Gaines S. Dobbins, "Facing Pastoral Problems," *The Review and Expositor*, Vol. 34, No. 2, April, 1937, pp. 222, 223.

11. Gaines S. Dobbins, "Theological Education in a Changing Social Order," *The Review and Expositor*, Vol. 32, No. 2, April, 1935, pp. 195, 196.

12. Frederick A. Agar, *The Minister and His Opportunity*, Fleming H. Revell Co., New York, p. 5.

13. Arthur Wentworth Hewitt, *Highland Shepherds*, Willett Clark and Co., New York, 1939, pp. 1-12.

14. Ibid., pp. 13-18.

15. Ibid., pp. 215-235.

16. Arthur Wentworth Hewitt, *God's Back Pasture*, Willett Clark and Co., 1941, pp. 62-95.

17. Halford E. Luccock, *In the Minister's Workshop*, Abingdon-Cokesbury Press, New York, Nashville, 1944, p. 16.

The writers of this period came to realize the importance of the person of the pastor as applied to the life of the people in trying and difficult days.

SUMMARY

The personal and pastoral life of the minister is of primary importance in order to be an efficient shepherd of souls.

B. Knowledge of Human Nature

In this period of application, special attention is given to the pastor's study and knowledge of human nature. W. Gladden saw the point and made bold the claim for a knowledge of human nature on the part of the pastor. He said:

> "The pastor must not get his knowledge of human nature wholly or mainly from books, though books may greatly aid him in interpreting phenomena. What other careful observators have seen will guide him. But first-hand knowledge is imperative."[18]
> "The individual and society in which he lives are as inseparable as the inside and the outside of a curve."[19]

A similar opinion was expressed by A. E. Garvie, in his book, *A Guide to Preachers.*

> "The preacher today must find out what it is that interests and impresses, perplexes and torments the men and the women to whom he is speaking. As a politician who never reads the newspapers is sure of courting disaster by bringing forward and carrying through a policy opposed to public opinion and popular sentiment, so that preacher who would morally and spiritually guide men must know and understand them."[20]

Likewise P. Brooks indicated that "the relation of the minister now is vastly more human and vastless more ecclesiastical than in the past."[21] And R. Z. Fahs made the same suggestion when he wrote that the home must be known by the pastor in order to work effectively in the life of the individual and the community.[22] A very important emphasis was given by F. W. Gunsaulus when he said that spiritual life comes only when the pastor comes near the human experiences of his parishioners.[23]

C. F. Rogers differentiated between pastors when he said:

> "Even from the beginning students will tend to divide themselves into two classes; one will show more practical ability, another more power of dealing with theories. The first will by preference get his material from intercourse with men and in the present; the second will rather gather his data from history of philosophical opinion. The one will prefer direct dealing with concrete facts; the other will find himself more able to deal with abstractions drawn from these facts."[24]

---

18. Washington Gladden, *The Christian Pastor and the Working Church,* Charles Scribners Sons, New York, 1903, pp. 93, 94.
19. Ibid., p. 100.
20. Alfred E. Garvie, *A Guide to Preachers,* Hodder and Stoughton, London, 1906, p. 275.
21. Philip Brooks, "The Minister and His People," *The Harvard Theological Review,* April, 1908, p. 226.
22. R. Z. Fahs, Suggestions for Pastoral Visiting," *Methodist Review,* July-August, 1908, pp. 531-537.
23. Gunsaulus, op. cit., p. 103.
24. Clement F. Rogers, *An Introduction to the Study of Pastoral Theology,* Oxford, at the Clarendon Press, 1912, p. 135.

His divisions of thought and action are excellent and to the point. With it he implies the importance of a knowledge of human nature, no matter how this is obtained.

In the language of O. L. Joseph:

> "Unlike the professional psychologist, these men with the religious spirit and the pastoral instinct united with the scientific mind, have diagnosed motives, analyzed emotions, interpreted desires, which give clearer perceptions of life, free from the prepossessions of theories and in closer accord with the actualities of life."[25]

Joseph meant that the pastor must have a thorough knowledge of his flock. He must know how the people live and work. It must be a "face-to-face" ministry and it may not be neglected. Additional evidence for this kind of thinking can be found in the work of H. Adams, *The Pastoral Ministry*, in which he wrote:

> "The pastor should not only know the truths that Jesus brought as 'good news' to the earth, but he must know human nature and the mind so that he can help people to acquire the release from old bondages and the force of the new faith."[26]

Adams raised a pertinent question, so often presented today and with it he gave a salutary answer when he wrote:

> "Would you substitute psychology for Jesus? is the silly query that we sometimes hear. No, of course, not, but we would make whatever knowledge we have of the mind serve Jesus, and those whom Jesus would serve."[27]

An important application of this interpretation was made by A. H. McKinney. He referred to the fact that Jesus knew people and thus could work with them. Christ knew human nature and because of his knowledge could work with people. For this reason he counseled pastors as follows:

> "We are urging our readers to study people seriously, sympathetically — for the purpose of learning how to approach them in order to present truth in such a way that they will accept Him who is the way, the truth, and the life, and through Him to come to the heavenly Father, for unless the worker leads others to God his best work is only partially successful."[28]

McKinney's entire book voiced the necessity of investigation. He insisted on the importance of knowing human nature in the pastor's own life and in the lives of others. His axioms concerning human nature are jewels of wisdom and shows that he understood the thing for which he pleaded.

Four writers combining their efforts in one book, *An Introduction to Pastoral Theology*, carried the same emphasis with respect to knowing human nature. One quotation will reflect their thinking on the subject:

> "Every year of practical experience of the ministry should make the priest more competent, as he widens his knowledge of his people's needs and tests the resources he already has."[29]

25. O. L. Joseph, *The Dynamic Ministry*, The Abingdon Press, New York, 1923, p. 117.
26. Hampton Adams, *The Pastoral Ministry*, Cokesbury Press, Nashville, 1932, p. 16.
27. Ibid., p. 18.
28. A. H. McKinney, *Human Nature in Christian Work*, W. A. Wilde Co., Boston, 1928, pp. 25, 26.
29. Henry Balmforth, Lindsay Dewar, Cyril E. Hudson, Edmund S. Sara, *An Introduction to Pastoral Theology*, The Macmillan Co., New York, 1937, p. 83.

These many references establish the proposition that the pastor must know human nature and he must study each individual in his parish. Every professional man must know the material with which he works, and the people with whom he works; so the minister must know human nature if he is to be an effective pastor. We can summarize the thought in a quotation from the versatile pen of G. S. Dobbins:

> "As a specialist it is the minister's function to discover religious need —
> if possible to put his finger on the one distinctive religious need that de-
> mands most to be met — and then to supply that need by bringing the in-
> dividual to the source of supply in Christ."[30]

SUMMARY

Knowledge of human nature by the pastor is an absolute necessity for effective ministerial work.

C. Individual Case Study

The knowledge of human nature is closely associated with the importance of individual case study. Continuing the thought of the previous period, we find a new interest in the application of the pastor to individual case study. Basing his urge for this study on the Bible, G. H. Gerberding wrote:

> "This individual soul cure has its foundation and warrant in the Scrip-
> ture. Not only that, but it is there laid down as the minister's special and
> solemn duty."[31]
> "All this requires personal effort in interviewing all who need his mini-
> strations and are in his reach. In this he must follow in the footsteps of
> Christ."[32]

The importance of individual care is clearly indicated in the book by J. O. Dykes, *The Christian Minister and His Duties*.[33] This individual care he catalogued as pertaining to household visitation, care of the sick, the bereaved, of the young and those of special trouble. In the same manner W. A. Quayle sensed the importance of individual work even though he did not specify classifications of individuals. Four of his chapters[34] are gems of understanding and practical guidance in meeting the needs of individuals.

Taking his idea from the study of medicine, C. E. Jefferson wrote:

> "Medicine has given us the clue. The modern physician is nothing if not
> individualistic. Physicians never deal with men in crowds. 'One patient at
> a time,' that is the rule in all hospitals through-out the world. Each
> patient has his own chart at the head of his bed. The temperature of his
> blood, the beat of his pulse, the number of his respirations are carefully
> noted."[35]

---

30. Gaines S. Dobbins, "The Problem of Pastoral Visiting," *The Review and Expositor*, Vol. XXXIV, No. 2, April, 1937, p. 222.

31. G. H. Geberding, *The Lutheran Pastor*, Fifth Edition, Lutheran Publication Society, Philadelphia, 1905, p. 373.

32. Ibid.

33. J. Oswald Dykes, *The Christian Minister and His Duties*, T. & T. Clark, Edinburgh, 1909, pp. 300-366.

34. William A. Quayle, *The Pastor-Preacher*, Eaton and Mains, New York, 1910, Chapters on "The Pastor," "The Pastor and the Sick," "The Pastor and the Child," and "The Pastor and Youth," pp. 134-172.

35. Charles Edward Jefferson, *The Ministering Shepherd*, Hodder and Stoughton, New York, 1912, p. 99.

He suggested that if the same policy were adopted in parish work, it would bring equally astonishing results. In much the same way W. Gladden recommended a thorough knowledge of the times, of educational and philanthropic circles and the needs of the individual. He wrote:

> "The needs of the souls to whom the pastor seeks to minister are many and various, not two cases are alike; each is a separate study but one may think of types which are always found in all congregations."[36]
> "One reason for the apparent waste of ministerial power is that the real events of the special field are not known, so are not ministered to. Each parish has its peculiarities, and so has each person in it."[37]

Likewise J. W. Kemp indicated the importance of reaching the individual just where he is. He recommended knowing the individual in his real condition. Said he:

> "Find out where the inquirer is. It is perfectly evident that in dealing with inquirers our first care must be to find out the real condition of the mind and heart; otherwise, how can we apply the Word of God with any hope of success? This is what the physician calls 'diagnosing his patient before prescribing his remedy.' "[38]

An unusual book indicating the increasing emphasis on the importance of case study is *The Work of the Pastor* by C. R. Erdman. Two chapters in particular describe the cure of souls pertaining to ten classifications of individuals needing such care. His classification reflects the thinking of his time and indicates at the same time the marked advance in this trend of thinking. He referred to the irreligious, the indifferent, the professed skeptics, the inquirers, the new converts, the doubter, the despondent, the deluded, the sick, the bereaved, the afflicted, the erring, the perplexed, the backsliders, and the mature Christians.[39] The same emphasis was given by T. W. Pym, when he wrote:

> "It is necessary to consider people's moral difficulties or spiritual needs against the background of the individual's past history and present circumstances."[40]

He urged the need of studying the individual cases, for, as the medical doctor makes a personal diagnosis, so pastors should make a personal diagnosis pertaining to spiritual life. He applied this in a realistic way when he concluded that pastor, like the doctor, should know the symptoms before he recommended a remedy.

In the book of J. H. C. Fritz, *Pastoral Theology*, the discussion dealing with the sick and the dying is very much like other treatises on the subject. His treatment of special cases comprehends a study of heredity, the influence of mind on the body, and fixed habits. His classification of individuals also

---

36. Gladden, op. cit., p. 180.
37. Washington Gladden, *Church and Parish Problems*, The Thwing Co., New York, 1911, p. 179.
38. J. W. Kemp, *The Soul Winner and Soul Winning*, George H. Doran and Co., New York, 1916, p. 75.
39. Charles R. Erdman, *The Work of the Pastor*, The Westminster Press, Philadelphia, 1924, pp. 67-90.
40. Pym, op. cit., p. 53.

included the following designations: poverty and wealth, health and illness, false religious convictions, various temperaments, sinful occupations, drunkeness, sinful amusements, coveteousness, gossiping, hysteria, insanity and offenders. His discussion of insanity and hysteria was approached from the Scriptural point of view. He described various cases and suggested remedial cures to be used by the pastor. His ideas of mental disorders and the cure for the same are noteworthy. A few sentences from his work indicate his position:

> "A pastor should be personally well acquainted with the individual members of his congregation, the children included. The pastor is a spiritual physician. He should know well each of his members, be able to diagnose any case of spiritual illness, and prescribe and apply necessary treatment."[41]
> "He should study the individual church-member in reference to his character, disposition, temperament, opinions, environment, education, friends and acquaintances, occupation, business associates, poverty or wealth, special hobbies, reading, physical conditions, etc."[42]
> "A pastor should not only have a thorough knowledge of the human being as such but as a true pastor, he also must know how to diagnose and treat the peculiar spiritual conditions of any individual soul."[43]

The trend of thought on individual case study was also specified by a quartet of authors writing the book, *An Introduction to Pastoral Theology*. Part II of this Anglican book was dedicated to the theme, "The Priest's Ministry to the Individual."[44] Chapters in this section deal with the care of the sick, the confessional, the ministry of reconciliation and the care of children. The emphasis on individual case study is the thrust of Part III, "The Treatment of Special Cases."[45] Special consideration is given to the nature of mental and spiritual disease, the priest as spiritual physician, some morbid types such as intellectual doubt, the scrupulous, the recidivist and sexual aberrations. Special case studies dealing with the problems of marriage, temperament and social life conclude this important section of the book.

O. Chambers gave strength to this trend of thinking with his book, *Workmen of God*. Under Scriptural texts for each chapter, the author indicated a working technique for the cure of souls. The emphasis on special case study and treatment is reflected in the chapter titles dealing with the abnormal, hardy annuals, backsliders, 'two-faced,' sick souls, and stupid souls.[46] Of special significance is the spiritual attitude of the author, particularly in his zeal to win lost souls.[47] The Scriptural basis and emphasis upon working with individuals for specific needs is the main characteristic of this book.

The title of R. H. Edwards' book, *A Person-Minded Ministry*, is a clear indication of the character of this writing. Chapter one, "Person-Mindedness," is the springboard for stressing the importance of individual case study. Basing the practice on the person-mindedness of Jesus, and on the necessity of seeing

41. J. H. C. Fritz, *Pastoral Theology, A Hand-Book of Scriptural Principles*, Concordia Publishing House, St. Louis, 1932, p. 185.
42. Ibid.
43. Ibid., p. 195.
44. Balmforth, Dewar, Hudson, Sara, op. cit., pp. 83-193.
45. Ibid., 197-298.
46. O. Chambers, *Workmen of God*, Dodd, Mead & Co., New York, 1938, pp. 15-85.
47. Ibid., pp. 85-108.

persons as ends in themselves, the author demonstrates how we should seek and help modern persons who are perplexed. Chapter three, "Getting and Facing the Facts,"[48] chapter four, "Realizing the Meaning of Facts,"[49] and chapter five, "Acting on the Basis of Facts,"[50] demonstrate the full significance of his specialization on individual case study. In each chapter he included the insight and practice of Jesus in relation to the person. The high value which the author places on individual case study is reflected on every page of these chapters. The importance of the knowledge of the facts, the background, the environment and the experience of the individual constantly confront the reader as the author interweaves a balanced discussion of this important trend. The need for a person-minded ministry is not only emphasized but fully explained and detailed in chapters six to ten. In the final chapter the author indicates how we should prepare ourselves for such an effective person-minded ministry. The entire book is a tremendous lift for the importance of knowing the individual in his environment, circumstance, and future possibilities.

One more book demands our attention in our examination of this trend. It is the most recent volume on the subject of pastoral theology. A. W. Blackwood has given us, *Pastoral Work*, a book intended as a source book for ministers. Only one chapter deals with the treatment of special cases,[51] but the discussion in this chapter is very much to the point. In view of the fact that the book covers the general work of the pastor, one could not expect more on the treatment of special cases. The spirit of individual attention is evident in the book and the variety of practical suggestions for the help of the individual is noteworthy.

Comparing the period of application with the period of development in relation to the particular interest of both in individual case study, we note a definite advance. The latter period was a time of specialized application, particularly with respect to the study and treatment of mental disorders of the person and the modern perplexing world in which people live.

SUMMARY

Specialized interest in and application to individual case study was evident in the growing concern for mental and physical characteristics and needs of the individual.

D. The Sociological Approach

Just before the turn of the century E. D. Weigle struck a note which became

---

48. Richard Henry Edwards, *A Person-Minded Ministry*, Cokesbury Press, Nashville, 1940, pp. 42-61.
49. Ibid., pp. 62-90.
50. Ibid., pp. 92-122.
51. Andrew Watterson Blackwood, *Pastoral Work*, The Westminster Press, Philadelphia, 1945, pp. 162-171.

a trend during the period of application. He gave a warning with regard to the social evils of his time by writing:

> "The attitude of the ministry to these current social problems should be that of Christlike and helpful sympathy in maintenance of a positive gospel as the only remedy for all the maladies which afflict society."[52]

This emphasis became a conscious feeling among writers of pastoral theology. F. Lynch sensed the spirit of the times and our necessary approach when he wrote:

> "The Epicurean philosophy has a great following in our land today, and especially in some of our great cities it is attracting so many devotees that it is creeping into our churches. The name is not used. Half the people who hold the philosophy would not know the word if one mentioned it. But all their thought and life is ordered by the old Epicurean pagan teaching. It is simply this; that life is for self-employment, not for altruism, service or sacrifice. Any man who lives simply for what enjoyment he can get out of life is an Epicurean . . . One cannot live long in the city without realizing that this philosophy of life has great hold upon fully half of the people in the city."[53]

Lynch contended that this new paganism ought to drive ministers to a better understanding of the community and the times which force and focus their atmosphere upon us.

That W. Gladden felt this influence of our time is evident from the fact that he wrote:

> "The forms of this life greatly vary as civilization changes. New occasions teach new duties. Ethical standards are purified and elevated; the emphasis of teaching is altered; modes of address, methods of administration that once were effective are no longer practicable, the work of the church must be adapted to the conditions by which it is surrounded."[54]

Gladden recommended a thorough knowledge of the times in which the minister serves. He did not forget the educational and philanthropic circles in which people moved.

Keen insight was revealed when R. Z. Fahs expressed the following statement in line with this trend of thinking:

> "Let us not forget that the habits and conditions of the people have so changed that the preachers of today cannot do their work as did the preachers of a past generation. There is as much difference between the pastoral work of today and that of fifty years ago as there is between methods of travel or warfare then and now."[55]

Similar discernment was expressed by A. J. Lyman in his discussion of the pastor as spiritual sponsor and social mediator. He sought to approach the pastoral spirit from "the plain, human ground floor of Christian experience and psychological law, rather than from the assumptions of an ex cathedra

---

52. E. D. Weigle, "The Ministry and Current Social Problems," *The Lutheran Quarterly*, October, 1894, p. 476.
53. Frederick Lynch, *The New Opportunities of the Ministry*, Fleming H. Revell Co., New York, 1912, pp. 44, 45.
54. Gladden, op. cit., p. v.
55. Fahs, op. cit., p. 531.

ordination."[56] He revealed that he felt the sociological implications of pastoral service when he wrote:

> "This mediation is distinctively social. Pastoral mediation has to do with the relations between man and man, class and class, as determined by the relation between man and God. The pastor helps everybody to understand everybody else, and is doing so to understand Christ most of all."[57]

This kind of thinking was termed "spiritual sociology" by C. F. Rogers. His slant needs re-emphasis:

> "We need besides an independent and purely spiritual sociology of the church, for 'we are each one citizens of one true city' and live as pilgrims on earth. This is to be created by the same methods that have done so much for the understanding of secular society by observation and comparison, by patient investigation and humble submission to facts."[58]

He contended that man as social being presents certain considerations for the study of a pastor. Because of man's social relations to fellow man, pastoral theology must take these into account and evidence how the minister must deal with such multiplied problems.

The same opinion was expressed by G. K. A. Bell:

> "I do not indeed forget that the minister of Jesus Christ is the minister of an eternal gospel, or that in its essential character that gospel is, rightly described as unchanging. But the truth which I would emphasize is; the men and women to whom Christ's word is spoken change, the conditions in which they live and are brought up change with them. There are changes of thought; changes of language; changes of habit; changes of a social and political character. All these things are bound to affect, not the essence of the gospel, but the manner of its expression, the method of presentation, and surely they must also to some degree great or small, affect the mental attitude and general equipment of the men to whom its preaching is entrusted."[59]

Bell sensed the social situation of the age and the opportunties which await the alert minister of an unchanging gospel.

G. S. Dobbins felt that the order of life was constantly changing and the minister should be one who could cope with this fluctuating social order. He indicated this in the following language:

> "No thesis is required to prove that ours is a changing social order. As a matter of fact every age has been an age of change. At no period of history has human life been completely static. Yet some epochs of history have been notable for the speeding up of changes. In the twenty years since the outbreak of the World War (I) more far-reaching changes have taken place in human affairs than in any century of preceding history. What we shall see when a plateau is reached God only knows; but we may be perfectly assured that we shall never again see the world of 1914."[60]

56. Albert Josiah Lyman, *The Christian Pastor in the New Age*, Thomas Y. Crowell and Co., New York, 1909, p. 67.

57. Ibid., p. 92.

58. Rogers, op. cit., pp. 208, 209.

59. G. K. A. Bell, *The Modern Parson*, Student Christian Movement, London, 1928, p. 2.

60. Gains S. Dobbins, "Theological Education in a Changing Social Order," op. cit., p. 182.

As we look about us today, we find that Dobbins' prophetic insight came to fruition in even greater measure than he anticipated. He understood the trend of the times and urged ministers to be alert to the situation. He gave warning in regard to the dominance of the group over the individual and the overshadowing of the spiritual by the material. Anticipating all of these conditions, he advised serious consideration of the sociological approach by pastors.

The period of application found its strong expression of this and other trends in a practical way. One additional reference will summarize the emphasis in the trend now under discussion:

> "He must know his community. Sometimes a knowledge of the traditions and customs of a community will go toward helping a preacher make important and necessary contacts. In a mining town he must know something of ores. In the country he should be interested in farming and live stock. In the city he would do well to have some acquaintance with commerce. Whatever the particular industry or the occupation of the people whom he serves, it should become a matter of interest to him. And for the sake of his people he should acquaint himself with their problems growing out of these things."[61]

The writers of this period evidenced a practical approach to the sociological issues and opportunities of the day. They had a social consciousness. They understood that the pastor had to take account of the changing social order.

SUMMARY

A new sociological consciousness reflected itself in the work of the average pastor and in the writings of pastoral theology.

E. Pastoral Counseling

The influence of present day psychology on counseling also touched the field of pastoral theology. Just before the turn of the century, J. Watson wrote concerning this important work of the pastor. He realized a growing responsibility in this respect and denounced the fact that Protestants are behind Roman Catholics in the *consultation approach* of our ministry. He also gave some suggestions how this consultation should be carried out.[62]

Two splendid chapters from the work of T. H. Pattison demonstrate the interest in pastoral counseling. His chapter on "Pastoral Intercourse,"[63] shows the adaptability which is required of a minister, and his chapter on "The Minister as Counselor,"[64] indicates the potentially wide range of pastoral contacts and the importance of counseling.

The drastic need for such counseling was expressed by H. Adams when he quoted Dr. C. Mayo, who had spoken on behalf of the American College of Surgeons:

---

61. Josiah Blake Tidwell, *Concerning Preachers*, Fleming H. Revell Co., New York, 1937, pp. 135, 136.
62. John Watson, *The Cure of Souls*, Dodd, Mead, and Co., New York, 1896, p. 235.
63. John Harwood Pattison, *For the Work of the Ministry*, American Baptist Publication Society, Philadelphia, 1907, pp. 397-415.
64. Ibid., pp. 481-502.

"Every other hospital bed in the United States is for the mentally afflicted, insane, idiotic, feeble-minded . . . There are an enormous number of people who are almost fit for the asylum . . . Who better than the well trained and sympathetic pastor could sit in conference with the man whose forces of mind and character are inhabited by fear, either conscious or sub-conscious, and show him how faith could unleash his powers."[65]

Adams saw the need, and although he did not prescribe the method to accomplish success, the manner in which he wrote indicated that he sensed the urgency of the matter.

T. B. Tidwell not only saw the importance of counseling but also suggested a method — a conference period. His reason was, "The pastor cannot succeed without frequent conferences with individuals and groups."[66] W. C. Martin likewise stressed the importance of visiting and counseling, indicating that no substitute has been found for pastoral calling. In the giving of a few rules for counseling, Martin was careful to avoid all temptations to indulge in amateur psychiatry.[67] From the Anglican point of view the quartet of writers, previously referred to, presented a chapter on, "Preparation for Confession,"[68] and a chapter on "The Hearing of Confessions,"[69] Both chapters reveal understanding insight into the technique of pastoral counseling.

SUMMARY

The importance of pastoral counseling was observed and brought to bear in the lives of people by enlightened writers and pastors.

Viewing the entire period of application it becomes very evident that many of the concepts and practices stressed by the writers of this period were not new. That is why this period has been called the period of application. During this particular time there was an intensification of application rather than the discovery of new techniques. It is striking to note that such matters as systematic visitation and the organized planning of pastoral theology were not predominant in the books of the twentieth century. Some books included this approach but in the main the attempt was to apply the technique of pastoral theology along the lines of specified interests of individual authors.

It is also striking that the Scriptural emphasis both by way of foundation for shepherding and as a guide for the application of techniques in the performance of the pastoral task was almost entirely lacking. This, of course, marks a distinct loss — for the Bible remains the foundation guide for all of pastoral work.

The trends during the last period are marked by a strong tendency toward the application of principles previously discovered and enunciated. The interest in applied psychology, the increased emphasis on the sociological approach,

65. Adams, op. cit., p. 138.
66. Tidwell, op. cit., p. 143.
67. William C. Martin, *To Fulfill This Ministry*, Abingdon-Cokesbury, Nashville, 1949, pp. 73-75.
68. Balmforth, Dewar, Hudson, Sara, op. cit., pp. 116-134.
69. Ibid., pp. 135-163.

the detailed interest in human nature and the knowledge of individual cases gave indication of the applicatory characteristic of this period of our study.

Looking back over the entire history of pastoral theology we conclude that many fine principles and policies were established by the writers and practitioners of this theological science. Modern students of pastoral psychology do well to review and remember their contribution to our thinking. We find that we are not as modern and up-to-date as we think, when we discover that many of the present day theories and techniques were practiced and tested by the writers and pastors of previous days. In essence, pastors of earlier days had most of what we call "strictly modern and new." Not in the same way, nor in the same degree, and surely not in the same language, but certainly with the same goal of bringing souls into a living and vital relationship with Jesus Christ, men of a previous day demonstrated remarkable contributions to the science of pastoral theology.

This does not minimize the new discoveries of psychology nor the importance of finding and fusing a new pastoral psychology for our age and generation. The point is, we must appreciate the rich heritage of the past in pastoral theology, and we must come to a new appreciation of the tremendous aid which psychology can give to this rich heritage in the formulation of a pastoral psychology worthy of the gospel of Jesus Christ and appropriate to the times in which we live.

Having viewed this historical heritage in the field of pastoral theology with genuine appreciation for the work of God through the leaders of the past, we are now ready to consider a research analysis of a specific area of service for the pastor. Not only must we understand the historical basis of pastoral theology in relation to pastoral psychology, but, as will be revealed in Part II, we must also explore and discover the area of experience in which people are sincerely desirous of help in our days of confusion and crisis. Therefore Part II gives an account of original research in the field of sickness, suffering and sorrow. This study will prepare us for a later consideration of Part III, "Constructive Analysis" and Part IV, a "Technique Analysis" of our subject,

Part II

RESEARCH ANALYSIS

Concerning Sickness, Suffering and Sorrow in Relation to Pastoral Psychology

CHAPTER V

Questionnaire Investigation on Sickness, Suffering and Sorrow

THE original purpose of sending forth a printed questionnaire on the subject of sickness, suffering, and sorrow was to obtain information for a book planned on this subject. During my serious illness in 1946 and 1947, many of my friends urged me to write a book on suffering. Because of these suggestions and because the Lord laid it on my heart as a responsibility, I decided to write my personal testimony in a book called, *Victory Over Suffering.*

I hesitated to write a book of this kind because I felt my experience was individual and specific and there were countless other people who had related experiences, just as real and just as vital. Many people came to me during my illness and told me of their personal experience as if theirs were the only and final pattern of Christian experience during illness. Theirs did not always coincide with my experience. This, of course, did not mark either mine or theirs abnormal; but it indicated a variety of Christian experiences during illness. Therefore, in order to obtain a true cross section of experience in the time of suffering, I constructed a questionnaire which could be circulated for the purpose of ascertaining the specific and personal experiences and impressions of afflicted people.

A. The First Questionnaire

The first questionnaire was a "trial" attempt. It was sent to thirty people who were asked to fill it out and to evaluate the technique. This was done in order to prepare the kind of a questionnaire that could ultimately be sent to hundreds of people. The first questionnaire contained a number of specific questions. They were as follows: Why are you sick? What were your reactions before and after the operation? How did faith play a part in your recovery? Can you be sure of your salvation? Did you experience recurrent feelings of frustration and inability to carry on? What was your experience of the grace of God? What were your reactions when you were at the door of death? What is the hardest part of sorrow? What is your advice to those who are in sorrow? How did the testimony of others at your bedside help you? What has been your experience in giving personal testimony during sickness? What are the problems of old age? What are the blessings of old age? What are your temptations now that you have recovered from your illness? What is your advice to others who have suffered? These questions were listed under specific headings of thought, such as, Sickness, Faith, Assurance, How can I take it? Death, Sorrow, Witnessing, Old Age, and Recovery. Under each of these sections a question was listed which asked for the Bible passage, hymn, and poem selections which gave the respondent blessing and strength.

As soon as the questionnaire was printed, it was evident that the form was not desirable. Nevertheless it was tested on thirty representative people in various walks of life, in the hope of discovering the right kind of form which should be used. The very purpose of sending forth the questionnaire was annulled in the first form used because the very thing I wanted to avoid, I invited. I did not want to set the pattern of reply, and the first form of the questionnaire clearly indicated the modes and attitudes I wished to discover.

Ever mindful of the limitations of the questionnaire method, and remembering the pitfalls of the psychologists, Starbuck, James, Stratton and Coe, in employing such methodology, I sought to discover the best possible way of obtaining the desired information on sickness, suffering and sorrow. The psychologists sought psychological and biological information in order to determine the experience of conversion. In addition, G. A. Coe in particular, used the method of interviews to clarify answers to his questionnaires. The consciousness of the pitfall of setting the pattern of reply and the failure of letting the respondent give personal, volitional and expressional reply, forced me to seek a better form. In addition, there was the desire and scientific necessity of obtaining a knowledge of the spiritual experience attendant on sickness, suffering and sorrow. This search, of course, was unfortunately entirely lacking in the procedure of the psychologists who sought information on conversion. This was the very search which was fundamental to my project.

B. The Final Questionnaire

By means of testing the first questionnaire in the way already indicated and by means of talking with people who had received them, the conclusion was clear. The questionnaire should be one which was "wide open" for any one who could and would write to the full concerning his experience in the school of affliction. After much study, prayer, and thought, the final questionnaire was constructed.

In order to present a friendly approach and a testimony of my experience, the first page appeared in the form of a typewritten letter, on letter-head paper with typewriter type face. A place for the date, the salutation and my signature in handwriting was left open so that each questionnaire would have a personal appeal. Folded, the questionnaire looked like a business or personal letter, standard eight and one-half by eleven inches in size. When the first page was turned over by the receiver, the questionnaire was open before him.

The following is a duplication of the material found in the questionnaire, although the space left for reply under each section cannot be indicated. Two sections appeared on the opened inside page to the left, and the other two sections appeared on the inside page to the right. The back of the questionnaire was left blank so that if any wished to respond at length there was sufficient space to do so.

(First page of questionnaire)

WESTERN THEOLOGICAL SEMINARY
OF THE REFORMED CHURCH IN AMERICA
HOLLAND, MICHIGAN

REV. WILLIAM GOULOOZE, D. D.
385 COLLEGE AVE.

Dear Friend:

You have been recommended as one who can help in a study that will benefit many people. My own recent experience of a very serious illness (cancer), my inability to do my work for nearly a year, my experience of the strength and blessing of salvation in Jesus Christ, and my recovery of health impel me to ask your assistance in an important research.

Many people have suggested that I place my experience in writing for the benefit of others. After much prayer on this matter, I have become convinced of my duty to write such a book. My experience was rich and deep, offering sufficient material for a book. However, rather than reflect just my own experience in this book, I desire to learn about the experiences of many others in sickness, suffering and sorrow. All of these experiences ought to render a balanced interpretation for the book.

This project is entirely a labor of love in thanksgiving to the Lord for granting me recovery from my illness. The author will receive no profit or royalty from this book. The plan includes the placement of this book for sale in the book stores, and the offer of a free copy to all sick and shut-in people who cannot afford to buy a copy. The few people who have heard of this plan endorsed it heartily and offered financial assistance to make it available for those who cannot afford to purchase it. The details will be worked out as the Holy Spirit directs and opens the way.

I am asking you to help me in this project. I would appreciate it if you would do four things.

1 — Very briefly, write your experience of sickness and sorrow.

2 — List the lessons you learned from your experience.

3 — Indicate your favorite Bible passage, hymn, and poem which helped you in your experience.

4 — Recommend a few selected people you know who would be just the right persons to make reply to this request.

I would appreciate it if you could send this back in the next few days. Accept my hearty thanks for your assistance.

Sincerely,

W. GOULOOZE.

(Second page of the questionnaire. When the folded questionnaire is opened,
this appears the left hand side)

A Confidential

QUESTIONNAIRE

Concerning

SICKNESS, SUFFERING, AND SORROW

(This can include accident, operation, invalidism, old age, etc.)
For additional writing space, use back side of letter page.

I — VERY BRIEFLY WRITE YOUR EXPERIENCE OF SICKNESS,
SUFFERING, OR SORROW.

....
....

II — LIST THE LESSONS YOU HAVE LEARNED FROM YOUR EXPERIENCE.

1 —
....
2 —
....
3 —
....
4 —
....
5 — ·
....
6 —
....

(Third page of the questionnaire)

III — LIST YOUR FAVORITE HELPS DURING YOUR EXPERIENCE.

1 — Your favorite and most helpful Bible passage..
2 — Your favorite hymn ....
3 — Your favorite poem ....
(If possible, send a copy of the poem, the author's name, the title of the book and
publisher from which it was taken.)

....
....
....

IV — LIST THE NAMES OF INDIVIDUALS YOU RECOMMEND
TO RECEIVE THIS QUESTIONNAIRE.

Name	Street Address	City	Zone	State

Your Signature..
Street Address ....City....................Zone........State ....
Name of Church of which you are a member........................Denomination........................
The people you recommend to receive a questionnaire will not be informed of your name.
Name of people making reply to this questionnaire will not be quoted by name in the book.
If you also prefer not to have me quote or refer to your particular experience. kindly check
here ☐.

Questionnaire and Book Plan
Copyright, 1948 by William Goulooze.

(Back side of questionnaire — left blank for additional remarks by respondent)

In analyzing this questionnaire we note that it presented the appeal in simplified form and asked for four things: (1) a description of the experience, (2) an enumeration of lessons learned, (3) an indication of the written helps during affliction, and (4) the recommendation of others to receive the questionnaire. The pattern of narration regarding experiences, and the subject matter of reply were not stimulated, anticipated, suggested or encouraged. This left room for a highly personal response. Since, as indicated, the reply to the questionnaire was considered confidential, there were no limitations which might keep the individual from unburdening his heart, if he chose to do so.

The distinct purpose in the construction and sending of this questionnaire was to obtain unbiased scientific data concerning the individual which might be enlightening for the development of pastoral psychology. As the psychology students and professors had eliminated the supernatural because of the nature of their questionnaires, so this kind of questionnaire could fall into the opposite danger, that of encouraging the individual to relate only the supernatural aspects of the affliction experience. But the simple fourfold classification, finally decided upon and used, left room for relating any and every experience, told in a personal way without limitations on expression, and without suggesting a pattern or mode of reply.

C. People Who Received the Questionnaire

The next problem was how to begin circulating the questionnaire in order to obtain the testimony from the most representative people. At first it was thought best to work through denominational headquarters with lists of names of their members, but this was so vast and impersonal that this plan was dropped.

The next step was to prepare a brief printed personal letter for ministers in order to present the idea, and ask them for names of people who would, perhaps, respond to the questionnaire. The letters were printed in typewriter type face, and, as in the case of the questionnaire itself, space was left for the typing of the date of letter issuance, the salutation, and the signature to be affixed in longhand. These letters, together with an enclosed questionnaire and a postage guaranteed return envelope, were sent to ministers in several denominations. The list of ministers from various denominations was drawn up with the aid of some one in the particular denomination who knew the people most likely to respond with coöperation. I also sent the letter and questionnaire to the ministers I knew personally, to those with whom I had some acquaintance or those I had chanced to meet. The ministers were asked to recommend names of afflicted people who should receive a questionnaire. The ministers were also invited to make a personal reply in case of personal experience in affliction.

In the case of two cities, Holland and Grand Rapids, Michigan, the letter of invited coöperation was sent to every one of the ministers without exception.

The returns proved that this procedure did not bring the best results. Consequently, this procedure was not continued.

A total of three thousand six hundred sixty-one questionnaires were sent in the period of fourteen months, May 1, 1948 to July 1, 1949. As the replies were returned, most of them contained names of recommended individuals to whom in turn a questionnaire was sent for reply and recommendation.

Having taken note of the method of constructing and sending the questionnaires, we now turn to study the returns and the content of the replies sent back. The following chapter contains this information in summary form and with interpretation.

CHAPTER VI

Questionnaire Returns on Sickness, Suffering and Sorrow

T HE returns to the request to fill out the questionnaire have been most gratifying. In the period of fourteen months, May 1, 1948, to July 1, 1949, 1,009 replies were received. No attempt has been made to judge the returns on a statistical level because the questionnaires were not sent to cover every denomination, or geographically to cover a state or a group of states. And by doing it nothing would have been proved for the purpose of the project. Statistical data was not an object of this study, nor is it important for the final result of the findings.

A. Experiences Reported

The purpose of this questionnaire was to ascertain what the average person experiencing sickness, sorrow or suffering, was thinking about and what his experiences had done to him and for him. The replies were given in confidence and, as the questionnaire indicated, were to be kept confidential after they were received.

Experiences reported in the replies indicate a tremendous amount of physical suffering. The total of human suffering experienced by an innumerable host of unsung and unknown heroes of the faith is simply staggering. It is so extensive and so intensive that the human mind cannot fully comprehend it. The replies indicate mountains of problems which daily confront people in ordinary life. Physical suffering in the form of pain and distress was recorded in nearly every questionnaire. Arthritis takes the lead in the kind of physical affliction reported, and some of the questionnaire answers represent years of untold suffering of pain and limited use of their body as a result of this dread malady. A large number of people reported operations with attendant pain and discomfort. This may seem usual and ordinary, but the questionnaire replies indicate a veritable host of people who have faced series of operations.

With physical suffering, we associate mental problems; and this going-together was also evident in the replies. Most people with serious mental problems do not like to report them, because of the unfortunate stigma which society has attached to such difficulties. Since it was promised that the replies to the questionnaire were to be strictly confidential, they have revealed a surprisingly large number of people who are troubled mentally. The mental problems of rebellion to God and opposition to His will, at least those of a temporary character, loom large in the reports. Particularly in cases of individuals who have been wonderfully restored after mental afflictions, the reply is character-ized by a real note of thanks to God. The large majority of cases reported tell of victory over mental problems and temptations because of the grace of God.

Spiritual vexations also loomed large in these reports. Spiritual problems in connection with physical afflictions and mental problems raised questions about the *why* of human suffering and the reason for personal affliction. Pro-longation of affliction, the inevitable problems of sinfulness of the human heart, and the need for personal self examination marked many of the replies to the first section of the questionnaire.

B. Lessons Learned from Affliction

The second part of the questionnaire dealt with the lessons learned from suffering and sickness. The statement read, "List the lessons you have learned from your experience." Countless lessons emerged from the multifarious conditions and manifold reactions to affliction. All of these had significance for the individual himself and are of tremendous importance for pastoral psychology.

In this survey of fundamental concepts of the sick and suffering, the ideas and convictions of the people who responded, will be given in quotation form under the summary conclusions which have been formulated after prolonged study and analysis of the replies. The conclusions were not preconceived or prepared by the author's choice, but they have emerged from the replies, and therefore they are of great significance. The quotations are exactly as given in the replies by the people themselves. Names and places are not identified because this information is strictly confidential. The questionnaire number is given to indicate source and breadth of information.

The quoted statements appearing under summary conclusions consist of simple short sentences. The material from which they have been chosen is voluminous. After studying the questionnaires each testimony and affirmation was copied and classified. When the task was finished, a complete filing was made of these typewritten classified affirmations and testimonies. Consequently the quoted statements which follow below constitute only a very small per-centage of the actual weight of conviction. In each instance three or four statements have been selected, and under each section such few statements were chosen from five to fifteen single spaced typewritten pages. The statements given here are brief and short, but testimonies of extended form could be supplied. So much excellent material has come through the questionnaire replies that instead of writing one book on, "Victory Over Suffering," there is sufficient testimony for an entire series of books. For the sake of brevity only short statements are reported in this research analysis on the problem of sickness, suffering and sorrow.

Here follow the conclusions of the sick and suffering together with affirmations of personal conviction and faith.

1. *God has a purpose in sending sickness and suffering to the individual.*

   a. "For seventeen years I have been a victim of arthritis. I've felt from the beginning of my illness that God chose me for some purpose and I can truthfully say, I'm glad God chose me."[1]

   b. "Eighteen years ago I was stricken with infantile paralysis, the type that is generally most fatal. I had many complications. God's way is the best way even though God's way is a mysterious way. No good thing will He withhold."[272]

   c. "We do not understand why, but we must know that what He does is right."[122]

2. *Satan troubles God's children in time of suffering.*

   a. "During a lingering illness, Satan came to tempt us so that we would faint under the pressure."[602]

   b. "Satan uses the tool of my affliction to trouble me."[995]

   c. "Satan tempted me many times even to commit suicide."[1000]

3. *Jesus Christ cares for our needs and our burdens.*

   a. "No matter what the affliction, Jesus is always near."[189]

   b. "Jesus Christ is the best friend I have."[419]

   c. "I was not alone; Jesus was with me all the way."[536]

4. *God answers the prayer of faith according to His divine will.*

   a. "God answers prayer in accord with the measure of our faith."[221]

   b. "We must be persistent in prayer and then wait upon God for the answer."[59]

   c. "I have experienced that prayer changes everything."[803]

   d. "God will answer prayer in a way that is best for us."[581]

5. *Pain and suffering lead us closer to God.*

   a. "I can bear this burden today with God's help, tomorrow new strength will be given."[56]

   b. "God gives strength to stand pain."[276]

   c. "When the pain is so severe and no one can give relief, He gives strength."[915]

6. *Balanced faith in God's power to heal is rewarded with recovery.*

   a. "If we have faith, we take God on the strength of His promises."[32]

   b. "I attribute my recovery to the grace of God."[162]

   c. "When the doctors said I could not live, the Lord restored me."[391]

7. *God gives sufficient grace for every trial.*

   a. "His grace is sufficient not only but abounding."[479]

   b. "God is sufficient for any circumstance."[574]

   c. "God's grace is sufficient for all our needs."[762]

8. *We can be sure of our salvation which is the gift of God.*

    a. "We are safe and secure in God's love and care."[372]

    b. "The fear complex of the unsaved should not unbalance the Christian."[477]

    c. "Through chastisement we have the assurance that we are His children."[793]

9. *We can face death with confidence and calmness.*

    a. "Death is hard to understand, yet I felt no bitterness toward God."[191]

    b. "How completely the Lord Jesus Christ has taken the sting out of death."[636]

    c. "For the child of God, death can be welcomed, realizing it is better to be with Christ."[560]

10. *The Bible is our great help in sickness and suffering.*

    a. "I love God's word and find it a great comfort."[342]

    b. "I have come to a deeper appreciation of the Scriptures."[357]

    c. "There is power in God's Word. I am convinced of it."[271]

11. *The Holy Spirit is the constant companion of the Christian.*

    a. "We must be thankful for the Comforter."[603]

    b. "The Holy Spirit who dwells in my heart is my Comforter and guide."[678]

    c. "The Holy Spirit prepares us for trials so that we may be submissive."[577]

12. *God gives us comfort for sorrow through His grace.*

    a. "Not God's blessing nor yet His word but God Himself is our real comfort."[221]

    b. "I have been sustained wonderfully by God's grace and comfort in my bereavement."[223]

    c. "My greatest comfort is that I with body and soul belong to my faithful Savior Jesus Christ."[231]

    d. "He can give serenity of mind in sorrow."[351]

13. *We can learn contentment through suffering.*

    a. "Faith in the Lord has given us contentment in all our affliction."[110]

    b. "After twenty-eight years of deformity due to arthritis, after four operations and two sons in the service, I can say, There is always a reason to be cheerful in the Lord and we should learn to overlook what is disagreeable in life."[72]

14. *Thinking health is very important for our mental and spiritual well-being in the Lord.*

    a. "Never give up and keep looking up."[103]

    b. "Be cheerful, always rejoicing in the Lord. Do not try to compare your ills with some one else. Do not groan when you suffer."[72]

c. "Waiting on the Lord is a technique that restores depleted energies."[33]

d. "As a blind person, I manage to find something to occupy my time. To me life is very interesting, more so than it is for a lot of sighted persons. I seldom think of my blindness and the world is, one might say, at my fingertips. I have felt God's guidance and nearness throughout the years."[123]

15. *Cooperation with the doctors and the nurses is a necessity and a Christian's duty.*

a. "My examination will tell if I must submit to surgery. I shall have to place my faith in the doctors, trusting that the Lord has given them wisdom to know what is best for me."[58]

b. "I always ask God to bless my doctors."[216]

c. "God guides the hands of those who perform surgery upon His children."[232]

d. "We should remember the blessings of modern surgery and the debt we owe the medical profession."[364]

e. "Coöperate with your doctor. Help the nurse all you can."[685]

16. *God is our strength for every circumstance.*

a. "In the time of weakness we can be made strong if we look to the Lord for our help."[371]

b. "The Lord can help us the most when we cannot help ourselves."[154]

c. "God wonderfully provides when one has special need."[221]

d. "God is my Saviour, a very present help in the day of trouble."[486]

e. "Here I stand at the end of the road, age seventy-nine. I trust in the Lord; He has always helped me."[597]

f. "God will supply all of our needs. Underneath are the everlasting arms."[507]

17. *"God gives His people songs in the night during suffering.*

a. "Not one night in all those seven years did I sleep well, but God gave me 'songs in the night.' "[530]

b. "On a bed of illness it is our comfort to know that He is near. It makes us think of the song, 'Count Your Many Blessings.' "[883]

c. "We can have songs in the night if we are truly His."[925]

18. *We can have fellowship in Christ's suffering.*

a. "I have learned the fellowship of suffering."[529]

b. "Jesus Himself suffered everything that can come to us; so He knows our weaknesses. He knows just how we need Him and just what we need from Him."[828]

c. "During my troubles I thought of Jesus and all He endured for us while He was on earth."[879]

19. *Sufferers who know, recommend Jesus Christ as the all sufficient Savior and the satisfying High Priest.*

　　a. "I believe in Jesus Christ. I believe His blood was shed for my sins."[530]

　　b. "I thank my Savior that He brought me from darkness to full and complete fellowship with Him."[732]

　　c. "It is wonderful and blessed to be a Christian."[753]

　　d. "A lost sinner must not place his confidence in man, but in the great Physician, Jesus Christ."[793]

　　e. "Christ satisfies."[596]

　　f. "How wonderful to know the Lord as your personal Savior even in the time of trouble."[895]

C. Choice Selections of Help to the Sick and Suffering

1. Hymn selections

A large number of hymn selections were given as helps for the experiences and sorrowing trials of shut-ins. These were indicated as having been taken from various hymn books, from the book of memory, and under various circumstances. The following hymns are listed according to the descending order of choice by the respondents to the questionnaires:

(1) "What a Friend"
(2) "All The Way My Savior Leads Me"
(3) "Have Thine Own Way, Lord"
(4) "Under His Wings"
(5) "Blessed Assurance"
(6) "Does Jesus Care?"
(7) "He Leadeth Me"
(8) "How Firm a Foundation"
(9) "Jesus Lover Of My Soul"
(10) "Abide With Me"

2. Poem Selections

This represented a wide and variant selection. Many of the selections were given without indicating authorship because they had come down as a family possession and tradition. Some respondents indicated that they had memorized their selections and cherished these poems for years. They had faced dangers, operations and death with the strength and inspiration of these poems.

The poems sent in came from various sources, such as Sunday School papers, books of poems, newspapers, magazines, and get-well greeting cards. In many cases people indicated a particular find of a specific poem under unusual circumstances. They kept them as their guide under special providence. And many who replied said they did not know from whence the poems had come, but they had kept them in mind and heart for all the years of their troubles.

It would be impossible to list choices of poems which were sent in. The main emphasis of the poems selected can be summarized in the following concluding statements:

(1) Frank recognition of afflictions, burdens and trials
(2) The fear of surgery and God's strength to meet it
(3) The reality of death and the inner conflict to meet it
(4) God's sustaining grace in time of trial
(5) The sufficiency of Jesus Christ for every trial
(6) Peace of mind through poems of author experience
(7) Complete surrender in the most trying circumstances
(8) Christian assurance of salvation and God's presence
(9) Scriptural comfort written in Scriptural language
(10) Christ gives victory over sin, death, and the world

There is one poem which was submitted so many times that amidst all the variation of selections, it stands out far ahead of all others suggested. Because of its singular popularity and because it so epitomizes the real spirit of the replies, it is quoted here.

> *"According to all that He promised there hath not failed one word . . ."* — I Kings 8:56.

> "God hath not promised skies always blue,
>   Flower strewn pathways all our lives through.
> God hath not promised sun without rain,
>   Joy without sorrow, peace without pain.
> But God hath promised strength for the day,
>   Rest for the laborer, light on the way:
> Grace for the trial, help from above,
>   Unfailing sympathy, Undying love."

3. *Selections from the Scriptures*

The selections of Scripture passages by the respondents to the questionnaire represents both a marked choice and a wide variety. Below is the listing of the favorite passages in descending order of choice by the respondents.

(1) Psalm 23
(2) John 14
(3) Psalm 91
(4) Isaiah 26:3
(5) II Corinthians 12:9
(6) Psalm 27
(7) Psalm 46:1
(8) Isaiah 41:10
(9) John 3:16
(10) Romans 8
(11) Psalm 42
(12) Psalm 103
(13) I Peter 5:7
(14) Psalm 121

D. Recommendation of Other Afflicted People

The fourth section of the questionnaire dealt with making recommendation of other people to whom the same inquiry should be sent. These names represent the acquaintance of individuals in the school of grace. Very few people failed to send names of individuals whom they recommended. Some pastors were very prompt in sending names of individuals and some were neglectful or ignored the request. In nearly every returned questionnaire, the entire blank space was filled out with names of recommended people.

In concluding our findings in this research analysis on sickness, suffering and sorrow, we must state the conviction that *as pastors* we have not begun to reach the actual conditions and circumstances of people under affliction. Some pastors, through personal experience, have been touched to a white heat in the fires of affliction; but others have failed to feel and understand the troubles of their flocks.

This research opens the door for a new evaluation of the need for a better approach to this age old problem. We must discover better ways and means of understanding the needs of and of ministering to people in trouble. It must be through pastoral psychology that a blending of the Biblical conceptions of grace, help, strength and spiritual life is to be interpreted in the light of the new means and aids presented by psychology. All of this has a definite bearing on and relationship to our subject, *pastoral psychology*.

In a consciousness of this relationship, we now turn to Part III, which seeks to make a "Constructive Analysis" of the content of a sound and workable pastoral psychology. Having seen the history of pastoral theology, and having studied the problem of sickness, suffering and sorrow with the questionnaire method of investigation, we proceed now to a constructive analysis of pastoral psychology based on the Word of God and on a solid theological basis.

Part III

A CONSTRUCTIVE ANALYSIS
OF PASTORAL PSYCHOLOGY

CHAPTER VII

Coordination Between Pastoral Theology and Psychology

IN PART I of this book we made an historical analysis of pastoral theology as it relates to psychology. We considered the crisis of our age and the importance of pastoral theology in relation to it. Part II of this book was devoted to a research analysis of the particular problems of sickness, suffering and sorrow which play so prominent a part in the lives of the constituent members of the pastor's flock. Naturally, there are many other areas of life in which the pastor works; but this particular area was studied by means of the questionnaire method in order to determine some fundamental concepts and conclusions for pastoral psychology.

We have now come to Part III of our subject and in this section we desire to make a constructive analysis of the relation of pastoral theology to psychology. We cannot cover the entire range of pastoral work, neither do we desire to do so. It is the purpose of this chapter to discuss some considerations which may guide us in formulating a pastoral psychology for our day and generation.

A. Our Times Require It

In chapter I we indicated that we are living in a time of sociological, psychological, and theological crisis. We wish to attempt a coördination of pastoral theology and psychology because of this present crisis. We may not isolate the ministry and the study of pastoral theology and psychology from the actual facts of life. In our day horizons have been raised; we are living in a new age. And, although some claim that the gospel cannot satisfy this generation, we maintain that the gospel is sufficient for every age. What seems to be lacking in the gospel as some interpret it, is but the result of inadequacy of understanding.

In our revolutionary days, amidst conflicting tendencies, pastoral work is becoming increasingly difficult. For example, our times present the knotty problem of behaviour. Our churches, our youth, and the world round about us have forced us to consider the tremendous problem of conduct and behavior. The psychologists have tried to meet this problem; and the ministers have virtually by-passed it, or pronounced a series of negations against the youth who are victimized by our times. The problem remains with us in a rapidly accentuating form.

Let us examine some sample observations made by a host of writers who sense the psychological and economical stress of our times, and withal, the responsibility of the pastor in this connection.

C. Bassett wrote:

> "Thousands of homes which are economically solvent are shaken and torn with serious problems which the participants themselves are helpless to untangle."[1]
> "With the increased practice among ministers of having regular conference hours when people are encouraged to come for the discussion of their concrete personal problems, the minister is in a strategic position to bring skilled service to the solution of many heart breaking situations."[2]

From another viewpoint, yet with the same duress, P. Bradley wrote concerning our fears:

> "The complexity of modern life makes ever increasing demands on the individual. The strain is evidenced not only in the failures of confidence and courage for business and social life, but also and most obviously, in the physical breakdown of many of our people."[3]

Calling attention to the noise of big cities, the pressures of social standing, and the crushing fears of modern civilization, he demonstrated that our times are frought with problems for every individual.

This brings us face to face with the problem of religious experience. In the words of L. Dewar:

> "It may perhaps be said that the religious problem of the second quarter of the twentieth century is the problem of religious experience. This fact is largely due to the greatly increased interest in and knowledge of psychology since the end of the last century."[4]

Face to face with the facts and the discoveries of psychology, we must utilize them for effective service in the kingdom of God. We must come to see that in our age of crisis and strain, there is an inherent challenge to produce an effective pastoral psychology. A quotation from W. F. Halliday touches upon that challenge briefly. He wrote,

> "We are living in an age of peculiar psychical unrest, and the religious mind will not deem it apart from the providential ordering of God that important psychological discoveries should give the key to the allaying of that unrest."[5]

He depicted the world as sick and in need of a physician. What an opportunity is ours for proper coördination of pastoral theology and psychology—for we are the ambassadors of the great physician who is available if only we will show Christ to the world and to the people of our parish.

---

1. Clara Bassett, *Mental Hygiene in the Community*, The Macmillan Co., New York, 1934, p. 270.
2. Ibid.
3. Preston Bradley, *Mastering Fear*, The Bobbs-Merrill Co., Indianapolis, 1935, p. 149.
4. Lindsay Dewar, Man and God, *An Essay in the Psychology and Philosophy of Religious Experience*, Society for Promoting Christian Knowledge, London, 1935, p. vii.
5. W. Fearon Halliday, *Psychology and Religious Experience*, Hodder and Stoughton, Ltd., London, 1929, p. 35.

Because of the very complexity of our times, psychology has a right to be considered in relation to pastoral theology. To ignore this consideration is to be blind to reality, since, in the last few years, psychology has come to be a real part of the practical affairs of men. Psychology, sociology, and psychiatry have opened up new areas of thinking and application for the Christian pastor. We must develop the proper coördination between pastoral theology and psychology because our times demand this. This concept of coördination is fundamental to the formulation of a pastoral psychology that is workable, thinkable and profitable.

B. Pastoral Theology Needs Psychology

The minister must remember that psychology can teach him much about the mechanism of man's action and purpose. The pastor has often overlooked the fact that abnormal religious experience frequently can be analyzed by means of psychology. While it is true that morbid and pathological psychology has been sadly overworked, it is also true that the best of psychology has been neglected by pastors. Pastoral theology needs exactly what psychology has to offer as a charge and a challenge. This does not mean the necessity of a wholesale infusion of psychology into the procedures of pastoral theology; but it does call for a serious consideration of that which psychology offers in the way of an aid to pastoral theology.

It is very necessary that pastors of our time see this important relationship. Time is fleeting and the psychologists are over-emphasizing their techniques. While we must use their proffered aid for greater effectiveness in our age of crisis, we must as zealously be on our guard against their exaggerations.

Generally the most important feature of the minister's work is preaching of the Word. This is the clear teaching of God's Word. This receives emphasis when we consider that preaching has been the central theme of many important books in recent years. Therefore, it is of primary importance for pastors to know the Bible and to preach the Word. But, in addition it is extremely important for pastors to know human nature and how best to reach individuals. "We would make whatever knowledge we have of the mind serve Jesus and those whom Jesus would serve."[6]

The modern pastor has a specific place to fill. Who better than the sympathetic and understanding pastor can consult and pray with disturbed individuals? And, who better than the *psychologically* trained and *psychologically* interested minister can give advice and comfort? This does not preclude a spiritual interest or the administration of spiritual blessings. Psychology must be employed as a means to a spiritual end. Pastors have rightly cherished their spiritual responsibility; but too many have discharged it without the aid of psychology. The minister holds the key, but he needs psychology as an aid to understand better how to use the key, and just when to turn it so that the door of the human heart may be opened for consultation and blessing. The pastor needs psychology as an aid to a better understanding of theory and practice.

---

6. Hampton Adams, *The Pastoral Ministry*, Cokesbury Press, Nashville, 1912, p. 138.

A pastoral psychology must be developed. This will raise the entire level of pastoral theology. In the words of C. F. Rogers:

> "It is not merely the standard of efficiency that needs to be raised to the level of that of other professions; the whole conception of pastoral theology needs to be lifted up to a higher plane."[7]

C. Obstacles in the Way of Proper Coördination Between Pastoral Theology and Psychology

It is to be expected that there will remain some differences of opinion between those who advocate the present efficiency of pastoral theology and those who propose to utilize the findings of psychology. Because "there is a glamour nowadays about psychology that tends to exaggerate its possibilities,"[8] many in the camp of pastoral theology are averse to the help that can come from psychology. Some of the exaggerations and arrogations of psychology serve as obstacles in the way of coordination between pastoral theology and psychology. We must discuss these if we are to construct a sound and tenable pastoral psychology for our times.

1. Imperfect Definitions of Religion

Psychologists too often appropriate to themselves the right and function to analyze and define *religion*. This is one of the objections we desire to raise and level at present day psychology. J. B. Pratt blazed a trail in his study of religion and yet he stated clearly in his work that he was not to be bothered with definitions as such. In speaking of psychology of religion he stated:

> "It does not concern itself with the nature or the definition of religion — a question that has resulted in so much smoke and so little light — but is limited to much more modest and concrete problem of the nature of belief in a god or gods, and a basis or bases on which this belief really rests."[9]

W. James, considered to be the foundational writer in the field of psychology as applied to religion, spoke of it in this way,

> "Religion, whatever it is, is a man's total reaction upon life, so why not say that any total reaction upon life is a religion?"[10]

For James, God was only the "absolute." He said:

> "This overcoming of all the usual barriers between the individual and the Absolute is a great mystic achievement. In mystic states we both become one with the Absolute and we become aware of our oneness."[11]

Similar indefiniteness is evident in his references to prayer. He said:

---

7. Clement F. Rogers, *An Introduction to the Study of Pastoral Theology*, The Clarendon Press, Oxford, 1912, p. 5.
8. Eric S. Waterhouse, *Psychology and Pastoral Work*, Cokesbury Press, Nashville, 1940, p. 5.
9. James Bissett Pratt, *The Psychology of Religious Belief*, The Macmillan Co., New York, 1907, p. vii.
10. William James, *The Varieties of Religious Experience*, Longman, Green and Co., London and Bombay, 1903, p. 35.
11. Ibid., p. 419.

"Prayer or inner communion with the spirit therefore — be that spirit 'God' or 'law' — is a process wherein work is really done, the spiritual energy flowers in and produces effects, psychological or material within the phenomenal world."[12]

One reference from C. C. Josey reveals that he falls in the same category:

"The evolution of the belief that human personality in some way survives death furnishes one of the best illustrations of the development that goes on in the conceptions of religion."[13]

G. B. Cutten said, "Religion is man's highest reach."[14] H. C. Miller put it this way, "A simpler and perhaps adequate definition would be "Man's recognition of conflict and his attempt to resolve it on a spiritual plane.' "[15] And R. H. Thouless passed it off by saying, "Religion is a felt practical relationship with what is believed in as a superhuman being or beings."[16] C. A. Wise wrote, "Religion is man's attempt to discover the nature and meaning of life and to formulate a way of life based on that discovery. Symbols are the tools available for that purpose."[17]

While such misconceptions of religion prevail, it is impossible to secure the proper coördination between pastoral theoligy and psychology. We appreciate the groping after light by the psychologists; but we emphatically assert that the Biblical view of Christianity and our relation to God must be accepted by the psychologists if they are to join efforts with us and we with them.

There are a few psychologists who have a genuine feeling for religion. H. Warner recognized the problem and left room for the concept of Holy Spirit who convicts of sin.[18] Likewise G. Steven[19] allowed Biblical truth to enter his discussion when he referred to Christ whose light helps us to know sin. Such writers are few and far between. The more common characteristic of the psychologists has been an indifference to definitions of religion, and a still greater indifference to a definition of Christianity. W. L. Jones indicated the spirit of the psychologists when he wrote

"Whilst it behooves the psychologist to take note of the problems which arise in these fields of inquiry, it is not incumbent upon him to take part in the controversy concerning the definition of religion which has been raised by anthropologists, sociologists, and theologians."[20]

12. Ibid., p. 484.

13. Charles Conant Josey, *The Psychology of Religion*, The Macmillan Co., New York, 1927, p. 122.

14. George Barton Cutten, *Instincts and Religion*, Harper & Brothers, 1940, p. 52.

15. H. Crichton Miller, *The New Psychology and the Preacher*, Thomas Seltzer, New York, 1924, p. 21.

16. Robert H. Thouless, *An Introduction to the Psychology of Religion*, The Macmillan Co., New York, 1923, p. 4.

17. Carroll A. Wise, *Religion in Illness and Health*, (Second Edition), Harper & Brothers, New York, 1942, p. 204.

18. Horace Emory Warner, *The Psychology of the Christian Life*, Fleming H. Revell, New York, 1910, p. 91.

19. George Steven, *The Psychology of the Christian Soul*, Hodder and Stoughton, New York, London, 1911, pp. 107, 108.

20. W. Lawson Jones, *A Psychological Study of Religious Conversion*, The Epworth Press, London, 1937, p. 23.

Jones further contended that in a psychological study of religion it is sufficient to outline the most general psychological characteristics of the religious
object and of religious response. He admitted that the boundary line of inquiry
must remain elastic because of the so-called anthropological and sociological
aspects of individuality, but he did not define them because he preferred to
identify what James called "personal religion" and R. H. Thouless called
"experimental religion" as that which is "distinguished from institutional and
traditional religion."

Many psychologists claim that they are not interested in definitions because,
so they say, definitions are not necessary. Yet we find these same psychologists
trying to define many of the things which they explore and study. And they
even try to formulate their own definition of religion. We agree with S. Norborg's observation when he wrote:

> "After reading some hundreds of volumes on the psychology of religion
> we begin to feel that every new psychologist gives a new but equally
> prejudiced definition of religion."[21]

The psychologists have not given clear definitions of religion and they have
ridiculed theologians for insisting on clarity of thought. With only a rare
exception, the attitude of psychologists continues to be anti-religious and anti-
definitive. The bungling of definitions by the psychologists is a stumbling
block to pastoral theology, and this obstacle must be removed if an effective
pastoral psychology is to be discovered and developed. We need to have the
aid of psychology for an effective ministry, but it must be a psychology that
will recognize the place of the Bible as God's revelation and the place of
Christianity as God's work of redemption.

In marked contrast to our American psychologists, some of the psychologists
of the Netherlands have revealed a clear conception of Christianity and man's
relation to God. H. Bavinck demonstrated the place of psychology in the
Bible and designated the importance of a Christian view of psychology.[22] J. H.
Bavinck urged the need of discovering a wholesome Biblical psychology.[23]
The same wholesome psychological viewpoint based on the Bible and thoroughly scientific is found in the work of J. Waterink,[24] also of the Free University of Amsterdam, the Netherlands. In order to construct a correct pastoral
psychology we must include this Biblical emphasis and this Christian viewpoint.

2. Imperfect Conception of God

Closely allied to the obstacle of imperfect definitions on the part of psychologists, is a second obstacle, namely, the psychologists' imperfect appreciation
and conception of God. James is our first evidence in the following quotation:

21. Sv. Norborg, *Varieties of Christian Experience*, Augsburg Publishing House, Minneapolis, 1937, p. 9.
22. H. Bavinck, *Beginselen der Psychologie*, J. H. Bos, Kampen, 1897, pp. 8-15.
23. J. H. Bavinck, *Inleiding in de Zielkunde*, J. H. Kok, Kampen, 1935, pp. 1-5, 20-22.
24. J. Waterink, *Hoofdlijnen der Zielkunde*, N. V. Gebr. Zomer & Keuning's Uitgevers
Mij, Wageningen, 1934, pp. 7-9.

"This is our own empiricist criterion; and this criterion the stoutest insisters on supernatural origin have also been forced to use in the end . . . In the end it had come to our empiricist criterion: By their fruits ye shall know them, not by their roots."[25]

"If there be higher powers able to impress us, they may get access to us only through the subliminal door."[26]

For James, God was merely the "absolute." God was looked upon subjectively and Jehovah was to him only the "other" and the "large" not the *infinite*. James believed in polytheism because the common people liked it. Similar vagueness was expressed by G. A. Coe:

"If there be a heavenly Father who yearns for fellowship with his children, what more effective method could there be of satisfying that yearning than to attach to adolescence an appetite for the infinite — the infinitely true, beautiful, and good . . . A passion for absolute truth, indubitable certainty, perfect righteousness, all that is most real — this is the mark of it. Then, too, there comes to adolescence a hint of the infinite in the form of beauty."[27]

Dealing very frankly with this problem, J. B. Pratt said,

"This view of the Supernatural so far as it concerns the outer world has been largely given up; and, it must be added, with no great harm to the cause of religion."[28]

However, Pratt felt that this view of the supernatural could not be dismissed or proved false. To use his own words:

"There are too many seeming gaps in our experience, too much that is unexpected and unaccountable in our lives, for us to be able to demonstrate in them an unbroken causal chain."[29]

Pratt felt no inclination to discover God because he was not concerned with the belief in God or even in gods. He left this to the anthropologists, the historians, and the theologians because he felt it was only a speculative and abortive study. He suggested that it would be easy to collect some definitions of deity from the creeds of Christendom and from dogmatic theologies:

"No one can for a moment suppose that these represent with any accuracy the living conviction of the mass of Christian people. Such definitions are almost invariably forms of words put together for the purpose of answering questions. They have a proper and important place in theology and philosophy; they may express what we ought to believe; they have their influence no doubt on what we do believe; but most of them are very far from expressing what God really means to us in our inner and practical living."[30]

Such reasoning, if it can be honored with that name, makes God very small; and while it can give "practical coloring" to life, our fundamental view of God is undermined. In fact, it really rules out God's being entirely. This was

---

25. James, op. cit., pp. 19, 20.
26. Ibid., p. 40.
27. George A. Coe, *The Spiritual Life*, Eaton & Mains, New York, 1900, pp. 54, 55.
28. Pratt, op. cit., p. 38.
29. Ibid.
30. Ibid., p. 200.

the attitude of J. H. Leuba when he wrote, "I cannot persuade myself that divine personal beings, be they primitive gods or the Christian Father, have more than a subjective existence."[31] For Leuba such understanding of the gods came from inductions drawn from "inner" life. Such "inner" experiences, according to Leuba, belong entirely to psychology and therefore such empirical gods belong entirely to science. No wonder K. R. Stolz said that Leuba was influenced by stark humanism. Quoting Stolz, we state the following:

> "He (Leuba) contends that all gods, including the Father-God of Jesus, are the products of the creative imagination of men. He supposes that the mystical core of religion is reducible to the mental processes of the theist himself."[32]

Similar humanism was demonstrated when A. Adler contended that life is merely a coöperation between human beings with endless possibilities in "the progress of our human association."[33] Likewise, J. B. Anderson asserted concerning psychology, "It has no expression to give regarding the Divine except as human consciousness conceives of it."[34] He believed that sin is only mental and outlawed all responsibility to the Divine. To A. E. Baker, "God is to be thought of, as a symbol of a certain amount of psychic energy or libido."[35] He agreed with Freud that this libido was nothing more or less than sexual craving, the urge or sexual need. According to him, religion is everywhere the same whatever name it may carry.

T. V. Moore said, "To the religious-minded man, God is the Supreme Intelligence in a universe of intelligent beings."[36] H. A. Overstreet said the same thing in other words,

> "None of these beliefs about the deity will any longer adequately serve us. Even the belief with which we have grown familiar, of God as a Heavenly Father, who orders our welfare and expects from us adoration and obedience, is, from the modern point of view inadequate."[37]

The conception of God according to the psychologists has come about through the process of evolution of the idea about God, rather than a revealed truth coming through the Bible by the power of the Holy Spirit. I. King stated this in the following words,

> "We would say that the character of Yahwey was built up rather than progressively revealed, for by such a statement we do account for the practical fact of the evolution of a deity, without becoming involved in

31. James H. Leuba, *A Psychological Study of Religion*, The Macmillan Co., 1912, p. 10.
32. Karl R. Stolz, *The Psychology of Religious Living*, Cokesbury Press, Nashville, 1937, p. 132.
33. Alfred Adler, *What Life Should Mean to You*, Little, Brown, and Co., Boston. 1931, p. 24.
34. James B. Anderson, *Applied Religious Psychology*, Richard G. Badger, The Gorham Press, Boston, 1919, p. 5.
35. A. E. Baker, *Psychoanalysis Explained and Criticized*, The Macmillan Co., New York, 1926, p. 154.
36. Don Thomas Verner Moore, *Personal Mental Hygiene*, Crune & Stratton, New York, 1944, p. 236.
37. H. A. Overstreet, *The Enduring Quest*, W. W. Horton & Co., New York, 1931, pp. 259, 260.

the insoluble problem of how an absolutely complete and perfect metaphysical being can possibly ever reveal himself in crude and partial forms, much less than any relation to that which is finite."[38]

The difficulty with such views is that they are untenable. They are foreign to the Bible and the true scientific analysis of all we know about God. The psychologist boasts of having studied the science of psychology; and doing this, he has failed to realize the power and recognize the person of God. The difficulty is that the psychologist has subjected religion to a subjective analysis in terms of his own particular brand of psychology. Psychologists should rather agree with J. G. McKenzie when he says, "I believe the source of all energy is in God, but I believe God works through the channels He has hewn out."[39]

E. S. Waterhouse made the point very clear when he wrote:

"Psychology as a science cannot recommend reliance on the power of God, yet psychology realizes that those who have a sense of help from a power greater than themselves are able to do what those who have not that sense can do."[40]

The average psychologist has not been willing to recognize God. In fact, he has challenged the idea that the old faith in Christ, in God and in the Bible is still possible for a thinking person. We are ready to admit that through psychology men have come to know how things are being done and how man acts in doing them. But this does not necessitate a denial of God who is over all and in all the doing. In fact, the Biblical conception of God is absolutely essential to a workable and effective pastoral psychology. As Weatherford so aptly stated:

"This conception of God, who dwells in our very souls, who lives by our sides, who is our very companion of life, means that all life is of one piece. Part of life is not sacred and part secular. All life which is legitimate for me is sacred and God like. God is as broad as life and fills all life with His sacred presence."[41]

This concept is of supreme importance for the pastor who deals with the sacred Bible and who is the agency of divine blessing for his people. In the words of R. D. Hollington:

"This groundwork must not be merely the conclusion of a philosophical or theological argument, but must become the integrating purpose and the ruling passion of one who would absorb and assimilate the life-giving energy of God in Christ in developing, preserving, and restoring physical, mental, and spiritual health, and in creating ideal social relations set forth by the Master as the kingdom of God."[42]

38. Irving King, *The Development of Religion, A Study in Anthropology and Social Psychology*, The Macmillan Co., New York, 1910, pp. 277, 278.

39. John G. McKenzie, *Modern Psychology and Achievement of Christian Personality*, Second Edition, The National Sunday School Union, London, no date given, p. 120.

40. Eric S. Waterhouse, *Psychology and Religion*, Elkin Mathews Marret, London, 1930, p. 85.

41. W. D. Weatherford, *Personal Elements in Religious Life*, Methodist Publishing House, Nashville, 1916, p. 25.

42. Richard D. Hollington, *Psychology Serving Religion*, The Abingdon Press, New York, 1938, p. 51.

Unless he places God at the center of life, a pastor cannot really minister to the needs of man. If we leave God out, our service will lead to absolute zero in both the goal of life and effective achievement. No wonder E. Barbour wrote:

> "Academic psychology, as such, cannot help us in our search, for it has limited itself very largely to the observable facts of the conscious minds of normal persons."[43]

We object to purely academic psychology because God is left out — both by way of definition and belief. For the child of God, and particularly for the minister, a belief in God is of primary importance. Stating it in the language of T. H. Hughes:

> "The truly Christian man is one for whom Christ has become central, whose master-sentiment is gathered around Him, so that He becomes the formative and directive force in life. The aim of every true minister should be to secure this place for Christ in the life of his people, and to do so if possible in the early days of their lives."[44]

If psychology is to be of help for pastoral theology in the formulation of a constructive, Biblical, scientific pastoral psychology — an integral part of both belief and practice must be focused upon God, the Lord of hosts. We should not forget that the eternal tension between God and man contains the heart-throb of physical victory but also the heartache of spiritual defeat. Like Asaph it puzzles and disturbs us till we go into the sanctuary of God.[45] It touches us in relationship to Christ as both "author and finisher"[46] of our faith. Some call faith in God a risk, while others find it a spiritual romance; but all of us should find and know God to be a personal, powerful and spiritual being. To deny this or negate this by refusing to discuss it, limits our understanding and service. Pastoral psychology to be genuine and true must include this faith in God.

We must recognize the God of Isaiah, high and holy, able to redeem and strengthen His people.[47] We must have the tremendous conviction of Jeremiah, so that we can trust in God, though difficulties of life press on every side.[48] We must minister to people who, like Job, have been bereft of all physical benefits, and in order to witness before them, we must have confidence in God, just like Job.[49] We must know God in the full Biblical revelation. The Bible informs us about God's knowledge, strength, righteousness, mercy, judgment, peace and holiness. Our objection to the psychologists is that they have left this out of their thinking and living. In the formulation of a correct pastoral psychology, faith in God is primary.

---

43. Clifford E. Barbour, *Sin and the New Psychology*, The Abingdon Press, New York, 1930, p. 31.
44. Thomas Hywel Hughes, *The Psychology of Preaching and Pastoral Work*, The Macmillan Co., New York, 1941, pp. 48, 49.
45. Psalm 73:17.
46. Hebrews 12:2.
47. Isaiah 6:1-13, 43:1-28.
48. Jeremiah 1:1-19.
49. Job 13:15.

D. Separation of Psychology and Pastoral Theology

The psychologists have expressed some objections to theology and therefore proper coördination between pastoral theology and psychology has been very difficult in the past. We do not admit that the claims of the psychologists are justifiable, but we must examine them in order to approach a solution to the problem of proper coördination.

G. A. Coe looked down upon religion as a "mass of ascertainable states of consciousness" and said:

> "What is needed is an examination of the facts as such, without reference to their possible bearing upon theology or philosophy. Until this work is done there will remain an important gap in the scientific knowledge of man."[50]

W. James was of the same opinion, and stated,

> "Now in these lectures, I propose to ignore the institutional branch entirely, to say nothing of the ecclesiastical organization, to consider as little as possible the systematic theology and the ideas about the gods themselves, as to confine myself as far as I can to personal religion, pure and simple."[51]

James endorsed liberalism, as is evident from his statement of the following:

> "The advance of liberalism, so-called, in Christianity, during the past fifty years, may fairly be called a victory of health-mindedness within the church over the morbidness with which the old hell-fire theology was more harmoniously related."[52]

James felt that the theological emphasis left in the church was "pessimistic." He believed in a God "who does wholesale, not retail business. He (God) cannot accommodate His processes to the convenience of individuals."[53] This is, of course, a marked departure from the concept of the fatherly love of God revealed in the Bible and individualized in providence.[54]

G. S. Hall recognized the gap between psychology and theology when he said, "We have permitted a chasm to yawn between our secular and religious life, between science and theology."[55]

Psychologists have been interested in *humanology* not in theology. They overlook that man is a unit, and that the natural and the spiritual cannot be separated. They ignore the importance of relating the two.

It is because of this fact that the psychologists have failed to recognize the place of the Christian church and the minister of the gospel. They have refused to accept the necessity of spiritual development. This viewpoint has separated them from the power and influence of Christianity.

---

50. George A. Coe, op. cit., p. 5.
51. James, op. cit., p. 29.
52. Ibid., p. 91.
53. Ibid.
54. Matthew 6:24-34.
55. G. S. Hall, *Adolescence*, D. Appleton and Co., New York, 1904, pp. xvii, xviii.

On the other hand, we maintain that C. E. Hudson was right when he said:

> "Christianity is a supernatural way of life, or it is nothing. What God offers to the human race in and through Jesus Christ is not, primarily, a moral code, nor a series of philosophical propositions, nor a system of philanthropy, but the opportunity of living at another and higher level than the 'natural.' 'Lay hold on eternal life' is one of those texts of Scripture in which the essence of Christianity may be said to be embodied."[56]

Psychologists would do well to adopt the conviction of C. Bassett:

> "The sincere minister can call to his aid in treatment the radiant and intimate picture of the ideal personality of Jesus, with all its contagious and inspiring implications for personal and social development, toward which the faltering progress of the individual may be measured."[57]

Very few psychologists are willing to take the position of S. Norborg who rightly recognized the difference between Christian experience and just "religious" experience.[58]

E. L. House was right when he said, "Psychologists have failed and will fail so long as they leave out of their philosophy the regeneration of man in Christ."[59]

Unless the psychologists descend from their high pedestal of criticism and come to see the need of coöperation and the basic principles underlying such coöperation, pastoral psychology will be limited. The gap between psychology and theology must be bridged and much can be done if psychologists will come to recognize the obstacles which they have placed in the way of coöperation.

E. Coördination of Pastoral Theology and Psychology, to Produce Pastoral Psychology

Because of the conditions which we have described it might appear that psychology and pastoral theology have no connection and should be separated. Our firm conviction is that they should not be separated. These two fields are not separate from each other in basic principles. We must come to realize that there must be a fusing of interests. The psychologists must recognize the spiritual as well as the natural, and the theologians must recognize the natural as well as the spiritual.

This does not mean that one is to take the place of the other but that both must be used to advantage. Men and women are not to be saved by any trick of psychology; yet through the means of psychology the pastor will be better qualified to understand the individual and minister to his spiritual needs. We have arrived at the juncture in history when psychology and pastoral theology must pool their findings and discover a new technique in pastoral psychology.

---

56. Cyril E. Hudson, *Recent Psychology and the Christian Religion*, George H. Doran Co., 1923, p. 67.
57. Clara Bassett, *Mental Hygiene in the Community*, The Macmillan Co., New York, 1934, p. 277.
58. Norborg, op. cit., p. 35.
59. Elwin L. House, *The Psychology of Orthodoxy*, Fleming H. Revell Co., New York, 1913, p. 29.

The counsel of W. M. Horton is very much to the point:

> "Theology must agree without reservations to alter, amend, or cancel altogether whatever there may be in the dogmas of the past that is flatly and decisively contradicted by any new facts that psychology may reveal . . . Psychology, on the other hand, must agree to recognize the limitations that are inherent in any specialized scientific point of view, and therefore grant the possibility that other points of view, and other explanations of the same phenomena, are possible and legitimate."[60]

With that kind of coöperation there can be no ultimate clash between the science of psychology and the art of pastoral theology. Then the extremes of both will fall by the way and a wholesome coördination will result. By the Spirit of God a new coördination must come about in order to formulate pastoral psychology.

This coördination requires considerable adjustment. F. Kunkel has the correct alternatives in the following statement,

> "Psychology, however, including the deepest kind of depth-psychology, cannot rescue us without the help of religion. It is doomed to deteriorate into mere psychologism, just as theology without psychology deteriorates into theologism. The depth is lost and only platitudes remain."[61]

The current feeling is that theology must make the biggest adjustment in relation to the science of psychology. There is certainly a technical adjustment which the proponents of theology must make for the proper work of pastoral psychology. There are many circumference adjustments which must be faced by ministers. But fundamentally the real adjustment must be made in relation to the Word of God. Wherever the pastor is out of line with the Bible, he must come back to its fundamental teachings and principles. In this respect the need for adjustment is even more necessary for the psychologist, because his natural inclination has been away from the Scriptures. The words of a medical doctor, F. Kunkel, are very much to the point in this discussion:

> "We have only one book which gives us the full description of the human situation, and of the way leading through all the troubles and frustrations, and finally into utmost light. It is the great textbook of depth-psychology; the New Testament. Without this religious knowledge, we cannot cure the more serious cases of anxiety and compulsive neuroses, we cannot help the dying person to face death, and we cannot hope to master the collective dark powers which threaten human culture today."[62]

With such a basis, we cannot go wrong in the formulation of a pastoral psychology. Then we will recognize the importance of guilt and redemption. God's covenant with man (Jeremiah 31:31-34) will come to a new emphasis. Man's eternal salvation will be given a careful place in the thinking and working of pastoral theology if the Bible is the foundational book of interpretation.

This does not mean that there need be a clash between psychology and pastoral theology on the subject of man's free will and God's directive decree.

---

60. Walter Marshall Horton, *A Psychological Approach to Theology*, Harper & Brothers, New York, 1931, p. 23.
61. Fritz Kunkel, *In Search of Maturity*, Charles Scribner's Sons, New York, 1943, p. 26.
62. Kunkel, op. cit., p. 28.

"This apparently irreconcilable antagonism between psychological determinism and the Christian concept of the freedom of the will is not an essential conflict.[63] It is only a matter of viewpoint. According to Barbour, psychology looks at the roots and theology at the flower. In a proper coördination man will be treated as a person who has a limited sovereignty and a binding freedom. Under God he will be free, and by God's direction he will be bound to serve the King.

As ministers of the gospel we must also share in the blame for the lack of coördination between pastoral theology and psychology. We have taken our task too much for granted, without opening our minds to the new findings and possibilities of a properly coördinated pastoral psychology. We have followed traditional lines, we have endeavored to labor as others before us, and we have considered our only task to bring Christ to a lost and lonely world. Our task of bringing this salvation is of primary importance, and our duty is first of all a spiritual ministry under the guidance and blessing of the Holy Spirit. However, this does not exclude the use of psychology. We have often carried an air of orthodoxy, without wielding the power inherent in a Biblical and spiritual conservatism. We have held ourselves aloof from the world and all that pertains to it, forgetting that the people whom we should seek to reach in every phase of their experience, actually live in the world of affairs and actions. We do well to remember the advice of W. S. Swisher:

> "The church must get more in touch with the world and its varied social problems, must face present issues, come directly into contact with contemporary life and seek to solve contemporary problems. Thus it may regain its ancient place of esteem in the world."[64]

It has been a tendency among many pastors to follow a set of rules or practices which have been handed to them in a seminary classroom without making adjustments such as they were warned would be necessary when they put the principles to actual test and working order. Our background of viewpoint and training is predominant in our technique. We cannot get away from our training. In the language of C. A. Wise:

> "It is characteristic of theologically trained persons to view religious experience in the light of some theological, psychological or social theory of life and religion. Clinical experience, in contrast, centers attention on the living person, and leads to the evaluation of religious ideas and behavior, in whatever degree of pathology or health, in the light of their function in the personality as a whole."[65]

Such a clinical approach, as suggested by Wise, has been shunned by the average minister. He has kept himself above or away from firsthand observation and study. It has been hard to molest his contentment. Our theology — including the practice and theory of pastoral theology — has been cast in a scholastic mold. We have come to worship at the shrine of logic and we forget that our present generation must be faced with psychological insight.

---

63. Barbour, op. cit., p. 14.
64. Walter Samuel Swisher, *Religion and the New Psychology*, Marshall Jones Co., Boston, 1920, p. 167.
65. Carroll A. Wise, op. cit., p. xii.

The power of God and the message of the gospel, whether given to an individual or to a group, can move more effectively if the channel is clear and conducting. Consecration to God's cause means that we, as the channels of God's person and power, must be informed, enlightened and open minded. Consecration to God's cause, without the proper knowledge of human nature and human situations does not necessarily spell success in the ministry. Success may be achieved, but it would be far more effective if a wholesome coördination of psychology and pastoral theology were brought about through a Christian pastoral psychology.

We must remember the advice of T. H. Hughes:

> "Psychological knowledge has made clearer and more accessible the roots of religion in the soul of man, and helped us to understand how the instinctive impulses of human nature and emotions connected with them have a place, and play their part in a healthy religious life. It has shown us also that there are three basic needs in every human being — the need for security, the need for love, and the need for power — and that, in the final issue, these needs can only find satisfaction as mind and heart are centered on a greater than self; in other words on a Perfect Being."[66]

This is the challenge for pastoral psychology. Pastoral theology has been working with the problems of the day for many centuries of the church's existence. Psychology has been unmindful of the place the church has played in this program of help, health and hope. On their part, the leaders of pastoral theology have been unconcerned about the new sciences of psychology and sociology and have let them go their merry way. F. Kunkel gave a striking expression and a ringing challenge concerning a more desirable relationship when he wrote:

> "The prophets of the Old Testament were practical sociologists. Jesus of Nazareth was the greatest psychologist of all times. But the riches of tradition, accumulated in religious literature and art, were neglected, and theology made no attempt to fight. It gave in, ignoring for many years the new sciences as they in turn ignored theology. Later, however, the ministers began to realize that they needed more knowledge of the human mind, as well as of social relations. So they began to study the secular psychology and sociology as they found them — instead of creating their own Christian sociology and psychology and teaching their secular colleagues the deeper truth and the stronger power that was entrusted to Christianity from the beginning."[67]

This is the challenge of our day to the church. Christian pastors should be alive to this marvelous opportunity. The pastor who studies life and human problems must come to the challenge with an awareness and a feeling of urgency, because all round about him are the stimuli that force the issue. "Back to the word of God!" is our cry for the basis of pastoral psychology. We must go back to the Lord Jesus Christ, the way the truth and the life for the maturity of life which we seek to bring through pastoral psychology. We must go back to the findings, faith, and the effective plans and measures used by great

---

66. Hughes, op. cit., pp. 17, 18.
67. F. Kunkel, op. cit., p. 12.

leaders in pastoral theology viewed in earlier chapters of this book. And, having these precious anchorings, we should use all the aid and the help psychology can give to the end that a proper pastoral psychology may be developed. Then we will be able to analyze constructively some principles and requirements of conversion, the problem of sickness, suffering and sorrow, and the proper manner of Christian living. In the successive chapters of Part III these matters will be discussed.

CHAPTER VIII

Conversion

W HEN psychology and pastoral theology meet, they find a battleground in the interpretation of conversion. This important area of thinking and experience needs careful analysis in our attempt to build a sound pastoral psychology. E. D. Starbuck opened the door to the controversy by saying,

> "Conversion is used in this study in a very general way to stand for the whole series of manifestations just preceding, accompanying and immediately following the apparently sudden changes involved."[1]

Starbuck said of his own definition,

> "Such a bungling use of this term and of others in this volume will be disappointing to those who demand nicety of definition . . . We have before us a purely inductive investigation, to take the bare records of this class of experience, without a thesis to be proved or anything to guide us but the axioms of scientific criticism, to compare them, to derive what conclusions seem forthcoming and to view these in the light of modern psychology."[2]

Starbuck was right. Such bungling of terms is objectionable to theological thinking and to real scientific analysis. This battleground of confusion with respect to the interpretation of conversion must be eliminated. This constitutes a real challenge and opportunity for pastoral psychology.

A. The Biological Interpretation of Conversion

A very important work of the Christian church is to bring all those who come into living contact with the gospel to a real conversion experience. It is therefore of primary importance to understand conversion — if pastoral psychology is to help accomplish this as far as man's abilities are concerned.

The understanding of conversion has been considered important for psychology. The particular questionnaire method of investigation used by the psychologists led them to a serious misinterpretation of conversion. It made no attempt to ascertain and analyze the spiritual importance of conversion. Only the natural and the experiential was sought and uncovered in the investigation. This was evident in the words of E. S. Ames when he said:

---

1. Edwin Diller Starbuck, *The Psychology of Religion*, Charles Scribner's Sons, New York, 1899, p. 21.
2. Ibid.

"Conversion designates the more sudden, intense and extreme emotional experience. It is the result of immediate and direct control and suggestion on the part of evangelists, parents and teachers. It is common among certain evangelical teachers. It is common among certain evangelical protestant denominations. It occurs chiefly in those communions which have cultivated an elaborate technique to produce it."[3]

Such an interpretation of conversion does not go beyond the physical and the tangible.

W. James was of the same opinion, and wrote:

"The mind curers have given the widest scope to this sort of experience. They have demonstrated that a form of regeneration by relaxing, by letting go, psychologically indistinguishable from the Lutheran justification by faith and the Wesleyan acceptance of free grace, is within the reach of persons who have no conviction of sin and care nothing for the Lutheran theology. It is but giving your little private convulsive self a rest, and finding that a greater self is there."[4]

With such a definition of regeneration, it is no surprise that James made the following observation concerning conversion:

"To say that man is converted means, in these terms, that religious ideas, previously peripheral in his consciousness, now take a central place, and that religious aims form the habitual center of his energy."[5]

This is a biological interpretation of conversion which considers only the things we experience to constitute the spiritual essence of conversion. The same thought was demonstrated by G. A. Coe who analyzed some seventy-seven converts to discover the experience of conversion in his subjects. He examined these people with repsect to hypnotic sensibility, hallucinations, odd impulses, and religious dreams experienced at the time of conversion. His conclusions proved to him and to W. James that sudden conversions were connected with the possession of an active sublimal self. No attempt was made to study the experience of conversion in its full meaning.

E. D. Starbuck, W. James, J. H. Leuba, J. B. Pratt, E. S. Conlin, G. A. Coe, and W. L. Jones advanced a biological interpretation of conversion without the proper theological understanding of its spiritual significance. Their interpretation can be expressed in the language of J. Howley:

"This unification and direction of psychic life is the basic fact in all religious conversion, be it gradual or sudden, ordinary and commonplace, or extraordinary and eccentric, in its manifestations."[6]

Such a discussion does not lift the experience of conversion above the biological point of view. It leaves it entirely in the realm of the exploratory

3. Edward Scribner Ames, *The Psychology of Religious Experience*, Houghton Mifflin Co., New York, 1910, p. 257.
4. W. James, *The Varieties of Religious Experience*, Sixth Impression, Longmans, Green, and Co., London and Bombay, 1903, p. 111.
5. Ibid., p. 196.
6. John Howley, *Psychology and Mystical Experience*, Kegan Paul, Trench, Trubner & Co., Ltd., London, 1920, p. 37.

and the explanatory. It fixes the study of conversion particularly in the field of the unusual. This led E. S. Waterhouse to observe:

> "Starbuck indeed actually restricted the word conversion to sudden conversion, and spoke separately of lives of growth not involving conversion. But the dramatic sense must not lead us to that error. Conversion means a change of direction, sometimes with, sometimes without a crisis."[7]

There is no doubt about it that when sudden conversion takes place there must of necessity be a tremendous psychological revolution. There is also no doubt that when such a sudden change takes place it touches every phase of psychological experience. The change must take place along psychological lines — and these must be studied; but this does not mean that God may be left out. Spiritual experience is as much a part of conversion as is the psychological experience. Such a dynamic power as was evidenced in Paul's conversion on the Damascus road[8] gives manifest demonstration of the power of God through His gracious providence; and such cannot be explained merely upon the basis of a biological interpretation. The psychologists have denied Christ's place in conversion. Both W. James and J. H. Leuba state that the conceptual belief of Christ's work, although often called efficacious, is really "accessory and non-essential"; and they believed that the joyous conviction of conversion could also come by entirely different channels.

As theologians and pastors we do well to study the psychological and biological aspects of the conversion experience, but we strongly object when we are told that this is the only way we must study conversion. With S. Norborg we say:

> "From the standpoint of Christian realism, we protest against the schematic methodism of the average psychology of conversion as a forging of the varieties of Christian conversion into a narrow, unrealistic frame of uniformity which decidedly does not exist in Christian conversion reality."[9]

We must realize that conversion may have diverse and even non-religious form of experience and expression. Certainly, conversion is not a simple process, and there are many variations in form, even as in other types of experience. Psychology has pointed to these different forms of conversion and students of pastoral theology have been slow to recognize these differentiations. This, however, does not permit a one-sided biological interpretation of conversion. While we insist that there is more to conversion than the psychologists admit, we do not mean, on the other hand, that the theologians can give us the complete picture. G. B. Cutten has well said:

> "In dealing with the subject of religious conversion, its very nature compels us to treat it incompletely. However, much we may believe in the

---

7. Eric S. Waterhouse, *Psychology and Religion*, Elkin Mathews & Marret, 1930, p. 88
8. Acts 9:1-9.
9. Sv. Norborg, *Varieties of Christian Experience*, Augsburg Publishing House, Minneapolis, 1937, p. 213.

divine element in conversion and in the religious life generally, it must remain an unknown quantity, and it can only be judged by the apparent effects upon the persons experiencing it."[10]

There is a completeness, an entirety about conversion which we must seek to understand even though from the outset we know that no one can grasp the full meaning of the conversion experience. And we must always strive for the analysis of the complete experience of conversion even with our human limitations. The observation of L. Dewar is very important:

> "The distinctions and divisions which we make in it (conversion) are solely for our convenience, and have no actual correspondence in reality. It is important, therefore, to endeavor to see the experience as a whole — to gain, as it were, a synoptic view of it."[11]

In order to formulate a true interpretation of conversion for the science of pastoral psychology, we must once more emphasize the fact that conversion is not a stereotyped experience. It may manifest a variety of forms. We must remember that

> "The data of the biological sciences are more variable than those of mechanics and physics and may call for special and elaborate modes of report and record as well as for special training and aids in observation. Psychological data, as we have seen, are still more variable, and the variety of necessary aids is great. There may be need of special observational skill, of unique apparatus, of delicate experimental techniques, modes of verbal, mathematical, and statistical analysis not required in all sciences."[12]

In the past many ministers have been oblivious to all of this, and the psychologists have been one-sided in their emphasis on this tendency. We do not outlaw the biological interpretation of conversion, but we do assert that it is not sufficient for a complete analysis. As will be seen later in this chapter, our interpretation must be complete — biological, spiritual, social and emotional. This is the Biblical emphasis, and reveals that the biological interpretation is not sufficient by itself.

B. Interpretation of the Soul

Closely allied to the psychologists' misconception of experience of conversion is their interpretation of the soul. This is a very important point for the correct understanding of pastoral psychology. We must examine the position held by psychologists.

Psychologists have largely denied or ignored the existence of a soul. J. B. Pratt denied the place of the soul and said it was indefinite and indescribable. W. James asserted that the universe had a soul, but never defined his idea. The main interest of psychologists, seems to have been, the relation of conscious to subconscious life — without so much as mentioning a soul. They

---

10. George Barton Cutten, *The Psychological Phenomena of Christianity*, Charles Scribners' Sons, 1909, p. 232.
11. Lindsay Dewar, *Man and God, An Essay in The Psychology and Philosophy of Religious Experience*, Society for promoting Christian Knowledge, London, 1935, p. 141.
12. Harvey Levi Hollingworth, *Psychology, Its Facts and Principles*, A. Appleton and Co., New York, 1929, p. 26.

tried to localize those states of experience and thus avoid a defined conception of the soul within man. F. L. Strickland raised the important question in this connection by asking whether a child who is two days old has a soul. He asserted that we may turn to theology for our answer and definition but psychology cannot give this answer, for the latter finds such answers unsatisfactory and seeks to find the difference between the child and the animal in terms of behavior.[13] This is exactly the point — psychologists are unwilling to recognize the soul as such. For them the soul is a soundboard on which influences of the world play and determine conduct. Such was the contention of A. Adler when he wrote:

"It seems hardly possible to recognize in the psychic organ, the soul, anything but a force acting toward a goal, and individual psychology considers all the manifestations of the human soul as though they were directed toward a goal."[14]

Adler went on to say that the goal toward which every human being's actions are directed is determined by the impressions which the child receives from environment. He contended that such was demonstrated by the ideal state during the first months of a child's life when such conditions are under control of the parents. C. G. Jung contended that we can only voice indefinite generalized statements about the soul.[15]

This kind of interpretation of the soul is a far cry from the Biblical conception. If this is the correct interpretation, there is no necessity for pastoral psychology. In the language of C. T. Holman, "It is useless to talk about the 'cure of souls' if there are no souls to cure."[16]

We must accept the Biblical conception of the soul such as G. Steven advanced when he said:

"The fundamental nature of the soul seems to involve a spiritual end, a personal talent by which the end may be reached, and an irresistible impulse to be up and doing."[17]

Without a fundamental Scriptural conception of the soul we cannot develop an effective pastoral psychology. Merely to call the soul, a "stream of consciousness" is not sufficient. If the psychologists continue to insist that the hypothesis of the soul is unnecessary because it does not relate itself to subjective expression and analysis, it follows that such psychologists cannot help us in the science of soul study. They deny the very thing they should define and analyze.

We do admit that the conception of the soul is one of the most difficult to discuss. Yet, that is no reason for avoiding the issue or for denying the reality

13. Francis L. Strickland, *Psychology of Religious Experience*, The Abingdon Press, New York, 1924, p. 30.
14. Alfred Adler, *Understanding Human Nature*, Greenberg, New York, 1927, p. 20.
15. Carl G. Jung, *Modern Man in Search of a Soul*, Harcourt Brace and Co., New York, 1939, p. 133.
16. Charles T. Holman, *The Cure of Souls*, The University of Chicago Press, Chicago, 1932, p. 3.
17. George Steven, *The Psychology of the Christian Soul*, Hodder and Stoughton, New York, London, 1911, p. 18.

of the soul. Most psychologists take that position. They have been unwilling even to discuss the probable existence of the soul. It is therefore refreshing to read the statement of R. M. Jones,

> "The problem of the real nature of the human soul is at the present moment probably the most important religious question before us, for upon the answer to it all our vital spiritual interests depend."[18]

This is a good analysis because the spiritual interest, which is a definite part of pastoral psychology, must include the proper conception of the soul. The real soul of man, the inner self, the handiwork of God, must be recognized. Unless we begin with that basic belief, we cannot serve man as *man*.

> "Let our psychologists and physicists not forget that the body is only an organ for the soul, and that the phenomena of the soul never can be explained by coördinated phenomena of the body."[19]

Our psychologists need not deny their historical lack of consideration of the soul for E. S. Conklin wrote

> "It is certainly true that the term soul rarely appears in contemporary reports of psychological researches and it is seldom discovered in the books which psychologists write."[20]

And it is well to remember that:

> "This repudiation of the soul hypothesis, though characteristic of the new psychology, is not by any means a novel position or an original contribution. From the time of Gautama, the Buddha, to the modern Hume, there have not been wanting men who espoused the position."[21]

In the language of W. Ellis,

> "The soul, according to an eminent philosopher, has worn out its welcome. Most modern philosophers would go further. Not only the soul, they would say, but all metaphysical ideas, have worn out their welcome."[22]

Their historic denial of the soul does not excuse the psychologists of today. A discussion and recognition of the soul may not be avoided.

> "While the soul and God are not the subject of psychology, psychologists need to remember that these are facts in another realm, and if they are to be true scientists they must recognize the existence of these facts."[23]

It is well to view the diagnosis of R. Muller-Freienfels in this connection.

> "Many of the new investigators did not even believe in the existence of the human soul in the earlier sense of the word. They pursued a 'soulless psychology,' and while utilizing the concept of the old-fashioned soul

---

18. R. M. Jones, "Psychology and the Spiritual Life," *The Journal of Religion*," Sept. 1921, p. 449.
19. D. W. Fisher, "The New Psychology and Personality," *Presbyterian and Reformed Review*, Vol. II, 1891, p. 623.
20. E. S. Conklin, *The Psychology of Religious Adjustment*, Macmillan Co., 1929, p. 1.
21. E. C. Wilm, "The Psychology and Personality," *Methodist Review*, Nov., 1908, p. 942.
22. William Ellis, *The Idea of the Soul in Western Philosophy and Science*, George Allen and Unwin, Ltd., London, 1940, p. 11.
23. Marion Hiller Dunsmore, "The Relation of the New Psychology to Religion," *Methodist Review*, Vol. 106, 1923, May, p. 418.

they sought to demonstrate that a thing did not really exist. But the most amazing result of these trends is the fact that in the course of the investigations the formerly ostracized soul won re-admission and with full honors, to the halls of science. Today, indeed, there are again psychologists who not only believe in a real soul but even openly grace their conviction with a metaphysical and religious coloring."[24]

This statement is very optimistic, and it is doubtful whether many modern psychologists are willing to accept it. On the other hand, it is encouraging to note this diagnosis of the issue and the hopeful words of prophecy, because, if psychology is to render real service in the world of today, it must return to the Biblical conception of the soul.

There are psychologists in the Netherlands who have consistently maintained the Biblical conception of the soul. J. Waterink defined the soul as that which God made as undivided, undying, unearthly, thus spiritual substance, which is the essence of man's personality.[25] This makes the soul the real life of the body and ties body and soul together as a unit. J. H. Bavinck, also of the Netherlands, agreed with the position of J. Waterink, declaring that the soul is the wonder work of God, thought and created by our Almighty God.[26] This is the Biblical view of the soul and without it our task and technique of pastoral psychology will be in vain.

C. *Biological-Psychological-Spiritual Nature of Conversion*

Having leveled our objections against the psychologists for their purely biological viewpoint of conversion and for their lack of belief in the soul in the Biblical sense, we come now to demonstrate that the true view of conversion maintains that the conversion experience includes biological, psychological, and spiritual elements. The battle line of difference is contained in the following statement from C. E. Barbour:

"The psychologist insists that man's soul is rooted in his animal nature. The Christian contends that man was made to be like God. The psychologist asserts that man is essentially of the earth earthly. The Christian says that heaven is his home."[27]

The viewpoint of the psychologist is definitely limited — because he sees man only in his actions and volitions. The pastor sees his people, as they experience conversion, from the spiritual point of view — sometimes with complete disregard of the biological findings in conversion as discovered and

---

24. Richard Muller-Frienfels, *The Evolution of Modern Psychology*, Translated by W Berean Wolfe, Yale University Press, New Haven, 1935, p. 3.
25. J. Waterink, "Maar nu wordt elke persoonlijkheid gedragen door een 'persoon. Deze persoon is de kern, het eigenlijke bewust handelende subject in den microskosmos (kleine wereld), dien wij mens noemen. Dit persoons-principe, deze 'onsterfelijke ziel, ook in samenhang met alle menselijke psychische functies en eigenschappen 'geest' genoemd, is datgene wat den mens het 'ik-bewustzijn' geeft; het is zijn eigenlijke diepste 'ik.'" *Ons Zieleven*, Zesde Uitgebreide Druk, N. V. Gebr. Zomer & Keuning's Uitgeversmij, Wageningen, 1946, p. 219.
26. J. H. Bavinck, *Inleiding in de Zielkunde*, J. H. Kok, Kampen, the Netherlands, 1935, p. 3.
27. Clifford E. Barbour, *Sin and the New Psychology*, The Abingdon Press, New York, 1930, pp. 23, 24.

analyzed by the psychologist. These two views must be harmonized, in pastoral psychology, if it is to be effective, Scriptural, and scientific.

We must come to recognize that the experience of individual conversion is fraught with *biological* motives, impulses, and reactions. The person lives in an environment which he cannot escape. Conversion takes place in a given situation and set of experiences. We cannot just say that God has made man with a living soul and therefore all are alike in their experiences and reactions. Man's physical being, his physical properties, his inherited body and his physical environment have a tremendous part in his attitude to and experience of conversion. The minister has often neglected this area of thought because he has not sensed the importance of the biological data of his people. Detailed and analyzed differentiations in individuals have been disregarded or overlooked.

The psychologists have over-stressed the *psychological* impacts and experiences of life in relation to conversion because they interpret everything in terms of psychological reactions and responses. Psychologists trace all involvements in conversion to psychological impulses and responses. While we must be on our guard against the one-sidedness of the psychologists, we will have to admit that these have an integral place in the experience of conversion, and that as ministers we have too often failed to recognize them in the experience of conversion. Besides, in those people whose experience in conversion has not been typical of the usual experience in conversion, we have failed to give diligent heed and to analyze the peculiarities of their biological and psychological experiences. We have not been willing to make full recognition of the abnormal phenomena in conversion.

The unity and totality of the individual must be understood by the minister as well as by the psychologist. This must not be a forced psychological analysis, as if that could give a full explanation of conversion. In the language of S. Norborg,

> "When we found Christian conversion in its decision and its opening to be a psychic totality-experience, we have — on the basis of factual Christianity, — once for all broken the methodistic chains that bound the old psychology of conversion. It is furthermore clear that we do not consider emotionalism and conversion identical. Repentance is definitely something more than feeling. The accompanying emotional feeling may be varicolored, ranging from despondency and utter panic to ecstasy and a grateful feeling of fellowship. The conviction of guilt may not seemingly dominate the conversion experience, still it may be there as a positive realization of indebtedness to God. It may express itself in a feeling, or, rather, a consciousness of utter indebtedness in fear and love toward God, because He created man to live in personal communion with Himself and in personal independence on His grace."[28]

The interpretation of Norborg includes a consideration of all the psychic processes and feelings. He is ready to study the total impact of the psychic experience, including the spiritual element in conversion.

---

28. Norborg, op. cit., p. 203.

The third component part of conversion, so easily neglected by the psychologists, is the *spiritual*. To approach this subject properly, we must accept the fact that man has a soul, and that the spiritual experience is just as much a part of conversion as the biological and the psychological. A true analysis of conversion includes the spiritual as well as the natural interpretation. Here again differences arise. The psychologist says this experience is only natural, while the pastor has a tendency to emphasize the spiritual at the expense of the natural. These differences can be resolved. Pastoral psychology based on the Bible and on the scientific facts of life must posit the position that conversion is biological, psychological, and spiritual. The vital force of conversion is spiritual because conversion is basically the supernatural working of the Holy Spirit; and its outward expression and its demonstration in the individual is regulated by the particular idiosyncracies and circumstances confronting the person. This position represents the Bible in its truest interpretation. It accepts the interpretation that God made the soul for His glory, making man different than the animals. It distinguishes man's personal life from mere animal behavior. And this view allows and includes all the varied psychological and biological impressions and reactions as a very important part of man's conversion. Pastoral psychology must have this triple interpretation of conversion to be true to science and the Bible.

Psychologists, with rare exception have refused to accept this position.

> "Psychology does not like to call itself the science of the soul for that has a theological tang and suggests problems that have so far not seemed accessible to scientific investigation."[29]

And yet, pastoral psychology accepts this "theological tang" because the Bible is clear on this theological emphasis of the soul and of conversion. We must see the experience of the soul in its entirety, at least as far as our human limitations permit. There is a point beyond which we cannot penetrate, even as Jesus explained to Nicodemus.[30] We cannot understand all the secret working of the Holy Spirit when we experience Him ourselves, or when we see Him operating in others; yet we recognize this as the work of God, and we praise Him for it.

We contend that a combination of biological, psychological and spiritual impressions and reactions take place in conversion. We do not say like Starbuck concerning the candidate of conversion,

> "He must relax, that is, he must fall back on the larger power that makes for righteousness, which has been welling up in his own being, and let it finish in its own way the work it has begun."[31]

Such analysis does not satisfy as an explanation of the real manifestation of conversion. It makes conversion a purely humanistic experience. It is a far cry from the Biblical interpretation of what takes place when confession and

---

29. Robert Sessions Woodworth, *Psychology, a Study of Mental Health*, Henry Holt and Co., 1921, p. 1.
30. John 3.
31. Starbuck, op. cit., p. 224.

repentance are made.[32] And it does not begin to touch the clear manifestations of the Holy Spirit in the experience of conversion which are so evident in the New Testament record.[33] S. Norborg gave a better explanation when he wrote:

> "As a Christian lives on in this life he will realize ever more fully that the miracle of the universe and of his own insignificant and limited life is the incomprehensible God of Love in Jesus Christ, under whom he will ever live in repentance and gratitude. That day-conscious personal life is ever filled with wonders and wondering. And over and over again the Christian will experience the humiliating and exhilarating leap into the depths of the Word of God: 'For God so loved the world, that he gave his only begotten Son, that whosoever believeth on him should not perish but have everlasting life.' John 3:16."[34]

Norborg described the spiritual phase of conversion in this quotation. The spiritual part of conversion is fundamental to the whole experience, since it is the Biblical basis of conversion.[35] This does not exclude the biological and the psychological phases of conversion, but includes them in their proper relation. This means that we accept a combination of phases in conversion — the biological, the psychological, and the spiritual. We who are of traditional and spiritual persuasion have the tendency to see only the spiritual and forget to accept and study conversion in the light of its three component parts. Not that we can separate them or study them independently; but we must see that there are three phases and expressions of the experience. Human data cannot cover this experience but as we study the biological and psychological facts, and the spiritual work of the Holy Spirit, we will obtain a better knowledge of conversion in the individual for the practical working of pastoral psychology.

The study and the practice of pastoral psychology must come to the rescue with respect to the proper understanding, analysis, and development of conversion in the lives of our parish people. The minister must come to a proper realization of the biological, psychological and spiritual phases of conversion, relating them properly for an understanding of the individual he serves. This is our commission from our Lord. This is making full proof of our ministry. This does not mean that the minister can explain all parts of conversion, nor does it mean that he can probe into the hidden recesses of the individual's life; but it does mean that in so far as these factors can be seen and evaluated, he will bring about a harmonious, unified, and related interpretation of conversion. Then, and only then, will he be in the proper position to minister to his people. He will then see the normal and the abnormal with proper insight. And he will be able with proper pastoral psychology to minister to the

---

32. Luke 13:3, Jeremiah 8:6, Luke 15:7, Acts 8:32.
33. Acts 2:14-21, Acts 9:4-6, Acts 10:44.
34. Norborg, op. cit., pp. 203, 204.
35. Acts 16:14, 15; 30-33, Acts 18:1-7.

totality of the individual's experience. This is our solemn duty in our day of physical, psychological and mental crisis.

Closely allied to the discussion of conversion is the important matter of sickness, suffering and sorrow. A study of this subject and of our obligation to those who experience sickness, suffering and sorrow either before or after conversion is very necessary to an understanding of the importance of pastoral psychology. Therefore we proceed to discuss this matter in the next chapter.

CHAPTER IX

Sickness, Suffering, and Sorrow

T HERE are many people who face the afflictions of sickness, suffering and sorrow and so a working pastoral psychology must be made effective to minister to their needs. Because of this fact Part II of this book was dedicated to the exploration of these needs as reflected in first hand information from those who are living in the school of affliction and grace. This present chapter is devoted to a constructive analysis and study of the working principles involved in the problem of sickness, suffering and sorrow. The actual technique involved in the solution of this problem will be discussed in a later chapter on the "Minister and the Doctor." Since sickness, suffering and sorrow form only a part of the total of Christian living, the totality of "Christian Living" will be discussed in the next chapter.

A. The Importance of Suffering, Sickness, and Sorrow

Our study of the questionnaire replies gave clear indication that the problem of suffering is gigantic and acute. The large number of people who responded and the ever widening circle of the family of suffering, make the importance of this subject of prime consideration for the minister. Problems of mountain proportion, and afflictions of intense suffering were written on every page of the returned questionnaires. Without the spirit of false boasting, or the martyr complex, these people of God unloaded·their burdens in their replies, with a fervor and an intensity that impressed itself indelibly upon the reader. All the aftermath of war casualties, all the gathering of the years of affliction, and all the acute broken heartedness of many years, was reflected in the replies. These folks did not desire to broadcast their problem, but in answer to a request for a description of their experience, they wrote confidentially, openly, and deliberately. It opened a new area of research, and revealed in a way that might not have been evident to one casually talking to them, that within the heart, down below the deepest of their expression, was a well of pent up sorrow and recurring trouble.

Not only from the questionnaires but also from the statements of authors, it is very evident that the problem of affliction is very important particularly for the pastor. Our first quotation is taken from A. T. Boisen:

"The problem of physical illness is for the pastor an ever-present one. No parish is without its share of sick people. The number of persons in our general hospitals at any one time may be less than in our mental hospitals, but if we consider the number of different persons cared for within a twelve months' period we get a different picture. Where the mental hospitals care for a total of perhaps 900,000, the general hospitals take care of about 15,000,000. (These figures were taken from the *Journal of American Medical Association* for April 20, 1946.) This figure does not include those who come to out-patient clinics and dispensaries. Neither does it take into account the multitudes who do not come to the hospitals but are cared for at home."[1]

C. A. Wise has given an estimate of this problem with particular concern for those who have mental problems. He wrote,

"We do know more today about illness than we have ever known before, but this does not prove that we are more healthy. The tremendous medical bill that is paid annually by the American public is just part of the evidence of our failure to master these factors in human existence which lead to illness. Additional evidence is found in the fact that of all the hospital beds in this country, more than one-half are occupied by patients suffering from mental and nervous diseases, and that the economic loss resulting from these diseases amounts to more than one billion dollars annually. To these should be added the losses sustained through crime, delinquency, poverty, family disorganization, and other expressions of individual pathology on the social level. And when such intangible factors as human suffering, misery and the destruction of human values are considered, much of our complacency in regard to the achievements of modern man should be reduced. For man may send the human voice through the ether to the far corners of the earth, or he may circle the globe in an airplane, or he may conquer certain diseases caused by bacteria. But until he has gone much farther in understanding the forces within himself and his society that lead to illness and how these may be turned into the direction of health, he is in danger of losing his own soul."[2]

We cite one more reference and it pertains to the total number of hospitals which are being supported by the church or are related to the church. S. Hiltner is the authority who wrote:

"There are at least four hundred and fifty hospitals in the United States under Protestant church auspices. And there are many more institutions for the care of children, of old people and of other groups."[3]

In addition, of course, there are many hospitals not under the care of the Protestant church. There are countless Roman Catholic hospitals and many Soldier hospitals. The F. Simons Hospital in Denver, Colorado represents a carrying load of 30,000 people. I have visited such hospitals in research for material on this subject, and one is amazed when he sees the great institutions, the staffs of workers, and the patients who carry in their body the marks of sickness, suffering and sorrow.

The pastor must face this tremendous problem. When the minister visits people in these hospitals, he hears the complaints of his people, and he sees

1. Anton T. Boisen, *Problems in Religion and Life*, Abingdon-Cokesbury Press, New York, Nashville, 1946, p. 85.
2. Carrol A. Wise, *Religion in Illness and Health*, Harper & Brothers, New York and London, 1942, pp. 3, 4.
3. Seward Hiltner, *Religion and Health*, The Macmillan Co., New York, 1943, p. 253.

the burdens which depress them. He comes into close contact with all the problems of suffering, because he is their confidant. The pity is that there are pastors who are oblivious to this problem because they approach it from the professional standpoint without the touch of human sympathy and under-standing. Too often the pastor despises calling on the afflicted and postpones calling on the sick because it "goes against the grain." It is very true that a pastor ought not to be a weeping prophet nor should he be the kind that will automatically make people cry in his presence. There are a few who approach their work with that kind of bearing and attitude which dethrones dignity and denatures the pastoral witness. On the other hand, the pastor must recognize the tremendous importance of suffering in the lives of those who are afflicted. Before our very eyes in the backyard of our own parish we find the people whom we love, loaded with burdens and bogged down with afflictions. We must sense the importance of their problem and the requirement of our sacred office. It is an important area of service and we may not neglect it.

B. Mental Illnesses Must Be Faced

Reference has already been made to mental illness in the quotation from C. A. Wise, because the problem of mental illness is closely associated with the difficulty of affliction usually classified as physical. We have also made mention of the "nervous tension crisis" in our first chapter.

As we face the problem of suffering, particularly in terms of mental dis-turbances, the minister must come to realize the gravity of the situation and the duty he has to his people so afflicted. The prevalence of nervousness, the strained condition in many homes, the multiplied worries of many individuals and the personal neuroses so manifest in our times confront every pastor. The serious minded minister who is a real confident of his people, knows that the "regular church-goers" are not immune to tragic problems and difficult burdens. Some are fear-ridden, some are definitely in need of advice on mental prob-lems, and some are desperate, even doubting their salvation. There are de-pressed spirits and wounded hearts in every congregation. At times the earnest minded pastor finds his heart almost at the breaking point because he knows and feels for the needs of his people.

Problems in this area face every average family in the average parish today. Our living is with such tempo that families formerly fortified against such onslaughts are face to face with them today. At the same time, even under normal conditions, there are problems which are natural to domestic situa-tions. In the words of G. Harkness,

> "The most fertile source of psychic disturbances is in the family. It is one of the deep paradoxes of our existence that the family, center and source of the best in human love, chosen by our Lord to symbolize God's loving relationship to his children, is likewise the lurking place of the most diabolical conflict and misery."[4]

---

4. Georgia Harkness, *The Dark Night of the Soul*, Abingdon-Cokesbury Press, New York, Nashville, 1945, p. 116.

The pastor finds that those difficulties which deal with mental aspects are the most difficult to solve. Mental perplexities, mental hazards, and mental idiosyncracies are found among his people — and as a family counselor, the pastor must be the first, and often the final agency to help them in their difficulty. Their hidden motives, their environmental difficulties, their anxieties and worries, confront the minister every time he talks to his people.

Our times are fraticidal. In the words of W. B. Pitkin,

> "An epidemic sweeps the world. Call it psychic cancer, if you like. (I do.) Minds are going to pieces. Diseased thoughts and emotions multiply, crowding out the normal tissues of mentality. Mild cases we call jitters. The advanced and hopeless cases are insanity, narcotic addictions and suicide. Two common symptoms of the oncoming ailment are confusion and fears."[5]

Some will say that a quotation such as this is too pessimistic, and claim that our times do not warrant it. Let us not bury our heads, like the ostrich, and deny these evident signs of our times. Let us go back to the first chapter of of this book and review the description of the crisis of our age. The nervous tension is around us, on all sides, and within us.

> "Today we cannot send people away from the danger zone for it is everywhere. All the world's a trap, and the men and women in it merely rodents. They have their entrances but no exits."[6]

We may argue that these problems are as old as time and pastors have always faced them, but authorities who have studied this matter make a claim that the mental crisis of our day demands special consideration by the minister. J. A. C. Murray made this claim in the following citation:

> "Mental disorder and nervous tension, though as old as humanity, have never been so frequent as they are at the present time. The all-too-familiar troubles of the day, national and international, have their repercussions on every part of our public and private life, repercussions which economist and politician endeavor in vain to mitigate. But underneath all the visible upheavals, and the surface currents of the storm, another and far more ominus tide is at work, disturbing the very foundations of being itself; for the stresses and the pace of modern life are producing dire confusions in the mind, and that to an extent which is at once more serious and more widespread than most men know."[7]

Murray wrote these words a decade ago and since that time the atomic age has enlivened and charged that quotation with additional meaning.

We must not mistake our times. The minister of today is face to face with a difficult generation and with multiplied mental problems. The victims of our suicidal generation are the subjects of his study and the objects of his help. People living under present conditions are bound to have tensions, nervous breakdown and frustration. The pastor must be adept at "spotting" the casualties of these conditions, since most people feel ashamed of the fact that they

---

5. Walter P. Pitkin, *Escape From Fear*, Doubleday, Doran and Co., Inc., 1940, p. 1.
6. Ibid, p. 8.
7. J. A. C. Murray, *An Introduction to a Christian Psycho-Therapy*, T. & T. Clark, Edinburgh, 1938, pp. 4, 5.

are victims of these conditions. The minister must nurture them back to normal healthful attitude and atmosphere. Social and cultural elements play a large part in man's thinking today, and the pastor must be able to sense the attendant mental perplexities so he can minister effectively to his people. The minister must stand in the gap and prevent breakdowns if he can. "The understanding of mental tensions, their causes, and their elimination is clearly required for the prevention of breakdowns."[8] This quotation is the verdict of a medical man and the spiritual minister must be fully aware of its importance. The minister must fortify his people with instruction on the grace and mercy of God, through sermon, personal counseling, and personal witness. Through preaching and personal conduct on the part of the pastor, he can do much to meet the needs resulting from the nervous tension of our time.

When the minister brings his witness to bear, he will meet opposition. Some even claim that Christianity is to blame for our tensions. S. Norborg referred to this when he said:

> "There is a very widespread criticism of all ages, that Christianity makes souls morbid and unhealthy. That criticism is even today a commonplace in the modern attacks on Christianity. It comes from Marxists, social reformers, mind-cure apostles, psychoanalysts, novelists and from the average citizen."[9]

Of course this criticism is unwarranted, but the pastor will have to meet it and have the answer. The very opposite of the statement is the correct view. Christianity and healthymindedness go hand in hand. Jesus said, "I am the way, the truth, and the life" (John 14:6). All of life is in Christ. Therefore the Christian pastor has a marvelous opportunity, and a ringing challenge in the field of pastoral psychology to meet the mental needs and tensions of our day. He must bring the individual into a full and complete spiritual relationship with Jesus Christ. He must bring the perplexed sufferer the message of Isaiah, "Thou wilt keep him in perfect peace, whose mind is staid on thee" (Isaiah 26:3). Then the individual will find life-full, satisfying, invigorating and permeating all of experience.

C. The Reason for Illness

Closely allied to physical and mental illness is the problem of the *why* and the *wherefore* of God's providence in sending affliction, or *the reason for* affliction. "Science recognizes over two hundred diseases: and all of us are at some time brought into touch with sickness."[10] And sure enough, when it strikes our home or personal experience, then we begin to ask the reason for such affliction. The questionnaire replies revealed this inner seeking, this soul

8. Milton Harrington, *The Management of the Mind*, Philosophical Library, New York, 1945, p. 114.

9. Sv. Norborg, *The Varieties of Christian Experience*, Augsburg Publishing House, Minneapolis, 1937, p. 119.

10. Samuel M. Shoemaker, *How You Can Help Other People*, E. P. Dutton, and Co., Inc., New York, 1946, p. 118.

longing for the light which seers have sought for ages. The deep philosophical problem of suffering confronts every thinking individual who is afflicted.

Often the minister and the church have implied and taught that the origin of disease is found in sin. Of course, disease came because of sin, but we know that personal affliction is not always due to personal sin. Job was not afflicted because of personal sin but to be used as an example of strength and security.[11] The man born blind was not afflicted because of his sin or the sin of his parents but that the glory of God should be revealed.[12]

The minister must give an answer that will satisfy the patient who is suffering. To do this the pastor must be steeped in the Word of God, and know the history of the exemplary leaders of the church of Jesus Christ who have served God joyfully through their tears. Pastors must know the secret of Paul's suffering[13] in order to give all that pastoral psychology can offer. We cannot solve the question of pain, we cannot dissolve evil, and we certainly cannot avoid the ills of life, but we can, as pastors, lead people into the perfect submission of the will to the will of God.[14]

Modern cults are giving reasons and seeking to explain away all semblance of evil and illness. Modern streamlined organizations and false leaders claim to have all the answers to these perplexing questions. The pastor must construct his practical understanding and scriptural answers in such a way that he can lead the burdened soul through the grace of the Holy Spirit to a surrender of heart, mind and life.

D. Attitudes of Afflicted People

Two attitudes prevail among suffering people with respect to their afflictions, and the pastor must understand both of them to minister effectively. There is the perennial "kicker," and faultfinder who will find fault with the doctor, quarrel with the nurse, criticize the meals, take issue with the members of his family, and constantly despise the very bed which makes him as comfortable as possible. He is determined to make the worst of his illness. It is true, there are attenuating factors. The sick person lives under constant apprehension. He does not know what the next moment will bring. He is always haunted by the fear that "they may not have told him everything." Yet some people, in spite of everything that is done for them, are constantly complaining and finding fault with circumstances and people around them.

We must not forget that at a time of sickness the emotions are always ready to flare and an uprising is easily started. S. Hiltner made a fine point when he wrote,

---

11. Job 2:3.
12. John 9:3.
13. II Corinthians 12:7.
14. Matthew 26:36-44.

> "Whatever emotions have been hovering about before illness, so to speak, generally come into prominence during it. If there has been anxiety, it may be accentuated. If there has been hostility, it may be brought into the open. If there has been guilt, it may come out."[15]

These and other feelings which lie buried, quickly come to the surface when the nerves are tested and physical strength is strained. People are then easily disturbed and feel the urge to "explode." The stern realities of sickness and pain, the indissoluble doubts and fears of the coming days, and the terrible affliction of being in the narrows of life with a hidden prospect of a defeated purpose, drive many to frustration and confusion.

The minister meeting these people in the deep valley must bring them out through the means of pastoral psychology. He has the wonderful privilege of ministering to such people with the realistic gospel, bringing the healing of God through Christ's blessing. The minister sees the people as they are, and he knows some of the impure and low thoughts that arise in people's minds — because they frequently express themselves freely before him. He may be deeply moved by their confusion and tremendously touched by the tremors which affect their spiritual conduct. Just here the pastor must bring the gospel of Jesus. Just here the minister can remind them that God "healeth all our diseases."[16] For exactly at this point the minister brings all his knowledge of psychology to bear upon his pastoral duties, and withal he brings Jesus Christ, whose presence and power can allay every problem and solve every difficulty. The pastor must sweeten his people when they are soured on life, he must bring peace to their perturbed hearts, and he must bring Christ for their crisis. This is the heart and hope of pastoral psychology for the people who are problemed with afflictions. For every sorrow and for every loss, Christ has the answer.

There is another attitude of suffering people which must not be forgotten. There is a cheerful, optomistic, genuinely spiritual attitude which the minister repeatedly sees in his people. Sometimes this attitude is found in the same people who at times are depressed and discouraged. More often it is found in the lives of those who are well schooled in the grace of God. Turn back to the quotes from the questionnaires in a previous chapter of this book and discover again the patient, powerful and perfect surrender of a host of people. See how God's wonderful sustaining grace is abundant and able to keep until the uttermost. Note these glowing words of trust:

> "One must sit back and allow the Spirit time to take these things as one seeks an answer to the problems of the why. Gradually the one question is answered and the next arises for a solution. Each time one is led to see that God is not unreasonable. God is just in all His doings." Questionnaire 179.
> "After an illness unto death, three operations, a serious relapse and a nervous breakdown, I can say, God's will, regardless of what it may be, is the best possible for us. My nervous breakdown caused the most agony. All I had left was, 'Though He slay me, yet will I trust Him.' It was sufficient." Questionnaire 213.

---

15. Hiltner, op. cit., p. 228.
16. Psalm 103:3.

Such wonderful testimonies could be multiplied by a thousand because God's people trusted and triumphed in Christ. Just at this point the minister has the opportunity to hear and honor such testimonies of his people. With proper psychological insight, he must know when to encourage such and how to develop them. There is a wonderful challenge in the testimony of these people and the minister must let these people "talk out" until they have told him all their heart. And with the true spirit of pastoral psychology, he can use their testimony to fortify the faith of other members of his flock.

E. *Cultivation of Mental, Physical, and Spiritual Hygiene*

The pastor is the key man for the development of a mental, physical and spiritual hygiene — because there must be a proper blending of these three in a well rounded ministry. There are practical helps and hints which the pastor needs to observe (These will be discussed in the last part of this treatise). Here we must content ourselves with a consideration of the proper relationship of mental, physical and spiritual hygiene for our people.

> "The duty of the spiritual physician must be twofold, that of teaching spiritual hygiene to the healthy and the cure of the diseased; for it is as important that the healthy be kept well as the sick be healed."[17]

Not many pastors will deny the significance of spiritual hygiene for the welfare of the soul, but there are many who will shun any and all responsibility for the constructive education and physical and mental hygiene for better living. Just here pastoral psychology stipulates our duty, and we must not be slow to perform it. As pastors we have a duty with respect to the physical health and well-being of our people. It is not our first duty but it is so intimately related to our spiritual responsibility that we cannot escape its obligation. The average pastor who denies this responsibility will nevertheless often be found going about giving his people practical health rules and home remedies which have come down as a tradition in his church or family. Far more than he realizes he is giving spiritual aid in addition to practical advice and training in physical hygiene. If done in a sane and sober way, the minister can be of inestimable service to his people as he guards their physical health, particularly if he knows when he should refer them to professional men for health knowledge and the detection of physical trouble. At the same time he is promoting their spiritual welfare.

The average person does much more than he realizes to intensify his own physical troubles and difficulties.

> "Man himself is the chief threat to man's mental health. It is not the ordinary vicissitudes of life, but the complications man has added to them that make trouble."[18]

Just at this point the minister can offer some preventative hygiene that will cover the individual's physical, mental and spiritual complications. He can

---

17. George Barton Cutten, *The Psychological Phenomena of Christianity*, Charles Scribner's Sons, New York, 1909, p. 9.
18. George H. Preston, *The Substance of Mental Health*, Farrar & Rinehart, Inc., New York, 1943, p. 5.

do much to help people meet and respond with resistance to the fears and frustrations which affect physical, mental, and spiritual health. The frequent need for mind cure on the level of the human situation, and the constant call for adjustment to the social conditions in which the individual finds himself, afford the minister a great opportunity to give constructive advice and con-secrated leadership.

The importance and value of religious influences in connection with physical, mental, and spiritual difficulties cannot be over-estimated; and the Christian pastor is the agency through whom the Lord works in His church and in the community. In the words of W. A. Sadler, a competent physician:

> "I would not know how to help many of the nervous sufferers I meet from year to year were it not for the aid of religious influences in strength-ening their wills, facilitating their decisions, and assisting them in getting their minds off themselves — in recovering from the tendency to chronic ingrowing of the thoughts."[19]

This doctor, a teacher of psychiatry in one of our theological seminaries also said:

> "If you are in need of a mind cure, if you are looking for a religious mind cure, turn not to some strange god or new fangled modern cult; but if you need the Balm of Gilead for your soul and spiritual consolation for your mind, get a religion that will not only heal your body just as well as any of these new fangled cults, but get a religion that also promises to do something for your soul, ever in the great beyond, in the sweet by and by, where you need no more healing for the body. And that religion, in my opinion, is not some new and modern psychic phantasma, but the simple, old-fashioned Gospel of the Lord, Jesus Christ."[20]

The minister is privileged to be the servant of the Lord and one of the agencies of this wonderful gospel. His very presence is the essence of its power, his ministry is the demonstration of its purpose, and his counsel for full physical, mental and spiritual hygiene demonstrate its real effectiveness. His very life, in its total impact and importance, should shine in the brightness of pentecostal power with the purpose of leading the individual to a better understanding of all of life. Our tensioned times need Christ's invitation to rest a while and the minister has the opportunity to extend this advice to his people in public and private exhortation.

The minister must be a technician in this field. He should present the de-mand for good living and clean morals. It affects the totality of life. We do well to remember the words of S. Hiltner in this connection.

> "People may be ill in mind, body or spirit. They are seldom ill in one way without being also ill in another. The practical distinction between 'illness,' or 'physical illness' and 'mental illness,' has some value so long as we realize that it relates more to the symptoms than to the causes. It is a pragmatic distinction, which arose in a day when people felt there was no real relationship between 'mental' and 'physical' disorders."[21]

---

19. William A. Sadler, *The Truth About Mind Cure*, A. C. McClure & Co., Chicago, 1928, p. 197.
20. Ibid., p. 206.
21. Hiltner, op. cit., p. 133.

Just at this point the minister can do much to practice balanced pastoral psychology. He knows the proper relationship of the physical, mental and spiritual problems in relation to complete personality development.

> "We ought really to talk of 'personality illness' or 'personality disorder' if we wish to speak from the point of view of causation. For we could make a distinction between those disorders whose causes are such that they can be attacked mainly by the use of psychological or 'spiritual methods,' and those whose causes are such that they can be attacked mainly by physical or physiological methods."[22]

In spite of all these admissions, we again emphasize that the spiritual remains the focal point of the minister's responsibility. The New Testament record indicates clearly that the minister must represent the victorious Christian life by stimulating noble thoughts,[23] by exemplary living,[24] by challenge to a complete consecration,[25] and by constantly reminding people of their obligation to spiritual perfection through the grace of the Holy Spirit.[26] The entire impact of New Testament living, interpreting the Old Testament principles and the teachings of Jesus Christ, emphasize the spiritual hygiene in which the minister should be the specialist. The pastor should instruct and exemplify this harmonized mental, physical and spiritual hygiene for his people. The spiritual ties the three together.

There are numerous cults which seek to minister to one or two phases of this triple relationship. The pastor should know these tendencies, speak of them from the pulpit by way of implication and instruction, and minister directly to the people who need his particular advice on some part of this relationship. Too often the minister has been in the habit of making a sweeping condemnation and open criticism of these cults without realizing that his people are driven to the cults by a need to which these minister. Regard for all the needs of the human organism and personality in its totality is a sound preventative.

This does not mean that the pastor must preach a gospel of psychotherapy as if by some slight of hand performance, he could bring healing to his people. Nor does it mean some kind of *gospel*, so called, whereby a psychotherapeutic philosophy is given, and whereby the pastor becomes the originator of health talks or the sponsor of health clinics. Indeed not, for this would belie the true calling and function of the minister. The pastor is first of all a spiritual minister and he must deal first of all in spiritual things. He must give advice on the total experience of life only as a means to an end. The mental, physical and spiritual will then receive their proper place so that his people may be men of God, "thoroughly furnished unto all good works."[27] The mental and physical health of the individual is most assuredly part of the purpose of the pastor as he seeks to help and shepherd his flock; but the end purpose and over-all goal will be to bring that improved individual into the proper place

---

22. Ibid., p. 123.
23. Philippians 4:4-8.
24. Acts 20:28.
25. Colossians 3:1, I Corinthians 15:58.
26. Philippians 3:12-21.
27. II Timothy 3:17.

and relation to the kingdom of God. His duty for himself, as well as for the people to whom he gives his ministry is "seek first the kingdom of God and His righteousness."[28] Then all things in his ministry will become clear, and all of his ministry will point and purpose his endeavor to that end. If this end purpose is lost, then all is lost and his ministry is not successful.

All of this has tremendous bearing not only on the problem of sickness, suffering and sorrow, but also on the wider sphere of life called *Christian living*. This we discuss in the next chapter, in order that we may understand the importance of pastoral psychology for all of life.

---

28. Matthew 6:33.

CHAPTER X

Christian Living

HAVING studied the importance and nature of conversion and the place of sickness and suffering, we turn now to the subject of Christian Living with a constructive analysis in search of directive principles for a pastoral psychology. Conversion and conduct during sickness are included in Christian living because both experiences reflect Christian life in a real way; yet, there are questions and conclusions which lie beyond the consideration of conversion and conduct under affliction. In this chapter we wish to emphasize the entire personality of the individual, the complete Christian life which is required of the individual by the Word of God, and the function of the individual in the society of God.

Psychologists have not been interested in Christian life other than the experience of conversion. They could estimate and evaluate the biological and psychological experiences in conversion. When it comes to Christian living, it is far more difficult to analyze and tabulate the impressions and reactions of individual. For this reason, academic psychology has not been interested in the art of Christian living, and has not deemed it important. It has not been concerned with forgiveness and guilt of sin. Atonement through Christ was ignored by the psychologists. The total impact of Biblical living has not registered in their thinking or research observation. Very few approximate the distinction which Sr. Norborg made between ordinary religious experience and Christian experience. Their very attitude has influenced the ministry, even as Mackenzie contended:

> "The trend of the popular volumes on psychology makes the minister wonder whether conscience and reason have any authoritative place in a world swayed by instinct and emotion; and it has had the effect of undermining and lessening the effectiveness of his convictions."[1]

Pastoral psychology must aim at helping man in Christian living. Therefore, the art and practice of Christian living is of tremendous importance for pastoral psychology. Through common sense methods, and through a general emphasis on Biblical living, Christian ideas and ethics have been preached and taught by pastors through the generations of church history. There is more to Christian living than has been traditionally cherished and encouraged; and in this area of emphasis, pastoral psychology can become an effective tool

---

1. John G. Mackenzie, *Souls in the Making*, The Macmillan Co., New York, 1929, p. 6.

in the hand of the minister. All too often the pastor views life with the yard-stick of his own personal experience.

A. The Meaning of Christian Living

Christian living means the full-orbed life, consecrated to Christ through sur-render, submission and service. It means the actual practice of Christianity unto the glory of God. Christian theologians look upon Christian living as the result of sanctification by the Lord. Theologian L. Berkhof defined sancti-fication thus:

> "Sanctification may be defined as that gracious and continuous operation of the Holy Spirit by which He delivers the justified sinner from the pollu-tion of sin, renews his whole nature in the image of God and enables him to perform good works."[2]

This gives the proper emphasis on the Holy Spirit as the prime mover of sanctification in the believer. It is also true, as L. Berkhof pointed out, sancti-fication is different from regeneration in that man's duty toward and in sancti-fication makes him work for and strive for an "ever-increasing sanctification by using the means which God has placed at his disposal."[3] While this is in absolute harmony with the Bible,[4] it is foreign to psychologists. They do not believe that the conscious and sub-conscious have a place in the process of sanctification.

Writers in pastoral theology, though few in number, have expressed them-selves on the importance of Christian living. A. N. Littlejohn merely mentioned the process as "re-establishing the equilibrium, and with it the regulating power which can preserve it."[5] F. E. Day suggested,

> "Wise tact will adjust the pastor's approach to his people, whatever their station, but the ultimate end of his mingling with his people will be the development of their spiritual life."[6]

A return to apostolic and post-apostolic activity of the church was suggested by W. Cunningham, and with that he did much to remove the mistaken notion that all in the church of that time were living a strong Christian life. He demonstrated that those people too were shepherded toward a sanctified life.[7] C. E. Jefferson spoke of it in this way:

> "Feeding of the sheep is an essential duty of the shepherd calling, and is known even to those who are least familiar with shepherds and their work. Sheep cannot feed themselves nor water themselves."[8]

---

2. Louis Berkhof, *Reformed Dogmatics*, Wm. B. Eerdmans Publishing Co., Grand Rapids, 1932, Vol. II, 1932, p. 131.
3. Ibid., p. 132.
4. II Corinthians 7:1, Colossians 3:5-14, I Peter 1:22.
5. A. N. Littlejohn, *Conciones Ad Clerum*, T. Whittaker, ——, 1880, p. 63.
6. Frank E. Day, "Pastoral Visiting and Pulpit Strength," *The Methodist Review*, 1902, Vol. 84, No. 6, p. 879.
7. W. Cunningham, *The Cure of Souls*, The University Press, Cambridge, 1908, pp. 5, 6.
8. Charles Edward Jefferson, *The Ministering Shepherd*, Thomas T. Crowell Co., New York, 1912, p. 58.

G. C. Morgan came the closest to the correct analysis when he said:

> "The true pastor will do much more than make social calls upon members of his flock. That he will do. Indeed he will seek to mix with his people in all the interests of their lives, that he may know them, not inquisitorially, but sympathetically. But he will do all this, never forgetting that his particular work is that of *perfecting them in Christ*, by admonishing them where necessary and always teaching them."[9]

From these references it is very evident that some of the writers in pastoral theology coveted the proper spiritual goal for their ministry even though they did not express the full meaning of Christian living in terms of sanctification.

The real meaning of Christian living was not even approached by the psychologists. This is evident in the statement by T. Newcomb:

> "Personality develops out of strivings which are made necessary because individuals find themselves thwarted; they face conflict. To a very considerable degree that which is unique in each personality is the result of strivings in the facts of social conflicts."[10]

E. D. Martin said we should keep alive our spirit of progress and to do this we should keep alive the spirit of liberalism[11] — as if this could be the power for Christian living.

When one reads the work of K. R. Stolz, *The Psychology of Religious Living*, particularly his chapter on "Religion as a Rallying Center," one feels an emphasis which does not approximate the Bible interpretation of sanctification. He stressed religion as a rallying center but did not include the radiant Christ as the center of life for fullness of experience and blessing in personality development.[12]

The concept of sanctification or the process of becoming holy are not understood by the psychologists. We have a typical illustration in the words of Halliday:

> "The difficulty lies in the popular conception of holiness. We believe that what is commonly called sainthood is achieved through the inhibition of instinctive forces. This inhibition is the result of a wrong attitude to nature, and consequently of a wrong attitude to the sex instinct which is the strongest of the natural forces within us. It is important to realize that this wrong attitude is psychological and not physical."[13]

This conception is far from the Biblical idea of holiness. Christian living is more than merely overcoming an inferiority complex or downing acquired fears. It is more than merely growing through pain, and absorbing the tension of our times. Christian living is growth in "wisdom and stature and in favor

9. G. Campbell Morgan, *The Ministry of the Word*, Fleming H. Revell Co., New York, 1919, pp. 123, 124.

10. T. Newcomb, "Christianity and Mental Hygiene," Conference Report, New York, 1939, p. 48.

11. E. D. Martin, *Psychology*, Peoples Institute Pub. Co., New York, 1924, p. 294.

12. Karl R. Stolz, *Pastoral Psychology*, Abingdon-Cokesbury Press, New York, Nashville, 1940, pp. 105-118.

13. W. Fearon Halliday, *Psychology and Religious Experience*, Hodder and Stoughton, London, 1929, p. 96.

with God and man" (Luke 2:52). It involves the necessity of joy in knowing Jesus Christ, as Bonnell suggests.[14]

The statement of H. C. Link is very important:

> "The greatest and most authentic text book on personality is still the Bible, and the discoveries which psychologists have made tend to confirm rather than to contradict the codification of personality found there."[15]

And yet Link did not speak of developing personality in the full meaning of sanctification. In the development of personality, psychologists have not considered the important doctrines of the depravity of man, his need of a higher being, and his utter inability to earn salvation. They have not urged the importance of becoming holy *unto the Lord*. Their cry has been:

> "Human beings of original nature seem to be neither good nor bad, responsible nor irresponsible, but they have in their original equipment the capacities for developing either or both kinds of characteristics."[16]

Such expressions of belief do not even touch the real meaning of sanctification. Such statements pervert the idea of Christian living into a generality of self-improvement. They indicate that what we call sanctification is to the psychologist only poise, balance, mental health, freedom from fear, personal happiness, and personality adjustment. We should not forget that all of these have a definite place in sanctification, because we cannot move far in the progress of sanctification under God's blessing without these qualities and achievements. Yet, these parts in themselves do not constitute the entire experience of sanctification, nor even the essence of it. L. D. Weatherhead gave a better view when he said;

> "Spiritually, we find universally a craving for God. This craving may express itself when as Augustine cried out, 'Thou hast made us for Thyself, and our hearts are restless till they find rest in Thee' or when some poor Indian pariah bows before his idol."[17]

But even this statement falls short of the truth. Real Christian living not only includes this craving of the human heart,[18] and the satisfaction of this craving by the grace and mercy of God; it also includes a heart response to the blessings of God.[19] There are many books[20] by psychologists today that deal with the subject of living and the better qualities of life that constitute whole-

---

14. John Southerland Bonnell, *Pastoral Psychiatry*, Harper & Brothers Publishers, New York, 1938, p. 179.

15. Henry C. Link, *The Return to Religion*, The Macmillan Co., New York, 1936, p. 103.

16. Harrison Sacket Elliot and Grace Loucks Elliot, *Solving Personal Problems*, Henry Holt and Co., New York, 1936, p 287.

17. Leslie D. Weatherhead, *Psychology in the Service of the Soul*, The Macmillan Co., 1932, p. 207.

18. Psalm 42:1, Psalm 63:1.

19. Psalm 27:8, Psalm 116:12-14.

20. Charles T. Holman, *The Religion of a Healthy Mind*, Round Table Press, Inc., New York, 1939.

S. H. Kraines and E. S. Thetford, *Managing Your Mind*, The Macmillan Co., New York, 1947.

Edward A. Strecker and Kenneth E. Appel, *Discovering Ourselves*, The Macmillan Co., New York, 1932.

some life in our day, but they do not so much as touch upon the real essence of Christian living in its Biblical implications and specifications.

B. The Place of the Pragmatic in Christian Living

The psychologists have manifested a strong interest in the pragmatic in life. There is a pro and con on this issue, and we do well to examine it for the construction of a tenable and effective pastoral psychology.

In examining the writings of the psychologists we note an over-emphasis on feeling or on the pragmatic. W. James expressed a profound respect for feeling in religion. He said:

> "Individuality is founded in feeling; and the recesses of feeling, the darker, blinder strata of character, are the only places in the world in which we catch real fact in the making, and directly perceive how events happen, and how work is actually done."[21]

This attitude of James was due in large measure to the kind of subjects he chose for questioning. He admitted this when he said,

> "The sentimentality of many of my documents is a consequence of the fact that I sought them among the extravagances of the subject.[22]

Even so, James was very enthusiastic about the pragmatic interpretation, and he wrote:

> "I believe the pragmatic way of taking religion to be the deeper way. It gives body as well as soul, it takes its claim, as everything real must claim, some characteristic realm of fact as its very own."[23]

This pragmatic interpretation led James to a dismal outlook on life and a belief about God that cannot stand the light of Scripture. Commenting on this he indicated:

> "Who knows whether the faithfulness of individuals here below to their own poor over-beliefs may not actually help God in turn to be more effectively faithful to his greater tasks."[24]

James has been quoted at length because he set the pace for this pragmatic interpretation of religious experience. He represents a large number of psychologists who maintain the pragmatic and empirical view. To them God is but an idea which is helpful to man's life and development. They project the idea of God so that they can receive "a lift" in their fears, hopes, ideals, and wishes. They consider the worship of God to be important because it helps man to improve himself. To them, sin is but a moral disease. In the language of W. B. Selbie:

> "It is an attempt to explain religion which really explains it away, and the air of scientific assurance with which it is done makes it very convincing to untutored minds."[25]

---

21. William James, *The Varieties of Religious Experience*, Longmans, Green and Co.. London and Bombay, 1903, pp. 501, 502.
22. Ibid., p. 486.
23. Ibid., p. 519.
24. Ibid.
25. W. B. Selbie, *The Psychology of Religion*, Oxford University Press, Oxford, 1924, p. 297.

Pragmatism has caused the psychologists to resort to the pathological and the psycho-analytic interpretations of religious experience. It has carried the idea to the extreme as evidenced in the Freudian emphasis on sex. They forget that such deductions are limited, and that "No psychological analysis of a sensation can reproduce its 'feltness', and no objective representation of religion can do full justice to the actual experience."[26]

Pragmatism has led to unbelief and therefore to a false evaluation of Christian life. It is time the psychologists came to the following realization:

> "Psychology is a science, and, as such of necessity empirical and purely immanent. However high may be the matters of which it treats, it is still of earth, earthly. The psychologist is often tempted to forget this. He may well be reminded of the recent exploit of the balloonists who succeeded in rising ten miles into the air. By so doing, no doubt, some of the substances which they sought to investigate came to them in purer form; yet this was only a matter of degree. They were still unable to transcend their earth-bound limitations. Even so, the psychologist may, if he is wise and enlightened, somewhat reduce his limitations, but he can never altogether rise above them. His method is descriptive and not explanatory; it is natural and never can comprehend the supernatural."[27]

The pragmatic test is not the final test. Psychologists forget that as human beings we are limited by time and in knowledge. They are blind to the fact that the kind of psychology usually proposed is totally oblivious to the real essentials of Christian living. F. Kunkel gave good advice when he wrote:

> "Religious experiences in particular can rarely be verified, and certainly cannot be understood by irreligious psychologists. The autobiography of a man like Saint Augustine is to men like Freud and Adler, what a painting by Raphael would be to a blind man."[28]

He is right, and if the psychologists could only realize this, they could be of tremendous assistance to pastoral psychology. The pragmatic test does not satisfy the soul response of the individual. The pragmatic test rules out the supernatural and seeks to find a norm only on the basis of appearances. James judged the reality of religion on the basis of external value. Psychologists since his time have tried to study the normal and the abnormal from this point of view.

Our objection to the extreme of pragmatism does not mean that we seek to avoid or deny the value of a proper evaluation of the individual with respect to feeling and experience. We should make a strong plea for a recognition of this important aspect of the individual. We of the traditional interpretation have been prone to outlaw feeling and experience in Christian life. We have failed to give proper regard to the element of the pragmatic in Christian life. On the other hand, we have insisted that belief, repentance, confession, and forgiveness shown to others are a real part of Christian life. Since these also manifest an experimental and pragmatic aspect, we need a pastoral psychology

---

26. Eric S. Waterhouse, *The Philosophy of Religious Experience*, Epworth Press, London, 1923, p. 29.
27. Lindsay Dewar and Cyril E. Hudson, *Psychology for Religious Workers*, Harper and Brothers, New York, 1934, p. 14.
28. Fritz Kunkel, *In Search of Maturity*, Charles Scribner's Sons, New York, 1943, p. 33.

that will include a study of them in the joint light of a true psychology and Biblical theology. The whole truth of the matter will be found when the two lights are brought into a single focus.

It is our duty to examine all of Christian living in the light of Scripture. The Bible must be the foundation of psychological knowledge. The fountain of human experience is found in the Bible, where we read about the image of God in man, the power of sin, the origin of false religions and the true way of redemption through Jesus Christ. The Christian life of regenerated people and the precepts which govern that kind of living have been given in the Bible. This does not mean that we must disregard the findings of psychologists such as Pratt, James, Coe and Ames. We must examine their findings, test their data, prove their fundamental interpretation of the facts, and determine from our theological Biblical viewpoint what we can use of their findings. Such of their findings and conclusions as fit into the proper theological Biblical interpretation of life may and must be used. Doing so we bring about a theological-experimental method of investigation. Then our moorings will be safely anchored in the Bible, and our investigation will be related to and coördinated with its revelation. This will give us a psychology with a soul. Then and only then, will we be in position wisely and effectively to examine and direct the individual by means of pastoral psychology.

C. The Importance of Sex in Christian Living

In recent years there has come to be a great deal of emphasis on sex information and sex education. There is reason for this, because our generation has been overstimulated in the matter of sex. Our loose living, the glamourized emphasis on sex by the theater and the movie stars, our sex-saturated literature, our two world wars within the span of a single generation, and the overemphasis upon sex by psychologists and psychiatrists have made the matter of sex critically important.

All of this has a tremendous influence on the kind of Christian living which people observe and practice. Therefore as ministers we must be alert to the situation. We face serious conditions in some of our churches.

The overemphasis on sex in the field of psychology can be traced back to Sigmund Freud. We can best indicate the influence of Freud by quoting L. W. Batten.

> "The scientific world owes a considerable debt to Sigmund Freud for his discoveries in abnormal psychology, but we must be on our guard against the too eager acceptance of his fundamental hypothesis. For Freud has reached the conclusion that the trauma in practically all nervous and mental disorders is of a sexual nature. He broadens the sexual field, it is true, till it covers almost all of life, and he carries the sexual motive back to a stage of infancy in which I believe the child is essentially as sexless as a plant. Unfortunately Freud has many followers who practice the sex cult to the limit and it is feared that much harm may result."[29]

Freud made a significant contribution to psychology by bringing to light areas of mental life which before his time had not been considered or fully

---

29. Loring W. Batton, *The Relief of Pain by Mental Suggestion*, Moffat, Yard and Co.. New York, 1917, p. 148.

explored. He contended that sex life actually begins long before puberty. Freud felt there was a hidden power in dreams and therefore his psychoanalytic therapy was advanced and practiced.

There has been widespread difference of opinion on Freud. For example, C. Carle claimed that Freudianism did not overemphasize the role of sex. He claimed that Freud talked about sex in order to "promote love, happiness and cultural progress."[30] On the other hand, C. Sidis made the bold analysis that Freud was extreme. Said he:

> "As a matter of fact psychoanalysis, by which Freud and his adherants have baptized their sexual theories and metaphysical wish-speculations, should be regarded as savage and barbaric."[31]

There has likewise been a warm debate between those who believe that religious faith and objects are real, and those who with Freud came to see man as a sex-propelled mechanism without a soul.

Freud has had a tremendous influence on psychological thinking for many decades. It has infiltrated all of psychological writing. To quote C. Carle:

> "Freud, without any doubt, has influenced psychological thinking more than anyone else in the last hundred years. His great achievement was to give the first fairly complete theory of human nature with the stress on mental equilibrium. But even geniuses are children of their time, and Freud was a typical child of nineteenth-century liberalism, with its advantages and short-comings."[32]

It is very unfortunate that a man with the power and influence of Freud should have been such an opponent of religion. He did much to establish the freedom of the human spirit, yet Freud disparaged religion.

> "Regarding religion, Freud says it is an illusion. He carefully distinguishes illusion from delusion. An illusion is the view we take of the universe, or of any aspect of it, under the influence of a wish."[33]

Freud taught a rigid biological determinism. Religion was to him "the obsessional neurosis of humanity." Freud left no room for the Biblical view of sex. "For the psychology of Freud the term sin has in fact no meaning at all."[34] Freud sought to know everything by the criterion of sex. In this regard, "Freud was guilty of two errors. The first is his assumption as to the impartiality of science and the utter impartiality of religion."[35] He sought to explain everything by means of a scientific analysis of sex life. He could explain matter but he could not explain the divine content of religious experience. Freud thought he was scientific, yet H. N. Wieman wrote:

---

30. Charles Carle, *Mysticism in Modern Psychology*, Psycho-Sociological Press, New York. 1943, p. 13.
31. Coris Sidis, *Nervous Ills, Their Cause and Cure*, Richard G. Badger, The Gorham Press, Boston, 1922, p. 8.
32. Carle, op. cit., p. 9.
33. William Brown, *Mind, Medicine and Metaphysics*, Oxford University Press, London, 1936, p. 208.
34. L. W. Grensted, *Psychology and God*, Longmans, Green and Co., London, 1930, p. 142.
35. Lindsay Dewar, *Man and God, An Essay in the Pschology and Philosophy of Religious Experience*, Society for Promoting Christian Knowledge, London, The Macmillan Co., New York, 1936, p. 116.

"Certainly the Freudian theories, however illuminating they have been in bringing human nature into the light, have been full of quite fantastic ideas, undisciplined by scientific method."[36]

We have not given a complete analysis of Freud because that would take us too far afield. We have shown that sex formed the basis for Freud's interpretation of life and from this he developed his psychoanalytic method. This emphasis, as stated before, has infiltrated all psychological thinking and study. It has also influenced psychological writing pertaining to pastoral work and we must constantly be on our guard for this pernicious danger. In the language of B. Sachs, quoted by H. C. Link:

"Altogether too much attention has been paid and is being paid to the question of sex, to the neglect of far more important facts . . . Much is said about this over-sexed age of ours, over-sexed chiefly in the amount of talk about it. Many of the groups instead of spending hours on sex education could spend time more profitably if they would consider how to develop in children absolute honesty, truthfulness, respect for authority, patriotism, love for one's neighbor."[37]

This quotation strikes an important truth. We must not overemphasize sex with the result that the total Christian life receives an unbalanced interpretation. Sex life is only one part of Christian living. Important as it is, there are also other drives that impel the individual, and these must not be overlooked. That is exactly what is meant in this chapter on Christian living. Psychologists have overemphasized sex to such an extent that they have not given due consideration to the totality of a wholesome Christian life.

On the other hand, even though we wrote with conviction in the previous paragraphs on Freud's extreme emphasis on sex, we hasten to assert that there are many ministers who are sadly unaware of the many and real sex questions which face their people. Whether we recognize it or not, our age is sex conscious. This is abetted by our modern literature, movie, and general mode of living. Birth control literature can be found on the counter of many drug stores. Companionate marriage, free love, and loose living are rampant. The display of contraceptive literature and aids places the question of sex before our people in a much different way than a generation ago. We live in a day when artificial sex stimuli are prominent. It is found in most everything we read. "Contemporary literature on this subject is voluminous and for the most part chaotic. It is too largely a literature of revolt."[38]

"The psychology of sex has an intimate connection with pastoral work."[39] There is a great need for sex education. A mass of wrong information has come to the average individual. The pastor is in the center of congregational life and he must face this problem realistically. Family troubles, and personal

---

36. Henry Nelson Wieman, *Religious Experience and Scientific Method*, The Macmillan Co., New York, 1935, p. 35.
37. Henry C. Link, *The Return to Religion*, The Macmillan Co., New York, 1936, p. 116.
38. H. Lichliter, *The Healing of Souls*, The Abingdon Press, New York, 1931, p. 72.
39. Clement F. Rogers, *An Introduction to the Study of Pastoral Theology*, The Clarendon Press, Oxford, 1912, p. 165.

problems of his people force him to have a working psychology on sex. At least he should understand the facts and know the problem.

> "It is most important that the pastor should have an understanding of the facts of sexual activities, not only those that may be classified as normal, but also those which are frequently described as abnormal or perversions. Only then is he able adequately to minister to those who come to him for help."[40]

Without a proper knowledge of the sex impulses and the sex problems that face himself and his people, the pastor cannot effectively minister to his congregation. The minister may want to evade this difficult problem and claim that this requires technical knowledge and should be handled by the physician. Yet, the pastor will find that he cannot avoid meeting this problem because it is foundational to many of the troubles of average people in congregational life. He will find in it a wonderful opportunity for service, because he can give sane and sober advice from the Biblical point of view. It affords him an opportunity to present the Scriptual teachings on morals and so do much to mold the thinking of his people. This is particularly true of the minister with respect to the family life of his parishioners. "It is still true that ministers play an almost unique part in the whole field of family relationships."[41] And today, more than ever before, the sex question is at the bottom of many of our family difficulties. A spiritual minister has a golden opportunity to meet this problem at a time when preaching and counseling can be the most effective.

This does not mean that the minister must of necessity become a sex specialist. Particularly the physical aspect of sex requires specialized attention. "Technical advice regarding sex adjustments belongs within the province of the physician and not of the minister."[42] But this does not lessen the responsibility of the minister to give careful and friendly counsel. Concerning this duty, A. T. Boisen wrote:

> "The right of the minister of religion to deal with the problem of sex is today being challenged, and there is need of rethinking carefully his function in relation to that of the doctor. In general the minister is no expert in the physiological aspects of the sex problem, but in so far as the problem relates to the philosophy of life and to the problem of sin and guilt, he is very much concerned and ought to be able to speak with as much authority as the physician or the psychiatrist."[43]

Religion and sex are intimately related. This does not mean that religion can be interpreted in terms of sex, as Freud maintained; but it does mean that the minister must understand sex life in relation to religion. Pastoral psychology demands this of the pastor if he is to work effectively. The modern divorce question forces these considerations on the minister with atomic explosiveness. The pastor of any average city church will evidence the fact that

---

40. Bonnell, op. cit., p. 97.
41. E. W. A. Dexter and R. C. Dexter, *The Minister and Family Troubles*, Richard R. Smith, Inc., New York, 1931, p. 88.
42. Anton T. Boisen, *The Exploration of the Inner World*, Willet, Clark & Co., Chicago, 1937, pp. 274, 275.
43. Anton T. Boisen, *Problems in Religion and Life*, Abingdon-Cokesbury Press, New York, 1946, p. 75.

behind many of the divorce tangles the sex question looms very large. Therefore the minister should know the various types of sex attitude and perversion. He should know the sex abnormalities among people. Knowing these he will be an understanding listener, having balance and poise before his people. Like J. S. Bonnell, he will be able to draw upon a reservoir of knowledge and case histories, giving point and purpose to consultative advice. Then he will, for example, be able to reach into his files for some medical statement on masturbation, and reading it to a young man who is troubled will calm his conscience and settle his religious life.

The average minister is not informed about the normal feminine climacteric and many do not recognize the same characteristic in men. Seemingly, this is a thing to be hushed and to be talked about only in whispers. The minister learns about such conditions only from his wife or he does not know about it at all. The masculine climacteric is not even considered important. Yet, the minister faces the results of the climacteric in the men and women who come to him for advice on spiritual things. A proper understanding of this background is an integral part of pastoral psychology. It need not be talked about with the frankness of a physician, yet it need not be avoided entirely in professional conversation with parishioners. There is an understanding way in which these problems can be discussed spiritually without the bluntness and uncouthness of a novice. This is constructive pastoral psychology and is of great importance for effective work.

Beneath many of the spiritual problems in Christian living are the sex problems which have their roots in the climacteric. So we discover that not only are young people faced with this problem of sex, but those in middle age of life are confronted with the same problem in a different way. The minister should be aware of this before he reaches that age himself.

In order that he may be well-informed, the pastor should be acquainted with such books as *The Second Forty Years*,[44] by E. J. Stieglitz, M.D., and *Making the Most of the Rest of Life*, by K. R. Stolz.[45] For instance, the chapter on "Sex and Age,"[46] in the book of Stieglitz is an eye opener for anyone not acquainted with this persistent problem. The minister should have standard books on marriage, sex life, and home happiness on his shelf for ready reference and constant consultation. One example of this kind of literature is the classic work of L. D. Weatherhead on *The Mastery of Sex Through Psychology and Religion*. The psychological-pastoral approach is predominant in this work. Such chapters as "Comradeship and Flirting," "The True Approach to Marriage," "A Message to Those Who Do Not Marry," and "The Mishandled

---

44. Edward J. Stieglitz, *The Second Forty Years*, J. B. Lippincott Co., Philadelphia and New York, 1946, 317 pp.

45. Karl R. Stolz, *Making the Most of the Rest of Life*, New York, Nashville, Abingdon-Cokesbury Press, 1941, 216 pp.

46. Stieglitz, op. cit., pp. 192-212.

Sex Life,"[47] are very important for the correct understanding of the sex problems which normal and abnormal people have daily.

We would not like to be misunderstood on this subject. We do not mean
that the minister must constantly preach on sex matters, but helpful counsel
will shine through his preaching with the proper psychological suggestions
for Christian living in this area of life. With adequate knowledge of people
in terms of sex life and disturbances, the pastor will be able to counsel his
people and avoid being shocked when his people actually unburden their
hearts in his presence. With proper pastoral psychology he will be an effective
minister of Jesus Christ in this area of Christian living.

It is necessary for every minister to keep his young people informed on
these questions. Instead of having his teen age boys and girls obtain the information on the story of life from the street or through filthy stories, lurid
magazines and suggestive pictures, he should see to it that the church takes
aggressive action to reach young people with proper enlightenment. In his
Christian education program the pastor should be alive to the question, and
at points of interest and advantage he should infiltrate sex information as may
be decently and conveniently possible in connection with Bible instruction.
The sanctity of marriage, the purity of youth, the fidelity of partners to each
other, and the lure of courting days, should receive proper attention as areas
of applied Christianity. With the knowledge and alertness of a true interest
from the psychological-spiritual point of view, such teaching and information
should be imparted from the Biblical point of view. The Bible is very plain
and very usable in explaining the fundamental spiritual and moral obligations
which form a definite part of Christian living in this regard.

It would be wise for a minister in the average parish to establish a period
of instruction, or a time when a conference is held for teen age boys and
another for teen age girls. If he did this every year it would not arouse unwarranted objection. He should engage a competent physician to talk to the boys
and girls in separate conferences in the church building and under the pastor's
auspices. Private conferences could be offered for any boy or girl who desired
to ask questions. The physician should be engaged to "just be around" for
a few days so that boys and girls could "casually" but really "on purpose"
meet him and ask their questions.

In some parish traditions this might not be the wise procedure because some
people do not want this question raised. But its very secrecy adds to its danger,
and emphasizes the demand that we face the question openly. The pastor can
then encourage young people to consult the physician in his office. If the
community physician is a competent man, he is the ideal person for the task.
Then the young people will always have confidence in such a person and feel
free to go to him in his own office for advice through the years. Such a procedure will bring an untold amount of good information at the proper time,
to the right people, and under the right auspices. Too often the church and

47. Leslie D. Weatherhead, *The Mastery of Sex Through Psychology and Religion*, The
Macmillan Co., New York, 1940, pp. 31-167.

her officers have held themselves aloof from wholesome sex information and because of this have lost golden opportunities and failed in spiritual responsibility.

Going back to Freud, the instigator of over-emphasis on the sex question, we note the following quotation which states the question and the answer:

> "Freud's vigorous emphasis of the role of sex in the emotional life of children and adults has so intrigued repressed psychiatrists and frustrated patients that sex has been assigned a grossly distorted and exaggerated importance . . . Without denying that we, as a species, are more vigorously biological than logical, sex is but one of the many aspects of successful and happy living."[48]

Just because it is important and because its importance has been so over-stressed as to unbalance our interpretation, we should view sex from the sane and scientific standpoint founded on the Biblical interpretation. Such an interpretation is found in J. Waterink's book, *Puberteit*.[49] In this masterpiece one finds the scientific understanding necessary to view sex in its proper relationships, and the proper Christian interpretation which has a justifiable Biblical foundation. Pastoral psychology demands that the minister should be alert to such a wise and careful study and instruction of sex with this kind of interpretation so that Christian living may be examined and explained for the total life of man.

D. Complete Christian Living Through Personality Development

Personality development has been much discussed by psychologists, and many books have been written by them on the subject. Details of the biological, educational, and emotional aspects of personality development have been treated in such books. The nature and development of personality traits, personality adjustment and integration, and the psychological appraisals of character and personality have received their proper attention in such writings. Psychological measurements of personality characteristics have not been lacking. The purpose of psychologists has been to present a complete study of personality development in the hope that mind and matter could be brought into perfect coördination for study and action.

The psychologists have claimed that the ministers have been interested in the soul of man and have forgotten the development of personality. To the psychologists, the epitome of success is found in the integrated personality moving about in our streamlined society with ease, comfort and poise. There is much truth in their claim, but it is not the whole truth, because there is also a spiritual development that belongs with this interpretation. Therefore it is of supreme importance that pastoral psychology bring this before students and pastors.

---

48. Stieglitz, op. cit., p. 211.
49. J. Waterink, *Puberteit,* Vierde Druk, N.V. Gebr. Zomer en Keuning's Uitgeversmij, Wageningen, 1948, pp. 181.

Books on this subject by C. G. Jung,[50] C. F. Leavitt,[51], S. H. Kraines-E. S. Thetford,[52] and K. A. Menninger,[53] treat the importance of personality but do not go far enough for complete Christian living. These books present a tremendous challenge to pastoral psychology because they stress the importance of the synthesis of the entire personality, and the minister should be the key man to stimulate and develop this synthesis.

At present the task of both the minister and the psychologist is hindered by antagonism between psychology and religion. This is evidenced in the following statement:

> "It is this belief in personality with its emphasis upon worth and reverence and altruism which furnishes the basis of religion, and Christianity is preëminently the religion of personality. A general recognition of this Christian belief in personality would greatly aid in the solution of the problem of the seeming conflict between the new psychology and religion."[54]

It is the role of pastoral psychology to bring about a synthesis of psychology and pastoral theology in order to accomplish instruction and technique for personality development as part of the program and art of Christian living.

The development of personality is specifically related to man's social environment. Much has been written by psychologists pertaining to this relation. We recognize with C. T. Holman that

> "Personality is achieved in the interaction of the individual with his social environment. Personality is the product of this dynamic relationship between what heredity bestows and what the social milieu presents."[55]

Man in his social environment presents a challenge to the minister. It is to the credit of the psychologists that this emphasis came to the front. C. T. Holman sensed this challenge when he wrote:

> "Personality is nurtured in social relationships and is inconceivable apart from them. Psychologists have felt keenly the need of such support for their patients, and some of them have even arranged regular social affairs for their recovered patients. Here religion always has been strong. The church is primarily a fellowship. Here, then, the pastor has ready at hand resources which any clinical practioner might well envy. Not only has he the opportunity to counsel with individuals, but he also has available all these social, educational and religious groups which form aspects of his program of work, and to the supporting and sustaining fellowship of such groups the needy individual may be introduced."[56]

50. Carl G. Jung, *The Integration of the Personality*, Farrar & Rinehard, Inc., New York, 1938, 313 pp.
51. C. Franklin Leavitte, *You and Your Unsuspected Powers*, Paul Beandel Printing Co., 1921, 38 pp.
    C. Franklin Leavitte, *Personality Plus*, Books of Merit Inc., New York, 1938, 152 pp.
52. S. H. Kraines and E. S. Thetford, *Managing Your Mind*, The Macmillan Co., New York, 1947, 375 pp.
53. Karl A. Menninger, *Man Against Himself*, Harcourt, Brace and Co., New York, 1938, 484 pp.
54. Marion Hiller Dunsmore, assisted by L. M. Crebe and E. O. Pearman, "The Relation of the New Psychology to Religion," *The Methodist Review*, 1923, May, Vol. 106, p. 424.
55. Charles T. Holman, *The Cure of Souls, A Socio-Psychological Approach*, The University of Chicago Press, Chicago, 1932, p. 55.
56. Charles T. Holman, *Getting Down to Cases*, The Macmillan Co., New York, 1942, pp. 186, 187.

The church should be alert to the truth of Holman's contention. The fellowship of the church offers the ideal environment for personality adjustment. Man must do much to become adjusted to society, and the church through pastoral psychology has a golden opportunity to promote this adjustment. We should not continue to let it slip out of our attention and interest. Psychologists have issued the challenge and we must not fail to meet it. The power of Christianity is able to alter the whole course of personality. The belief is all too common that it is not so.

> "In many religious circles there is a sickly sentimental belief in the power of religion to change any personality. But in its more realistic moments religion has had insight that a life may reach a point beyond which there is no turning back."[57]

Pastoral psychology offers the way of meeting the real challenge of molding individuals, by the grace of God, to become new creatures in Christ Jesus and better citizens for God.

> "If any man be in Christ Jesus, he is a new creature: old things are passed away; behold, all things are become new."[58]

And pastoral psychology seeks to relate the total person to Jesus Christ in Christian living. In the language of B. Condé:

> "Psychology makes the plea to live integrated lives. One of the goals of psychology is to attain what it calls 'integration,' the unifying of the self. But countless people are so divided and helpless in the clutch of conflicting desires that some power outside of themselves must help them to this unity. Jesus gives us the picture of God as the Father of love with whom we are meant to live as a little child in His protecting arms . . . Love takes away all fear and centers our desire on God and a close fellowship with Him. Life becomes unified and focused in trusting ourselves wholly to him."[59]

This is the importance of pastoral psychology. Jesus integrates life perfectly for Christian living.[60] Jesus interprets true freedom and brings the whole of life into relationship with the Almighty. But throughout it all, we need the aid of modern psychology to give us the complete picture of man. In the words of W. V. Richmond,

> "Modern psychology does not, to be sure, have all the answers to the riddle of human nature, but it has enough to enable people to understand far more about themselves than most of them do at present, and to guide their lives toward greater degrees of happiness and efficiency."[61]

Pastoral psychology is dedicated to the purpose of bringing spiritual happiness and efficiency to the individual in order that he may live and enjoy a

---

57. Carroll A. Wise, *Religion in Illness and Health*, Harper & Brothers, New York, 1942, p. 203.
58. I Corinthians 5:17.
59. Bertha Condé, *What's Life All About*, Charles Scribner's Sons, New York, 1931, pp. 101, 102.
60. Ephesians 1:4, 5, 7, I Peter 2:5, Matthew 5:48, II Corinthians 13:11.
61. Winifred V. Richmond, *Making the Most of Your Personality*, Farrar & Rinehard, Inc., 1942, p. vi.

wholesome Christian life. To do this we need technical knowledge readily available in the pastorate. We need to know something about the "Last Four Laps"[62] of life, as described by K. R. Stolz, if we are to minister effectively toward bringing complete Christian living to our people. Stolz reminded his readers that "personality either declines or develops fresh vitality and expands in new directions,"[63] and therefore we must know the four laps or periods described by him as adjustment, achievement, conservation and retirement. Every pastor knows that these laps exist if only he will reflect on the experiences of his people.

The Bible has all we need in essence but we need an explanation of Scriptural implications and statements in order to actuate pastoral psychology. This is the thought of J. G. McKenzie:

> "We must confess that modern psychology and psychotherapy tell us no more about the incompatible motives that tear the human soul asunder than was already in the Scriptures for all to read; but we lacked the perceiving eye and the understanding mind and the believing heart. Modern psychology has elucidated how human motives work, how they become perverted, how they 'split' our personality into flesh warring against the spirit and spirit against the flesh. It has added no knowledge of new motives; albeit it has helped us tremendously to realize how motives in the unconscious may work their havoc in our spiritual life."[64]

Expressing a similar opinion, C. T. Holman wrote,

> "Religion has always been the most powerful of all available resources in winning victory for men in all these areas of need. It unifies their discordant impulses about noble purposes; it effects satisfying social adjustments, both in human and cosmic relationships; it gives life meaning and value."[65]

> "Religion, then, and above all the Christian religion provides a cause to which a man can devote his life with unqualified loyalty."[66]

While there is no reference to the full import of Christianity in the saving power of Jesus Christ in this quotation, there is recognition of the power of our faith and the Christian religion. The Bible believing Christian asserts the full power of Christianity. No wonder G. Harkness said, "The Christian gospel interpreted in love and accepted in faith is relevant to every human situation,"[67] and "Let us trust God, not less but more, with knowledge of these facts."[68] The foundation of pastoral psychology includes the Biblical conceptions of life and the aid of modern science to understand life as it is. And for the individual

---

62. Stolz, Making the Most of the Rest of Life, op. cit., pp. 28-41.

63. Ibid., p. 28.

64. John G. McKenzie, *Psychology, Psychotherapy and Evangelicalism*, The Macmillan Co., New York, 1940, p. 218.

65. Holman, The Cure of Souls, etc., op cit., p. 220.

66. Ibid., pp. 221, 222.

67. Georgia Harkness, *The Dark Night of the Soul*, Abingdon-Cokesbury Press, New York, Nashville, 1945, p. 23.

68. Ibid.

in relation to these findings we offer the gospel of Jesus Christ. With W. A. Sadler we say:

> "Call a halt in this business of taking a page out of psychology to start a new religion: taking the heart out of the teachings of Jesus Christ to start a commercial system of religious mind cure."[69]

Another evidence that medical men are recognizing the help of religion has been given by S. N. Stevens:

> "The therapeutic value of religion in re-establishing harmony and unity in lives that have become emotionally unstable through fear, anxiety, worry and the like has been recognized by medical men as well as by ministers."[70]

The Christian religion is the source and substance of complete Christian living. Christianity can work soundness of mind, singleness of heart, stability of character and supreme poise in the conflicts of life. All of this is true because Christian living in Christ means a new life through Him. This influences our experience both in this life and for the life to come. S. Hiltner made a plea for the importance of religion to health in his chapter, "Some Contributions of Religion to Mental Health."[71] He indicated that theologians usually do not seek to explore this influence because they are interested mainly in salvation beyond time and beyond the usual considerations of health in the temporal order. On the contrary, the theologian and the minister should be interested in the total life of the individual. When Christ takes over, there is newness of power and life for all things and in all circumstances. The purpose of pastoral psychology is to bring the soul into living fellowship with God through Christ. Academic psychology does not lead to that fellowship since it is merely a natural science, not a religion. In the language of W. L. Northridge:

> "Psychology can show us many of the obstacles that prevent spiritual or mental health and how these may be removed, but it supplies neither a sufficient integrating ideal, nor an adequate dynamic for life. Merely to carry out a reductive analysis on a soul may leave the last state worse than the first. We should not forget that no soul is completely cured until it has been brought into a fellowship with God so intimate and real that life henceforth shall become an unbroken pilgrimage with Him."[72]

Then the Christian faith is more than a prophylactic, and is more than merely an escape mechanism to allay fears and frustrations. The contention of this thesis is that Christianity in its Biblical and historical sense is the secret to the world situation and to the experience of every individual. This means that we must see man in his lost condition,[73] we must recognize that he has guilt and the need of divine redemption.[74] The very ideas and doctrines

---

69. William A. Sadler, *The Truth About Mind Cure*, A. C. McClurg & Co., Chicago, 1929, p. 205.
70. Samuel Nowell Stevens, *Religion in Life Adjustments*, The Abingdon Press, New York, 1930, p. 111.
71. Seward Hiltner, *Religion and Health*, The Macmillan Co., New York, 1943, pp. 22-41.
72. W. L. Northridge, *Health for Mind and Spirit*, The Abingdon Press, New York, 1938, p. 191.
73. Matthew 10:6, Jeremiah 50:6, Luke 19:10, Isaiah 53:6.
74. Romans 8:1, Acts 4:12, II Thessalonians 2:13, Hebrews 1:14.

which modern psychologists have disregarded must be recognized. We must come to see the real impact of man's lost condition and his frustrating sinfulness. Man needs redemption; then and only then can man come to complete Christian living. Then the atonement of Jesus becomes real and the key for better Christian living.

In a widely quoted statement Jung admitted that when people really found religion they found life. He said,

> "During the last thirty years people from all civilized countries of the earth have consulted me . . . Among all my patients in the second half of life — that is to say, over thirty-five — there has not been one whose problem in the last resort was not that of finding a religious outlook on life. It is safe to say that every one of them fell ill because they had lost that which the living religions of every age have given to their followers, and none of them has been really healed who did not regain his religious outlook."[75]

This is going far for a psychologist, and yet it is not far enough; because the only religion that can give peace to a disturbed soul is the Christian religion through Jesus Christ. Jesus made bold the claim:

> "I am the bread of life: he that cometh to me shall never hunger and he that believeth on me shall never thirst."[76]
> "I am the resurrection, and the life: he that believeth in me, though he were dead, yet shall he live: and whosoever liveth and believeth in me shall never die."[77]

Complete Christian living can only be through Jesus Christ our Lord and Master. This is the cornerstone of pastoral psychology. We may say with the psychologists that all the religions of the world are helpful, but we must say with emphasis that only the way of Christianity through the atonement and sacrificial work of Christ is really helpful for man's frustration under the guilt of sin. Christianity is made of one piece — not eclectic, not evolutionary, nor materialistic. It is a spiritual testimony and triumph for the believer. Pastoral psychology is firmly based on these principles, otherwise we might as well close shop before we open the door for spiritual business.

When we speak of Christianity and the Christian faith we mean exactly what the Bible says in its revelation about this way of life. These are fundamental conceptions in the construction and application of pastoral psychology. We must be sure not only of our terminology but also and particularly about the meaning of our terms. It is so easy to be talking about the same thing and still have different meaning. For instance, C. T. Holman indicated that in the past all human failure has been traced by most ministers to Adam's fall. Quoting Romans seven, Holman contended that most ministers sought to bring souls to repentance and thus avail people of God's only remedy. He added:

> "It is not the intention to brush all this aside with a superior gesture. As a matter of fact, this 'plan of salvation' reveals a penetrating insight into the needs of the human soul. The literal transformation of thousands

---

75. Jung, op. cit., pp. 264, 265.
76. John 6:35.
77. John 11:25, 26.

of lives under the preaching of this gospel demonstrates its pragmatic values. At the same time, the traditional theory in which it is formulated rests back upon an utterly inadequate knowledge of human nature and its actual processes of normal development. Consequently, while it has met many notable successes, it has also met many, perhaps avoidable, failures."[78]

Revealing his non-Biblical interpretation, Holman also wrote:

"The view of human nature, then, which the social sciences are contributing as over against the traditional theological formulation which has been presented, is briefly as follows: instead of original being seen as 'sinful,' it is seen as neither 'good' nor 'bad.' The new-born babe is simply a bundle of biological impulses entirely non-moral in themselves. Through untold ages an evolutionary process has been preparing and shaping this tiny bundle of life. Inner organic drives, hungers, impulses, compel it to behave in characteristic ways. It sucks, grabs, aimlessly moves arms and legs. It behaves as it must, according to the inner law of its being. But 'good' or 'bad' are not the terms which can properly be applied either to its native behavior or to its original nature. This little biological bundle, in its original nature is neither moral nor immoral: it is amoral."[79]

Such language is in direct violation to the revelation of God in His word. The Bible is very plain with respect to the curse of Adam's sin,[80] and the curse of sin due to Adam's transgression.[81] Man is conceived and born in sin.[82] How can man therefore be called neutral or amoral? It is simply preposterous to entertain such a modernistic position — because it flaunts at Scripture. Man is inclined to all manner of evil from his youth to his dying day.[83] "This little biological bundle, in its original nature" is against God, and is sinful by nature.

This fundamental difference between the viewpoint of the social scientists in the field of psychology and the conservative Biblical theologian is the battle line on which the interpreter of pastoral psychology must take his stand. That stand must include a firm belief in the inability of man, the total depravity of human nature, and the need of divine supernatural redemption through Jesus Christ. Apart from Christ, through the working of the Holy Spirit sinful man cannot be redeemed because he is lost in trespasses and sins. Christian living means dynamic, effervescent and spiritual living through Jesus Christ.

The words of T. W. Pym serve as a fine conclusion to our emphasis in this chapter:

"Psychology itself is the science of efficient living; it does not include the study of right living. The part cannot include the whole. But Christianity, the science of right living, should include the study of efficient living. No Christian can be said to be living rightly if he is not living efficiently; nor is psychology likely to be spiritualized until Christians take psychology into their own religious life, or at any rate expect efficiency in daily life as one of the marks of Christian belief and practice."[84]

78. C. T. Holman, The Cure of Souls, etc., op. cit., 79.
79. Ibid., pp. 80, 81.
80. Genesis 3:17, 8:21.
81. Romans 3:11-18; 7:1-25.
82. Psalm 51:5, 10.
83. Isaiah 1:1-9, Psalm 25:7; 110:9, John 16:8, Romans 5:20.
84. T. W. Pym, *More Psychology and the Christian Life*, Student Christian Movement, London, 1925, p. 7.

The right living, which psychologists have not stressed according to this quotation from Pym, is the Christian living exemplified in the Bible. This complete Christian living is the fundamental basis for happiness according to true pastoral psychology. Paul outlined Christian living in some of his outstanding chapters such as Romans 7 and 8, I Corinthians 13 and 15, Colossians 3, Ephesians 4 and 5, Philippians 3 and 4. Christian living in the light of God's revelation through these and other Pauline writings reflect the life of Jesus Christ and the grace of the Holy Spirit. These passages represent fallen man, redeemed in action and consecration in order to live the Christian life. It is not a picture of helpless man, but of man, though lost in himself, hopeful of victory through God unto His glory. This describes man in complete personality development, in perfect relationship with God and man. With such a conception pastors can do pastoral work with a psychological interpretation and application. With that basis, we are ready to analyze the technique of pastoral psychology in the following chapters.

Part IV

TECHNIQUE ANALYSIS
OF PASTORAL PSYCHOLOGY

CHAPTER XI

Qualifications of the Pastor

WE have viewed pastoral theology from the historical viewpoint, we have made an investigation in the area of sickness, suffering and sorrow, and we have sought to make a constructive analysis of pastoral psychology. Now we come to analyze the technique by which we may accomplish a working application of pastoral psychology.

Our first area of study in the technique of pastoral psychology is the person of the pastor. In the historical analysis of our study it was evident that the person of the pastor was considered by so many writers in each of the three periods of pastoral theology that it became the main continuing trend of emphasis. Present day books and articles continue to stress the importance of the pastor as the key for success.

A. The Minister Himself

The technique of a minister in working out the principles of pastoral psychology are helped or hindered by his own person. The minister must first of all study his own personal habits, personality characteristics, and spiritual devotion to his work and to the Lord Jesus Christ.

> "He who is sound in his knowledge of himself is most likely to meet successfully the social problems that confront him in life. His willingness to scrutinize himself shows a fact-finding disposition which augurs well for any undertaking."[1]

Pastors should not feel that by virtue of their exalted office they are immune to the necessity of self examination.

> "The idea that a minister, just because he is a minister, has not to solve the problem of his own honesty before God is one of the greatest fallacies which vitiate religious thought."[2]

The minister has often held himself aloof from such personal examination even when he felt in his heart that it was very necessary. The difficulty has been that some pastors have thought of their work as a career rather than a calling. They have not sufficiently consecrated themselves to their task.

1. Ernest R. Groves, *Understanding Yourself*, Emerson Books, Inc., New York, 1941, p. 14.
2. W. Feardon Halliday, *Psychology and Religious Experience*, Hodder and Stoughton, Ltd., London, 1929, p. 164.

Pastoral psychology demands that the minister examine his own life and conduct. If the pastor cannot discover his own needs, if he cannot evaluate his own feelings, and if he cannot face the intricacies of his own dark experiences, he cannot successfully serve others. "The mere reading of a book will not make you popular or skillful in handling people."[3] Academic research, and careful psychological analysis cannot give this to the minister. Essentially, he must be a consecrated person, fully dedicated to the life which Christ called him to live. He must know himself. His faith must be deeply rooted in the word of God.

> "The pastor must himself have a deep religious faith and experience. Only with such support will he be able to carry the burdens, his own and those which others pour out on him."[4]

A minister can never lift other people to a higher plane than the one on which he himself lives. The minister must therefore maintain a sense of God in his life and conduct; he must live consciously in the presence of God. Pretense of sincerity or demonstration of an external relationship without the inner fellowship with Jesus Christ will not suffice. In the words of T. H. Hughes,

> "Reality and sincerity are basic in any man's relation to God. So he can only make God real to others when his own character is charged with God-like powers, when his manhood is irradiated with divine potencies, and his spirit is in harmony with the Eternal Spirit. He can only fulfill his function when he lives in close fellowship with God."[5]

A deep religious faith must at all times emanate from the pastor. The minister's oratory from the pulpit, his business dealings in administration, his leadership with young people, his social contacts with his people, and his calling on the sick and bereaved will reflect this inner spiritual relationship and integrity. No fanfare or demonstration will cover or hide any lack of personal devotion and conduct. The pastor's personal and public appearances will always reflect his inner life.

E. S. Waterhouse in discussing pastoral personality emphasized this important point that the minister should know himself, by saying that he should understand his calling in Christ Jesus, and know that God wants him to exercise powers of self-control and use his gifts for the glory of the kingdom. Waterhouse likewise stressed the need of Christ-likeness in the person of the pastor. Waterhouse said, "The finest type of Christian character has always been that of a man who reflects the spirit of Christ through his own inborn temperament."[6]

There is a particular phase of pastoral psychology which automatically reveals the real person of the pastor. It is at the point of counseling. The new

---

3. Harry Walker Hepner, *It's Nice to Know People Like You*, D. Appleton-Century Co., 1939, p. 9.
4. Murray H. Leiffer, (Editor), *In That Case*, Willett, Clark and Co., Chicago, 1938, p. 16.
5. Thomas Hywel Hughes, *The Psychology of Preaching and Pastoral Work*, The Macmillan Co., 1941, pp. 249, 250.
6. Eric S. Waterhouse, *Psychology and Pastoral Work*, Cokesbury Press, Nashville, 1940, p. 57.

emphasis of applied psychology on the importance of the person of the counselor is appropriate to our discussion. R. May suggested some fine qualities
for the counselor. He advised good training, calmness under tension, understanding of the sex problem, care for details, good moral judgment, and the
ability to see good in others rather than being ready to condemn.[7] All of this
is important practical advice for the pastor, but it lacks the spiritual emphasis
which God, as revealed in His Word, requires of spiritual stewards. C. J.
Schindler struck the right note when he said, "The pastor-counselor must have
reached full religious manhood himself, if he is to lead others into wholesome
Christian experiences."[8] It is regrettable that some writers of repute do not
stress sufficiently the spiritual aspect of counseling. S. Hiltner, in his book,
Pastoral Counseling,[9] gave many suggestions regarding the multiple duties of
the pastor but failed to indicate properly the essential attention that should
be given to the person of the counselor. No mention is made of the pastor's
duty to sanctify himself through consecration for his high task. Hiltner said,

> "Broadly speaking, the special aim of pastoral counseling may be stated
> as the attempt by a pastor to help people to help themselves through the
> process of gaining understanding of their inner conflicts."[10]

Counseling, from this point of view, becomes merely "emotional re-education" and merely shows people how to help themselves. We need "emotional
re-education"; but counseling by the pastor is much more than that. It must
be a heart to heart relation which glows with the light of Christ's presence
and power.

It is more than passing strange that C. R. Rogers entirely misses this point
in his book, *Counseling and Psychology*.[11] It is important to remember that
the great men who have been successful as preachers have also been spiritual
pastors at heart. A glance at our historical analysis and the sections on the
person of the pastor reflecting the three periods of history of pastoral theology,
ought to convince the reader that those who recommend spiritual leadership
and those who practiced it were themselves outstanding leaders in the ministry.
One cannot help but come to the same conclusion when he reads the book,
Physicians of the Soul, by C. K. Kemp. The author gives "A History of Pastoral Counseling," and in case after case of ministerial leadership, Kemp
demonstrated that the person of the pastor was the motivating and moving
force for professional success.[12]

"The Minister Himself" really means what the real minister is *within* —
spiritually, morally, and devotionally. This reflects the importance of the

7. Rollo May, *The Art of Counseling*, Cokesbury Press, Nashville, 1939, pp. 165-178.
8. Carl J. Schindler, *The Pastor as a Personal Counselor*, (Second printing), Muhlenberg
Press, Philadelphia, 1942, p. 18.
9. Seward Hiltner, *Pastoral Counseling*, Abingdon-Cokesbury Press, New York, Nashville,
1949, pp. 123-170.
10. Ibid., p. 19.
11. Carl R. Rogers, *Counseling and Psychotherapy*, Houghton Mifflin Co., New York,
1942, 450 pp.
12. Charles K. Kemp, *Physicians of the Soul*, The Macmillan Co., New York, 1947,
pp. 108-123, 188-212.

pastor as a person in the true Biblical light of God's will. Ministers who seek
to be such before God follow the advice of Paul to Timothy:

> "Thou therefore endure hardness as a good soldier of Jesus Christ."[13]
> "Thou therefore, my son, be strong in the grace that is in Christ Jesus."[14]
> "Be instant in season, out of season."[15]
> "But watch thou in all things, endure afflictions, do the work of an evangelist, make full proof of thy ministry."[16]

B. Seminary Training

Having established the fact that the person of the pastor is of primary significance for pastoral psychology, we come to see at this point the importance of
seminary training for every minister. Not only must the pastor be spiritually
and morally strong in heart, mind, and life; he must also have a working
basis whereby as a professional person and as a sympathetic minister, he can
bring this inner life to bear effectively in the lives of those he seeks to serve.

A few writers of pastoral theology were early aware of the need of better
seminary training to enhance the minister's effectiveness in personal life and
in service of the church. But there remained a wavering between the importance
of training and experience. In 1831 C. Bridges said:

> "Medical skill is gained much more by practical experience than by any
> system of abstract study even of standard works; and thus, whatever value
> belongs to an accurate and well-directed course of reading (and the writer
> is far from depreciating its value), yet he is persuaded that the study of
> the human heart — of our own heart most essentially — is, far more im-
> portant."[17]

S. Miller suggested that in order to do pastoral work one should "be familiar
with practical books, and especially with the lives of eminently pious men."[18]
G. T. Bedell said, "The minister will make the most of his own experience, and
must chiefly depend on it."[19] And C. E. Hewitt emphasized experience at the
expense of scientific training by saying, "Experience also proves the essential
importance of this kind of work in the pastorate."[20]

Later writers of pastoral theology came to see the importance of psychological insight and training for the minister. H. Adams indicated the need for
courses that would fit the student for the applications needful in the areas of
sociology, economics, philosophy and psychology.[21] Even so, very few expressed
themselves on the importance of better seminary training for the pastor and

---

13. II Timothy 2:3.
14. II Timothy 2:1.
15. II Timothy 4:2.
16. II Timothy 4:5.
17. Charles Bridges, *The Christian Ministry*, Vol. II, Jonathan Leavitt, New York, 1831, p. 134.
18. Samuel Miller, *Letters on Clerical Manners and Habits*, Presbyterian Board of Publication, Philadelphia, 1852, p. 135.
19. Gregory Thurston Bedell, *The Pastor, Pastoral Theology*, J. B. Lippincott and Co., Philadelphia, 1880, p. 435.
20. C. E. Hewitt, *"The Personal Work of the Pastor,"* Baptist Quarterly Review, Vol. 12-13, October, 1890-1891, p. 411.
21. Hampton Adams, *The Pastoral Ministry*, Cokesbury Press, Nashville, 1932, p. 7.

his personal work among people. Not till the modern movement of the new psychology forced the issue, have theological seminaries come to see the importance of psychological training. C. A. Coe said in this connection:

> "Training in doctrine, in philosophy, in history, and even in the questions of the day, constitutes only a logical equipment; there is still necessary a psychological equipment in order that one may appreciate the vast mass of mental states and processes of a non-logical sort."[22]

Coe reminded his readers that up to this time the religious worker had relied almost entirely upon instinctive sympathy with human nature and the personal insight of tact. T. W. Pym suggested that every theological student should have a course in "moral pathology" as well as the medical student his hospital course. Quoting J. C. Mackenzie, L. H. Weatherhead said:

> "The time has come when every minister ought to have some knowledge of the psychology of the human soul; when he ought to receive in his curriculum a thorough grounding in the conflict which leads to the divided soul; when he ought to know the principles of mental healing."[23]

G. B. Cutten made the complaint that the seminary does not train the student sufficiently, and observed, "He must stumble along through years of trying experience and look back over countless mistakes before he understands even in a general way."[24] And C. T. Holman indicated that seminaries need to overhaul their theological training. "Certainly," said he, "the seminaries should greatly improve their programs for the training of men in this important field of service."[25] In another book, C. T. Holman wrote:

> "The traditional theological curriculum does not meet the need. The psychological and social sciences, in our day, have thrown a new flood of in the cure of souls."[26]

Another discernment of the need in this area is reflected in the writing of F. Kunkel:

> "The average minister since the Reformation has had to rely on his common sense and on superficial traditions as far as his efforts in helping people were concerned. His training in theology was thorough, but in handling individual cases his training was insufficient."[27]

---

22. George A. Coe, *The Spiritual Life*, Eaton and Mains, New York, 1900, p. 6.

23. Leslie D. Weatherhead, *Psychology in the Service of the Soul*, The Macmillan C(., New York, 1930, pp. 22, 23.

24. George Barton Cutten, *The Psychological Phenomena of Christianity*, Charles Scribner's Sons, New York, 1909, p. 7.

25. Charles T. Holman, *Getting Down to Cases*, The Macmillan Co., New York, 1942, p. 201.

26. Charles T. Holman, *The Cure of Souls, A Socio-Psychological Approach*, The University of Chicago Press, 1932, p. x.

27. Fritz Kunkel, *In Search of Maturity*, Charles Scribner's Sons, New York, 1943, p. 14.

C. A. Wise made the statement that the average theological institution is not training candidates to deal with persons.

> "They are not trained to deal with the fundamental material of the ministry — the human personality. Their thinking and work become book-centered, idea-centered, or program-centered, whereas it should be centered in personality."[28]

While we disagree with this statement from Wise concerning personality training as the needful emphasis of all theological training, Wise did well in reminding us that this kind of training has been neglected in the average seminary. Many other authors could be quoted who make similar contentions concerning deficient seminary training.[29] Pastoral psychology must minister to this deficiency not only by revealing the need for such training, but supplying the necessary technique to improve the condition.

One method of improving our seminary training is to incorporate in the seminary curriculum the services of a trained psychiatrist who has Christian convictions. He will enable the students to see the problems as they really are, and he will be able to give them instruction along technical lines with Christian foundation. He will be able to relate such scientific knowledge to the rest of the student's theological education so that they are syncronized and not detached.

In addition, every student should spend some time as an observer and worker in a mental hospital. The claim had been made that a theological student should spend a full year in a mental hospital to gain sufficient training; but this contention is one-sided. The average pastor is not a specialist on mental cases and spending a year as student observer in a mental hospital would have a tendency to lead to an abnormal ministry. Some students might have a special interest along this line of study, and for them it would be profitable; but the average theological student need not spend a year in such study. He should have some specific study and training in the viewpoints, principles and practice of hospital procedure.

There is another method which might be employed to improve the future pastor's technique in this respect. The student might profitably serve an internship with a minister in an average pastorate. The ministerial student will then receive practical training with a minister who understands the normal and abnormal cases of human experience. All of this training should be blended and dovetailed together for the proper technique of pastoral psychology. Then the young man will have a proper balance between theory and practice

---

28. Carroll A. Wise, *Religion in Illness and Health*, (Second Edition), Harper & Brothers, New York, London, 1942, p. 263.

29. Jerome Henry Simpson, *Pastoral Care of Nervous People*, Morehouse-Gorham Co., New York, 1945, p. 45 ff.

Richard Henry Edwards, *A Person-Minded Ministry*, Cokesbury Press, Nashville, 1940, p. 231 ff.

John G. Mackenzie, *Souls in the Making*, The Macmillan Co., New York, 1929, p. 13 ff.

John Rathbone Oliver, *Psychology and Mental Health*, Charles Scribner's Sons, New York, London, 1936, p. 7 ff.

for both the normal and the abnormal of his study and internship in preparation for his future ministry. Then he will know how to relate conversion, affliction and sanctification by means of inner personal spiritual consecration and by means of a trained mind steeped in the teachings of Scripture in order to effectively minister to our generation.

C. Ministerial Training

Closely allied to the seminary training needed by the student to become an effective pastor, is the training which is needed by the minister who is out on the field. Some are willing to concede that young men need special training, but they are not willing to admit that men who have been out of the seminary for a while and older men, need specialized training in the field of pastoral psychology. The contention of this chapter is that ministers need scientific, psychological, spiritual training to meet the problems faced by the average pastor. There is an ever increasing emphasis on the social implications of Christianity, and we should keep pace with these interests. There is an ever increasing interest in mental hygiene, and the minister should have the proper training and insight to minister to this situation. Often the minister has not been consulted because, though his person and willingness were beyond reproach, his ability to handle a psychological situation did not warrant their taking the risk of having him handle the case. Many people prefer to go to the professional psychiatrist instead of to their minister just because the minister has not stayed abreast of the times. This is not a broad-side criticism of the ministry, but it is an obstacle which people find in many ministers.

We forget that there are many people, particularly of the middle class of society, for whom there is very little help available along this line of counseling. The rich employ psychiatrists, the poor are served by social agencies, but the middle class people are often neglected. The minister should receive training to meet their situation. He should understand the nature of personality development and the overwhelming importance of family relations. Not only for the middle class people but for all classes, the minister must be trained to give help. The psychiatrist has his place of importance, but more than we realize, the minister has a unique place to fill in service to man.

We need not be afraid that the new psychology and this new approach to the problems of man's need will overthrow our religious principles. The principles of psychology and the psychological application as found in the Bible agree in a remarkable way. The teachings of Jesus on the moral, spiritual, ethical and sociological principles of life do not conflict with the true interpretation offered by psychological insight.

The pastor must obtain some training of technical kind to meet the needs of the average parish today. It is not as simple as the average minister thinks. Psychotherapy is not as easy as the untrained mind may imagine. For example, the very common affliction called *neurasthenia* should be thoroughly understood by the minister, since he will face this repeatedly in his church and he must give an answer for this problem. The pastor must know the tools, and he must know how to use them. In addition he must know the needs of his people in such a way that he can recommend the proper people to care for such individuals.

There is much that can be done in the way of pastoral training. The first that must be done takes place within the life of the minister himself. He must live a clean, moral, spiritual, social life himself. His relation to God and to fellow men must be in the best spirit and with the finest of fellowship. This takes personal training and careful living, but with all its requirements, it is an absolute "must" in terms of ministering effectively to the welfare of God's people. The importance of this kind of personal training has been missed by the modern movement of psychology, and is very important for the proper technique of pastoral theology.

The minister should also have available on his shelf for ready reference, and for constant availability for the people who need it, such books as treat the problems of life and their answers. It is just as important to buy such books as to buy commentaries for sermons to be preached on Sunday. There are many problems of our people that could be remedied by the aid of such books. Preaching is very important, and buying all the aids essential for effective preaching are part of the minister's duty to his church and his profession. It is also very true that books on practical psychology and a working psychiatry should have an important place on his study shelves. These do not take the place of the Bible, but they will, if they are the right books, throw light on the Bible, and will give the minister the right kind of trained mind to meet the situations he confronts daily.

Another way for the minister to a trained mind is to seek clinical training under the supervision of a psychiatrist or psychologist. This has been recommended for theological students, but it would be of even greater value for ministers who have extensive experience with the raw material of case studies. If ministers could have a periodic training school with some psychiatrist who is of Christian persuasion, they could profit in such a way that their congregation would notice a marked change in the attitude and ministry of their leader.

The last suggestion for a better technique is for the minister to be associated with a psychiatrist in the actual field of endeavor. Norman Vincent Peale and Smiley Blanton have effected such an arrangement in the parish of the Marble Collegiate (Reformed) Church of New York City. Here minister and psychiatrist work together, each in his own realm, and each in a contributory way to solve the problems of the people in the parish and of the city at large when they come for help. In some cosmopolitan areas such an ideal arrangement can be used as a functioning agency for the benefit of many people. It takes money and cooperation to do this; and not all parishes will allow money for it, and not all can afford to pay. In some smaller traditional churches, this arrangement would not work and would not be accepted if it were tried. In such cases, it would be an excellent arrangement if the minister had access to the consultative services of a psychiatrist, either at the expense of the church or on his own expense. This in itself would afford practical training for the minister, and it would bring help and blessing to those who in turn were served by the minister.

Pastoral psychology requires improved training and cultivated leadership in this field of service. This does not mean that the minister must become a trained psychologist. Pastoral psychology does not require a technique of the pastor that will qualify him to take the place of the psychiatrist. Nor does it mean that in attitude or training he should ever lessen his spiritual ministry or his devotional responsibility over against his flock. It means the very opposite. It construes this relationship in such a way that the pastor will improve his spiritual ministry with a knowledge of psychology to the glory of God and the welfare of men. Pastoral psychology requires continued training on the part of the minister, but not a one-sided training that will minimize his effective service as a spiritual leader among his people. True pastoral psychology prescribes the proper combination for which God's spiritual servants seek — and which they feel in their hearts incompetent to meet in our swift moving and super-sensitized psychological times without some knowledge of the total human personality and a better working technique in pastoral psychology for the blessing of God's people.

CHAPTER XII

Knowing Life Situations

THE title of this chapter might appear non-technical in aspect, definition and scope of thought, but that is not the intention in the choice of this subject, knowing that life situations demands a technical interest and understanding by the pastor. This is not something new in the field of pastoral theology nor in the field of psychology. Yet, it needs a stronger emphasis, particularly in respect to the working technique of pastoral psychology.

A. Emphasis in Pastoral Theology

Our historical survey indicated that the writers on pastoral theology were mindful of the important matter of knowing the life of the individual and understanding case histories of people. In the third period of pastoral theology we noticed a particular interest in human nature and the sociological approach to the problems of the pastorate. Some classifications of individuals by writers of pastoral theology were general, such as the converted and unconverted, and others were more specific. Their approach might be summed up in the words of J. M. Hoppen,

> "This pastoral skill is something different from a Shakespeare's knowledge of the human heart; it is something which must be given a man from above; it is a spiritual insight, a knowledge of the soul and its wants, that is communicated only by the Spirit that searcheth the deep things of God and man."[1]

Man's problems are essentially spiritual, but in addition they must be viewed in the total situation of life. And to this the writers of pastoral theology applied the common sense method of analysis. A typical evaluation of this technique is contained in the words of E. Pond:

> "A good judgment, sound discretion, plain practical common sense, the whole being under the guidance of the Word and Spirit of God, will be a minister's best dictionary in regard to his intercourse with those various characteristics which go to constitute his flock."[2]

It was clearly evident from our historical study of pastoral theology that knowledge of a particular situation was thought to depend on intuition rather

---

1. James M. Hoppen, *Pastoral Theology*, Funk and Wagnalls Co., New York and London, 1869, pp. 392, 393.
2. Enoch Pond, *The Young Pastor's Guide*, Ezra Collier, New York, 1844, p. 77.

than scientific psychological information. A. H. McKinney saw the deeper significance when he said:

> "It is perfectly evident that in dealing with inquirers our first care must be to find out the real condition of the mind and heart; otherwise, how can we apply the Word of God with any hope of success? This is what the physician calls 'diagnosing his patient' before prescribing his remedy."[3]

But such a clear understanding of the problem was not common to the earlier writers of pastoral theology. C. R. Erdman in his work, *The Work of the Pastor*,[4] gave a list of individual needs represented in classifications of people, but by and large most of the writers of pastoral theology did not analyze the spiritual and psychological needs which must be discovered in the individual situations which surround people. It is generally true, as W. S. Bruce has indicated,

> "There are preachers and evangelists who have denounced people as wholly irreligious and have consigned them to uncovenanted mercies."[5]

There are many ministers today who have sensed the importance of a scientific knowledge of life situations. The earlier writers on pastoral theology were reaching for this kind of information even though they sought to obtain it through unaided common sense. The modern psychologist has gone the opposite extreme of seeking to know only the individual life situation without a proper spiritual knowledge of the subject under observation. Both of these positions are a combination of truth and error. The truth in both positions must be combined in developing a technique for pastoral psychology.

B. Individual Life Situations

We must know the individual in the situation and surroundings which environ his experience. This is exactly what is meant by the title of our chapter, "Knowing Life Situations." Every person is tremendously affected by his emotional reactions. There is a reciprocal influence which comes to the body and to the spirit of the individual. The moral and the physical impulses react on each other. All of this is involved in relation to the nervous tension of our time. Nervous disorders have tremendous influence on our physical and mental life. Modern psychology has thrust a consideration upon us that we must not forget; but modern psychology has not given the answer because this problem has not been related to the power and faith of Christianity. This is the task of a pastoral psychology, and this chapter is dedicated to the discovery of the importance of knowing the individual as he is in his environment.

---

3. A. H. McKinney, *Human Nature in Christian Work*, W. A. Wilde Co., Boston, 1929, p. 101.
4. Charles R. Erdman, *The Work of the Pastor*, The Westminster Press, 1924, pp. 76-91.
5. W. S. Bruce, *The Psychology of Christian Life and Behavior*, T. & T. Clark, Edinburgh, p. 14.

Psychology has taught us that varied conditions face individuals in our day of frustrated living and confused thinking.

"The life of religious feeling is not uniform. It moves in great rhythms; the exaltation is followed by depression. The saint falls sometimes from an immediate consciousness of the divine presence to the blackest depths."[6]

Georgia Harkness has indicated this variant experience for different people by saying:

"There is no uniform way in which this new life expresses itself. According to your temperament, you may feel a great wave of emotional exaltation; or you may simply feel that you have adept and steadiness of purpose you did not have before; or you yourself may be less aware of change than are others who note the transformation in you. God does not run all into one mold in the deep things of religion any more than he does in the rest of our living."[7]

The modern anthropologist has done much to unearth the hidden tensions and trials of the individual. The clinical psychologist and the professional psychiatrist have explored the thinking and activity of many people, bringing to light many hidden fears and apprehensions. They have done this very often at the expense and sacrifice of Christianity; but nevertheless, they have exposed these impulses to investigation. Some of these deep-lying causes of personality disorder and behavior reactions have been brought to light and the pastor must come to a new realization of their presence in the individual.

The busy pastor does not take time, and often does not have time to look at the individual from such variant circumstances and viewpoints. Yet he must know the individual in the inextricable tangle of mental, psychical, moral and spiritual factors of Christian life. Within the individual and behind the conduct of the person, there is a mental process stimulated by a mental impression and reaction. Psychology has functioned as the agency to discover this process, and pastoral psychology must utilize this discovery in the best possible approach to the individual — in order that the person being helped may come into proper contact with God and Jesus Christ.

Pastoral psychology prescribes that the individual must be intimately known by the pastor. The individual must be seen in the school of life under the grace of God. The problem of the minister is to discover and adjust differently endowed individuals by counseling, training and encouragement so that such people may find their proper place in society, in the church, and in the circle of their own family. In order to obtain the maximum of spiritual life, social productivity and personal satisfaction must be developed by the pastor in individuals; and in order to do this the circumstances of the people who fall under his ministry must be known and observed. There are intricate combinations in individuals, and the pastor must know these. People are not like a combination lock, set to open when a standard combination of numbers has been dialed in counseling. because the combination is often different under

6. Frank Granger, *The Soul of a Christian,* The Macmillan Co., New York, 1900, p. 23.
7. Georgia Harkness, *Religious Living,* The Edward W. Hazen Foundation, Inc., New York, 1937, p. 43.

different circumstances. We cannot say that we understand the individual fully until we have seen him in the throes of variant conditions and under the pressure of different circumstances. This makes our knowledge of these circumstances of greater importance.

Modern psychology has opened our thinking to this kind of approach, and pastoral psychology demands our interest in and technique of pastoral leadership in this important phase of our work. Serious minded leaders sense this importance for our times.

> "We struggle heroically for a way out and forward, seeking to give expression to our many sided desires. We are not simple creatures like the prosaic characters of a Victorian novel. We are endowed with titanic forces, capable of fierce hungers, greedy for great satisfactions. We have capabilities that lift us so far above the humdrum needs of daily existence that we seem like gods. Also, alas, we still bear marks of the jungle, primitive appetites and elemental passions."[8]

There is a modernistic touch to this language, of course; yet we cannot escape the central thrust of the reference. We do have titanic forces within us, for there are powers which engulf us in our days of tension. We must know these conditions which play so large a part in the experiences of our parishioners. And we must aspire to reach these people. In the language of J. R. Oliver:

> "You cannot judge cases justly unless you know the past lives of your penitents; unless you know them as individuals; unless you are familiar with the reactions, the mental habits, the trains of thought that have made your penitent or your parishioner what he or she now is, and that makes him or her different from the other members of your congregation."[9]

Such a study takes time, sympathy and careful appreciation of individual differences. A wise understanding pastor will develop these in order to be the most effective with his people. This means a study of individual, family and community environment. It means an evaluation of spiritual capacities, inclinations, and experiences. It will do much for the people who are served and it will help the minister who serves them.

> "Intensive study of particular cases should provide one of the minister's chief opportunities to serve as well as one of his chief sources of understanding."[10]

Pastoral psychology demands the obligation of the minister to study the individual in his particular and sometimes peculiar circumstance because then he will be able to render greater service to such persons, and the minister himself will be alert and alive to the needs of all his people.

---

8. David Seabury, *What Makes Us Seem So Queer?* Whittlesey House, division of Mcgraw-Hill Book Co., London, 1934, p. 20.

9. John Rathbone Oliver, *Psychiatry and Mental Health*, Charles Scribner's Sons, New York, 1932, p. 9.

10. Anton T. Boisen, *Problems in Religion and Life*, Abingdon-Cokesbury Press, New York, Nashville, 1946, p. 38.

C. Group Study

Closely allied to the important study of individual situations is the related subject and technique of group study. There are general groups of individuals. One grouping has been indicated by J. R. Oliver who discussed the Psychoses of Schizophrenia, Paranoi, Epilepsy, Paresis, and Alcoholism. He also dealt with such Psychoneuroses as Hysteria, Psychasthenia, Psychogenic States, Phobias, Inhibitions and Obsessions. There is a wealth of information about these afflictions for which the minister must always have an open mind. Further-more we must remember that these types change.

> "As there is no finality in, so there is no unchanging form or type of, the religious life. It runs into many moulds. It is shaped by temperament, education, individuality. In every age there is a prominent type. But the next age seems a change, and what was before pronounced falls into shade and secondary place. At the root of all these typical characteristics lies the personal factor. As a man is, so does he think and act."[11]

Thus we see that we must group people, but within the very group there are differences of characteristic and inclination. Therefore we must be careful in our grouping, and we should be cautioned lest we keep people classified in a group when, because of changes, they no longer belong to the same group.

This matter of group study is very important within any given congregation. Each particular congregation has such groupings whether we recognize them or fail to see them. In a general way we may accept the classifications of S. Norborg who said that groupings divide themselves into a three-fold mold; (1) the healthy-minded Christian personalities who have balanced minds and live with a personal faith in Christ with forgiveness and release, (2) the would-be healthy minded who do not know themselves, do not know that they need help and usually are "blue," "nervous," and "lonely," and (3) Christians with severe personality distresses who protest against any psychological or personal approach to their Christian experience. They are the souls who are sick and think they have been healed.

> "Christians of the third group are in desperate need of ministerial and medical help; they need the help of psychologically trained ministers and very often also that of an expert psychiatrist."[12]

It is not our purpose to discuss these groups, but to call attention to the fact that they exist and we must recognize them as part of our pastoral study and responsibility.

The minister can use the technique of working through the group with profit. He can give personal counseling to individuals within the group, and implied pulpit counseling through preaching to the groups within the church. This does not mean that he will publicly single out such groups in his preach-ing; but it does mean that he will be conscious of them, and through the total

---

11. Bruce, op. cit., p. 215.
12. Sv. Norborg, *Varieties of Christian Experience*, Augsburg Publishing House, Minne-apolis, Minnesota, 1937, p. 22.

impact of his ministry speak to these groups. This will help to bring them into line with the normal experience of Christian living.

This involves a personal study by the pastor of his entire congregation, with particular interest in the groups within his parish. In his own mind he should arrange such groups and classifications as best serve his understanding and ministry. It may take a long time to determine these groupings and who belong to each. It may be possible for a minister to visit a person for a number of years without being sure of his classification because of a variant response under different circumstances. Yet, somehow he will soon classify most of his people. Part of this will come automatically as he serves them and meets them:

> "As the minister looks about him in even a small parish he can hardly escape a sense of bewilderment at the great number of individual temperaments and behavior patterns which he meets on every side. This great variety of individual differences has always puzzled and fascinated students of human nature and attempts at classification are probably very old. They help to reduce to a certain system and order what would otherwise seem endless confusion."[13]

Next, it is the duty of every pastor to study the groups in his church. This may not mean that the pastor will have a complete knowledge of each of these groups, or have a perfect technique to deal with them. Yet he should have knowledge of these, and he should be careful that he is not blinded by the seeming importance of one of the groups, thus closing his mind to a perfect understanding of all of them in their proper relationship.

> "The parish minister, if he is to be a true pastor, a real spiritual guide, a lover and a physician of souls, must have a knowledge of these types of behavior, and some technique attained by study, experience, or personal gifts that will make it possible for him to deal with them."[14]

Even if such knowledge is only a practical acquaintance with such terms and characteristics of psychiatry as outlined in the book, *How Psychiatry Helps*, by P. Polatin and E. C. Philtine,[15] the minister will be in position to render great service to his people. He will then be able to understand the groups within his church, and the characteristic of his community. He will be better able to counsel and advise for conduct, activity, and service. The minister must therefore study his field and tabulate his results. All of this is essential for the proper presentation of Jesus Christ, before the congregation of groups on Sunday and always before the individuals of the flock and community.

---

13. Carl J. Schindler, *The Pastor a Personal Counselor*, Muhlenberg Press, Philadelphia, 1942, p. 37.
14. Oliver, op cit., p. 5.
15. Phillip Polatin and Ellen C. Philtine, Harper & Brothers, New York, 1941, particularly chapter I, Types of Psychiatric Disturbances, pp. 1-22.

CHAPTER XIII

Systematic Counseling

THE necessity and art of counseling has been emphasized in every field of endeavor for the improvement of the individual and his relations with other people. Personnel workers, social leaders and even politicians have gone the full length in their enthusiasm for counseling. The matter of counseling has also engaged the attention of those who have been interested in applied Christianity. Pastoral psychology must incorporate the best in pastoral counseling.

A. Significance of Counseling in Pastoral Theology

We must not minimize the consideration which writers on pastoral theology have given to pastoral counseling. Our historical review demonstrated that pastoral counseling was part of the program and technique of earlier writers in the field of pastoral theology. In each period of our historical survey, it was evident that pastors and writers were interested in more and better counseling. Not in modern terms, but still with sincere earnestness, these writers sought to emphasize the importance of pastoral counseling.

As we study the history of pastoral theology, we marvel that these writers were so far advanced in their views and techniques with respect to pastoral counseling. Most of them wrote without the aid of the new psychology, and without its help developed a technique that was commendable.

It is not our purpose to review the material on pastoral counseling given earlier in this book. A glance at the findings reveals that the pastors and writers sensed the importance of giving counsel to parish people with the best means at hand and in the best way possible. Common sense methods and pastoral intuition often were the prime movers in the urge to do this work; but in addition these men recommended a knowledge of human nature, and the best possible approach to people in individual situations. In the second historical period great strides were made in the matter of counseling because the writers saw the possibilities and opportunities of the average pastor, and they recommended means and methods to accomplish this task. One would think they had benefited from the modern movement of psychology when one reads their interest in and application of pastoral counseling. Not many writers saw the light, but the few who explored the subject and practiced the technique were far ahead of their time.

To this wholesome interest in pastoral counseling as has been evidenced in pastoral theology, we must now add the findings of psychology in order to produce a pastoral psychology that will be a real aid and blessing to pastors and people. In the words of W. C. Martin:

> "The newest and in many respects the most alluring method of helping people with moral and spiritual difficulties is pastoral counseling. Its basic techniques are as old as the Christian religion but the effort to apply the findings of modern psychology to the problems of pastoral guidance has resulted in this new approach. It brings with it both exciting possibilities and subtle dangers."[1]

While it is true that there are both "exciting possibilities and subtle dangers,"[2] it is also true that the Lord Jesus Christ calls us to such ministry to help people in trouble and to point them heavenward.

B. The Benefits of Psychology for Pastoral Counseling

Through the influence of psychology a new interest has been manifested in pastoral counseling. We cannot discuss all the books and articles which engender this spirit, but we will evaluate a half dozen books which have appeared in the last decade to indicate the importance of the growing interest in counseling, with particular emphasis on pastoral counseling.

In 1939 R. May wrote *The Art of Counseling*. This book explains underlying principles, practical steps and ultimate considerations of counseling. Of special importance for our study in his discussion on ministerial counseling are the chapters on "Personality of the Counselor,"[3] "Morals and Counseling,"[4] and "Religion and Mental Health."[5] This book was not written particularly for ministers but pastors can profit greatly from a study of the principles which the author gave.

Counseling and Psychotherapy, written by C. R. Rogers, is a fine source book for ministers on the use of counseling techniques. The author sought

> "to formulate a definite and understandable series of hypotheses in regard to counseling which may be tested and explored. For the student it aims to provide a consistent framework for thinking about counseling, with illustrative, analyzed examples of procedure."[6]

This book represents the author's experience of working in the field of child guidance for a dozen years. The basic hypothesis of the book is as follows:

> "Effective counseling consists of a definitely structured permissive relationship which allows the client to gain an understanding of himself to a degree which enables him to take positive steps in the light of his new orientation."[7]

1. William C. Martin, *To Fulfill This Ministry*, Abingdon-Cokesbury Press, New York, Nashville, 1949, pp. 72, 73.
2. Ibid., pp. 73.
3. Rollo May, *The Art of Counseling*, Cokesbury Press, Nashville, 1939, pp. 165-178.
4. Ibid., pp. 179-206.
5. Ibid., pp. 207-224.
6. Carl R. Rogers, *Counseling and Psychotherapy*, Houghton Mifflin Co., New York, 1942, pp. 16, 17.
7. Ibid., p. 18.

The book was written by a professor for students, research workers and for workers in the field, and as such it deserves the serious attention of the minister in order that he may improve his counseling technique.

In the same year, C. J. Schindler wrote, *"The Pastor as Personal Counselor,* which was intended as a manual of pastoral psychology. It was not planned to present original research in either field of theology or psychology, but was designed as a treatise by a pastor for pastors. This book deserves to be studied by pastors for technique with regard to preparation for counseling, differences in people, psychological types and the therapeutic value of group experience. This book suggests numerous practical applications for the minister in seeking to serve his constituency. The author indicates that allowance is to be made for individuality in the minister as well as among his people in the following expression, "Because pastoral care is an art rather than a science, allowance must be made for individual differences."[8]

Pastoral Work and Personal Counseling was written by R. L. Dicks. He wanted to write on the total work of the pastor, particularly because of the war situation at the time. He wrote the book, "for the purpose of assisting the average clergyman serving the average church to take advantage of the opportunity and meet the responsibility of the pastoral work from the call to this work through the various applications, with special emphasis on personal counseling.[10] Its practical advice and interpretation can be used with profit.

J. S. Bonnell's, *Psychology for Pastor and People,* is outstanding in the field of counseling. With his usual deftness in this field and his ability to write interestingly, he treats this subject with challenging attention for every pastor. Beginning with the need for and the resources of the counselor, the various techniques of asking questions, listening, consulting and ministering to others are discussed with completeness and interest. These characteristics mark this book the most outstanding in the field. Its spiritual flavor, the usual characteristic of his books, is a predominant feature of this important volume on pastoral counseling. The place of the Bible and the application of Christian principles are not lacking but feature the main thrust of this wholesome volume. The chapter on "Some Principles of Counseling,"[11] sets forth sane and helpful spiritual counseling principles which every minister should know. Bonnell has given in a nutshell the concrete and fundamental principles of counseling which are basic to the technique of pastoral psychology.

S. Hiltner's book, *Pastoral Counseling,* is complete with accounts of interviews from real experience. The book is divided into three parts dealing with the *principles, preparation* and *resources* for counseling. While the book con-

8. Carl J. Schindler, *The Pastor as Personal Counselor,* Muhlenberg Press, Philadelphia, 1942, from the preface — no page reference given.
9. Russell L. Dicks, *Pastoral Work and Personal Counseling,* The Macmillan Co., 1945, p. viii.
10. Ibid., pp. 31-120.
11. John Southerland Bonnell, *Psychology for Pastor and People,* Harper & Brothers Publishers, New York, London, 1948, pp. 172-190.

tains "Religious Resources for Pastoral Counseling,"[12] the spiritual note is lacking and a spiritual pastor will find a chasm between this work and the proper emphasis outlined in the Bible. Having given this criticism, it is still important for every pastor to read this book for its sociological and psychological interpretations.

There is one more book that deserves our attention. *Every Pastor A Counselor*, by S. E. Anderson places a strong emphasis on the Christian viewpoint of counseling. Christ and the Bible are the guides for counseling according to this author. The author showed this spirit when he wrote,

> "The pastor who wishes to improve his counseling program needs to magnify the distinctive Christian and spiritual factors or he will be another victim of prevailing secularism. The New Testament contrast between good and evil is as black and white, but contemporary Christendom is instead a dull, monotonous gray. The counselor must know how to separate ethical values according to the New Testament pattern."[13]

This volume seeks to give practical advice from the Biblical point of view and is very important for the spirit of pastoral counseling.

The books just reviewed and others in the field, stimulate the thinkers and writers in the field of pastoral psychology to an increased interest and challenge. The benefits which we should appreciate from these books may be summarized in the following conclusions:

1. The tremendous importance of pastoral counseling must not be overlooked, because this age old practice is ready for a new technique to help burdened and distressed souls.

2. The advances and benefits of psychology for pastoral psychology must be studied, examined, and infused into the pastoral counseling program of the Christian Church.

3. The importance of social case work, long overlooked by the Christian minister, must be seen in the light of Scripture and with possible practical application to pastoral psychology.

4. The technique of interviewing as explained and demonstrated by those who are not in Christian work must be studied and analyzed for its possible implications for pastoral work, in order to derive the greatest amount of blessings from pastoral contacts with people.

5. Vocational guidance, long neglected by pastors, should be important to the minister as well as to secular leaders and corporations.

6. Understanding human behavior is as much the duty of the Christian pastor as the duty of the secular psychologist.

---

12. Seward Hiltner, *Pastoral Counseling*, Abingdon-Cokesbury Press, New York, Nashville, 1949, pp. 187-226.
13. Stanley E. Anderson, *Every Pastor a Counselor*, Van Kampen Press, Wheaton, 1949, p. 9.

C. Distinct Advantages of the Minister as Counselor

Having seen some of the appreciative lessons from counseling, we now study the important proposition that the minister has a distinct advantage as counselor.

> "The Minister, as counselor, has some important opportunities and resources not so readily available to other counselors. These opportunities and resources are to be found in the religious faith which he proclaims, the religious practices which he directs, and the religious fellowship which he organizes."[14]

This evaluation is exactly right — except that we would write the word *Christian* where Holman uses the word "religious" — because the Christian minister has unbounded opportunities. This does not mean that the pastor has merely the wonderful opportunity of bringing social adjustment to people in society. He can go beyond the social level. He will seek to bring spiritual balance, poise, and peace to those who love the Lord Jesus. The pastor will be able to show them by means of the Scripture that they have a corrupt nature and need Jesus Christ to have and live a cleansed life. It is just here that the Christian pastor has a golden opportunity. Most psychologists and many modern ministers are not aware of the real sinful character of human nature. To that extent they fail to touch the heart of human ills. In the words of H. A. Overstreet,

> "In the delicate matter of influencing human behavior, most of us fall short, not so much from a profound ignorance of human nature — such ignorance does, unfortunately, exist — as from a failure to use the simplest and most obvious techniques."[15]

Just at this juncture of theological and psychological thinking, the Christian pastor has the important position and responsibility of counseling his people. The pastor has the stategic place because pastoral counseling touches all of life. The spiritual sphere does not have another representative on the field to help man. The pastor is the key person to bring relief and resolve to troubled hearts. Pastoral counseling is of far greater importance than S. Hiltner indicated when he said:

> "Pastoral counseling is the endeavor by the minister to help people through mutual discussion of the issues involved in a difficult life situation, leading toward a better understanding of the choices involved, and toward the power of making a self-chosen decision which will be as closely bound up to religious reality as the people are capable of under the circumstances."[16]

This statement does not convey the full meaning of pastoral counseling because the minister has the tremendous advantage and duty of leading the troubled soul to the real source of light and life, Jesus Christ — the bread of life

---

14. Charles T. Holman, *Getting Down to Cases*, The Macmillan Co., New York, 1929, p. 15.
15. H. A. Overstreet, *Influencing Human Behavior*, W. W. Norton & Co., Inc., New York, 1925, p. 9.
16. Seward Hiltner, *Religion and Health*, The Macmillan Co., New York, 1943, p. 167.

(John 6, 35). No other counselor has this privilege or this professional duty. The pastor owes it to himself, to his Lord and to his people to be this kind of a counselor to tried hearts. In the language of G. S. Dobbins:

"As a specialist it is the minister's function to discover religious need, if possible to put his finger on the one distinctive religious need that demands most to be met, and then to supply that need by bringing the individual to the source of supply in Christ."[17]

Anything less than this purpose is not pastoral counseling in the full Biblical sense. For the pastor, the supreme purpose is to bring his parishioners into saving knowledge with Jesus Christ. Counseling for moral improvement and social adjustment is important, but without the spiritual direction and devotion of the subject fixed on Jesus Christ, counseling will be in vain.

The minister comes with the real weapon of spiritual victory when as counselor he uses the Word of God. It is very important for people to realize that they must live with themselves, with their neighbors and most of all with God. In this triple relation of the individual, the pastor has the unusual method and means of helping people when he points them to the Word of God. The Christian pastor has the answer to the problem of sickness, sorrow, suffering, and death such as no other counselor. All of this help and power is found in the life of the Lord Jesus Christ, who is brought to the individual by a spiritual pastor. In that sense our ministry must be fashioned after the ministry of Christ.

"A Christian ministry will be successful to the degree to which it is modeled after the ministry of Him who came among men as Teacher, Counselor, Physician and Friend. If we judge men by His standards and deal with them in His spirit, we have proved ourselves not only good interpreters of human nature but have taken that essential step which leads from theory to practice."[18]

This is the advantage of the Christian pastor. Using all available helpful aids from psychology, he is the best qualified to minister to our decrepit and decadent generation. The minister has the opportunity and the duty of leading the individual into the fullness of Christian living with Jesus Christ, under the blessing of the Holy Spirit. He holds the key given by God in the Bible for the interpretation of God's truth to the psychological, social and spiritual needs of a particular parishioner. For students and practitioners of pastoral psychology, this is the primary consideration. It is the thrust of the Holy Spirit in the commission one receives by going into the ministry. It is our holy task, and we must not fail to seize it as an opportunity of service to man for the glory of God.

D. A Protestant Conference

The Roman Catholic Confessional is known to all students of Church History as an integral part of that church to call the individual to a sense of

---

17. Gaines S. Dobbins, "Facing Pastoral Problems," *The Review and Expositor*, April, 1937, p. 222.
18. Schindler, op. cit., p. 147.

sin, the importance of confession, and the benefit of sharing fellowship with God's servant. Technically speaking we do not have a Protestant confessional. We ought to have something that compares with the practice of the Roman Catholic Confessional. Purposely we wrote, "We ought to have *something that compares*," rather than something like the Roman Catholic Confessional. We do not want hierarchical authority in the ministry and we do not believe that an officiating clergyman has the power to forgive sins.

We should realize that the Roman Catholic Confessional reveals a conscious or unconscious use of a great many laws, principles and practices of modern psychology. Long before modern psychology came to its own, these interpretations and applications were a part of the Confessional. Therefore, we Protestants would do well to give consideration to something that means to us a place of confession, of sharing spiritual fellowship, and a way of consulting with the minister.

Many of our people would welcome such a procedure. In the words of J. Watson:

> "It is the custom of Protestants to denounce the confessional, and not without reason for the claim of a priest to hear confessions and absolve is a profane interference between the soul and the Christ, — but it would be wise to remember that there are times and moods and circumstances when every person desires to open his heart to some brother-man, when some persons cannot otherwise get relief."[19]

In Protestantism, the pastor is not the priest (except to the Anglicans and the Episcopalians) and we do not make claim that the minister belongs to a sacred cast of men. We do not claim for him some high elevated position above other people which gives the minister an exalted power of forgiveness. Yet, it is true, that for many people, the minister is the most approachable person who understands human tensions and spiritual problems. He should be such for all; and he could become such for many more, if there were greater opportunity for people to come to him for advice and spiritual counsel.

The duty to facilitate release from tension through confession of sin, sharing of guilt, and opening of the heart to sympathetic understanding, is as much a part of a Protestant pastor's responsibility as it is of the Roman Catholic priest. If the pastor can display the sympathetic understanding of a spiritual father, the warm hearted fellowship of a friend, the wisdom of a theologian, and the skill of a physician, he will be well on the way to helping people in time of great need. Of course we have just described ideal characteristics for the minister and every servant of God should strive to achieve them. Yet it is also encouragingly true, that in spite of his limited abilities and faulty techniques, people have come to their minister just because they viewed him as that kind of person. To them he was as water in the desert, and strength in the valley of need.

The Protestant ministry should seek to develop a technique in this area. A few pioneers have launched forth in the noble venture of receiving people

---

19. John Watson, *The Cure of Souls*, Dodd, Mead and Co., New York, 1896, p. 235.

at stated office hours; but much more must be developed along this line. It takes time and adjustment on the part of the pastor as well as on the part of the people, but there are many who are ready for this innovation. If ministers will develop a proper bearing and establish confidence among their people, they will find the members of the flock and "outsiders" from the community coming to take advantage of their kind attention and interest. Such service must not carry the professional stamp of time, place, ritual, formality, sacramentalism, or superstition. It must represent a sympathetic heart and a ready spirit to share spiritual fellowship. It must provoke and challenge spiritual unleashing of tension and spiritual fellowship, or it will be of no lasting value.

W. L. Northridge called attention to the fact that Jung once sent out a questionnaire asking:

> " 'Would you, in a serious difficulty in life, seek the advice of a physician qualified in psychology, or of a priest or minister of the gospel?' The majority of answers from Protestants were in favor of a doctor, while Roman Catholics showed that they preferred the priest."[20]

Northridge made the point concerning this observation of Jung, that the Protestant church does not have a recognized confessional as an institutionalized part of our religious system. For that fact we rejoice because the institutionalization of the Roman Catholic Confessional has done violence to its spiritual significance. No, we must not have an institutionalized confessional, that would lead to its becoming sacramental and would give the minister an overlordship over the people. But Protestantism should be receptive to a technique whereby the weak and the wayward, the tried and triumphing people of God, may have open access to the minister's services in a way that will be attractive, inviting and spiritually uplifting. We must recognize that we have much to learn in this area of technique. In this connection the words of K. R. Stolz are pertinent:

> "Protestantism, has yet a great deal to learn about the structure and function of religious confession. As it is, most members of the Protestant church, when they wish to unburden themselves, consult a lawyer or the physician."[21]

This does not mean that pastors should pose as mind healers, but it does require of all of us to be at our best when we help burdened people. Pastors are not specialists in the field of psychology, and pastoral psychology does not demand a complete swing in that direction. Yet if pastors opened the door for a Protestant conference, there is no doubt that the people would welcome the innovation and make good use of it.

To make this Protestant Conference of lasting value the minister should take it seriously. It can be called by any name that is suitable to the pastor

---

20. W. L. Northridge, *Health for Mind and Spirit*, The Abingdon Press, New York, 1938, p. 173.
21. Karl R. Stoltz, "The Church and Psychoanalysis," *Methodist Review, Vol. III*, 1928, p. 180.

and the community or church. The designation *Protestant* Conference is in distinction to the Roman Catholic Confessional. The word *conference* represents the idea of freedom of conversation, open hearted discussion, and interchange of spiritual fellowship. This removes the idea of institutionalism from the procedure and though it makes the appointment official, it does not make it traditional. Other names which could be used are Spiritual Interview, Spiritual Fellowship, Pastoral Appointment, and Spiritual Retreat Hour. The name does not matter, if only the name used will suggest a spiritual check-up for God's people and any who wish to come to make use of it.

Such a technique should be dignified by the minister's making himself available by being "in his office" just like a doctor, at certain times and on certain days. The old traditional type church will not welcome such a radical change, and in some places it will not work even with the kindliest means of introducing the procedure. In such places, it should not be used, for certainly a fundamental rule of pastoral psychology is that the acceptability of a practice determines its effectiveness — all things being equal. To those who will not even consider this new emphasis, let them remember that the old traditional manner of a minister calling in a home is very important, but let them also remember that a new day brings new techniques.

This is no ridicule or belittling of the home-going pastor. It is a fact that a home-going pastor makes a church going people. And it is also possible to take the idea of a conference into the home; this will be discussed later in this chapter. But the plea here is for the idea of a Protestant Conference, to which people may come along with freedom and ease knowing that in such a face to face relationship the person may "unload" to the pastor, and "reload" with spiritual power and blessing. All of us have at times wished we had met a sin-burdened individual alone, because being in the company of others we were hindered from counseling sufficiently and effectively. We have heard individuals say, "I hope I can catch the minister alone," or, "Perhaps I can meet him on the street alone, so that I can talk more freely." It is to this need that the conference hour speaks with satisfaction and power.

The pastor should therefore have a stated time and place where he may be found. The place is very important. All the requirements of the place have been aptly described by J. S. Bonnell. His chapter, "In the Consulting Room",[22] should be read by every minister. He recommends a quiet room with street entrance and exit, or at least the possibility of the individual leaving the room without meeting others who know the party and happen to be waiting for a similar appointment. Room arrangement, furniture, lighting effect, and literature are very important.

Old line churches and denominations have not welcomed such an arrangement, and the plans for their church buildings include a sanctuary, and a few rooms that happen to fit in with the general design of the building. Besides, the idea of such conference rooms with suitable furniture and proper setting might even

---

22. Bonnell, op. cit., pp. 84-97.

be revolting to some people, just because it is not in harmony with the practice or the tradition of the church or denomination.

In the past we have let people go to the parsonage with great embarrassment. The minister's family moved about, even though futile attempts at privacy were made. Children of the minister, not knowing about the conference, raced through the house, and the loud talking in the poorly built parsonage resounded through the room. Common sense alone would tell us that spiritual conferences held in such an environment could not produce the kind of results pastoral psychology desires. The medical man would not and could not conduct a physical examination under such conditions. The spiritual leader, God's chosen minister, should not conduct a spiritual examination under such conditions.

A Protestant Conference or meeting plan should be announced to the members of the church and should be known to the people in the community so that all may feel free to come for consultation. A minister who has his study "in the church" will soon find people drifting to his office to consult and talk about matters which would never be discussed "in the presence of others."

It would be very effective if the pastor would ask all his people to come to his office for a periodic, spiritual check-up. Medical clinics recommend this and in many cases demand it to keep the case history intact, and to watch progress, recurrence, and manifestations related to the physical problem under diagnosis. Even after restoration, many clinics require such a physical check-up at regular times or when the patient discovers recurrent trouble. One of the amazing features of the Mayo Brothers Clinic at Rochester, Minnesota, is this important practice of returning for a periodic check-up. Case history, attendant physicians, condition of the patient, and comparison with other case histories are kept in constant relationship in order to watch the patient's recovery and to guard the patient's physical well-being. Having been a patient at this clinic, one comes to have great admiration for the system, and one has the feeling of security, at least as far as human medical skill is concerned. Pastors should inaugurate a spiritual check-up for their people patterned after the practice in this clinic. It would give people the impression that this business of spiritual life and spiritual health is of extreme importance and it would help them know that the pastor really is concerned about their welfare.

In some of our churches this check-up is covered by family visitation once a year. This will be discussed a little later in this chapter; but it is in point to say now that there are times and circumstances when this check-up should be personal, individual, and specific with no one else in the room. We have made a fetish of ministers visiting in people's homes — good as the intention and the visitation has been. Often the home is the most difficult place to "handle a situation." The conference room with a periodic check-up would take care of many problems and difficulties. People should go to the minister's study or conference room as freely as they go to the medical doctor for a periodic check-up.

The conference hour would save the minister much travel, endless time "bucking traffic," and delayed service because people are not at home when he calls. He could see some people after working hours in the afternoon, and he could dovetail many other calls in off-hours when a call in the home would not be appropriate or effective. If the program were carried on regularly with a check-up scheduled each year for every person in the congregation, a tremendous amount of work could be done effectively through the coöperation of God's people with the pastor. Spending the same time now consumed by "chasing around" to cover his parish, the pastor could spend more actual time with his people in serious conversation and pastoral counseling. It would unearth many problems which now remain buried just beneath the surface or deep down in the human heart and conscience — just because the minister does not see his people alone, eye-to-eye, when no one else is near. This kind of procedure would do a job of shepherding that is not being done at the present time because of the press of duties, because of business of our people, and because the job is so colossal that it looks impossible to accomplish.

It is a foregone conclusion that many churches will not welcome such a program, and it is also understandable that many ministers will not attempt such a systematic conference check-up because it would be exacting. Nevertheless, in communities and churches where it could be operated, it would bring untold blessing through effective systematic counseling. Then the young people, boys and girls, would get the habit of "running in to the pastor" to see him about little things, and as life developed, on the great issues of Christian living.

A secretary would be a great help in arranging such appointments with the people of the parish so that they would come in at stated time, and the minister would be able to have continuous consultation while he was on duty for conference hour appointments. Case records would keep the visits connected and the counseling of greater value. Religious reading material in the "waiting room" would offer growth of Christian living and fellowship of the saints—a neglected feature in many of our churches. Waiting in the office for an unusual appointment because of some spiritual emergency would not appear to others to be extraordinary, because the ordinary custom would be to go to the pastor for a yearly or periodic check-up.

Do not say that such a program will not work. C. Bassett said:

> "Thousands of homes which are economically solvent are shaken and torn with serious problems which the participants themselves are helpless to untangle. With the increased practice among ministers of having regular conference hours when people are encouraged to come for the discussion of their concrete personal problems, the minister is in a strategic position to bring skilled service to the solution of many heartbreaking situations."[23]

My plea is that we should not only have a conference hour when people are encouraged to come; we should also request people to come. It would take a little time to accustom people to such a procedure, but once established it

23. Clara Bassett, *Mental Hygiene in the Community*, The Macmillan Co., New York, 1934, p. 270.

would bring untold blessings of happiness, release from tension, confession of sin, and a growing spiritual life. It would have to be adapted to the needs of a particular congregation. To inaugurate such a program, one would have to begin slowly, first by inviting the people to such a proposed conference, then by specially urging some people to come, and later by trying to get the entire congregation to respond. The establishment of this habit would do much for the parish people in time of emergency. It would give them the feeling of freedom and the urge to see the pastor in his conference room because of having been there before for a "regular check-up"; and neither the pastor nor any one else seeing them go, would consider the emergency appointment of special or unusual significance. This kind of procedure, adapted to the needs and the attitude of each particular parish, would give the minister a greater technique to really fulfill his ministry of shepherding.

E. Systematic Family Visitation

This subtitle may seem like a contradiction to the material just discussed with respect to the conference hour. On the contrary, systematic family visitation brings the conference hour into the home. While it is more difficult to do personal work in family visitation, there are some compensations which make systematic home visitation of great value and effective service. In the historical division of our discussion we discovered that the writers of pastoral theology advocated family visitation. Chapter II C, "Systematic Visitation" and Chapter III C, "Pastoral Visiting", clearly indicated that the writers on pastoral theology before the twentieth century felt the urge and importance of this work in the church. During our present century this matter of systematic family visitation has largely been lost and writers have not stressed its importance. One writer, P. Y. De Jong, has written, *Taking Heed to the Flock,* an important treatise on this work. This book appeared in 1948 and presents a challenge to revive this neglected custom in our churches. The author discussed the following features of the subject, the name, nature, history, Scriptural basis, spiritual purpose, necessities, requisites, objections, value, proper practice, and supreme ideal of family visitation. The book is small but powerful in presenting the important position that family visitation is needed in the church today. The author stated his conviction of the value of family visitation in the following way,

> "In spite of all the objections which have been raised against the practice of family visitation as we have come to know and love it in our churches, so much spiritual value inheres in the work if conducted properly that we greatly impoverish ourselves by either carrying it on carelessly or neglecting it altogether.
> "Spiritual blessings, we are convinced, will accrue not only to the members of the church but quite as much to the consistory which zealously seeks to perform this part of its calling."[24]

Any minister who is not sure or who has been neglecting his family visitation, should read and study this book by P. Y. De Jong. It will refresh his

---

24. Peter Y. De Jong, *Taking Heed to the Flock,* Baker Book House, Grand Rapids, Michigan, 1948, p. 65.

mind with respect to his duty, and it will challenge him to go out and do the job carefully and systematically. A balanced view is presented in this book. Personal work is not cast overboard. The author states:

> "We should never forget that family visitation may and often must be supplemented with calls of a more personal character. Such follow-up work yields rich and satisfying results for all concerned. The good under-shepherd will learn to know his sheep better as he meets them regularly and will be prepared to help them when occasion requires."[25]

De Jong related the personal call to the family call by continuing his contention just quoted:

> "But this can hardly be successfully realized, unless the ground-work of mutual trust and respect has been laid. For this last no time is so propitious as that of the annual visit to all families of the church."[26]

Of course such personal work can be done in the conference room, but this does not diminish the importance of family visitation. De Jong has revived the emphasis on the good custom which has been entirely overlooked by writers on pastoral theology during the present century.

It is interesting to note that the importance of the ministerial-family tie is recognized by those who do not prescribe a technique to utilize the opportunity. C. T. Holman indicated the open door of welcome which the minister has among the homes of his people in the following quotation.

> "The pastor is intimately and affectionately bound to his people. The doors of his church family homes, and indeed of many other homes, are open to him. He visits in time of sickness and trouble, he shares the family joy at births and marriages, he brings courage to the dying and comfort to the bereaved. He is bound to his people by many and tender ties through facing with them the greatest crises of life. His council is sought as people confront all kinds of baffling problems. There is no one whose integrity and disinterestedness are more unquestioned. If he will take pains to acquire a real skill as a personal counselor, and demonstrate by his wisdom and sound judgment the value of the service he renders, he will find people coming to him in steadily increasing numbers."[27]

This is the evaluation of one who looked at the importance of pastoral work from the viewpoint of social improvement and moral betterment without the full emphasis of a spiritual transformation and the joy of eternal life. If you added these last named spiritual features to the purpose and program of pastoral family visitation, and ministerial technique, the value of the quotation just given will be immeasurably increased.

It is also well to remember the importance of the home in our day and generation. The minister must understand his task; and to do so, he must know the home. In the words of W. F. Halliday:

> "To understand this from the psychological point of view as a living reality, it is necessary to understand the home, which is the ground-form of ordinary life. It is not without significance that the decay of the old

---

25. Ibid.
26. Ibid.
27. Holman, op. cit., p. 20.

home life, which is a marked feature of society in many parts of the modern world, is accompanied by a restlessness and a lack of religious certainty."[28]

The big problem in our civilization today is the home. One of the most predominant factors causing unrest and psychoneurosis is the unhappy home. It accounts for many a "breakdown." Surface observation will not reveal these tensions in the average family. When the minister knows the family as a family, and when he has had family contact, he can do much to understand the individual members of the family, and he can accomplish much toward a greater family unity. Therefore, we ought to be concerned with the problems of the family.

> "Christianity and the family is a plea to the Protestant ministry for a more practical understanding interest in the family and a greater appreciation of its relation to Christianity. The clergy are not lacking in concern for the welfare of marriage and the family, but they, like other people, are too apt to be content with spasmodic, occasional efforts to conserve the family instead of planning and carrying out a detailed, deliberate program. A sentimental attitude toward domestic relations, that is not translated into concrete activity, does not go far in helping a family to fulfill its spiritual mission."[29]

This places before us the importance of the family in modern civilization, and the way to keep posted with the life of the families of the church is to maintain a continuous family contact. "Without this sustained interest no parish can be held together as a living organism."[30] There are no substitutes for effective pastoral work within the families of the church. The conference hour will not cover all the needs of the family, because the conference hour will reveal some family background that must be checked and evaluated by a family call. And there are some family problems that may, by cleverness and closely guarded conversation, be hidden in the conference room. Personal pastoral work will not eliminate family contact. A pastor cannot have a conference hour in order to meet all his people, and in addition make the rounds of family visitation. Therefore he must devise the system which best suits his parish, and in following either method must not exclude the other. Conference work with individuals should include some family visitation, and family visitation includes conference consultations to complete the technique for helping people spiritually for improved Christian living. The two are related. In the words of R. L. Dicks,

> "Pastoral work consists more in the pastor going to the people than it does in their coming to him, for the pastor who goes to his people ultimately will find them coming to him."[31]

This reciprocal relation must be studied by the minister and he must apply it to the proper balance between the conference hour or appointment, and the family call which he makes in the home.

---

28. W. Fearon Halliday, *Psychology and Religious Experience,* Hodder and Stoughton, Ltd., London, 1929, p. 171.
29. Ernest R. Groves, *Christianity and the Family,* The Macmillan Co., New York, 1942, p. vii.
30. Martin, op. cit., p. 72.
31. Dicks, op. cit., p. 31.

Family visitation must be systematic. A clear cut system of sick, bereavement and family calling must be arranged or it will defeat itself before one starts. By observing rigid rules, self imposed and carefully followed, in order to cover all the families of the church, a spiritual program will be advanced for a shepherding service which benefits all. It has been argued by the modern busy pastor that such visitation is not possible. Indeed, it is a tremendous task and one not easily accomplished. It is also true that some people merely want a social call, a hurried visit, and a professional "chat" rather than a settled and sustained call on the spiritual verities of faith. While it is true that people sometimes prefer this kind of visit to the regular systematic family visitation program, often, it must be said, the ministers are to blame for inculcating this desire because that is all people have had. Systematic visitation has often deteriorated into a glorified "coffee klets." On the other hand, such visits have been made only rigid and formal. I remember such family visitation from my boyhood days. It stifled me when such calls were announced from the pulpit, and it worried me the night the elder and minister came to call. They came to talk to my parents about spiritual matters, and last of all, at the close of the visit, a few words of superior advice, above my head and my heart, were addressed to me. This family visitation caused every young lad to fear the minister, to "shake in his boots" when he called, and to heave a sigh of relief when the "whole business" was over for another year. Both, extreme sociability and rigid formality must be avoided in the family call. In the one the conversation often drifts into the social aspects of living, without genuine spiritual consideration and Biblical uplift. In the other the opening of the heart door for spiritual conversation is not accomplished because people are afraid, reserved, and hold back.

Based upon personal experience as a lad and as a young man, and from first hand experience in the pastorate, I inaugurated a system of systematic family visitation. It is explained in my *Manual for Ministers, Elders and Deacons*.[32] This book includes an explanation of tne necessity of visitation both for the members of the church and for the officers of the church. The choice of the theme or material to be discussed can be made from the selection of fifteen proposed plans, on fifteen different subjects of spiritual significance for the life of the individual in the church.

Before such a campaign, usually held in the fall and winter season of the church year, the minister and the elders should sit in consultation together, determine which plan is the most necessary for the congregation, and then discuss the necessary amplifications and applications of the suggested topics and questions under the chosen plan for the year. This will give system to the project, and will make the plan adaptable for the particular congregation at the particular time when such a plan is to be inaugurated. This will make it up-to-date and psychologically effective for the people in a given parish at a given time for the best benefit of all concerned. This will not make it

32. William Goulooze, *Manual for Ministers, Elders, and Deacons*, Wm. B. Eerdmans Publishing Co., Grand Rapids, Michigan, 1937, pp. 79-106.

stereotyped but will allow for application and alteration in the carrying out of the plan when the house to house spiritual visitation is made.

After the plan has been adopted, and just before the campaign is launched, the minister should present the general theme of the thought to be discussed at one or two of the worship services of the congregation. This will be challenging to the people and they will anticipate something of the spirit of the program of visitation for the year. This will likewise present a renewed incentive to the officers of the church who assist in this kind of calling program.

In addition, the entire membership of the church should be reviewed and carefully evaluated. When the minister and the elders consult together on the spiritual condition of the members, each can contribute knowledge and opinion so that the team scheduled to visit a particular person or family may be properly briefed.

Part of the planning for the visit should be the fixing of a definite length of time for the visit, with a somewhat fixed mode of beginning and concluding the visit — such as prayer, Bible reading, one member of the team being responsible for a particular part and the other coöperating with delegated responsibility. A definite plan of what should take place in each family should be discussed briefly just before going into the home. There are some routine questions which should be asked in one form or another, depending on the nature of the family to be visited. These questions pertain to the enjoyment of the worship services, the organizational life of the church, and the Christian welfare of the entire family. A list of such usual questions and topics[33] has also been suggested in my manual for this kind of work. In addition a Scripture passage should be read in each home. These also have been listed and printed in my manual.[34] More will be said about the use of Scripture in the next section of this chapter, but suffice it to say at this point that such a systematic procedure is very necessary in order to complete the spiritual family visit.

Such a plan will make for variety and for system. It will sustain and support the work of the church; it will be stimulating for people, pastor and assistant workers. It will finish a task that ought to be done well. It will be personal counseling brought home to the family as a unit. Such a plan will reach out into the needs of the congregation and of the individuals. The fifteen plans which I have suggested in the manual give some idea of the breadth and scope of possible interest and discussion. The following optional units of discussion for the year indicate the different plans: "Christian Growth," "Lessons from our Afflictions," "Religious Reading," "Prayer," "Education," "Christian Exemplary Living," "Giving," "Personal Soul-Winning for Christ," "The Christian Family," "Lessons from Our Blessings," "Popular Amusements," "Scripture Exposition," "The Means of Grace," "The Church," and "Special Spiritual Problems."[35] A combination of any of these for a given year can be effected according to the needs which are particular for that time. When

---

33. Ibid.
34. Ibid., pp. 11-66, 69-78.
33. Ibid., pp. 86-88.

emergencies arise in the visit itself, the formulated plan can be set aside for that particular call, and the matters at hand be discussed.

In some large congregations it is required of the minister that he serve on one of the visitation teams. In other large churches it is the responsibility of the minister only to do some follow up work, the basic and initial work of necessity being left to the elders or spiritual leaders.

When the visits have been completed, the officers of the church with the minister should sit in counsel together again and report their discoveries. These should be evaluated, recorded for future reference, and followed with repeat visits where such are necessary. In large churches where the minister cannot cover all the families in a short period of time, he should be informed about cases requiring his special attention. Such can be handled in the conference hour or in a visit by the minister to the home. Following the report on the families and persons visited, a profitable series of sermons should be arranged by the minister, by means of which he can cement and certify the spiritual warnings and spiritual gains which his congregation should receive. This will afford a new opportunity for indoctrination of Bible truth and presentation of good psychological suggestions pertaining to Christian living. The whole program will then have system, strength, stimulus, and supervision. The following year, as a new plan is adopted for systematic visitation, it can be carried out as a continuation or follow-up of the preceding plan; or if necessary variation should be found desirable, such can be done for the text technique of pastoral psychology. The full discussion of this plan and technique can be found in my manual.[36]

F. Systematic Use of Scripture

One of the most effective techniques for pastoral counseling is the use of Scripture. This is not a new method, for it was used by Jesus in His ministry. Christ constantly referred to the Scriptures in his work of evangelizing, and in his conversations with those who were already a part of the kingdom of God. He used this as an effective weapon against Satan in the hour of temptation. In his book, *How Jesus Dealt with Men*, R. Calkins gave ample proof of Christ's use of Scripture in his ministry.[37] He was always mindful of the Old Testament Scriptures and used them when necessary. He wove into his dealings with men the tender words which later became Scripture. By so doing he set before us a great example.

The writers on pastoral theology were mindful of this important feature of pastoral counseling. This was clearly evident in our historical survey, particularly in Chapter II F, "Biblical Application," and Chapter III F, "Applied Scripture." However, very little was done in the way of arranging systematically the passages of Scripture which could be used in the technique for reaching people effectively.

---

36. Ibid., pp. 79-85.

37. Raymond Calkins, *How Jesus Dealt with Men*, Abingdon Cokesbury Press, New York, Nashville, 1942, pp. 54-72.

The writers on psychology have not manifested an interest in this technique, because they do not feel the need of the Scripture. K. Stolz, C. Rogers and S. Hiltner did not mention the Scripture as an invaluable aid for pastoral counseling. S. E. Anderson evidently took it for granted in his spiritual and Scriptural emphasis of the pastor as counselor, but he did not recommend it as a systematic technique to help people.[38]

Authors interested in the application of psychology to the field of pastoral work have mentioned the use of Scripture. We call attention to the book, *The Art of Ministering to the Sick*, by R. C. Cabot and R. L. Dicks. These two authors indicated the importance of Scripture by devoting Chapter XVII, "Scripture,"[39] to this important feature of pastoral work. They wrote, "The Bible can be used effectively with the sick, but not wholesale."[40] By this they meant that passages should be selected and recommended to people with wisdom and discretion. These authors called attention to the fact that some of the great Psalms and words of Jesus bring comfort and release in time of trouble and suffering. These passages should be placed before the patient so that his mind can be tied to God through their experience.

Another author, J. S. Bonnell, demonstrated the importance of using Scripture. His book, *Pastoral Psychiatry*, reveals his constant use of the Scriptures in the effective technique of helping people. In the case histories reported it is very evident how Bonnell used Scripture in the accomplishment of the spiritual cure for those to whom he brought his ministry.[41] Bonnell varied the method of using Scripture to suit the occasion and purpose. Sometimes he quoted it informally, and at other times he wrote it out on a card — like a prescription card of the doctor. He also read portions of the Bible before his patients and when occasion presented itself, he wrote Bible passages in personal correspondence. In Bonnell's book, *Psychology for Pastor and People*, the author likewise indicated his esteem for the Scriptural method by including a chapter on "How to Read the Bible."[42]

Other references to the practice of using Scripture in pastoral counseling are few. W. S. Sadler suggested Scripture passages which he used in comforting the sick,[43] and H. C. Link said that as a psychologist who experienced conversion, he found himself using Bible language and Bible doctrine when he counseled the unfortunate.[44]

From these brief references it is perfectly clear that very few writers of our generation understand and appreciate the value of using the Bible as a technique for pastoral counseling. It is an alarming fact that so few ministers

38. Anderson, op. cit., pp. 25-37.
39. Richard C. Cabot and Russell L. Dicks, *The Art of Ministering to the Sick*, The Macmillan Co., New York, 1937, pp. 234-243.
40. Ibid. pp. 234, 235.
41. John Southerland Bonnell, *Pastoral Psychiatry*, Harper & Brothers Publishers, New York, 1938, pp. 127, 128, 208, 209, 211, 212, 218-220, 223-226.
42. Bonnell, *Psychology for Pastor and People*, op. cit., pp. 191-196.
43. William S. Sadler, *Theory and Practice of Psychiatry*, C. V. Mosby Co., St. Louis, 1936, pp. 1079-1081.
44. Henry C. Link, *The Return to Religion*. The Macmillan Co., New York, 1936, p. 5.

actually use this technique for effective pastoral work. We have lost the fine art of using "the sword of the Spirit, which is the Word of God."[45] I know this is true from personal experience because so few used the comfort and blessing of the Scriptures when they called on me during my prolonged illness. A few made references to the promises from the Bible, but only two ministers of the large number who called on me, read the Word of God in my presence to comfort and sustain me. Of course, they may have been timid about it because they called on a fellow minister; but even so, it appeared that many were not using the Bible as the first aid in spiritual ministration.

We must come to a renewed appreciation of the Bible in the technique of pastoral psychology. The pastor must understand human nature, he must know the situation in which the individual finds himself, he must know all that psychology can give as an aid for better service; but most of all and best of all he should know and use the Bible passages for occasions of pastoral counseling. Knowing the Bible is his primary task. He should memorize passages of Scripture which may be used effectively for different needs and circumstances. He should know the favorite passages of the members of his congregation. It would be well for the minister to memorize these passages and use them with these individuals. It will double and triple his effectiveness with such people. It will have a surprisingly wholesome influence in his own life and in the lives of others whom he visits. The least the minister can do is to read such passages before his people, because we know that we have the promise that God's word will not return to him void.[46]

In addition, the minister should obtain the aid of carefully selected Bible passages to help people with specific problems. I have made an attempt at furnishing these for the ministry in two books. The one book, already referred to, *Manual for Ministers, Elders, and Deacons*, is in the form of a handbook and contains printed Scriptural passages for various occasions which arise in pastoral counseling. These passages cover the range of our general experience and specific problems. The following titles appearing at the head of each section of printed Bible passages indicates the scope of the book. The titles are: "We Are Lost in Sin," "We Feel the Need of God," "Repentance and Confession of Sin," "Regeneration," "Conversion," "The Marvelous Christ," "The Duty to Have Faith in God," "Excuses for Not Accepting Christ," "The Duty of Complete Surrender," "The Experience of Forgiveness and Justification," and "The Need of Confessing Christ." All of these titles and the selected passages[47] under each fall under the general heading, "Winning the Unsaved, Non-Confessing, For the Lord Jesus Christ."[48] Under the second main heading, "Sanctification,"[49] the following titles with selections of Scripture appear: "We Have a Duty to be Holy, or Sanctified," "Afflictions, Sickness, Trials," "Sorrow," "Spiritual Growth," "Prayer," "Living by the Spirit," "The Means

45. Ephesians 6:17
46. Isaiah 55:11.
47. Goulooze, op. cit., 11-27.
48. Ibid., p. 11.
49. Ibid., p. 28.

of Grace" ("The Church," "The Bible," "The Lord's Supper"), "Popular Amusements," "Temptations," and "Education."[50]

Section three represents "Service in God's Kingdom,"[51] and describes with titles and Bible passages just what it means for the child of God to do effective service for Christ. The subtitles are: "The Duty of Service," "God's Requirement," "The Duty of Expressing Thankfulness to God," "Our Duty to Be an Example," "Testify for Christ," "Win Souls for Christ," "Give to the Kingdom," and "Duties for the Entire Family."[52]

In the fourth or remaining section of the manual attention is given to "Special Spiritual Problems,"[53] with specialized concern for "Doubts of Christians," "Faultfinding," "Settling Disputes," "Assurance," "Sin Against the Holy Ghost," and "Suicide."[54] This manual is indexed according to topic and Biblical references, so that while a pastoral or workers conference with the individual is in progress the one using the Manual can turn to the index for the desired passage on the subject needing Biblical light. The Manual appears in the form of a miniature Bible so that it is dignified and makes the receiver feel he is being told about the Word of God directly.

My extended reference to this Manual was solely to call attention to the wide range of subjects and purposes for which the minister should have available definite selections of Scripture. It will be impossible for some ministers, in fact for most of them, to memorize all these passages; therefore such a small book should accompany the minister when he calls and counsels. It will fortify his position, it will give point to his counsel, and it will give balance to the parishioner who listens and heeds the Word of God. Using a manual of this kind, a pastor will become steeped in the Word of God, and by that very fact he will be a reservoir of spiritual strength to his people, always overflowing with the word of Life, the Bible, God's book of salvation and spiritual strength.

The pastor must also devise a means of leaving the Scripture with his people. J. S. Bonnell has often written out a Bible text which was appropriate to the individual. Written on a card or nearby letter envelope, it remained with the patient as a boon and blessing. It was repeatedly read, re-read and applied because God's servant left it as a blessing.

Another way is to leave or provide some good book on the problem facing the individual. This book should have the proper Scriptural emphasis, with appropriate Bible quotations so that the individual may come to discover by re-reading and meditation, that the word of life is found in God's truth.

As a result of my experience of sickness and suffering, as already indicated, I decided to write the story of God's wonderful grace and the power of the

---

50. Ibid., pp. 28-47.
51. Ibid., p. 47.
52. Ibid., pp. 47-61, 70-78. (The latter section deals with giving pertaining to sacrifices, the tithe, the love offering, New Testament principle of giving, covetousness, giving for the church and for missions.)
53. Ibid., p. 61.
54. Ibid., pp. 61-66.

Bible. As a result, two books of the series on suffering were prepared, *Victory over Suffering*,[55] and *Blessings from Suffering*.[56] These books came about, as already indicated in the Research Analysis, because of my personal experience and on the basis of the replies received from over a thousand people on the subject and the experience of suffering. The people who replied to the questionnaire indicated choice Scripture passages of great variety and of repeated choice. The top selections of the people have been indicated in the Research Analysis of this book. In these two books of suffering an attempt was made to place and interweave the various Scripture passages in such a way that the suffering patient and the shepherding minister could have a common meeting ground on the Word of God.

We must firmly contend for an adequate use of the Scriptures when we minister to the sick and the afflicted. Research on this question through the questionnaires has proven conclusively that people live by the Bible and need the ministry of the Bible in order to live. Only when we use the Bible properly and effectively before our people and in our counseling will they become fully aware of the grace of God through the Word for all of life.

---

55. William Goulooze, *Victory Over Suffering*, Baker Book House, Grand Rapids, 1949, 150 pp.
56. William Goulooze, *Blessings of Suffering*, Baker Book House, Grand Rapids (forthcoming).

CHAPTER XIV

Minister and Doctor

THE goal of a close relationship of minister and doctor in the common work of helping people is a modern development. The writers on pastoral theology were aware of the need of proper coöperation between ministers and doctors, but they did not prescribe a technique for this association. In the past both professions have been to blame for the distant feeling between them. In the past, ministers have been considered necessary for consultation in spiritual matters in the time of serious sickness, during a crisis or when death seemed approaching. The doctor has been considered necessary in case of physical ills, illness of grave character, or when death was near. But these two, ministering to the same people, and often under the same circumstances have been far apart in terms of fellowship, understanding and coöperation.

Doctors have felt that ministers brought a depressing spirit upon the patient and that as far as medical purposes were concerned, ministers were better off the premises than near the patient. G. B. Willcox described their attitude when he said, "Being irreligious men, having no sympathy with a pastor's work, they assume that his mere presence in the sick room will depress the spirits and retard the recovery of the patient."[1]

This attitude is to be expected because, as Willcox stated, the average doctor is not religious and is antagonized by the minister's presence. However, Willcox added a note of warning for ministers when he said:

"But Christian physicians sometimes join the complaint, and that for good reasons. The minister is sombre and solemn, or he is careless in speech or act, or shows in other ways want of good sense."[2]

As pastors we must admit that sometimes we do not understand, we blunder, and we do not bring the kind of cheer that is helpful to the patient or the work of the physician. This antagonism and misunderstanding between doctor and minister has hindered proper coördination. It must be removed.

A. Emphasis in Pastoral Theology

A few writers on pastoral theology realized the importance of the proper relation between doctors and ministers. A. Vinet wrote,

"The pastor ought not to omit to learn of the physician the state of the patient; from his relations and friends he should learn his moral and religious condition."[3]

1. G. B. Willcox, *The Pastor Amidst His Flock*, The American Tract Society, New York, 1890, p. 146.
2. Ibid.
3. Alexander Vinet, *Pastoral Theology*, T. & T. Clark, Edinburg, 1852, p. 253.

And W. Gladden advised,

> "Be careful to coöperate in every possible way with the attending physician, to whom belongs the chief responsibility and whose orders should be scrupulously respected."[4]

G. H. Gerberding said, "The pastor is not to play the physician or to interfere with him. But he can aid him by giving a few hygienic directions."[5] A more specific coöperation was indicated by J. A. Beebe:

> "The relation of the pastor to the physician should be one of cordial coöperation. Most physicians recognize the therapeutic value of the pastor's call and welcome it, except where a pastor has proven himself to be a wretched bungler, who irritates more than he soothes by his coming."[6]

A warning was given by L. C. Douglas, lest the minister meddle with the work of the doctor:

> "The minister must never prescribe. He is not the doctor. He must not assume to know anything about the treatment or care of this or any other malady. If he has any business there at all, it relates to the patient's soul."[7]

Along the same line of thinking, J. D. Wells expressed himself in the following way:

> "It is clear enough that unless a physician knows a minister to be wise in dealing with the sick — one who at once perceives what is helpful and what is hurtful — he must decline taking the responsibility of encouraging, or even permitting his visits. He is waging a battle with disease."[8]

At the same time Wells cautioned,

> "The physician in all ordinary cases has no more reason or right to exclude the minister, who seeks the salvation of the soul for eternity, and of the body with it, than has the minister to exclude the physician, who aims to heal the body for a few and uncertain years appointed it for life on earth."[9]

From these quotations it will be seen that a few of the writers on pastoral theology felt the importance of the right relation between doctor and minister, even though they did not anticipate the close coördination which is demanded by pastoral psychology.

It is more than passing strange that the same church has been for centuries interested in a healing program for the mission fields. In that area of endeavor, the missionary doctor and the missionary evangelist work hand in hand to

4. Washington Gladden, *The Christian Pastor and the Working Church*, Charles Scribner's Sons, New York, 1903, p. 187.
5. G. H. Gerberding, *The Lutheran Pastor*, Lutheran Publication Society, Philadelphia, 1905. p. 231.
6. James Albert Beebe, *The Pastoral Office*, The Methodist Book Concern, New York. 1923, p. 286.
7. Loyd C. Douglas, *The Minister's Everyday Life*, Charles Scribner's Sons, New York, 1924, p. 113.
8. J. D. Wells, *Pastor in the Sick-Room*, Presbyterian Board of Publication and Sabbath-School Work, Philadelphia, 1893, p. 94.
9. Ibid., p. 95.

accomplish one purpose — the salvation of souls and the healing of the body, both for the glory of God. Yet, while the average minister preaches missions, both evangelistic and medical, the kind of coöperation that is necessary between doctor and minister does not prevail on the home field. For this reason, pastoral psychology has a challenge for both minister and doctor in fostering a coöperation of understanding, technique, and purpose.

B. Coöperation Between Doctor and Minister

In this section of our analysis we seek to understand a better relation between doctor and minister for full coöperation and coördination. A. T. Boisen treated this question in the following way:

> "My own view is that the religious worker, with all his limitations and with his waning influence, has yet in his keeping three things that are of fundamental importance in dealing with this problem: 1 — A message with regard to the ultimate realities of life that has brought comfort and hope and strength to many a sufferer . . . 2 — An effective means of re-education through suggestion in prayer . . . 3 — A group of socially minded people of whom the religious worker is the chosen leader and through whom he can greatly multiply his own effectiveness. Such a group can be utilized to provide a wholesome environment for the man in distress."[10]

This is an important position because the doctor really treats a person, not just a body or a pain. The minister also treats a person, not just an experience, or a feeling within the individual. Therefore, according to G. G. Dawson,

> "Pastor, physician and nurse ought to have some psychotherapic knowledge. The pastor might have some medical training and the physician and nurse some pastoral knowledge. Thus healing would cease to be departmental."[11]

To this the same author makes the following wise conclusion:

> "All medical agents, all surgery, all hygiene, all physical, mental, moral and spiritual education must, where valid and true, fit in with the redemptive scheme of God the Father, who is Eternal Love, until Christ completes the final act of Divine Redemption by offering up the Kingdom to God, that He may be all in all."[12]

The total life of the individual must be brought under the power of Christ. The bodily, the mental, and the spiritual aspects of the individual's experience must be brought into perfect harmony with each other and with God. Therefore the minister and the doctor must coöperate to bring this to pass. The tension of our times, and the nervous complexes of our generation must find a solution in the dual work of the minister and the doctor. The church must help the medical man because it has the organization, the spiritual leader in the pastor, and the proper spiritual environment to educate and inspire people

10. Anton T. Boisen, "Concerning Relationship Between Religious Experience and Mental Disorders," *Mental Hygiene*, Vol, 7, April, 1923, *Quarterly Magazine of the National Committee for Mental Hygiene, Inc.*, New York City, pp. 309, 310.

11. George Dawson, *Healing, Pagan and Christian*, The Macmillan Co., New York, 1935, p. 300.

12. Ibid., p. 308

with spiritual life, under the grace and blessing of God. On the other hand the medical profession should give technical knowledge and scientific research to the individual for the total improvement of life and health.

This need of coöperation between doctors and ministers is pressing upon us daily. Doctors are required to give more than mere advice and treatment for the physical ailments, and ministers are asked to give more than spiritual advice. In the words of C. G. Jung:

> "Here, then, the clergyman stands before a vast horizon. But it would seem as if no one had noticed it. It also looks as though the Protestant clergyman of today was insufficiently equipped to cope with the urgent psychic needs of our age. It is indeed high time for the clergyman and the psychotherapist to join forces to meet this great spiritual task."[13]

While our forces and our assets should be joined for effective leadership, the one should not be considered a substitute for the other.

> "To assist in overcoming the mental and moral difficulties of individuals, we thus see the necessity for closer coöperation between the doctors who are working to restore mental normality and physical health, and the clergy and educationists whose work lies in the development of the mental and spiritual capacities of the individual within a social group."[14]

If only we could harmonize and harness the findings of the fields of pastoral theology and psychology for the correct formulation of pastoral psychology, we could do much for our decadent civilization.

> "It would be an enormous step toward the synthesis which modern thought and life are seeking if the medical profession and the clergy could act as allies and not as enemies, act as fellow-workers and not as jealous opponents."[15]

When these two agents of the Lord coöperate with the proper technique under pastoral psychology, we will experience a new confidence on the part of our people, and we ourselves as ministers and doctors will feel the challenge of a new consecration to a high and holy task. If these two agents would seek to help each other and maintain a counseling service which would serve as a clearinghouse for tangled nerves and tried hearts, we would be well on the way to a better understanding and a guaranteed service of efficient helpfulness to our people.

The goal of the physician should be the goal of the pastor. There should be no quarreling about aims and purposes. G. W. Jacoby stated it thus:

> "All that medicine asks of religion is that it face fearlessly the results of scientific research and appreciate its high aims. Religion, in turn, asks of medicine an open mind where moral and spiritual evolution is concerned. In the final analysis, their object is the same: the physical, mental and spiritual well-being of man."[16]

13. Carl G. Jung, *Modern Man In Search of a Soul*, Harcourt, Brace and Co., New York, 1939, pp. 264, 265.
14. A. Graham Ikin, *Religion and Psychotherapy*, Student Christian Movement Press, London, 1935, p. 20.
15. Ibid., p. 109.
16. George W. Jacoby, *Physician-Pastor and Patient*, Paul B. Hoeber, Inc., Medical Book Department of Harper & Brothers, New York, London, 1936, p. 10.

If only such open mindedness could be developed, then pastoral psychology would be ready for a new day of help, understanding, and blessing. There should be no rivalry between the minister and the physician.

It is sure that the average physician is using some methods of pastoral theology without giving credit to that study and information. There have been physicians who knew that the particular patient needed, not medicine, but good Christian balance and interpretation, and giving such, the doctor found recovery rapid. Yet it would be hard for them to admit this to the community minister because it might appear beneath his professional standing to do so. Likewise the minister, in seeking to give spiritual advice, has many times recommended simple hygiene and good health rules to his people, knowing that observing such would help the person live a better Christian life. And the pastor did not credit this bit of good advice to the medical profession because he himself would like all the credit. What we need is a close coöperation between the two, a constant cross recommendation of both so that people will know that their advice stands together, and both professions work in harmony. Each must remain authoritative in his own field, and each must complement the other. After all, we cannot divide man into separate compartments — turning over the body to the doctor and the soul to the minister — expecting the person to thrive on compartmental treatment. Man is a unit, body and soul, and to do the most for this person, the doctor and the minister must work together in harmony.

> "In a hundred different ways members of the two professions may work hand in hand, but each should be able to mutually esteem the other and give to each his proper place and function. They ought never to despise one another, because they ought never to encroach on one another's province."[17]

Pastoral psychology demands a close coöperation between the medical and the ministerial professions. The very spirit of Christianity breathes coöperation. The Bible is the foundation book for the kind of coördination that will bring blessing, health, and happiness to the individual. Not only should this coöperation exist for the sake of a better technique, but it should be exercised because it is the spirit of Christ. Just as on the mission field medical missions and evangelistic missions are combined and coördinated for the sole purpose of bringing spiritual salvation and Christian living to the subjects coming under the influence of the gospel, so in the home church, in the neighborhood community, and in the large city, minister and doctor should coördinate their efforts for the betterment of man's physical health and spiritual life.

C. The Duty of the Physician in This Cooperation

In this coöperation both the doctor and the pastor have specific responsibilities toward the success and effectiveness of both. Doctors, particularly those who are not Christian, fail to realize the welcome they should give to the proper place of the ready and gifted minister. It is to be understood that

---

17. Groffrey Rhodes, (Editor), *Medicine and the Church*, Kegan, Trench, Trubner & Co., Ltd., London, 1910, p. 48.

some pastors do more harm than good in the sick room, but it is also to be remembered that some pastors are gifted and talented with the ability to handle people and these have given wonderful assistance to the doctor, though unnoticed by many in the very experience of sickness. Often, when the doctor has prescribed a course of action, such as a surgical operation or a prolonged stay in a sanitarium, it has been the minister who persuaded the patient to surrender to the doctor's required procedure. Because of a personal and spiritual confidence in the minister, he, even more than the doctor, could get the patient to make the personal surrender to drastic measure for health. It is not always so; but more than many doctors admit, ministers have been instrumental in quietly helping people with their medical problems.

Doctors should also remember that our conception of God, and our conception of the worth of man must be right before we can really be whole. They should value the help of ministers, particularly in the mental disorder cases, knowing that through the power of the gospel, people can be transformed. The doctor should appreciate the fact that in these days of nervous tension, the pastor carries the supreme medicine — the tonic for the soul — the promises of God, the power of the Holy Spirit, the blessings of the Lord and spiritual advice given in consecration to a spiritual commission.

Doctors have been trained in a special field, and for the most part have been estranged from religion. Secular training, the experience of dealing objectively and impersonally with the human body, and the cold facts of life have hardened the average doctor to the power of Christ and the influence of Christianity. Now, not all doctors carry this spirit, for there are Christian physicians who permeate their services to the body with the fine Christian attitude and atmosphere which Luke displayed as "the beloved physician" in the gospel record of our Lord Jesus Christ. There are doctors who begin surgery with prayer that the Great Physician may guide a deft hand and control the human mind while the operation is in progress. There are doctors who know and express their faith in God, their allegiance to Jesus Christ, and the belief in the Virgin birth of our Lord Jesus Christ, even though this is a medical mystery. But in proportion to the total number of physicians, such doctors are few and far between.

Some doctors who convey the Christian spirit because they are Christian at heart have spoken to the entire profession, and their injunctions should be heeded by all. M. A. Liotta, a doctor, wrote the following:

> "Physicians should be interested in the supernatural as well as the physical or natural order; they should have a knowledge of medical science. God is the Author of true religion and real science."[18]
> "Our body is the abode of the soul. The condition of the soul is frequently dependent on the condition of that abode. Man is bound to take precautions for the preservation of his health and of his life."[19]

---

18. Matthew A. Liotta, *The Connection Between Religion and Medicine*, J. J. Little and Ives Co., New York, 1935, p. 15.
19. Ibid., p. 23.

In much the same spirit, J. R. Oliver, M.D., writing the introduction to Weatherhead's book, *Psychology in the Service of the Soul,* stated:

> "We physicians are, therefore, all the more ready to welcome into the field of psychiatry a clergyman who has done his best to acquaint himself with the method in which psychiatrists deal with various types of mental problems. The old ideal of the priest-physician may be a very beautiful and desirable one. It is, however, very difficult to realize. A physician cannot, in dealing with his mental patients, force upon them his own personal religious attitude. It is far easier for the priest or the minister who has a working knowledge of individuals from the religious stand-point."[20]

In the foreword to Weatherhead's book, *Psychology and Life,* the same emphasis was given by H. B. Brackenbury, M.D. He wrote:

> "Medicine has become a social service as well as a science and an art; and the doctor must do his part in intimate association with all sorts of other social workers, the teachers and the clergy above all."[21]

We repeat the words of another doctor, a well known psychiatrist, who has also taught this subject in a theological seminary. He said concerning his work:

> "In this work, while the approach to personality problems is made through psychology, their final conclusion is found to involve not only social situations but moral implications, spiritual experience, and even cosmic attitudes and relationships. A human being, as we visualize him, is something more than a machine, and therefore must the psychiatrist prove himself to be something more than a mere master mechanic."[22]

Not all doctors are willing to recognize the necessity of a close relationship of medicine to Christianity, such as has been described in the above quotations "from Christian doctors." Too often doctors are interested in the body and not in the human personality living in that body. They analyze symptoms and seek to trace troubles to causes. The psychiatrists often seek to discover mental processes and the causes for mental disorders without proper relation to the character of the person and the spiritual implications of personality. They forget that man is not a machine, but that he is a human being, body and soul. We have been made in the image of God,[23] and with eternity in our heart. We need more than the surgeon's knife and the X-ray of the body to tell the full story of our affliction. Doctors must come to recognize the therapeutic value of Christianity, and the power of an endless life through the grace of the Holy Spirit and the atonement of Jesus' death.

Physicians should also remember that they are on an equal basis with the pastors in relation to the patient. Too often the doctor is the "boss" in the case. The doctor resents being told anything or even asked anything by the

20. John Rathbone Oliver, In the Foreword to *Psychology in the Service of the Soul,* by Leslie D. Weatherhead, The Macmillan Co., New York, 1930, p. xiii.
21. H. B. Brakenburgy in the Foreword to *Psychology and Life,* by Leslie D. Weather-head, The Abingdon Press, New York, 1935, p. xi.
22. William S. Sadler, *Theory and Practice of Psychiatry,* C. V. Mosby Co., St. Louis, 1936, p. viii.
23. Genesis 1:26.

minister. To the doctor, even an intelligent and understanding minister is merely to be an observer and he is supposed to know very little, much less take any intiative in the search for the cure of the individual. Too many doctors demand that the minister must stay out of the way, out of sight, away from contradiction regardless of the technique of the physician. To them the minister should assume the attitude, "leave well enough alone," and "mind your own business." Certainly the minister should "mind his own business," but part of that business is to assist the patient and to work along with the doctor for the best interest of a common friend.

When both doctor and minister assume the attitude of helping each other, then much can be done in the field of pastoral psychology. This has been evidenced in the working of E. Worcester, a minister, and S. McComb, a doctor. Their book, *The Christian Religion as a Healing Power*, is a defénse of the Emmanuel Movement but at the same time it is a demonstration of their ability to work together harmoniously, concertedly, and understandingly. They wrote:

> "The meaning and aim of our work may be expressed in a single sentence. It is to bring into effective coöperation the physician, the psychologically trained clergyman, and the trained social worker in the alleviation and arrest of certain disorders of the nervous system which are now generally regarded as involving some weakness or defect of character or more or less complete mental dissociation."[24]

A similar working team has been constituted by S. Blanton, a physician, and N. V. Peale, the minister of the Marble Collegiate (Reformed) Church in New York City. Their books, *Faith is the Answer*, and *The Art of Real Happiness*,[25] are the outcome and record of their mutual interest in guidance in the clinic they conduct at the Marble Collegiate Church. They seek to help normal people in trying to keep them normal, and they attempt to help the abnormal to bring them to perfect poise and balance in Christian living. Their book is an evidence that they are a perfect working team.

The last two evidences could have been listed under the previous heading in this chapter, under the coöperation which should exist between minister and doctor. They have been recorded here to evidence the important step which the doctor must take in order to effect the desired coördination. Doctors should be willing to work coöperatively in the church clinic. Often it is the doctor whose inclination must first be awakened and whose willingness must first be engaged, before a working coöperation can be effected.

D. The Duty of the Minister in This Coöperation

In the coöperation between doctor and minister there are some specific things the pastor must learn and develop as his responsibility.

1. *He Must Develop the Proper Attitude*

24. Elwood Worcester and Samuel McComb, *The Christian Religion as a Healing Power*, Moffat, Yard and Co., New York, 1909, pp. 48, 49.

25. Smiley Blanton and Norman Vincent Peale, *Faith Is the Answer*, New York, Nashville, Abingdon-Cokesbury Press, 1940, 233 pp., and *The Art of Real Happiness*, Prentice Hall, Inc., New York, 1950.

The minister should cherish his God-sent opportunity of helping people. The difficulty has been that pastors frequently do not cultivate the proper attitude with respect to their work. Ministers have a golden opportunity to bring Jesus Christ to a lost generation, but too often we are not joyful in our presentation. Too often we are interested in the ministry merely as a job and a profession.

> "The clergyman now has an opportunity to recover what may be termed 'the lost art' of his important work, a true pastoral relation to his flock. It may be said safely that very few ministers know anything about real pastoral visitation. In the cities and larger towns such visitation is often largely of a conventional social character."[26]

Ministers have been too perfunctory without persuading themselves or the people among whom they minister that to them the call to the ministry and the performance of the ministerial work is a high privilege, worthy of all consecration and devotion. Today, if ever, we should open our eyes to the vistas of opportunity and the golden harvest of troubled souls waiting for the reaper who represents Jesus Christ, the spiritual and physical healer of life.

> "The opportunity of the clergyman has come. He can bring a divinely human Bible as the ground of his faith and appeal. He can bring the Lord, the Healer, not a dumb and deaf and blind principle, but a loving Father, to the help of his needy children. He can bring the real Christ of the New Testament — Emmanuel — God with us, to speak again the words, and give again the touch, and extend the hand, to those possessed with the demons of unrest, disquiet, and bodily ills."[27]

This is the high calling of the minister, and he should not fail to appreciate this blessed opportunity, utilizing it to the full advantage of blessing, service, and the joy he can bring to himself and others.

The minister, more than any other worker, has the golden opportunity of being able to seek out his parishioner when he senses a problem or when he seeks to improve the conduct of such a person. The physician must wait till his patients come to him, but the pastor has the privilege and the responsibility of shepherding the fold. To him the opportunity and the challenge of complete shepherding is a Biblical commission of the Lord. At any time, within the limits of common sense, and in any reasonable circumstance, the pastor need not apologize for approaching his member and discussing spiritual matters with him. The pastor is in control of the situation. He can direct the thought he wishes to advance. This is an enviable position. No psychiatrist in the world has this opportunity.

Furthermore, the minister has the opportunity of presenting spiritual truth of therapeutic value to this person on Sunday when he brings God's message through sermon or suggested hymns. All the power of the minister can be brought to play on the life of the individual. His knowledge of human affairs, his perception about human nature, his insight into situations, his intuition for remedy, and his spiritual application by means of the Bible, can be used

26. Samuel Fallows, *Health and Happiness, or Religious Therapeutics and Right Living*, Third edition, A. C. McClurg & Co., Chicago, 1909, p. 84.
27. Ibid, pp. 78, 79.

by the minister for the benefit of the individual. Both on Sunday when he preaches to this person in his audience, and during the week in the conference hour or in the man's home, the minister has the golden leverage of bringing mental and spiritual health through Jesus Christ. The minister is the sole judge when he wants to apply his technique, and the situation is in his hand. The minister has a coveted opportunity in working with people, and we do well to cultivate the proper attitude in cherishing it.

The attitude of the minister must also be correct in relation to his opportunity in exercising practical psychotherapy. The minister's work is the cure of souls. While he may and should help his people in the time of trouble, his main solution to this and all other problems in the lives of his people, is the salvation of souls for eternity through the blood of Jesus Christ. It is his work to see that people are helped socially and that through their circumstances God's people are developed into wholesome conduct to meet the sociological adjustments of our generation. But most important of all, the pastor must maintain the attitude of shepherding his sheep toward a full experience of Jesus Christ and His saving power. Only when this attitude is cultivated by the pastor can the minister work harmoniously with the doctor. Only when he is true to his commission, can the minister be called a worthy professional man, of equal rank with the doctor.

The attitude of the minister must also be checked with respect to his habits and practices of dealing with people.

> "The techniques of the clergyman in the sickroom or in the privacy of his own office need to be examined in the light of modern knowledge of personality in health and illness."[28]

This is good advice, because so often the minister does things a certain way because he has been taught to do so and he has never changed just because he despises changing. In order to stay fresh in the technique of his work, he, like doctors, must constantly study to stay abreast of the times, and to keep in touch with the newer techniques of service.

The pastor should welcome the advice of the doctor. The pastor must stand by the decision of the physician regarding the case, without placing the obstacle of a questioning attitude and criticism on the matter. The pastor ought to have the highest regard for his mutual friend, the physician in the case. He should consult the physician and open the door to a friendly companionship. Never should he release the fundamental conviction that Christianity is the final hope of the patient. The minister must have the conviction of C. H. Valentine who said:

> "The individual who is convinced that apart from religion, psychology cannot help him, is fundamentally right. He may be mistaken in what he understands to be religion, but in a deep sense, and in a sense that psychology is coming more and more to recognize, religion is the only cure."[29]

---

28. Carroll A. Wise, *Religion in Illness and Health*, (Second Edition), Harper & Brothers, New York and London, 1942, p. 255.
29. Cyril H. Valentine, *The Treatment of Moral and Emotional Difficulties*, Student Christian Movement Press, Ltd., London, 1937, p. 41.

Such a conviction will cultivate the proper attitude within the mind and life of the minister. Having the real blessing of spiritual life, and possessing that which the physician usually does not claim, the minister should not be boastful. With that kind of attitude, he would disturb the doctor and frustrate a real spirit of coöperation. The minister should know his spiritual wares, and he should understand that the doctor has a specific place to play in the administration of the physical and mental life of the individual. Every pastor should study the chapter, "What the Doctor is Like," in the book, *The Art of Ministering to the Sick*,[30] by Cabot and Dicks. This short chapter will give insight and understanding regarding the work of the doctor and it will help the minister to cultivate the correct attitude over against the physician of the body.

2. *The Minister Must Overcome the Preaching Complex*

Preaching is very important and absolutely essential to the ministry. This is commanded by our Lord in the Bible,[31] and is an integral part of the minister's ordination vows. This writing is not a brief for the neglect of preaching, because one of the causes of our anemic times is the very lack of efficient, dynamic, evangelistic-doctrinal preaching. The world needs fervent, spiritual, Biblical preaching because our first problem is sin. We need expositional, evangelistic, doctrinal preaching and the minister must give himself to this unreservedly. We must have preaching which presents the whole counsel of God. The Bible must be presented in all its fullness and evangelical warmth. But withal the pastoral viewpoint must not be lacking — for only as this emphasis permeates our preaching, can it be real preaching for conversion and Christian living through our Lord Jesus Christ. Our Lord was sympathetic, understanding, congenial, and spiritually warm toward all people. Christ was "moved with compassion," when he saw the people as sheep without a shepherd.[32] Christ has the pastor heart. Paul followed this custom with great success, and the ministers of the Christian church down through the corridors of history who have demonstrated the pastor heart, have moved people and stirred communities.

This does not mean that preaching must become a sentimentalism with experience centered messages. It does mean that we must base our sermons on the Bible and fuse them with experience so that they will speak to the individual in the pew. Biblical preaching with doctrinal content and evangelical warmth is still the spiritual diet which the minister must furnish in every message he presents to his people, whether from the pulpit to the entire congregation or to an individual as a person to person communication. Such messages must have a deep devotional tone and a sympathetic touch that will impel people to claim them as their own. The "feeling" of the minister must be reflected in his message, and the attitude of the minister will be molded by experience — his own and those of his people. God's word will have a new meaning, and shed a new

---

30. Richard C. Cabot and Russell L. Dicks, *The Art of Ministering to the Sick*, The Macmillan Co., New York, 1937, pp. 45-51.
31. Luke 9:60, Matthew 28:19, 20, I Corinthians 1:21, II Timothy 4:2.
32. Matthew 9:36.

light on all who hear. And the minister will reveal a pastor heart — a character-istic which is essential to successful service in the kingdom of God.

Psychology gives us concepts for a better understanding of the individual. Medical science helps us see the problems of the human body and the importance of health. The profession of the ministry ought to sense these elements with a spiritual emphasis so that we come to realize and cherish the pastor heart. With such a presentation and with that attitude we will say with Paul as pastor and people,

> "What? know ye not that your body is the temple of the Holy Ghost which is in you, which ye have of God, and ye are not your own? For ye are bought with a price: therefore glorify God in your body, and in your spirit, which are God's."[33]

This attitude is closely allied to our attitude over against the members of the congregation. We must have a "soul consciousness" which reflects itself in an individual relationship with our people. The doctor sees people one by one, and the minister should likewise see his people as distinct individuals. In our professional attitude as ministers, particularly when we preach, we generally fail to see and sense this. We look upon the congregation as an "audience" that needs "to be preached to." When we stand before them we should be deeply mindful of individual needs, and individual blessings. We should sense somehow that there is a composite whole, a combined need, and yet we should also feel the independent tributaries to such combined and corporate need. We should speak to the "audience" as though we were speaking to each individual soul by himself. The INDIVIDUAL seeks after God, according to Psalm 28:1,2, and the INDIVIDUAL must have this searching satisfied. The pastor stands before such an individual to minister to him, and to serve as the channel through which flows the blessing the person craves.

Our "preaching complex" must be removed. We must feel the love of God flowing through our message so that it is more than a "take it or leave it" proposition. It should become a must for our people because of an impelling challenge from God through us. All of this is very important for the minister on Sunday when he preaches, and of equal significance when he visits his people, particularly the sick and the afflicted.

Exactly at this point, doctors have objected to the attitude of the ministers. Too often pastors have preached to their patients in the sick room. Far too frequently the pastor does all the talking in the sick room and does not so much as give the patient a chance to respond or to "talk out" concerning his experience. One illustration from actual life, told me by an eye witness of the experience, is that of a minister preaching his Sunday sermon to a polio victim in the busy and noisy corridor of an overcrowded hospital. The sermon was more than a half-hour in length and dealt with the betrayal of Judas. To be sure there were some applications of God's word appropriate to that patient; but the "preaching complex" had so seized that minister that he could not refrain from preaching on such an occasion and under very strange

---

33. I Corinthians 6:19, 20.

circumstances. A short devotional message, particularly adapted to the individual would have been far better. If the individual was to be edified by an entire sermon, then certainly a better message could have been chosen, and a more opportune time. This is but one illustration of the preaching complex with which ministers are often afflicted.

Ministers, we must preach—that is our calling—but in our preaching we must indicate that we seek to reach individuals with the blessed and satisfying result of knowing and loving Christ. Our preaching complex often leads to a procedure which may be compared to turning a garden hose on a number of milk bottles in the hope that some water will run into the bottles. Under certain conditions it may be necessary and wise to go over to each milk bottle and pour some water in carefully, watchfully, and with individual attention. If we follow his technique in dealing with individuals, we can coöperate more properly with the doctor and so apply more effectively the principles of an improved pastoral psychology.

3. *The Minister Must Not Pose as a Psychiatrist*

While we have emphasized in this thesis that the minister should study psychology for its benefits, and psychiatry for its help to pastoral psychology, we make the firm assertion that the minister himself should not play the role of a psychiatrist, pretending to be more or other than his calling requires. We face this temptation, particularly if we have a strong interest in psychology.

> "Some ministers have become so engrossed by the needs of the maladjusted that they have stepped into the field of psychiatry. I believe that every minister should have a background knowledge of psychiatry. Very few of them should try to become psychiatrists. This is a very highly developed profession."[34]

The minister must recognize at the very outset that psychiatry belongs to the medical field and not to the discipline of theology.

> "A psychiatrist is a physician who has specialized in what are known loosely as nervous and mental disorders . . . As an adjective it has been used in other connections recently, notably in the case of 'psychiatric social worker.' But as a noun it should still be reserved for the physician who specializes in mental disorder."[35]

We must remember the distinct sphere and method of activity between the doctor theological and doctor medical. The minister is not a psychiatrist either by training or by calling; this belongs to the medical department of study and practice.

Although the minister should not be a psychiatrist himself, he still has a direct relation to the technique and purpose of psychiatry. J. S. Bonnell gave the proper distinction when he wrote:

34. William H. Leach, *The Making of the Minister*, Cokesbury Press, Nashville, 1938, p. 130.
35. H. Bone, "Personality Reconstruction," *Christianity and Mental Hygiene*, Committee on Religion and Health, Federal Council of the Churches of Christ in America, New York, 1939, p. 11.

"Pastoral psychiatry is the ministry of pastors directed to the healing of the soul. It is distinguished from the practice of the psychiatrist and the physician by the fact that the pastor works to bring his parishioner into contact with God and the spiritual resources that flow from him. A minister devoted to the service of God has neither the intention nor the desire to limit himself to the work of either the psychiatrist or the physician."[36]

The intriguing challenge of this field of study has led many ministers to attempt psychiatry in a semi-professional way. They forget that the ministry is greater than psychiatry, and that they have no right to make psychiatry a substitute for our ministry. We should avoid becoming so interested in psychiatry that we lose the theme and thrust of our ministry. When we wade to depths beyond our swimming ability, we jeopardize our profession. It certainly is true, even as J. D. Mulder, M.D., wrote, "The field of psychiatry is large, obscure, and full of difficult problems, even to the specialist."[37]

On the other hand, the minister must know enough about psychiatry to recommend a good psychiatrist to his people when necessary. He should know something of the symptoms of the various mental and physical troubles so that he can direct people properly. Often under the pressure of duties, the minister cannot give sufficient time to the complete study of individual cases. Yet, he should be willing to sacrifice time and effort in order to be of coöperative service to the doctor. When the minister sees an inextricable tangle of moral, mental, physical and spiritual factors, he should know sufficiently well how to take care of the spiritual phase of the patient's trouble, and then he should be willing to refer the patient to other professional persons for assistance in the complete recovery program.

This does not require some miracle knowledge of supernatural power. It simply means that the man of God who seeks to pastor his people in the ways of normal Christian living, should know when the patient needs advice and vitamins from the doctor, and when such an individual needs to go to a psychiatrist. Naturally the minister should also know when the individual is most in need of spiritual vitamins from the Bible; and that when this is the real problem, the individual need not be sent to the physicians for either a mental or a physical examination. The spiritual needs are always present, but the point is that the needs of the body and the mind may be proportionately greater at given times and under peculiar circumstances.

The real point in question is whether the pastor will approach this problem with a scientific-spiritual combination viewpoint, or whether he is going to continue as the church too often has done in the past — to deal with the combined serious problems of human nature in a superficial and half-hearted manner. This does not disparage the excellent service that has been done by many of God's pastors. It does bring into judgment those who have refused to approach this scientific age without a scientific approach to pastoral psychology.

---

36. John Southerland Bonnell, *Pastoral Psychiatry*, Harper & Brothers Publishers, New York, 1938, p. 199.

37. Jacob D. Mulder, *Psychiatry for Pastors, Students and Nurses*, Wm. B. Eerdmans Publishing Co., Grand Rapids, 1939, p. 12.

We forget as Christian leaders that we have the key to the problems of our day. We have the theology which is necessary for our consumptive world condition, we have the Bible which is the spiritual powerhouse of faith, and we have the technique which can bring our Christian way of life to individuals in the proper way. Our shame is that we have not put our technique to practice.

The twofold technique of W. L. Northridge is in essence the position maintained in this book and particularly in this chapter. In meeting people who came for consultation, he always asked whether they had seen a doctor to determine whether there was anything organically wrong. If they had not been to a doctor, he would require them to do so before talking with him. In this way he used the physician to do the proper work which is his responsibility, and thus he maintained a friendship with the doctors. Northridge also advised,

"A knowledge of the characteristic symptoms of the most common types of mental and nervous diseases is, in our opinion, most essential for ministers if pastoral work is to be efficiently done."[38]

4. *The Minister Must Have Proper Bearing*

One could say that the minister must have proper appearance, for this is a vital part of what we mean by "proper bearing." Appearance does much to give tenor and atmosphere. But having a "proper bearing" for the minister means more; it includes the entire emphasis and influence of the man of God. The influence of the pastor depends so much on the impression he makes with his people. This does not refer to the initial impression through demonstration and suave conduct, but to the real impression that continues through the years of service and personal contacts. We sense a difference. When some ministers enter the presence of the sick, or move about with other professional men, one can immediately sense that a man of God has entered the room. Not what he says, or even the character of his tone of voice, but the sum total of things for which he stands, and the principles by which he lives make him important and distinctive. This is pastoral psychology in action.

More can be done and undone by the personal bearing of the pastor than a year of preaching or many visits and consultations. The sick are particularly sensitive to this. When one is sick, or in sorrow he is super-sensitive to the real and the genuine. It seems as if one's emotions are laid bare and one feels the difference in persons who come to visit. Immediately and almost instinctively, one can feel the devotion of the minister whose personal bearing is firm, steadfast, reserved, and yet sympathetic, outreaching, understanding, and full of kindness with love.

A minister does not cultivate this without having some talent for it. Yet, he can do more to cultivate this spirit than one might think. The older generation of ministers simply called a man with such personal characteristics "a person of talent"; and such he is. But it is more than just talent, because even the man with this talent will do much, devotionally and spiritually, con-

---

38. W. L. Northridge, *Health for Mind and Spirit*, The Abingdon Press, New York, p. 15.

sciously or unconsciously, to develop that talent. For such bearing and conduct will necessitate the elimination of arrogance and the "know it all" spirit. It will require a purging of the inner life. All professionalism must disappear, and the true profession of the pastor must rise to the surface, so that everyone, including the attending physician, will welcome the presence of the pastor. A holy hush of welcome and expectancy steals over the patient when that kind of a pastor comes into the room for consultation and prayer. It involves the person of the pastor, though it means more than just his person. It includes his technique, though it is more than technique. It is so difficult to describe, yet we all know it when we see it in action.

N. B. Harmon came close to a description of it when he quoted the good rule of a Dr. Osler of Baltimore, from an address of the medical man to young doctors:

> "Imperturbability means coolness and presence of mind under all circumstances, calmness amid storm, clearness of judgment in moments of peril, immobility, impassiveness . . . The physician who has the misfortune to be without it, who betrays indecision and worry, and who shows that he is flustered and flurried in ordinary emergencies, loses rapidly the confidence of his patients."[39]

From this rule for doctors, Harmon concluded, "If this be a good rule for the doctors medicae, it applies equally well to doctors theologiae."[40]

J. S. Bonnell quoted D. Saleeby, a well-known eugenist, who stated the same thing in another way,

> "There ought to be a difference even in the way a physician rings a doorbell and walks into a home. His proved medical skill is a source of the confidence he inspires."[41]

That is the point we wish to make. If the medical man must display "imperturbability" and "confidence," certainly the minister should demonstrate such security and faith in providence and the God of all things. The bearing of the minister is very important. The very conduct, the very atmosphere he carries with him and leaves with the home, the fragrance of his counsel and the way he does things, should mark the minister as one who is different. We do not mean that he should be considered sacred and of hierarchial standing by means of dress or intonation, ceremony or tradition. No, the minister himself must be different. With a devotional tone, born of a rich faith in God, the pastor should have a personal bearing which make people feel that with him come the spiritual breezes from heaven, the rich promises of God, and the personality of a man who first of all believes and lives the gospel in his heart and life.

---

39. Nolan B. Harmon, Jr., *Ministerial Ethics and Etiquette*, Cokesbury Press, Nashville, 1928, p. 93.

40. Ibid.

41. John Southerland Bonnell, *Psychology for Pastor and People*, Harper & Brothers Publishers, New York, London, 1948, p. 146.

5. *The Minister Must Have Purposed Conversation*

This is closely associated with the personal bearing of the minister, because usually the way he talks and the things he says represent the man as he really is. The technique of pastoral conversation needs to be studied and exercised with care and skill. The medical doctor does this; he guards his words, he is careful about what he tells the patient, and he is always professional in his contacts with his people. Pastoral psychology has a technique for pastoral conversation which is in direct relation to the coöperation which should exist between doctor and minister.

Previously, and even now, a minister often approached a consultation or a visit, and thought, "If only I can get started to talk, the rest will follow." Usually it has followed, because of the versatility of the minister, and thanks to the Holy Spirit who makes up for our deficiencies at many places, the visit and consultation was completed with a fair degree of success. But today with specialists in every field, we as ministers should strive for better conversation with our people. If we are to be considered on an equal professional basis with the doctors, we do well to give heed to our manner of communication. One thing is needful for us to remember in this regard. We must begin with people where they are, and not from where we came or the way we look at life.

> "The minister has to take sick people where he finds them and work up the ladder rung by rung. In some respects they may be many rungs ahead of him. People are dull in one line and sharp in another, strong in certain muscles and paralyzed in others close beside them. So it is with their spiritual powers, that is with their impulse to size up life as a whole and steer for the best in sight. They are superstitious in one matter and sensible in another, perhaps one where the minister himself is weak. He will be especially keen to find points of superiority in the patient and to learn from him. Nothing heals sick minds more than serving others."[42]

Exactly at this point we pastors fail to begin our work properly. We often have little or no personal experience with sick people and our techniques are very poor. I have watched the techniques of ministers in my sick room and discovered the difference. So often pastors begin with the sick from the elevation of the outside world or the particular experience of the visitors themselves, instead of where the patient is and his experiences of the last days and weeks. Our conversation is forced upon the patient, and it is fused with personal feelings and often complaints about life. We so often look down on people rather than viewing them on our level and from their experience point of view.

In order to carry on proper conversation with the patient, one must know the attitude and condition of the sick room. We should consult the family before we enter the private room of the afflicted, or we should contact the attending nurse in the hospital; and it will be surprising how it will give point to pastoral conversation, and new life to the patient. Then, too often we have that attitude of "all will be well," regardless of the actual condition of the patient. S. Hiltner gave good advice in this regard when he wrote:

---

42. Cabot and Dicks, op. cit., p. 178.

"The emotion and attitude of the patient must be accepted before one can proceed. It does no good and sometimes much harm to tell the patient that everything is going to be all right, if he feels despondent about his condition. That merely cuts the minister off from any real chance to help. The basic attitude may not be evident at first; much of it will be in that 'unconscious' area which cannot be comprehended without deductions from little signs that are perceptible. But unless one accepts the basic attitude of the patient as a fact, it will be impossible to establish contact."[43]

The intimate relation which the pastor is trying to establish with the patient through conversation is very important for the individual and of particular interest to the physician. Unless the pastor senses this, his visit will not be complete or really accomplished. The technique to accomplish this will come through the spiritual life and interest of the pastor. Whether the conversation takes place by telephone, or whether it is a face to face contact, the understanding and sympathy of a pastor are very important. So often pastors at the conclusion of a visit heave a sigh of relief and think or say, "Another call is done; there are so many more to do." But was the call really "done," or just performed in the traditional manner?

This matter of purposeful conversation from the viewpoint of the patient is of tremendous importance for effective pastoral consultation. It represents a technique which the doctor is quick to notice and the patient is sensitive to experience. It is an integral part of the coöperation between minister and doctor. When a minister knows how to converse with people, when through that conversation he reflects the light and life of Jesus Christ, and he carries and clothes it in the best technique of pastoral psychology, there will be a new coöperation between minister and doctor. The doctor will call for the service of such a minister because he knows its therapeutic effect on the patient. Under God, a new blessing will come to patient, minister and doctor, because such coöperation results in spiritual, scientific and psychological coördination.

43. Seward Hiltner, *Religion and Health*, The Macmillan Co., New York, 1943, p. 230.

CHAPTER XV

Commissioned Spiritual Ambassadors

IN THIS volume we have been discussing the interchange and interplay of psychology and pastoral theology. At times we examined one branch of learning, and at other places along the way of our investigation we explored the benefits of the other, but always we sought for a proper union, a pooling of interests and a coördination of efforts in order to come to the proper formulation and technique of pastoral psychology. Just a blending of the benefits of both sciences in itself will not produce a proper pastoral psychology; nor will the absorption of the essence and technique of both produce a perfect pastor. It takes more than that, because the work outlined by pastoral psychology is more than a science and a method. It has a spirit and a goal.

Having discussed the interflow of pastoral theology and psychology into the stream of pastoral psychology, we must seek to understand something of the goal and purpose of spiritual ministers commissioned to do Christ's work on earth. We come now to place the capstone in the arch of our study of pastoral psychology. On both sides of the doorway we have built ascending stones so that pastoral psychology might rest and be built on the highest and best in the two sciences of pastoral theology and psychology. Now that we are ready to place the capstone, we should see its character, its beauty, its strength and its necessity. The title of this capstone chapter is, "Commissioned Spiritual Ambassadors." There are three characteristics of this subject which demand our interest and consecration, and the first is,

A. The Minister Must Know God

The first requisite of the writer and practitioner of pastoral psychology is that he must know God. To the Bible believing Christian this is simple, grand, and necessary. To many others reading these lines it will appear as a naive conjecture, and a futile technique for the efficient working of pastoral psychology. The point must be well taken, because we can have many ideas about God, we may even define our concept about God in a way that would be acceptable to many interpreters and still not be right with God ourselves. Many modern writers of pastoral work will ridicule the plea of this chapter, and yet it must be considered fundamental to the construction and technique of a sound pastoral psychology.

The success of real pastors in the history of pastoral theology reflects their relation to God as persons. It was so in Bible times. Elijah knew God and talked with the Lord during his ministry.[1] John the Baptist spent his time in the wilderness and fellowshipped with God in order to know Him and be known by Him.[2] This gave him a fearlessness and a technique all of his own. Paul was captivated by Jesus Christ[3] and this moved and moulded his life and ministry — making it dynamic, devotional and determined.

This is the kind of ministry we must have today or our construction and technique of pastoral psychology will be of no avail. The capstone of our knowing God personally with a radiant faith and a resolute confidence is absolutely essential to a successful ministry. Something has to happen to us; we must be born-again ministers of Jesus Christ, or we can never really describe the necessity of the rebirth for others. This rebirth is not only a requirement to enter the kingdom,[4] it is fundamental to an ongoing ministry. We must be part of the working of God's Holy Spirit, or we might as well close shop. Fellowship and companionship with the Spirit gives us the dynamic of service. We must know the Spirit to be really successful in the Christian ministry. Sad to say, just as in Bible times, there are some who do not know that the Holy Spirit has come.[5] Pastoral psychology, in order to be properly applied, must be in the hands of ministers who believe in the blood bought redemption of Jesus Christ,[6] and in the Pentecostal ministry of the Holy Spirit as the supporting, sustaining, and culminating blessing on the ministry.[7]

The ministry must move by this power and by this energy. It may be argued that this is only religious palaver and cannot stand up to scientific study and analysis. Over against such a false conception B. Conde asserts the following:

> "Out of the depths of the unconscious life within us the Spirit brings ᴛ. our memory those things which will guide us to the life of spiritual victory. It is not a theory but an experience, which the best men and women of countless generations have known as the secret of their power to live like Jesus Christ. It is the miracle of the Christian religion. Just as Jesus transcended human life by the God within Him, so we too may pass from death to life and immortality by receiving as a child the gift of God's Spirit. By it we live in perfect unity with the whole universe, bound by love to the heart of God and to all humanity."[8]

This is the secret of Christian living, and the secret of a Christian pastor. If one's heart is tuned to God, and if one knows God as He really is, as far as we can know Him, then he is in a position to practice pastoral psychology. Without it he is lost, condemned, unclean, and without the worth of Christ's

---

1. I Kings 17, 18, 19.
2. Matthew 3.
3. II Corinthians 10:5, Philippians 3, 4, Colossians 3.
4. John 3:1-16.
5. Acts 19:2.
6. Luke 22:20, I Corinthians 11:25, Acts 20:28, Romans 5:9, Ephesians 1:7, Colossians 1:14, 1 Peter 1:19.
7. Acts 2:4, 6:3, 10:44, 15:28, Titus 3:5, II Peter 1:21.
8. Bertha Conde, *What's Life All About?* Charles Scribner's Sons, New York, London, 1931, pp. 113, 114.

salvation. We must come back to the Biblical conception of sin, salvation and service for the Christian minister. This goes beyond the mere person of the pastor though it is an integral part of his personality. Inside, way down below the depth, the heart, mind and life of the individual must know God and be led by the Holy Spirit to a greater knowledge and greater life with God. We cannot do this of ourselves, we are dependent on God for this revelation and affirmation.[9]

Knowing God, we will know the sufficiency of His plan of salvation for lost humanity. This is part of the capstone for pastoral psychology. This will take care of the mind cure, the cure for Christian living, and the cure for sin. This is the heart of pastoral psychology, because it is the gospel which we believe. It is the only way to be saved and happy.[10] If we have that faith and confidence we are ready to meet a world with pastoral psychology because then we know God and His answer to the needs of the world. Too many are prescribing a technique that does not include such a grand and glowing reality, fully based on the Bible. Only this can satisfy the human heart,[11] and only with this kind of faith, knowing God, dare we face our dangerous generation. In the language of W. A. Sadler,

> "If you are in need of a mind cure, if you are looking for a religious mind cure, turn not to a strange god or newfangled modern cult; but if you need the Balm of Gilead for your soul and spiritual consolation for your mind, get a religion that will not only heal your body just as well as any of these newfangled cults, but get a religion that also promises to do something for your soul, ever in the great beyond, in the sweet by and by, where you need no more healing for the body. And that religion, in my opinion, is not something new and modern psychic phantasma, but the simple, old-fashioned Gospel of the Lord, Jesus Christ."[12]

This is the heart of the matter. The essence of the Bible for the application to all of life is found in this quotation. That is pastoral psychology as it should be, a firm belief in God, a thrust in Christ's salvation, and the "old-fashioned gospel" for lost sinners. No wonder W. S. Sadler continued the clarion call of knowing God when he said:

> "Call a halt in this business of taking a page out of psychology to start a new religion: taking the heart out of the teachings of Jesus Christ to start a commercial system of religious mind cure."[13]

If one really knows God he will not substitute psychology for the religion of Christ Jesus, he will use the benefits of psychology for the application of Christianity. Therefore the minister who seeks to practice pastoral psychology must know God. Too many people are like Israel of old — they do not really know God;[14] they are not waiting to perceive God's presence and power.[15]

---

9. I Corinthians 2:7-16.
10. Acts 4:12.
11. Psalm 42:5, 62:1, 2.
12. William A. Sadler, *The Truth About Mind Cure*, A. C. McClurg & Co., Chicago, 1929, p. 206.
13. Ibid., p. 205.
14. Isaiah 1:3.
15. Psalm 46:10.

We know the way even as Thomas if we will only look and see.[16] Then we will come to know Christ as our personal redeemer,[17] and we will know the certainty of His return.[18] This is the full requirement laid upon the ambassador of Christ. If we have these Biblical elements, then we are spiritual — in the calling and developing of our faith, in the challenge and the consumation of our ministry through pastoral psychology.

B. *The Minister Must Know Himself*

We have written concerning the importance of knowing God in order to be effective instruments of pastoral psychology. Part of knowing God is knowing ourselves. The complete technique of pastoral psychology includes the spiritual technique of knowing one's self. Proper self examination of God's grace and revelation should lead us to exclaim as David did in his song of repentence,[19] and to cry out with Isaiah:

> "Woe is me for I am undone: because I am a man of unclean lips, and I dwell in the midst of a people of unclean lips: for mine eyes have seen the King, the Lord of hosts."[20]

The minister cannot understand repentance and faith, sin and salvation, unless he has experienced it in his own heart and life. The pastor cannot come to grips with life in the experiences of others, unless he has seen himself in the light of God's word. He must know himself, how weak and frail he is, full of evil inclinations and a tendency to do wrong. Likewise, Paul, though a wonderful servant of Christ, an ambassador of the first order, and a leader of men, confessed that he was "chief" among sinners,[21] one who knew the power of sin and the release that comes through Jesus Christ.[22]

It has been said correctly that the biggest problem of the parishioner is to have him know himself. When he comes to see himself as God sees him, in the light of God's Word,[21] he is humble, pliable, teachable, and fit for the kingdom of God. This is certainly true of the servants of the Lord, His ministers. They, too, must know themselves under the close scrutiny of the Word of God by the direction of the Holy Spirit. Only when Paul knew his sin and uselessness, could he become strong in the Lord.[23] God's servants must likewise sense this self examination of heart, mind and life. We must pray for this like the Psalmist,[24] because then we will be consecrated in service for Christ Jesus. This means full surrender and with it a belief in the redeeming victorious work of Christ. When we know ourselves in this light, then we will have the fortitude and the grace to labor on for Christ and His kingdom.[25]

---

16. John 14:4-14.
17. II Timothy 1:12.
18. I John 3:2.
19. Psalm 50:10-12.
20. Isaiah 6:5.
21. I Timothy 1:15.
22. Romans 7, 8.
23. Romans 4:20, II Corinthians 12:10.
24. Psalm 139:23, 24.
25. I Corinthians 15:58, Ephesians 5:1, 2, Philippians 3:13, 14.

All of this self knowledge is very beneficial for our relationship to God and to fellowmen. One can sense the difference immediately in those who practice the fellowship with God and those who merely "tip the hat" to this kind of devotional consecration. It will help us come to maturity of Christian faith. Such experience will season us and prepare us for a richer, fuller ministry among God's people.

This is not only true of spiritual leadership in relation to spiritual dependence upon God, it is also true on the level of sympathy and understanding which comes through experience. R. C. Cabot, M.D., said:

> "If I had my way, I would see to it that every doctor, nurse, social worker and clergyman became seriously ill themselves. They'd know something about their jobs then."[26]

And R. L. Dicks, wrote,

> "Out of suffering comes maturity of soul and the need to help others who suffer. It is doubtful if any person reaches a depth of living, an appreciation for life, a spiritual quietness and poise, without suffering — the type of suffering whether it be pain, fear, guilt, feelings, loneliness, does not matter."[27]

I can testify that Cabot and Dicks have spoken the truth in the foregoing quotations. Not till one becomes desperately ill, and at the point of death, does one really know the realities of life. Then he comes to see himself in the light of God's revelation, a poor, condemned, unclean sinner in need of divine redemption. Then the glow of his ministry is seen in its proper balance, then the service which he has rendered comes to set itself forth through grace, and one feels the tenderness of God. Then in reality he knows himself, his weakness, his fraility, his human nature, and his real ambitions. The temporary and the trivial soon taper off; the real and the lasting remain. Each day lived after that is a fresh gift from God, fully appreciated and fully utilized for Christ's glory. Then he can minister to others, because he knows their thoughts, their inner struggles, their worries, and their temptations.

I thought I was sympathetic before I was seriously ill. I thought my ministry to others was one of understanding because I sought to feel what they felt, and those who received my ministry characterized me as sympathetic and kindly. But the difference between my feeling then and now, is the difference between daylight and night. Automatically I sense the sufferers pain and poverty of strength. Physical frustration, mental exhaustion, and moral futility, outside of the grace of Christ is plainly evident when one has been in the valley himself. Cabot was right — only when one has gone through the valley himself, can he really understand others when they pass through. Seeing it in others without personal experience does much, but it does not give the finishing touch of self-examination, self-knowledge, and self-condemnation. Going through the valley one learns not to say, "Lord, restore me," or "Grant

---

26. Russell L. Dicks, *Pastoral Work and Personal Counseling*, The Macmillan Co., New York, 1945, p. 145.
27. Ibid.

me all these needed things," but one comes to pray, "Lord, show me what you want me to do, and give me grace to do it." Then you come to really know yourself, and come to the point of absolute surrender.

This does not mean to say that all pastors who have not personally trod the path of sorrow are devoid of sympathy and understanding of others. But even the best and most talented of God's servants, understanding as they seem to be, do not really know the full technique of the Holy Spirit with human hearts, nor the technique of talking to the sick and afflicted unless they themselves have gone through the experience. We do not really know ourselves until we are completely "undressed" before the Lord. We are so important when we walk around and greet each other. We appear to be so significant when we professionalize and do our work in a perfunctory manner. But, let me inform you that when you are in a hospital bed, dressed in a hospital shirt, with a dreaded disease plaguing your body and mind you come to see yourself as you really should and as you really are — a sinner in need of divine redemption.

Now for the healthy and well, and those who have not faced such serious difficulty, it is worthwhile and necessary to know the real stature of man. J. A. C. Murray has given a good description in the following quotation:

> "It is we ourselves who are maladjusted, and not only the neurotics; we live like strangers, in a new earth, with new heavens above us. Scientific knowledge is creating a hostile environment round the mind, one to which the mind reacts in terms of overstrain and breakdown, simply because we have not begun to know ourselves one hundredth part as well as we know the forces of nature and the face of the stars; a humiliating thought."[28]

This quotation reflects the Biblical viewpoint of man. If we knew ourselves as God knows us, we would see God's portrait of man, recorded by Paul.[29] If we judge ourselves by the standard of the Sermon on the Mount spoken by Jesus, we will discover that we as pastors need to have a spiritual adjustment as well as the neurotics. We are not fit vessels for the Master's use, unless and until we have been cleansed, purified, adjusted, and sanctified for His glory. We cannot be real spiritual ambassadors unless we know the real character of Christian living, and vow to try to live our real thanks to God through victorious service in the name of Christ. We must know ourselves as unworthy servants, if we must deal with God's people.

> "If we have to receive, and deal with, the very worst in our patients, without flinching, we have to be ever mindful of our own dark spots, and walk humbly side by side with him. Too many analyses have been spoiled because the analyst has dealt with patient 'de haut en bas'; judge not, because your patient is your judgment, and if you fail with him, you fail with yourself."[30]

---

28. J. A. C. Murray, *An Introduction to a Christian Psychotherapy*, T. & T. Clark, Edinburgh, 1938, p. 260.

29. Romans 3, 5.

30. Murray, op. cit., p. 261.

Look inside, servant of God, for the Lord often reveals dark spots which we did not notice even when we were told about them. Such was the experience of David.[31] The Bible reveals our wicked tendencies, even though we are walking in the presence of Christ, and claim to give him full allegiance, like Peter who followed from afar.[32] We must know these tendencies in human nature, and we must see ourselves as we really are. Otherwise we are not qualified to be the conveyors of pastoral psychology.

We have a spiritual goal to reach; we have high standards to achieve. We must seek to bring people into living relation with Jesus Christ, our Lord and King. This is the aim of pastoral psychology if it is Biblical. To do this we may not dream or drift. We face a solemn duty in this hour of crisis. To do our task well and for the glory of Christ, we must be humble, we must know ourselves, and we must know how to decrease.

> "If we believe that we are making straight the way for the Creator to come and deal with His creature, we must, like the Baptist, decrease, that He may increase. A Christian analyst, above all men, must keep down, lest he get between God and his ailing child, must be humbly careful of stating his own conclusions, in case his voice overpower a certain still, small sound."[33]

This is the real spirit of the New Testament pastor. It requires a thorough self-examination, and a constant spiritual humiliation before the Christ. This does not mean a false piety, or a sham devotion, but a genuine contrition and a real sense of unworthiness outside of Christ. We come to that when we see the real significance of Christ, and with the Baptist begin to exalt Christ in the following words:

> "I am the voice of one crying in the wilderness, Make straight the way of the Lord, as said the prophet Esaias."[34]
> "I baptize with water: but there standeth one among you, whom ye know not; He it is who coming after me is preferred before me, whose shoe's latchet I am not worthy to unloose."[35]
> "Behold the Lamb of God, which taketh away the sin of the world."[36]

Then we come to a perfect pastoral psychology. The Baptist came to practice it because he knew himself in the light of the glorious Christ whom he introduced. By comparing himself with the spotless Lamb of God, he saw himself in the true light. Then he could be humble, then he was effective, and then he was used of the Lord. His technique with individuals and with the multitude stands as a model of pastoral psychology which is enviable and filled with wonderment. The secret of his success was that he understood his standing and personal relationship to Jesus Christ. Therefore, pastor, know yourself in the light of God's Word and God's Son, for then true pastoral and psychological insight can infiltrate and enable us to do Christ's work as He planned and for His glory. Pastoral psychology demands this of us for a better tech-

---

31. II Samuel 12:1-15.
32. Matthew 26:58.
33. Murray, op. cit., p. 261.
34. John 1:23.
35. John 1:26.
36. John 1:29.

nique. More important still, the Bible demands it of us if we really wish to be ambassadors. It is our solemn duty, and our spiritual requirement.

Then our personal bearing discussed in Chapter XI, pp. 141-144, will be fused with a spirituality, anticipated in that discussion, but now impelled with a commission of personal salvation and stewardship for our high and holy task.

C. The Minister Must Know His Commission

As an ambassador of Jesus Christ it is important that the minister know God and know himself. We have evaluated the same in this chapter. The minister must also be reminded of the sacred commission by which he came into the office and by which his life should be regulated. That is the urge and the impelling power which should drive him forward to practice pastoral psychology. The minister is God's representative on earth. No other stands in such direct relation to God and to God's people as God's servant, set aside and dedicated for this holy purpose. By virtue of his commission from the Lord through the visible agency of the church of which he was a member, the candidate for the ministry received his charge to go forward as a good minister of Jesus Christ. This should enthuse his entire ministry so that he desires to be the best and do the best for his Lord Jesus Christ. This conception and this commission is part of the capstone of pastoral psychology.

Viewing our commission from the Biblical point of view we remember the challenge which came to the early disciples. All of that remains as a divine commission. Jesus gave the first "brief" of that commission in his own words when the twelve were sent forth with power and comfort. Jesus said:

> "Go not into the way of the Gentiles and into any city of the Samaritans enter ye not: but go rather to the lost sheep of the house of Israel.
> "And as ye go, preach, saying, The kingdom of heaven is at hand.
> "Heal the sick, cleanse the lepers, raise the dead, cast out devils: freely ye have received, freely give.
> "Provide neither gold, nor silver nor brass in your purses,
> "Nor scrip for your journey, neither two coats, neither shoes, nor yet staves: for the workman is worthy of his meat."[37]

These words were strange to the disciples, and stranger still to the man of the world because they seemed like idle challenges to a strange and sacrificial task. Jesus predicted in the verses[38] immediately following the above commission, that His followers would be misunderstood, presecuted, scorned, and brought to judgment. He also reminded them that if they remained faithful, they would receive a prophet's reward.[39]

Jesus prepared his apostles for greater service and for a deeper understanding of this commission by training them when they returned from this ministry. Jesus took his followers with Him during His public ministry, through the days of suffering, in the experience of the last days of condemnation, and beyond the resurrection experience so that they might come to perceive what

---

37. Matthew 10:5-11.
38. Matthew 10:11-42.
39. Matthew 10:42.

was the meaning of their position and purpose in life. After the resurrection He appeared unto them to prepare them for His final departure from the earth and for their great task to carry on this commission. Peter found it hard to grasp the full meaning of this commission because he was bold and foolhardy. Jesus knew this, and because of Peter's foolish and cowardly denial in the hour of great witness to fidelity, Jesus taught him the real spirit of the commission when before all the apostles He said, "Simon, son of Jonas, lovest thou me more than these?"[40] Jesus gave this charge three times, and it was a renewal of the commission to the disciples for their service soon to be rendered without the visible presence of Jesus. The charge to Peter and to all of them represented the great spirit of love. Today this challenge holds stimulus for us, because the very secret of practicing pastoral psychology in its full meaning requires the spirit of love, the tact of a genius, and the devotion which Jesus required of His apostles.

At almost every resurrection appearance, Jesus manifested to His followers that they carried the responsibility of going forth to represent Him on the earth. This was the continued thrust of the commission. When the time of His ascension drew near, Christ appointed them to go to Galilee, into a mountain.

> "And Jesus came and spoke unto them, saying, All power is given unto me in heaven and in earth. Go ye therefore, and teach all nations, baptizing them in the name of the Father, and of the Son, and of the Holy Ghost:
> "Teaching them to observe all things whatsoever I have commanded you: and, lo, I am with you alway, even unto the end of the world."[41]

This was the great commission which Jesus gave to His apostles, and which He gives to His servants in our day. The challenge of this commission has never been altered; its ringing call to service remains as the watchword of every called minister of Jesus Christ. This is the greatest commission which could ever be given to any man. Far greater than any portfolio or commanding word from Washington to a delegated ambassador to a foreign country, and of more enduring importance than any high command in military circle, our Lord's commission remains as the challenge of the centuries, given once for all to His followers as the watchword for service. It is the great commission which is the capstone of our pastoral psychology. Without this great commission, there is no need of pastoral psychology, for without it our responsibility and our technique would evaporate into the thin air of man's words.

Jesus outlined the program of carrying out this great commission when He said:

> "It is not for you to know the times or the seasons which the Father hath put in his own power.
> "But ye shall receive power, after that the Holy Ghost is come upon you: and ye shall be witnesses unto me both in Jerusalem, and in all Judea, and in Samaria, and unto the uttermost part of the earth."[42]

---

40. John 21:15.
41. Matthew 28:18-20.
42. Acts 1:7, 8.

This missionary commission found application through the pastoral ministry
of God's great leaders as the program which Jesus outlined was developed in
the early church. Paul practiced this missionary challenge, and as he established
churches gave them the fullness of his ministry. He also was used of the Holy
Spirit to define the Biblical conception of pastoral psychology in the challenge
concerning the ministry which he gave to young Timothy in the following
words:

> "I charge thee therefore before God, and the Lord Jesus Christ, who
> shall judge the quick and the dead at his appearing and his kingdom;
> "Preach the word; be instant in season, out of season; reprove, rebuke,
> exhort with all long-suffering and doctrine.
> "For the time will come when they will not endure sound doctrine; but
> after their own lusts shall they heap to themselves teachers, having itching
> ears:
> "And they shall turn away their ears from the truth, and shall be turned
> unto fables.
> "But watch thou in all things, endure afflictions, do the work of an
> evangelist, make full proof of thy ministry."[43]

These words remind one of the first commission given by Jesus to the apostles
when he sent them forth to do their first work for the kingdom of God. These
words of Paul harmonize perfectly with the spirit and the challenge which
Jesus gave to the apostles in the first commission and in the great commission
when He was about to leave the earth. This is the thrust of pastoral psychology.
We must remember our divine commission as ambassadors of Jesus Christ or
the heart and the hope of success for pastoral psychology will never be realized.

Down through the corridors of history, through the ongoing development of
the Christian church, this ministry has come with the challenge of the commission of Jesus Christ as the compelling urge to serve. This ministry has
appeared in various forms, and with various interpretations depending on the
denominational emphasis and the circumstances of the times. But always the
centrality of God's true servants voiced the consecration of lives wholly dedicated to the thrust of Christ's commission. Only in that power was the gospel
ministry cherished, and only through the grace of God was that ministry rendered unto the glory of Christ Jesus, the commissioning Lord of heaven.

Viewed in the light of our historical survey of pastoral theology, we discovered men of God, moved by the Holy Spirit, consecrated through God's call,
thoroughly victorious in the conception and completion of the gospel ministry.
These men were challenged by the great commission to carry forth the best
kind of ministry they knew. And it should be remembered that the impulse
that moved them, and the driving force that stirred them was the great commission to be spiritual ambassadors of Jesus Christ.

We have made many references to Richard Baxter in this book because he
set the pace for so much of American pastoral theology, and his leadership,
though unknown and unrecognized in that area, has been outstanding for the
real principles and technique of pastoral psychology. He outlined the duty of

---

43. II Timothy 4:1-5.

the minister by quoting from the Directory of the Westminster Assembly about the visitation of the sick:

> "It is the duty of the minister, not only to teach the people committed to his charge in public but privately, and particularly to admonish, exhort, reprove, and comfort them upon all seasonable occasions, so far as his time, strength, and personal safety will permit. He is to admonish them in time of health, to prepare them for death. And for that purpose, they are often to confer with their minister about the estate of their souls."[44]

This represents a breath of knowledge and spirit. It contains all the seed thoughts of present day pastoral psychology, and it carries the very spirit of the great commission of Jesus Christ.

The church today lives by the great commission of Jesus Christ, and ministers in the service of Christ are bound by this commission. The ordination vows which we take as ministers bind us to this requirement. Ministers of constituted churches are bound by the constitutional requirements of their particular church. The traditional churches are alike in their conception of this ministry, and their requirements are similar in creedal statement, in doctrinal requirement and in application of the Spirit to those called for this special service. One reference from a church constitution will indicate how this fundamental requirement of ministers is important for pastoral psychology. The reference is taken from the constitution of the Reformed Church in America, the church of which I am a member and a minister. This part of the constitution, even as that part of the constitution of the church to which you belong, contains the thrust of our pastoral, psychological, spiritual ministry. And all of us should repeat and renew our allegiance to it in order to maintain our ministry in its true spirit. Here is the requirement of the constitution, already mentioned.

> "The office of a minister is to preach the Word of God, and to administer the Sacraments; to watch over his brethren the elders and deacons as well as over the whole congregation, and in conjunction with the elders to exercise Christian discipline; to be careful that all things be done decently and in order. Every minister must consider himself devoted wholly to the Lord Jesus Christ in the service of the Church, and shall faithfully fulfill the obligations of his call in preaching, teaching and visiting his sick. He shall persevere in prayer, be urgent in season and out of season, and by word and example promote always the spiritual welfare of his people."[45]

This is explanatory of the great commission which Jesus left His apostles and servants of all generations. It is a binding commission, and it is spiritual in every part of its original statement and interpreted explanation. This gives depth to pastoral psychology because it is forever binding on the candidate, and it is forever challenging to a life of full service to Jesus Christ. Note how binding the constitution of the previously mentioned denomination, makes the commission for the candidate.

---

44. Richard Baxter, *The Reformed Pastor or the Duty of Personal Labors for Souls of Men.* Revised and abridged by William Brown, American Tract Society, New York, 1829, pp. 80, 81.

45. *The Constitution of the Reformed Church in America*, The Board of Publication and Bible School Work, New York, 1932, Section 7, p. 6.

"Only those persons shall be allowed to exercise the office of a minister who have been inducted into that office by ordination, according to the Word of God and the order established by the Church. No person who has once been ordained shall be at liberty to relinquish the active work of the ministry or to relinquish the office of a minister by demission, unless for reasons of weight concerning which the Classes shall inquire and determine."[46]

In some form or other every candidate for the ministry formally obligates himself to be true to this great challenge. By doing this he asserts that he feels he is called of God to be Christ's servant, thus obligating himself to the great commission as an ambassador of the Word. Only when it is based on the Word of God carrying the commission of Jesus Christ, can our ministry be successful and blessed by the Lord.

We must come back to this conception if we have lost it, and it is a shame to state that many have lost or never possessed a conception of the great commission. Without it we are floundering about without faith for the future. Without it, there can be no construction of principles and technique or pastoral psychology. With this commission we present the gospel of Jesus Christ to a lost world. We must go back to the Bible for our commission and all that it implies: a solid gospel, a stimulating Christ, a consecrated ministry, a consuming zeal for lost souls, and a continuing outpouring of the Holy Spirit. Only then can pastoral psychology be of worth and value for our generation.

The words of W. A. Sadler are very appropriate at this point. He concluded his book, *The Truth About Mind Cure*, in the following way:

"I would, therefore, say this in closing this discussion on mind cure: Since fear is the foundation of nerves and since faith is the only known cure for fear, and since religious faith is the master mind cure, I would therefore make this recommendation — that we call a halt in this business of taking a page out of psychology to start a new religion: taking the heart out of the teachings of Jesus Christ to start a commercial system of religious mind cure; and further, that we call you people back to your long neglected Bibles with their 'exceeding great and precious promises,' wherein is written: 'Cast all your care upon Him, for He careth for you': 'Come unto Me all ye that are weary and heavy laden, and I will give you rest': and that 'He healeth all our diseases': and that you get a new vision of the carpenter's Son, going up and down this world two thousand years ago healing the sick and comforting the afflicted."[47]

Unless this be the message of the commissioned ambassador he has no commission and no message. But we who believe in the New Testament conception of the pastor have a pastoral psychology which emulates the life and technique of the Lord Jesus Christ.

We need the technique of present day scientific investigation to make our pastoral psychology of effective usefulness in the kingdom of God. Every technique we can muster for the glory of God must be studied and used in the service of pastoral work. We have sought to discover these in the formulation of pastoral psychology in this book. Basing our findings on the Scriptures, through an analysis of writings by authors in the field of pastoral theology,

46. Ibid.
47. Sadler, op. cit., p. 205.

we have come to appreciate God's great leaders of the past, and great foundational principles of perennial service in the kingdom of God. In our constructive analysis we sought to analyze and syncronize the findings of the past with the research findings in the field of sickness, suffering, and sorrow. With a new evaluation of the techniques of pastoral psychology, an attempt was made to bring these techniques up-to-date not only but also in line with the fundamental conceptions of pastoral work as outlined in the Bible, particularly by Jesus Christ, the Master of life, of psychology, and of the technique of helping others. The conceptions, principles, and techniques of pastoral psychology, as outlined in this book, stand or fall by this chapter on the capstone of our presentation. If we do not believe in the Biblical conception of "Commissioned Spiritual Ambassadors," our pastoral psychology is of little value in the real help and service needed by man and prescribed by God. To accomplish our technique of pastoral psychology, and to maintain the fundamental Biblical principles which God has given one for all, we must exercise our responsibility and use our talents for the technique of pastoral psychology. But some will say, God's sovereignty must take care of our task, and we are limited in our work and effort. We must remember:

> "God's sovereignty in history is not an opiate for our minds, but an operation for life. Our interpretation of it must not mystify our minds, but mirror the grace of God, miracle the experience of God in history, and move us to march valiantly forward. This does not liquidate the sovereignty of God, but liberates it from the shackles of traditionalism. It does not swerve us from our historic faith but nerves us to propagandize it. This is not only a crucial doctrine, it is the dynamic power which should give us a challenging devotion. We are either constructive or corruptive. God's sovereignty constrains us to be creative Christians. The sovereignty of God is therefore not only a blessing but a battle cry."[48]

We who have a spiritual commission as ambassadors of Christ may not sit still or be slovenly. We have a tremendous task to perform, we have a high calling to fulfill. We need the strength and the stimulus of the Word of God to remind us of sacred responsibility and challenging faith. We may not sit idly by and think that God will bring people into His kingdom without our work and service. God demands our time and talents, as well as our trust. Pastoral psychology will not be effective unless we as ministers of the gospel are interested, enthused, and unswerving in our service.

There is so much need around us, and there are so many opportunities at hand, that we may not fail in this essential responsibility. We should look into the back yard of our own parish and next door in our own experience, to discover that the world is dying for a little bit of love brought with the sympathetic touch of a pastor, and the technique of pastoral psychology. What a privilege we have as Christian pastors, Bible believing and Christianity affirming ministers, to bring our wonderful Christ, "who healeth all our diseases." The

48. William Goulooze, *The Sovereignty of God in History*, The Western Theological Seminary, Holland, 1944, pp. 24, 25.

world needs this gospel brought in the best possible way through the agencies of pastoral psychology.

"The world is sick and in need of a physician, and we know that there is one who is still available for it is the healing of the Great Physician which waits only on the confession of our disability and our faith. The people of our day are bewildered, as sheep that have no shepherd, and the tragedy of it is that the Shepherd and the fold are there."[49]

We are the conveyors of this good news. We as pastors are the commissioned officers of Christ's spiritual army to bring people into an acquaintance of the way of salvation under God's blessing. We have been given the revelation of God, and we carry a holy responsibility to bring it to others. So many have been given a watered gospel and a traditional interpretation. And so many have been fed the cheap diet of a psychological housecleaning which does not give genuine conversion. We must remember our duty because there are contrary winds.

"Conversion is not merely the re-shuffling of the conscious and subconscious motives which determine our conduct. Such an experience might mean an amendment of life, but not the new life in Christ."[50]

As ministers of Jesus Christ, we have the charge to bring the Lord Jesus Christ in His fullness and power to lost people and disturbed individuals. We must show them by the grace of God how to experience genuine conversion, and we must demonstrate the Biblical spirit of Christian living. This is our solemn obligation and task. We are commissioned for this task.

It is not of ourselves that we have chosen to do so; we are divinely called as ambassadors. We should cherish this divine call and exercise our human limited sovereignty of stewardship and service to accomplish it. This must be the goal of our ministry.

"I am a stranger here, within a foreign land;
My home is far away, upon a golden strand;
Ambassador to be of realms beyond the sea,
I'm here on business for my King.

"This is the message that I bring,
A message angels faint would sing:
'Oh, be ye reconciled,'
Thus saith my Lord and King,
'Oh, be ye reconciled to God.' "[51]

This is the spirit of Christ's great commission, and we must catch the vision in order to be true practitioners of pastoral psychology. If you do not agree with this philosophy of the Christian pastor, do not laugh it out of court, because

---

49. W. Fearon Halliday, *Psychology and Religious Experience*, Second Edition, Hodder and Stoughton, Ltd., London, 1929, p. 308.

50. John G. McKenzie, *Modern Psychology and the Achievement of Christian Personality*, The National Sunday School Union, London, no date given, p. 103.

51. E. T. Cassel, *The King's Business*, Hope Publishing Co., Chicago, 1926, p. 196.

in the great day of days, we will be held accountable for this spiritual commission as ambassadors of Jesus Christ. We must therefore be convinced of our commission to be spiritual ambassadors of Jesus Christ. Without this commission our work will be maimed and our message will be missing, and of all men, we will be the most miserable. Without it we will have a profession without power, a service without a Savior, and a job without a real spiritual joy. With it we will have Pentecostal power for a great purpose, and spiritual strength for a great service. This was the motivating power for Paul. He had a message and a method because he was convinced concerning his great spiritual commission as an ambassador of Jesus Christ. Let his words sink down deep into our lives. Hear him say to us:

> "Therefore if any man be in Christ, he is a new creature: old things are passed away; behold, all things are become new.
> "And all things are of God, who hath reconciled us to himself by Jesus Christ, and hath given to us the ministry of reconciliation;
> "To wit, that God was in Christ, reconciling the world unto himself, not imputing their trespasses unto them; and hath committed unto us the word of reconciliation.
> "NOW THEN WE ARE AMBASSADORS FOR CHRIST, as though God did beseech you by us: we pray you in Christ's stead, be ye reconciled to God.
> "For he hath made him to be sin for us, who know no sin; that we might be made the righteousness of God in him."[52]

This is our great commission in action. This is pastoral psychology in its basic principles and its spiritual appeal. This is the capstone of pastoral psychology. We must know ourselves, we must know God, and we must sense our commission as spiritual ambassadorship. Then method and message will bring glory to God — in the church, in the community, in the world and in heaven. Then we will "fulfill" our ministry in bringing Christ to others.

---

52. II Corinthians 5:17-21.

SELECTED BIBLIOGRAPHY

SELECTED BIBLIOGRAPHY

I. The Psychological-Social Crisis

Biederwolf, W. E., *Whipping Post Theology*, W. B. Eerdmans Company, Grand Rapids, 1934.

Case, Shirley Jackson, *The Christian Philosophy of History*, The University of Chicago Press, Chicago, 1943.

Clark, Elmer T., *The Small Sects of America*, Cokesbury Press, Nashville, 1937.

Covert, William Chalmers, *Facing Our Day*, The Abingdon Press, New York, 1934.

Fosdick, Harry Emerson, *Living Under Tension*, Third Edition, Harper & Brothers, New York and London, 1941.

Fosdick, Harry Emerson, *A Great Time to Be Alive*, Harper & Brothers, New York and London, 1944.

Goulooze, William, *The Sovereignty of God in History*, The Western Theological Seminary, Holland, 1944.

Hammond, William A., *Spiritualism and Allied Causes and Conditions of Nervous Derangement*, G. P. Putnam's Sons, New York, 1876.

Harkness, Georgia, *The Dark Night of the Soul*, Abingdon-Cokesbury Press, New York, Nashville, 1945.

Horney, Karen, *The Neurotic Personality of Our Time*, W. W. Norton & Co., Inc., New York, 1937.

Horton, Douglas, *Out Into Life*, The Abingdon Press, New York, Cincinnati, 1924.

Hough, Lynn Harold, *Wither Christianity*, Red Label Reprints, New York, 1929.

Kelly, Robert L., *Theological Education in America*, George H. Doran Co., New York, 1924.

Mackay, John A., *A Preface to Christian Theology*, The Macmillan Co., New York, 1941.

Mackay, John A., *Heritage and Destiny*, The Macmillan Co., New York, 1943.

Martin, John, *From Failure to Fulfillment*, The Macmillan Co., New York, 1948.

Masaryk, T. G., *Modern Man and Religion*, George Allen & Unwin Ltd., London, 1938.

McKenzie, John G., *Nervous Disorders and Character*, Harper & Brothers, New York and London, 1947.

Pitkin, Walter B., *Escape from Fear*, Doubleday, Doran & Co., Inc., New York, 1940.

Sorokin, P. A., *The Crisis of Our Age*, E. P. Dutton and Co., Inc., New York, ...

Sorokin, P. A., *Man and Society in Calamity*, E. P. Dutton and Co., Inc., New York, 1943.

Trueblood, Elton, *Alternative to Futility*, Harper & Brothers, New York and London, 1948.

Trueblood, Elton, *Foundations for Reconstruction*, Harper & Brothers, New York, 1946.

Trueblood, Elton, *The Predicament of Modern Man*, Second Edition, Harper & Brothers, New York, 1944.

Wolfe, W. Beran, *Nervous Breakdown: Its Cause and Cure*, Farrar & Rinehart, New York, 1933.

II. Pastoral Theology

Adams, Hampton, *The Pastoral Ministry*, Cokesbury Press, Nashville, 1932.

Adams, Hampton, *You and Your Minister*, The Bethany Press, St. Louis, 1940.

Agar, Frederick A., *The Minister and His Opportunity*, Fleming H. Revell Co., New York, 1932.

Allnatt, F. J. B., *Studies in Soul Tending*, The Macmillan Co., New York, 1922.

Anderson, Stanley E., *Every Pastor a Counselor*, Van Kampen Press, Wheaton, 1949.

Anderson, William K., Editor, *The Minister and Human Relations*, General Conference Commission on Courses of Study, The Methodist Church, Nashville, 1943.

Anderson, William K., Editor, *Pastor and Church*, The Methodist Publishing House, 1943.

Bailey, Ambrose Moody, *The Pastor in Action*, Round Table Press, Inc., New York, 1939.

Balmforth, Henry; De War, Lindsay; Hudson, Cyril E.; Sara, Edmund S., *An Introduction to Pastoral Theology*, The Macmillan Co., New York, 1937.

Barrett, Alfred, *Essay on the Pastoral Office*, John Mason, London, 1839.

Baxter, Richard, *The Reformed Pastor or the Duty of Personal Labors for Souls of Men*, Revised and abridged by Wm. Brown, American Tract Society, New York, 1829.

Beck, J. T., *Pastoral Theology of the New Testament*, Translated from the German by James A. M'Clymont and Thomas Nicol, Scribner and Welford, New York, 1885.

Bedell, Gregory Thurston, *The Pastor — Pastoral Theology*, J. B. Lippincott & Co., Philadelphia, 1880.

Beebe, James Albert, *The Pastoral Office*, The Methodist Book Concern, New York, 1923.

Bell, G. K. A., *The Modern Parson*, Student Christian Movement, London, 1928.

Benson, C. H., *Techniques of a Working Church*, Moody Press, Chicago, 1946.

Bernard, T. A., *Homiletical and Pastoral Lectures*, A. C. Armstrong and Son, New York, 1880.

Berkhof, L., *Reformed Dogmatics, Vol. II.*, Wm. B. Eerdmans Publishing Co., Grand Rapids, 1932.

Biesterveld, P., *Het Huisbezoek*, J. H. Bos, Kampen, 1900.

Blackwood, Andrew Watterson, *Pastoral Leadership*, Abingdon-Cokesbury Press, New York, 1949.

Blackwood, Andrew Watterson, *Pastoral Work*, The Westminster Press, Philadelphia, 1945.

Blaikie, William Garden, *For the Work of the Ministry*, Strahan & Co., London, 1873.

Bonar, Andrew A., *The Visitors Book of Texts*, Fourth Edition, Robert Carter & Brothers, New York, 1867.

Bridges, Charles, *The Christian Ministry*, Vol. 1 and 2, Jonathan Leavitt, New York, 1831.

Brown, Charles Reynolds, *The Making of a Minister*, The Century Co., New York & London, 1927.

Brown, John, Editor, *The Christian Pastor's Manual*, J. Whethram, Philadelphia, 1837.

Brown, U. S., *If the Minister is to Suceed*, Wm. B. Eerdmans Publishing Co., Grand Rapids, 1937.

Brown, William Adams, *The Minister, His World and His Work*, Cokesbury Press, Nashville, 1937.

Bruce, W. S., *The Psychology of Christian Life and Behaviour*, T. and T. Clark, Edinburgh, 1923.

Buckham, John Wright, *Personality and Psychology*, George H. Doran Co., New York, 1924.

Buckham, John Wright, *Religion as Experience*, Abingdon Press, New York, 1922.

Burkhart, Roy A., *Guiding Individual Growth*, The Abingdon Press, New York, 1935

Burkhart, Roy A., *Ministerial Counselling and Planned Parenthood*, National Clergymen's Advisory Council, New York, ...

Burnett, Bishop, *A Young Minister's Companion or a Valuable Collection of Scarce Treatises on the Pastoral Office*, Samuel T. Armstrong, Boston, 1813.

Calkins, Raymond, *How Jesus Dealt with Men*, Abingdon-Cokesbury Press, New York, Nashville, 1942.

Cameron, W. A., *The Clinic of a Cleric*, Ray Long and Richard R. Smith, Inc., New York, 1931.

Cannon, James Spencer, *Lectures on Pastoral Theology*, Charles Scribner, New York, 1853.

Chambers, O., *Workmen of God*, Dodd Mead & Co., Inc., 1938.

Clausen, B. C., *The Technique of a Minister*, Fleming H. Revell Co., New York, 1925.

Crosby, Howard, *The Christian Preacher*, Anson, D. F. Randolph & Co., 1879.

Cunningham, W., *The Cure of Souls*, The University Press, Cambridge, 1908.

Cuyler, Theodore L., *How to Be a Pastor*, The Baker and Taylor Co., New York, 1890.

Davis, Peter Seibert, *The Young Parson*, Smith, English & Co., Philadelphia, 1863.

Dearmer, Percy, *The Parson's Handbook*, Humphrey Milford, New York, 1932.

DeBlois, Austen Kennedy, *Some Problems of the Modern Minister*, Doubleday, Doran & Co., Inc., New York, 1928.

De Jong, Peter Y., *Taking Heed to the Flock*, Baker Book House, Grand Rapids, 1948.

Demarest, David D., *Pastoral Theology*, J. Heidingsfeld, New Brunswick.

Dewar, Lindsay and Hudson, Cyril E., *A Manual of Pastoral Theology*, Philip Allan, London, 1932.

Dexter, Elizabeth W. Anthony and Dexter, Robert Cloutman, *The Minister and Family Troubles*, Richard R. Smith, Inc., New York, 1931.

Donaldson, Andrew, *Glimpses of Pastoral Work in Covenanting Times*, James Nisbet and Co., London, 1877.

Doney, Carl Gregg, *An Efficient Church*, Fleming H. Revell Co., New York, 1907.

Douglas, A. F., *The Pastor and His People*, James Nisbet & Co., London, 1868.

Douglas, Lloyd C., *The Minister's Everyday Life*, Charles Scribner's Sons, New York, 1924.

Dykes, J. Oswald, *The Christian Minister and His Duties*, T. and T. Clark, Edinburg, 1909.

Edwards, Richard Henry, *A Person-Minded Ministry*, Cokesbury Press, Nashville, 1940.

Ellicott, C. J., (Compiler) *Homiletical and Pastoral Lectures*, A. C. Armstrong & Son, New York, 1880.

Erdman, Charles, *The Work of the Pastor*, The Westminster Press, Philadelphia, 1924.

Everts, W. W., *Pastor's Handbook*, Lewis Colby & Co., New York, 1848.

Fairbairn, Patric, *Pastoral Theology*, T. and T. Clark, Edinburgh, 1875.

Fenn, Don Frank, *Parish Administration*, Morehouse-Gorham Co., New York, 1938.

Fritz, J. H. C., *Pastoral Theology*, Concordia Publishing House, St. Louis, 1932.

Furfey, Paul Hanley, *New Lights on Pastoral Problems*, The Bruce Publishing Co., Milwaukee, 1931.

Garvie, Alfred Ernest, *A Guide to Preachers*, Hodder and Stoughton, London, 1906.

Garvie, Alfred Earnest, *The Christian Preacher*, Charles Scribner's Sons, New York, 1923.

Gerard, Alexander, *The Pastoral Care*, Long, printed for T. Cadell Jun. and W. Davies, in the Strand: and A. Brown, Aberdeen, 1799.

Gerberding, G. H., *The Lutheran Pastor*, Fifth Edition, Lutheran Publication Society, Philadelphia, 1905.

Gilbert, George B., *Forty Years a Country Preacher*, Harper & Brothers, New York and London, 1940.

Gladden, Washington, *Church and Parish Problems*, The Thwing Co., New York, 1911.

Gladden, Washington, *Hints and Helps for the Pastor and People of the Churches*, Wilbur B. Ketcham, 2 Cooper Union, 1897.

Gladden, Washington, *The Christian Pastor and the Working Church*, Charles Scribner's Sons, New York, 1903.

Goodell, Charles L., *Pastor and Evangelist*, George H. Doran, 1922.

Goodlife, J. B., *The Parson and His Problems*, Society For Promoting Christian Knowledge, London, 1933.

Goulooze, William, *Manual for Ministers, Elders and Deacons*, Wm. B. Eerdmans Publishing Co., Grand Rapids, 1937.

Goulooze, William, *Victory Over Suffering*, Baker Book House, Grand Rapids, 1949.

Graham, Henry, *The Preacher and His Work*, Eaton and Mains, New York, 1906.

Granger, W. A., *Practical Papers on Parish Problems*, The Judson Press, Philadelphia, 1919.

Green, Peter, *The Man of God.*, Hodder and Stoughton, Ltd., London, 1935.

Green, Peter, *The Town Parson*, Longmans, Green and Co., London and New York, 1814.

Greer, David H., *The Preacher and His Place*, Edwin and Gorham, New York, 1904.

Gunsaulus, *The Minister and Spiritual Life*, Fleming H. Revell Co., New York, 1911.

Hall, Charles Cuthbert, *Qualifications for Ministerial Power*, Hartford Seminary Press, Hartford, 1895.

Harmon, Nolan B. Jr., *Ministerial Ethics and Etiquette*, Cokesbury Press, Nashville, 1928.

Herbert, George, *Country Parson*, Henry Washbourne, London, 1832.

Hewitt, Arthur Wentworth, *God's Back Pasture*, Willett, Clark & Co., Chicago, New York, 1941.

Hewitt, Arthur Wentworth, *Highland Shepherds*, Willett, Clark & Co., New York, 1939.

Hoppin, James M., *Pastoral Theology*, Fifth Edition, Funk and Wagnalls Co., New York and London, 1909.

Hoppin, James M., *The Office and Work of The Christian Ministry*, Sheldon & Co., New York, 1869.

How, W. Walsham, *Lectures on Pastoral Work*, Wells, Gardner, Darton and Co., London, 1883.

Humphreys, G. W., *A Pastor Speaks Out*, The Blakiston Co., distributed by Henry H. Revell, 1943.

Huntington, F. D., *Personal Religious Life in The Ministry and in Ministering Women*, Thomas Whittaker, New York, 1900.

Inskip, James Theodore, *The Pastoral Idea*, The Macmillan Co., New York, 1905.

Jacoby, G., *Physician, Pastor and Patient*, P. B. Hoeber, Inc., New York, 1936.

James, John Angell, *An Earnest Ministry*, M. W. Dodd, New York, 1848.

Jefferson, Charles Edward, *The Minister as Shepherd*, Thomas Y. Crowell Co., New York, 1912.

Jefferson, Charles Edward, *The Ministering Shepherd*, Hodder and Stoughton, New York, 1912.

Joseph, O. L. *The Dynamic Ministry*, The Abingdon Press, New York, 1923.

Keedy, Edward E., *Moral Leadership and the Ministry*, Horace Worth Co., Boston, 1912.

Kemp, Charles F., *Physicians of the Soul*, the Macmillan Co., New York, 1947.

Kemp, Joseph W., *The Soul Winner and Soul Winning*, George H. Doran Co., New York, 1916.

Kempthorne, J. A., *Pastoral Life and Work Today*, Longmans, Green, and Co., New York, 1919.

Kidder, Daniel Parrish, *The Christian Pastorate*, Methodist Book Concern, New York, 1871.

Knox, Edmunt Arbuthnott, *Pastors and Teachers*, Longmans, Green and Co., New York, 1902.

Latham, Henry, *Pastor Pastorum*, James Pott & Co., New York, 1891.

Leach, William H., *The Making of the Minister*, Cokesbury Press, Nashville, 1938.

Lefroy, William, *The Christian Ministry*, Funk and Wagnalls, New York, 1891.

Lichliter, McIlyar Hamilton, *The Healing of Souls*, The Abingdon Press, New York, 1931.

Littlejohn, A. N., *Conciones Ad Clerum*, T. Whittaker, 1880.

Lowrie, Walter, *Ministers of Christ*, The Cloister Press, Louisville, 1946.

Luccock, Halford E., *In the Minister's Workshop*, Abingdon-Cokesbury Press, New York, 1944.

Lyman, Albert Josiah, *The Christian Past in The New Age*, Thomas Y. Crowell & Co., New York, 1909.

Lynch, Frederic, *The New Opportunities of the Ministry*, Fleming H. Revell Co., New York, 1912.

Macfarland, Charles S., (Editor), *The Christian Ministry and the Social Order*, Yale University Press, New Haven, 1909.

Mackenzie, John G., *Souls in the Making*, The Macmillan Co., New York, London, 1929.

Macleod, Norman, *A Highland Parish*, Robert Carter & Brothers, New York, 1867.

Martin, William C., *To Fulfill This Ministry*, Abingdon-Cokesbury Press, New York, Nashville, 1949.

Mason,—"Student and Pastor," *Young Minister's Companion*, Samuel Armstrong, Boston, 1813.

McAfee, Cleland Boyd, *Ministerial Practices*, Harper & Brothers, New York, 1928.

McClure, James G. K., *The Growing Pastor*, The Winona Publishing Co., Chicago, 1904.

McDowell, William Frauser, *Good Ministers of Jesus Christ*, The Abingdon Press, New York, 1917.

McKinney, A. H., *Human Nature in Christian Work*, W. A. Wilde Co., Boston, 1928.

Meade, William, *Lectures on the Pastoral Office*, Stanford and Swords, New York, 1849.

Miller, Samuel, *Letters on Clerical Manners and Habits*, Presbyterian Board of Publication, Philadelphia, 1852.

Moore, William Thomas, *Preacher Problems or The Twentieth Century Preacher at Work*, Fleming H. Revell Co., New York, 1907.

Morgan, G. Campbell, *The Ministry of the Word*, Fleming H. Revell Co., New York, 1919.

Mueller, Frederick F. and Hartschorne, Hugh, *Ethical Dilemmas of Ministers*, Charles Scribner's Sons, New York, 1937.

Murphy, Thomas, *Pastoral Theology*, Presbyterian Board of Publication, Philadelphia, 1877.

Murphy, Thomas, *People and Pastor*, Presbyterian Board of Publication, Philadelphia, 1887.

Murray, David A., *Christian Faith and the New Psychology*, Fleming H. Revell Co., New York, 1911.

Oman, John, *Concerning the Ministry*, Harper & Brothers, New York, 1937.

Owen, John Wilson, *The Pastor's Companion*, The Otterbein Press, Dayton, 1935.

Oxendam, Ashton, *The Pastoral Office, Its Duties, Difficulties, Privileges, and Prospects*. Bible House, New York and Philadelphia.

Palmer, Albert W., *The Minister's Job*, Willett, Clark & Co., Chicago, New York, 1937.

Parkhurst, Charles H., *The Pulpit and the Pew*, Yale University Press, New Haven, 1913.

Pattison, T. Harwood, *For the Work of the Ministry*, American Baptist Publication Society, Philadelphia, 1907.

Pleune, Peter H., *Some to be Pastors*, Abingdon-Cokesbury Press, New York, Nashville, 1943.

Plumer, William S., *Hints and Helps in Pastoral Theology*, Harper & Brothers, New York, 1874.

Pond, Enoch, *The Young Pastor's Guide*, Ezra Collier, New York, 1844.

Powell, Lyman P., *The Emmanuel Movement in a New England Town*, G. P. Putnam's Sons, New York and London, 1909.

Pym, T. W., *Our Personal Ministry*, Student Christian Movement Press, London, 1935.

Pym, T. W., *Spiritual Direction*, Morehouse Publishing Co., Milwaukee, 1928.

Quale, William A., *The Pastor-Preacher*, Eaton and Mains, New York, 1910.

Rees, W. G. Edwards, *The Parson's Outlook*, Longmans, Green & Co., New York, 1906.

R. E. X., *Morals for Ministers*, The Macmillan Co., New York, 1920.

Riley, W. B., *Pastoral Problems*, Fleming H. Revell Co., New York, 1936.

Schenck, Ferdinand S., *Modern Practical Theology*, Funk and Wagnalls Co., New York, 1903.

Shedd, William G. T., *Homiletics and Pastoral Theology*, Eighth Edition, Scribner, Armstrong & Co., New York, 1876.

Sheepshanks, John, *The Pastor and His Parish*, Hodder and Stoughton, London, 1908.

Sheppard, H. R. L., *The Human Parson*, John Murray, London, 1924.

Skrine, John Huntley, *Pastor Ovium*, Longmans, Green & Co., New York, 1909.

Smith, Henry Wallis, *The Pastor as Preacher*, William Blackwood and Sons, Edinburgh and London, 1882.

Smith, John, *Lectures on the Nature and End of the Sacred Office, and on the Dignity, Duty, Qualifications and Character of the Sacred Order*, A. Neal, Baltimore, 1810.

Smith, Reuben, *The Pastoral Office*, Presbyterian Board of Publication, Philadelphia, 1859.

Spann, J. Richard, Editor, *The Ministry*, Abingdon-Cokesbury Press, New York, Nashville, 1949.

Spencer, Ichabod S., *Pastor's Sketches, or Conversations with Anxious Inquirers*, Dodd and Mead, New York, 1850.

Spencer, Ichabod, *Pastor's Sketches, or Conversations with Anxious Inquirers*, Dodd and Mead, New York, 1853.

Spooner, Edward, *Parson and People*, Bunce and Huntington, New York, 1866.

Sweet, Louis Matthews and Sweet, Malcolm Stuart, *Pastoral Ministry in Our Time*, Fleming H. Revell, New York, 1949.

Taylor, T. S., *For Parsons Only*, Allenson & Co., Ltd., London.

Taylor, William M., *The Ministry of the Word*, Anson, D. F. Randolph and Co., 1876. 1876.

The Constitution of the Reformed Church in America, The Board of Publications and Bible School Work, New York, 1932.

The Pastor's Manual, *A Selection of Tracts on Pastoral Duty*, Sawyer, Ingersoll and Co., Hudson, Ohio, 1852.

Thomas, W. H. Griffith, *The Work of the Ministry*, Hodder and Stoughton, New York, 1910.

Thompson, Henry, *Pastoralia*, Second Edition, C. J. G. and F. Rivington, London. 1832.

Tidwell, Josiah Blake, *Concerning Preachers*, Fleming H. Revell Co., New York, London, and Edinburgh, 1937.

Tilden, W. P., *The Work of the Ministry*, George H. Ellis, Boston, 1899.

Tucker, William Jewett, *The Making and the Unmaking of the Preacher*, Houghton, Mifflin & Co., Boston and New York, 1899.

Tying, Stephen H., *The Christian Pastor*, Harper & Brothers, New York, 1874.

Underhill, Francis, *Feed My Sheep (Essays in Pastoral Theology)*, The Morehouse Publishing Co., Milwaukee, 1927.

Vinet, Alexander, *Pastoral Theology*, translated from the French, John Robertson, Dublin, 1752.

Wallace, C. C. S., *Pastor and People*, Broadman Press, Nashville, 1936.

Ware, J. F. W., *The Silent Pastor, or Consolations for the Sick*, Third Edition, Walker, Wise and Co., Boston, 1864.

Waterink, J., *Plaats En Methode Van De Ambtelijke Vakken*, J. B. v. d. Brink & Co., Zutphen, 1923.

Waterhouse, Eric S., *Psychology and Pastoral Work*, Cokesbury Press, Nashville, 1940.

Watson, John, *The Cure of Souls*, Dodd, Mead, and Co., New York, 1896.

Watson, John, *The Clerical Life*, Dodd, Mead & Co., New York, 1898.

Wayland, Francis, *Letters on the Ministry of the Gospel*, Sheldon and Co., New York, 1863.

Waynne, Frederick R., *Our Sacred Commission*, James Pott and Co., New York, 1891.

Webb, Robert Lee, *The Ministry as a Life Work*, The Macmillan Co., New York, 1922.

Weidner, Revere Franklin, *Practical Theology*, Fleming H. Revell, New York, 1891.

Wells, John D., *Pastor in the Sick-Room*, Presbyterian Board of Publications and Sabbath School Work, Philadelphia, 1892.

Willcox, G. B., *The Pastor Amidst His Flock*, The American Tract Society, New York, 1890.

Wilson, James M., *Six Lectures on Pastoral Theology*, The Macmillan Co., New York, 1903.

Wilson, James Steward, *Ministerial Life and Work*, Oliphan, Anderson & Ferrier, Edinburgh and London, 1901.

Zimmerman, L. M., *The Gospel Minister*, Meyer and Thalheimer, Baltimore, 1930.

III. Psychology

A. Principles of Psychology

Adler, Alfred, *The Neurotic Constitution*, Moffat, Yard and Co., New York, 1921.
Adler, Alfred, *The Practice and Theory of Individual Psychology*, Translated by P. Radin, Harcourt, Brace & Co., Inc., New York, 1929.
Adler, Gerhard, *Studies in Analytical Psychology*, W. W. Norton & Co., New York, 1948.
Allan, Frederick H., *Psychotherapy with Children*, W. W. Norton & Co., New York, 1942.
Alexander, Franz, *Archives of Neurology and Psychiatry*, American Medical Association, Chicago, 1931.
Ames, Edward Scribner, *The Psychology of Religious Experience*, Houghton Mifflin Co., New York, 1910.
Angell, James Rowland, *An Introduction to Psychology*, Henry Holt and Co., New York, 1920.
Barrett, Boyd E., *Man His Making and Unmaking*, Thomas Seltzer, New York, 1925.
Barrett, Boyd E., *The New Psychology, How It Aids and Interests*, P. J. Kenedy & Sons, New York, 1925.
Bascom, John, *The Principles of Psychology*, G. P. Putnam and Son, New York, 1869.
Batten, Loring, W., *The Relief of Pain by Mental Suggestion*, Moffat, Yard and Co., New York, 1917.
Bavinck, H., *Beginselen der Psychologie*, J. H. Bos, Kampen, 1897.
Bavinck, H., *Bijbelsche en Religieuze Psychologie*, J. H. Kok, Kampen, 1920.
Bavinck, J. H., *Inleiding in de Zielkunde*, J. H. Kok, Kampen, 1935.
Beers, Clifford Whittingham, *A Mind That Found Itself*, Doubleday & Co., Inc., New York, 1933.
Boring, Edwin G., *A History of Experimental Psychology*. A. Appleton-Century Co., New York, London, 1929.
Bouquet, A. C., *Religious Experience, Its Nature, Types and Validity*, H. Heffer & Sons, Ltd., Cambridge, 1932.
Brooks, Harry C., and Charles Ernest, *Christianity and Auto Suggestion*, Dodd, Mead & Co., New York, 1923.
Brown, William, *Mind, Medicine, and Metaphysica*, Oxford University Press, Humphrey Milford, London, 1936.
Brown, William, *Psychology and Psychotherapy*, Fourth Edition, The William & Wilkins Co., Baltimore, 1940.
Brown, William, *Suggestion and Mental Analysis*, Second Edition, George H. Doran Co., New York, 1922.
Carrington, Hereward, *Modern Physical Phenomena*, Dodd, Mead and Co., New York, 1919.
Christian, H. A., *Psychiatry for Practioners*, Oxford University Press, New York, 1936.
Cutten, George Barton, *Instincts and Religion*, Harper & Brothers, New York, 1940.
Cutten, George Barton, *The Pychological Phenomena of Christianity*, Charles Scribner's Sons, New York, 1909.
De Montet, Ch., *The Primary Problems of Medical Psychology*, Translated by A. Newbold, John Bale, Sons & Danielsson, Ltd., London.
Dewey, John, *Psychology*, Harper & Brothers, New York, 1892.
Dresser, Horatio W., *The Religion of the Spirit in Modern Life*, G. P. Putnam's Sons, New York and London, 1914.

Dubois, Paul, *The Influence of the Mind on the Body*, Funk and Wagnalls Co., New York, 1906.

Ellwood, Charles, *The Psychology of Human Society*, D. Appleton & Co., New York, London, 1926.

Flower, J. Cyril, *An Approach to the Psychology of Religion*, Kegan Paul, Trench, Trubner & Co., Ltd., London, 1927.

Flugel, J. C., *A Hundred Years of Psychology*, The Macmillan Co., New York, 1935.

Forsyth, David, *Psychology and Religion, A Study By a Medical Psychologist*, Watts & Co., London, 1935.

Freienfels, Richard Muller, *The Evolution of Modern Psychology*, Translated by W. Berean Wolfe, Yale University Press, New Haven, 1935.

Freienfels, Richard Muller, *Mysteries of the Soul*, Translated by Bernard Miall, Alfred A. Knopf, New York, 1929.

Garrison, Karl C., *Psychology of Adolescence*, Third Edition, Prentice-Hall, Inc., New York, 1946.

Gulick, Luther H., *Mind and Work*, Doubleday, Page & Co., New York, 1908.

Hall, G. S., *Adolescence*, D. Appleton & Co., New York, 1904.

Halliday, James L., *Psychosocial Medicine, A Study of Sick Society*, W. W. Norton & Co., Inc., New York, 1948.

Harriman, Philip Lawrence, Editor, *Twentieth Century Psychology, Recent Developments in Psychology*, McLeod, Toronto, 1946.

Harrington, Milton, *The Management of the Mind*, Philosophical Library, New York, 1945.

Hart, Bernard, *Psychopathology, Its Development and Its Place in Medicine*, University Press, Cambridge, 1927.

Healy, William, *Mental Conflicts and Misconduct*, Little, Brown & Co., Boston, 1917.

Heidbreder, Edna, *Seven Psychologies*, D. Appleton-Century Co., New York, 1933.

Henry, G. W., *Essentials of Psychopathology*, William Wood & Co., Baltimore, 1935.

Herrick, C. Judson, *The Thinking Machine*, The University of Chicago Press, Chicago, 1929.

Hinsie, Leland E., *Concepts and Problems of Psychotherapy*, Columbia University Press, New York, 1937.

Hollingsworth, Harvey L., *Psychology, Its Facts and Principles*, D. Appleton & Co., New York, London, 1928.

House, Elwin Lincoln, *The Psychology of Orthodoxy*, Fleming H. Revell Co., New York, 1913.

House, Richard and Miller, H. Crichton, *Christian Experience and Psychological Processes*, Student Christian Movement, London, 1920.

Howley, John, *Psychology and Mystical Experience*, Kegan Paul, Trench, Trubner & Co., Ltd., London, 1920.

Jacoby, George W., *Physician-Pastor and Patient*, Paul B. Hoeber, Inc., New York, London, 1936.

James, William, *Psychology*, Henry Holt and Co., New York, 1920.

James, William, *The Varieties of Religious Experience*, Sixth Impression, Longmans, Green & Co., London and Bombay, 1903.

Jones, W. Lawson, *A Psychological Study of Religious Conversion*, Epworth Press (Edgar C. Barton), London, 1937.

Josey, Charles Conant, *The Psychology of Religion*, The Macmillan Co., New York, 1927.

Jung, C. G., *Modern Man in Search of a Soul*, Harcourt Brace & Co., New York, 1939.

Jung, Carl Gustav, *Psychology and Religion*, Yale University Press, New Haven, 1938.

Jung, Carl Gustav, *Psychological Types*, Fourth Edition, Harcourt, Brace & Co., New York, London, 1933.

King, Irving, *The High School Age*, The Bobbs-Merrill Co., Indianapolis, 1914.

King, William P., Editor, *Behaviorism a Battle Line*, Cokesbury Press, Nashville, 1930.

Kraines, S. H., and Thetford, E. S., *Managing Your Mind*, The Macmillan Co., New York, 1943.

Kranefeldt, W. M., *Secret Ways of the Mind*, Kegan Paul, Trench Trubner & Co., Ltd., London, 1934.

Leiffer, Murray H., Editor, *In That Case*, Willett, Clark, & Co., Chicago, New York, 1938.

Leuba, James Henry, *A Psychological Study of Religion*, The Macmillan Co., New York, 1912.

Leuba, James Henry, *God or Man?* Henry Holt & Co., New York, 1933.

Leuba, James Henry, *The Belief in God and Immortality*, Sherman, French & Co., Boston, 1916.

Leuba, James Henry, *The Psychology of Religious Mysticism*, Harcourt, Brace & Co., Inc., New York, 1925.

Leuba, James Henry, *The Psychological Origin and the Nature of Religion*, Constable & Co., Ltd., London, 1915.

Leuba, James Henry, *A Psychological Study of Religion*, The Macmillan Co., New York, 1912.

Levey, David M., *New Fields of Psychiatry*, W. W. Norton and Co., New York, 1947.

Mackenzie, Murdo, *The Human Mind*, The Blakiston Co., Philadelphia, 1941.

Martin, E. D., *Psychology, What It Has to Teach You About Yourself and Your World*, Peoples Institute Publishing Co., New York, 1924.

McDougall, William, *Body and Mind*, Third Edition, Methuen & Co., London, 1915.

McDougall, William, *The Frontiers of Psychology*, D. Appleton Century Co., New York, 1934.

McDougall, William, *Outline of Psychology*, Charles Scribner's Sons, New York, 1923.

Menninger, Karl A., *Man Against Himself*, Harcourt, Brace & Co., New York, 1938.

Menninger, Karl A., *The Human Mind*, The Literary Guild of America, New York, 1930.

Menninger, William Claire, *Psychiatry In a Troubled World*, Macmillan Co., New York, 1948.

M'Hardy, George, *The Higher Powers of the Soul*, Charles Scribner's Sons, New York, 1913.

Miller, Emanuel, *Modern Psychotherapy*, Jonathan Cape, Ltd., London, 1930.

Mitchell, T. W., *Medical Psychology and Psychical Research*, Methuen & Co., Ltd., London, 1922.

Montgomery, E. A., *Can Psychology Help*, Rich and Cowan, Ltd., London, 1938.

Moore, John Morrison, *Theories of Religious Experience*, Round Table Press, Inc., New York, 1938.

Morgan, John J. B., *Keeping Sound Mind*, The Macmillan Co., New York, 1934.

Munsterberg, Hugo, *Psychology and Social Sanity*, Doubleday, Page & Co., New York, 1914.

Murphy, Gardner, *A Historical Introduction to Modern Psychology*, Third Edition (Revised), Harcourt, Brace & Co., New York, Kegan Paul, Trench, Trubner & Co., Ltd., London, 1932.

Murray, Alfred L., *Psychology for Christian Teachers*, Round Table Press, Inc., New York, 1938.

Murray, David A., *Christian Faith and the New Psychology*, Fleming H. Revell Co., New York, Chicago, Toronto, London, Edinburgh, 1911.

Northridge, W. L., *Modern Theories of the Unconscious*, Kegan Paul, Trench, Trubner & Co., Ltd., London, 1924.

Overstreet, H. A., *The Enduring Quest*, W. W. Norton & Co., Inc., New York, 1931.

Pillsbury, W. B., *The History of Psychology*, W. W. Norton & Co., Inc., New York, 1929.

Polatin, Phillip and Philtine, Ellen Co., *How Psychiatry Helps*, Harper & Brothers, New York.

Pratt, James Bissett, *The Psychology of Religious Belief*, The Macmillan Co., New York. 1907.

Pratt, James Bissett, *What Is Pragmatism?* The Macmillan Co., New York, 1909.

Putnam, James Jackson, *Human Motives*, Little, Brown & Co., Boston, 1915.

Rosanoff, Aron J., *Manual of Psychiatry and Mental Hygiene*, Seventh Edition, John Wiley & Sons, Inc., New York, 1938.

Ruch, Floyd, *Psychology and Life*, Scott, Foresman & Co., Chicago, 1941.

Sadler, William A., *The Truth About Mind Cure*, A. C. McClurg & Co., Chicago, 1928.

Sadler, William S., *The Mind at Mischief*, Funk & Wagnalls Co., New York, 1929.

Sadler, William S., *Theory and Practice of Psychiatry*, C. V. Mosby Co., St. Louis, 1926, 1936.

Saunders, K. J., *Adventures of the Christian Soul*, University Press, Cambridge, 1916.

Schofield, Alfred T., *The Force of Mind*, Funk and Wagnalls Co., New York, 1908.

Schofield, Alfred T., *Unconscious Therapeutics: or, the Personality of the Physician*, Second Edition, P. Blakiston's Son & Co., Philadelphia, 1906.

Selbie, W. B., *The Psychology of Religion*, Oxford University Press, London, 1924.

Sheldon, William H., *Psychology and the Promethean Will*, Harper & Brothers Publishers, New York, 1936.

Snowden, J. H., *The Psychology of Religion*, Fleming H. Revell & Co., New York, 1916.

Stalker, James, *Christian Psychology*, Hodder and Stoughton, New York and London, 1919.

Starbuck, Edwin Diller, *The Psychology of Religion*, Charles Scribner's Sons, New York, 1899.

Stevenson, J. G., *Religion and Temperament*, Cassell and Co., Ltd., New York, 1913.

Stratton, G. M., *The Psychology of the Religious Life*, The Macmillan Co., New York, 1911.

Streeter, Burnett Hillman, *The Church and Modern Psychology*. The Nineteenth Annual Hale Memorial Sermon, delivered March 26, 1934, Seabury-Western Theological Seminary, Evanston, Illinois.

Strickland, Francis L., *Psychology of Religious Experience*, The Abingdon Press, New York, Cincinnati, 1924.

Thouless, Robert H., *An Introduction to the Psychology of Religion*, The Macmillan Co., New York, 1923.

Thouless, Robert H., *The Control of the Mind*, Hodder and Stoughton, London, 1927.

Underwood, Alfred Clair, *Conversion, Christian and Non-Christian*, The Macmillan Co., New York, 1925.

Uren, Rudolph A., *Recent Religious Psychology*, Charles Scribner's Sons, New York, 1928.

Waterhouse, E. S., *The Philosophy of Religious Experience*, Epworth Press, London, 1923.

Waterink, J., *Ons Zieleven*, N. V. Gebr. Zomer & Keuning's, Wageningen, 1946.

Waterink, J., *De Oorsprong en het Wezen van De Ziel*, Wageningen, N. V. Gebr. Zomer & Keuning's, Uitgeversmij, 1930.

Watson, John B., *Psychology from the Standpoint of a Behaviorist*, J. P. Lippincott Co., Philadelphia and London, 1919.

Wells, H. G.; Huxley, Julian S.; Wells, G. P., *The Human Mind and the Behaviour of Man*, Doubleday, Doran & Co., Inc., New York, 1932.

White, William A., *An Introduction to the Study of the Mind*, Nervous and Mental Disease Publishing Co., Washington, D.C., 1924.

White, William A., *Mechanisms of Character Formation*, The Macmillan Co., New York, 1916.

White, William A., *Outlines of Psychiatry*, Fourteenth Edition, Nervous & Mental Disease Publishing Co., New York, 1935.

White, William A., *Twentieth Century Psychiatry*, W. W. Norton & Co., Inc., New York, 1936.

Woodburn, Angus Steward, *The Religious Attitude, A Psychological Study of Its Differentiation*, The Macmillan Co., New York, 1927.

Woodworth, Robert Sessions, *Contemporary Schools of Psychology*, Ronald Press Co., New York, 1931.

Woodworth, Robert Sessions, *Dynamaic Psychology*, Columbia University Press, New York, 1918.

Woodworth, Robert Sessions, *Psychological Issues*, Columbia University Press, New York, 1939.

Yeaxlee, Basil, *A Religion and the Growing Mind*, Nisbet & Co., Ltd., London, 1939.

Zilboorg, Gregory, *A History of Medical Psychology*, (in collaboration with George W. Henry), W. W. Norton & Co., Inc., New York, 1941.

B. Applied Psychology

Adler, Alfred, *The Science of Living*, Greenberg, New York, 1929.

Adler, Alfred, *Understanding Human Nature*, Greenberg, New York, 1927.

Adler, Alfred, *What Life Should Mean to You*, Little, Brown & Co., Boston, 1931.

Appel, Joseph H., *Living the Creative Life*, Robert M. McBride & Co., New York, 1918.

Ash, Edwin Lancelot Hopewell, *Mental Self-Help*, Macmillan, New York, 1920.

Brewster, Edwin Tenney, *Vocational Guidance for the Professions*, Rand McNally & Co., Chicago, New York, 1917.

Crane, George W., *Psychology Applied*, Northwestern University Press, Chicago, 1941.

Davis, Jesse Buttrick, *Vocational and Moral Guidance*, Ginn and Co., New York, 1914.

Dresser, Horatio W., *Psychology in Theory and Application*, Thomas Y. Crowell Co., New York, 1924.

Dubois, Paul, *The Psychic Treatment of Nervous Disorders*, Funk and Wagnalls Co., New York and London, 1908.

Folsom, Joseph K., *Social Psychology*, Harper & Brothers, New York and London, 1931.

Hepner, Harry Walker, *Psychology Applied to Life and Work*, Prentice-Hall, Inc., New York, 1943.

Hoffman, Frank Sargent, *Psychology and Common Life*, G. P. Putnam's Sons, New York. and London, 1907.

Hollingworth, H. L., and Poffenberger, A. T., *Applied Psychology*, D. Appleton & Co., New York, 1920.

Jastrow, Joseph, *Keeping Mentally Fit, a Guide to Every-day Psychology*, Second Printing, Greenberg, New York, 1928.

Katz, Daniel and Schanck, Richard L., *Social Psychology*, John Wiley & Sons, Inc., New York, Chapman & Hall, Ltd., London, 1938.

King, Henry Churchill, *Rational Living*, The Macmillan Co., New York, 1905.

King, Irving, *The Development of Religion, a Study in Anthropology and Social Psychology*, The Macmillan Co., New York, 1910.

Krout, Maurice H., *Introduction to Social Psychology*, Harper & Brothers, New York, 1942.

Lowrey, Lawson Gentry, *Psychiatry for Social Workers*, Columbia University Press, New York, 1946.

McDougall, William, *An Introduction to Social Psychology*, John W. Luce & Co., Boston, 1917.

McDougall, William, *Character and the Conduct of Life*, G. P. Putnam's Sons, New York, London, 1927.

McDougall, William, *Social Psychology*, John W. Luce Co., Boston, 1918.

Moss, Fred A., *Applications of Psychology*, Houghton, Mifflin Co., New York, 1929.

Munsterberg, Hugo, *Psychology, General and Applied*, D. Appleton & Co., New York and London, 1918.

Neustatter, W. Lindesay, *Modern Psychology in Practice*, P. Blakiston's Son & Co., Inc., Philadelphia, 1937.

Newcomb, Theodore M., and Hartley, Eugene L., co-chairmen of editorial committee, *Readings in Social Psychology*, Henry Holt and Co., New York, 1947.

Peale, Norman Vincent, *The Art of Living*, The Abingdon Press, New York, 1937.

Peale, Norman Vincent, *A Guide to Confident Living*, Prentice-Hall, Inc., New York City, 1949.

Peale, Norman Vincent, Editor, *Guideposts, Personal Messages of Inspiration*, Prentice-Hall, Inc., New York, 1948.

Platt, Charles, *The Psychology of Social Life*, Dodd, Mead & Co., New York, 1922.

Poffenberger, A. T., *Principles of Applied Psychology*, D. Appleton-Century Co., New York, 1942.

Powers, Francis F., *Psychology in Everyday Living*, D. C. Heath & Co., New York, Chicago, 1938.

Seashore, Carl Emil, *Psychology in Daily Life*, D. Appleton and Co., New York, 1927.

Stevens, Samuel Nowell, *Religion in Life Adjustments*, The Abingdon Press, New York, 1930.
Trout, David M., *Religious Behavior*, The Macmillan Co., New York, 1931.
Van Keuren, Floyd, *Outfitting for Spiritual Marriage*, 3rd Edition, Morehouse-Gorham Co., New York, 1941.
Varnum, Walter C., *Psychology in Everyday Life*, McGraw-Hill Book Co., Inc., New York and London, 1942.
White, Wendell, *Psychology in Living*, The Macmillan Co., New York, 1944.
White, Wendell, *The Psychology of Dealing with People*, The Macmillan Co., New York, 1936.
Young, Kimball, *Sociology*, American Book Co., New York, 1942.
Zahniser, C. R., *The Soul Doctor*, Round Table Press, 1938.

C. Psychoanalysis

Alexander, Franz and French, Thomas Morton, *Psychoanalytic Therapy, Principles and Application*, The Ronald Press Co., New York, 1946.
Baker, A. E., *Psychoanalysis Explained and Criticized*, The Macmillan Co., New York, 1926.
Bradby, M. K., *Psycho-analysis and Its Place In Life*, Henry Frowde, Oxford University Press, London, Hodder & Stoughton, Ltd., New York, 1920.
Brill, A. A., *Fundamental Conceptions of Psycoanalysis*, Harcourt, Brace & Co., New York, 1921.
Forsyth, David, *The Technique of Psycho-analysis*, Kegan Paul, Trench, Trubner & Co., Ltd., London, 1922.
Fridon, André, *Psychoanalysis: Its History, Theory and Practice*, B. H. Buebsch, New York, 1919.
Healy, William, *The Structure and Meaning of Psychoanalysis as Related to Personality and Behavior*, A. A. Knopf, New York, 1930.
Hingley, R. H., *Psycho-analysis*, Second Edition, Methuen & Co., Ltd., London, 1922.
Horney, Karen, *New Ways in Psychoanalysis*, W. W. Horton & Co., Inc., New York, 1939.
Horney, Karen, *The Neurotic Personality of Our Time*, W. W. Horton & Co., Inc., New York, 1937.
Peck, Martin W., *The Meaning of Psychoanalysis*, Alfred A. Knopf, New York, 1931.
Tridon, Andre, *Psychoanalysis*, B. W. Huebsch, Inc., New York, 1921.

D. Freud

Bridwood, Wilbur D., pseud., *Euclid's Outline of Sex; a Freudian Study*, H. Holt & Co., New York, 1922.
Brill, Abraham Arden, *Freud's Contribution to Psychiatry*, W. W. Horton & Co., Inc., New York, 1944.
Dunlap, Knight, *Mysticism, Freudianism and Scientific Psychology*, 1920.
Freud, Sigmund, *Psychoanalysis*, Garden City Publishing Co., Inc., New York, 1938.
Freud, Sigmund, *The Basic Writings of Sigmund Freud*, Ed., with an Introduction by A. A. Brill, New York Modern Library, New York, 1938.
Freud, Sigmund, *The Psychopathology of Everyday Life*, The Macmillan Co., New York, 1917.
Jastrow, Joseph, *The House That Freud Built*, Greenberg, New York, 1932.
Jastrow, Joseph, *Freud, His Dream and Sex Theories*, The World Publishing Co., New York, 1948.
Ludwig, Emil, *Doctor Freud, an Analysis and a Warning*, Williams & Co., 1948.
Walker, Helen, *Freud; His Life and His Mind*, a Biography, Walker, Puner, Howel, Soskin.
Wittels, Fritz, *Freud and His Time*, Translated by Louise Brink, H. Liveright, Inc., New York, 1931.

E. Personality Development

Allan, Denison Maurice, *The Realm of Personality*, Abingdon-Cokesbury Press, New York, Nashville, 1947.

Allport, Gordon W., *Personality, a Psychological Interpretation*, Henry Holt and Co., New York, 1937.

Bagby, English, *The Psychology of Personality, an Analysis of Common Emotional Disorders*, Henry Holt and Co., New York, 1928.

Bradley, Dwight J., *Your Problem — Can It Be Solved?* The Macmillan Co., New York, 1945.

Bradley, Dwight J., *Freedom of the Soul*, Association Press, Fleming H. Revell Co., New York, 1943.

Bradley, Preston, *Mastering Fear*, The Bobbs-Merrill Co., Indianapolis, New York, 1935.

Brierley, J., *The Life of the Soul*, The Pilgrim Press, Boston, The James Clarke & Co., London, 1912.

De Ovies, Raimundo, *Maybe You're Not Crazy*, Tupper & Love, Atlanta, 1947.

Dewey, John, *Human Nature and Conduct*, Henry Holt & Co., New York, 1922.

Groves, Ernest R., *Understanding Yourself, the Mental Hygiene of Personality*, Emerson Books, Inc., New York, 1941.

Haggard, Howard W., and Fry, Clements C., *The Anatomy of Personality*, Harper & Brothers, New York, 1936.

Healy, William, *Personality in Formation and Action*, W. W. Norton & Co., Inc., New York, 1938.

Hocking, William Ernest, *Human Nature and Its Remaking*, Yale University Press, New Haven, 1918.

Horney, Karen, *Self-Analysis*, W. W. Norton & Co., Inc., New York, 1942.

House, Elwin Lincoln, *How to Heal One's Self and Others*, Fleming H. Revell Co., New York, 1924.

Jung, Carl G., *The Integration of the Personality*, Farrar & Rinehart, Inc., New York, Toronto, 1939.

Kunkel, Fritz, *Conquer Yourself*, Ives Washburn, New York, 1936.

Kunkel, Fritz, *God Helps Those . . . Psychology and the Development of Character*, Ives Washburn, New York, 1936.

Ladd, George Trumbull, *The Secret of Personality*, Longmans, Green and Co., New York, 1918.

Leavitt, C. Franklin, *Personality Plus*, Books of Merit, Inc., New York, 1938.

Leavitt, C. Franklin, *You and Your Unsuspected Powers*, Paul Brandel Printing Co., New York, 1921.

Lester, Muriel, *Dare You Face Facts?* Harper & Brothers, New York, London, 1940.

Ligon, Ernest M., *The Psychology of Christian Personality*. The Macmillan Co., New York, 1935, 1937.

Lockhard, Earl G., *Improving Your Personality*, Walton Publishing Co., Chicago, 1939.

Murphy, Gardner and Jensen, Friedrich, *Approaches to Personality*, Coward-McCann, Inc., New York, 1933.

Overstreet, H. A., *Influencing Human Behavior*, W. W. Norton & Co., Inc., New York, 1925.

Rhoades, Winfred, *The Self You Have to Live With*, J. B. Lippincott, Philadelphia, New York, 1938.

Richmond, Winifred V., *Personality, Its Study and Hygiene*, Farrar & Rinehart, New York, 1937.

Seabury, David, *What Makes Us Seem So Queer?* Whittlesey House, London, 1934.

Shellow, Sadie Myers, *How to Develop Your Personality*, Harper & Brothers, New York, London, 1932.

Stuart, Grace, *The Achievement of Personality in the Light of Psychology and Religion*, The Macmillan Co., New York, 1938.

Symonds, P. M., *Diagnosing Personality and Conduct*, The Century Co., New York, 1931.

Thorpe, Louis P., *Personality and Life*, Longman, Green and Co., New York, 1941.
Thorpe, Louis P., *Psychological Foundations of Personality*, McGraw-Hill Book Co., Inc., New York, 1938.
Valentine, P. F., *The Psychology of Personality*, D. Appleton and Co., New York, 1927.
Vaughan, Richard M., *The Significance of Personality*, The Macmillan Co., New York, 1930.
Wieman, Henry Nelson, *Methods of Private Religious Living*, The Macmillan Press, New York, 1928.
Wolff, Werner, *The Expression of Personality*, Harper & Brothers, New York, 1943.

IV. Pastoral Psychology

A. Principles

Barbour, Clifford E., *Sin and the New Psychology*, The Abingdon Press, New York, Chicago, 1930.
Barry, F. W., *Christianity and Psychology*, George H. Doran Co., New York.
Beck, J. T., *Outlines of Biblical Psychology*, Translated from Third Corrected German Edition, T. & T. Clark, Edinburgh, 1877.
Boisen, A. T., *The Exploration of the Inner World*, Willett, Clark & Co., Chicago, 1937.
Bonnell, John Southerland, *Pastoral Psychiatry*, Second Edition, Harper & Brothers, New York, London, 1938.
Carle, Charles, *Mysticism in Modern Psychology*, Psychosociological Press, New York, 1943.
Cattell, Raymond B., *Psychology and the Religious Quest*, Thomas Nelson and Sons, Ltd., London, New York, 1938.
Chambers, O., *Biblical Psychology*, God's Bible School and Reveralist, Cincinnati, 1914.
Coe, George Albert, *The Motives of Men*, Scribner, New York, 1930.
Coe, George Albert, *The Psychology of Religion*, The University of Chicago Press, Chicago, 1916.
Coe, George Albert, *The Spiritual Life*, Eaton & Mains, New York, Cincinnati, 1900.
Collins, E. T., *The Soul*, Jennings & Pye, Cincinnati, Eaton & Mains, New York, 1901.
Conklin, E. S., *The Psychology of Religious Adjustment*, The Macmillan Co., New York, 1929.
Conn, J. C. M., *The Menace of the New Psychology*, The Inter-Varsity Fellowship, London, 1939.
Cooley, Charles Horton, *Social Process*, Charles Scribner's Sons, New York, 1918.
Dawson, George Gordon, *Healing, Pagan and Christian*, Society for Promoting Christian Knowledge, London, The Macmillan Co., New York, 1935.
Dearden, Harold, *The Doctor Looks at Life*, Doubleday, Page & Co., New York, 1924.
Dearmer, Percy, *Body and Soul*, Sir Issac Pitman & Sons, Ltd., London, 1912.
Dewar, Lindsay, *Man and God, an Essay in the Psychology and Philosophy of Religious Experience*, Society for Promoting Christian Knowledge, London, The Macmillan Co., New York, 1935.
Dewar, Linsay, and Hudson, Cyril E., *A Manual of Pastoral Psychology*, Philip Allan, London, 1932.
Dewar, Lindsay, and Hudson, Cyril E., *Psychology for Religious Workers*, Harper & Brothers Publishers, New York, London, 1934.
Dresser, Horatio W., *Outlines of the Psychology of Religion*, Thomas Y. Crowell Co., New York, 1929.
Edward, Kenneth, *Religious Experience; Its Nature and Truth*, T. & T. Clark, Edinburgh, 1926.
Ellis, William, *The Idea of the Soul in Western Philosophy and Science*, George Allen and Unwin, Ltd., London, 1940.
England, F. E., *The Validity of Religious Experience*, Harper & Brothers, New York, London, 1938.

Everett, Charles Carroll, *The Psychological Elements of Religious Faith,* The Macmillan Co., New York, London, 1902.

Faunce, D. W., *The Christian Experience: An Inquiry Into Its Character and Its Contents,* American Baptist Publication Society, Philadelphia, 1881.

Findlay, Arthur, *The Psychic Stream, or the Source of Growth of the Christian Faith,* Psychic Press, Ltd., London, 1939.

Fisher, R. H., *Religious Experience,* George Doran Co., New York, 1924.

Foster, Randolph S., *Philosophy of Christian Experience,* Hunt & Eaton, New York; Cranston & Stowe, Cincinnati, 1890.

Gardner, Percy, *The Interpretation of Religious Experience,* Williams & Norgate, Ltd., London, 1931.

Gates, A. I., *Psychology for Students of Education,* The Macmillan Co., New York, 1924.

Granger, Frank, *The Soul of a Christian,* The Macmillan Co., New York, 1900.

Gregory, Marcus, *Psychotherapy, Scientific and Religious,* The Macmillan Co., London, 1939.

Grensted, L. W., *Psychology and God,* Longmans, Green & Co., London, New York, 1930.

Hadfield, J. A., *Psychology and Morals,* Fifth Edition, McBride & Co., 1925.

Halliday, W. Fearon, *Psychology and Religious Experience,* Hodder and Stoughton, London, 1929.

Hardman, O., Editor, *Psychology and the Church,* The Macmillan Co., New York, 1925.

Harmon N. Bishop, *Religion and the New Psychology,* The Lindsey Press, London, 1924.

Hickman, Frank S., *Introductions to the Psychology of Religion,* The Abingdon Press, New York, Cincinnati, 1926.

Hiltner, Seward, *Clinical Pastoral Training,* Commission Religion and Health, Federal Councl of the Churches of Christ in America, New York, 1945.

Hollington, Richard D., *Psychology Serving Religion,* The Abingdon Press, New York, 1938.

Holman, Charles T., *The Cure of Souls, a Socio-Psychological Approach,* The University of Chicago Press, 1932.

Holman, Charles T., *The Religion of a Healthy Mind,* Round Table Press, Inc., New York, 1939.

Horton, Walter Marshall, *A Psychological Approach to Theology,* Harper & Brothers, New York, London, 1931.

House, Edwin L., *The Psychology of Orthodoxy,* Fleming H. Revell Co., New York, 1917.

Hudson, Cyril E., *Recent Psychology and the Christian Religion,* George H. Doran, New York, 1923.

Hughes, Thomas Hywel, *Psychology and Religious Origins,* Charles Scribner's Sons, New York, 1937.

Hughes, Thomas, Hywel, *Psychology and Religious Truth,* George Allen & Unwin, Ltd., London, 1942.

Hughes, Thomas Hywel, *The Psychology of Preaching and Pastoral Work,* The Macmillan Co., New York, 1941.

Ikin, A. Graham, *Religion and Psycotherapy,* Student Christian Movement Press, London, 1935.

Ikin, A. Graham, *The Background of Spiritual Healing,* George Allen & Unwin Ltd., London, 1937.

Inge, Ralph William, *Faith and Its Psychology,* Charles Scribner's Sons, New York, 1910.

Johnson, Paul E., *Psychology of Religion,* Abingdon-Cokesbury Press, New York, Nashville, 1945.

Johnston, Donald Kent, *Religious Aspects of Scientific Healing,* Richard G. Badger, The Gorham Press, Boston, 1920.

Keyser, Leander S., *A Hand Book of Christian Psychology,* The Lutheran Literary Board. Burlington, Iowa, 1928.

Liebman, Joshua Loth, editor, *Psychiatry and Religion,* Beacon Press, Boston, 1943.

Liebman, Joshua Loth, *Peace of Mind,* Simon and Schuster, New York, 1946.

Link, Henry C., *The Rediscovery of Man,* The Macmillan Co., New York, 1938.

Link, Henry C., *The Return to Religion,* The Macmillan Co., New York, 1936.

Mackay, W. M., *Bible Types of Modern Men*, First-Second Series, Doubleday Doran & Co., Inc., New York, 1920.

Macmurray, John, *The Structure of Religious Experience*, Yale University Press, New Haven, 1936.

Mahoney, C. K., *The Religious Mind*, The Macmillan Co., New York, 1927.

Matthews, W. R., *Psychology and the Church*, The Macmillan Co., New York, 1925.

Matthews, W. R., *The Pychological Approach to Religion*, Longmans, Green and Co., New York, 1925.

McComas, Henry C., *The Psychology of the Religious Sects*, Fleming H. Revell, New York, 1912.

Miller, H. Crichton, *The New Psychology and the Preacher*, Thomas Seltzer, New York, 1924.

Mulder, Jacob D., *Psychiatry for Pastors, Students, and Nurses*, Wm. B. Eerdmans Publishing Co., Grand Rapids, 1939.

Murray, J. A. C., *An Introduction to a Christian Psychotherapy*, T. & T. Clark, Edinburgh, 1938.

Northridge, W. L., *Recent Psychology and Evangelistic Preaching*, The Epworth Press. London, 1924.

Powell, Lyman P., *The Emmanuel Movement in a New England Town*, G. P. Putnam's Sons, New York, 1909.

Pym, T. W., *Psychology and the Christian Life*, George H. Doran Co., New York, 1922.

Pym, T. W., *More Psychology and the Christian Life*, Student Christian Movement, London, 1925.

Rogers, Clement F., *An Introduction to the Study of Pastoral Theology*, The Clarendon Press, Oxford, 1912.

Sherrill, Lewis Joseph, *Guilt and Redemption*, John Knox Press, Richmond, 1945.

Shillito, Edward, *You Can Find God*, Willett, Clark Co., New York, 1937.

Shoemaker, Samuel, *How You Can Help Other People*, E. P. Dutton & Co., Inc., New York, 1946.

Steven, George, *The Psychology of the Christian Soul*, 4th Edition, Hodder and Stoughton, New York, London, 1911.

Stolz, Karl R., *Pastoral Psychology*, Abingdon-Cokesbury Press, New York, Nashville, 1940

Stolz, Karl R., *The Church and Psychotherapy*, Abingdon-Cokesbury Press, New York, Nashville, 1943.

Swisher, Walter Samuel, *Religion and the New Psychology*, Marshall Jones Co., Boston, 1920.

Valentine, Cyril H., *Modern Psychology and the Validity of Christian Experience*, Society for promoting Christian Knowledge, London, The Macmillan Co., New York and Toronto, 1926.

Waterhouse, Eric S., *Psychology and Pastoral Work*, Cokesbury Press, Nashville, 1940.

Waterhouse, E. S., *Psychology and Religion*, Elkin Matthews & Marrott, London, 1930.

Weatherhead, Leslie D., *Psychology and Life*, The Abingdon Press, New York, 1935.

Weatherhead, Leslie D., *Psychology in the Service of the Soul*, The Macmillan Co., New York, 1930.

Weatherhead, Leslie D., *This is the Victory*, Abingdon-Cokesbury Press, New York, Nashville, 1941.

Weld, H. P., *Psychology as a Science, Its Problems and Points of View*, Henry Holt & Co., New York, 1928.

Yellowlees, David, *Psychology's Defence of Faith*, Richard R. Smith, Inc., New York, 1930.

B. Christian Life

Anderson, James B., *Applied Religious Psychology*, Richard G. Badger, The Gorham Press, Boston, 1919.

Balmforth, Henry, *Is Christian Experience an Illusion?* Student Christian Movement. London, 1923.

Beaven, Albert W., *Remaking Life. A Challenge to the Christian Church,* Cokesbury Press. Nashville, 1940.

Betts, George H., *Religion and Conduct,* The Abingdon Press, New York, 1930.

Blanton, Smiley and Peale, Norman Vincent, *The Art of Real Happiness,* Prentice, Hall, Inc., New York, 1950.

Blanton, Smiley and Peale, Norman Vincent, *Faith is the Answer,* Abingdon-Cokesbury Press, New York, 1940.

Boisen, Anton T., *Problems in Religion and Life,* Abingdon-Cokesbury Press, New York, Nashville, 1946.

Brightman, Edgar Sheffield, *Personality and Religion,* The Abingdon Press, New York, 1934.

Bruce, W. S., *The Psychology of Christian Life and Behaviour,* T. & T. Clark, Edinburgh.

Burnham, William H., *The Wholesome Personality, A Contribution to the Mental Health,* D. Appleton, & Co., New York, London, 1932.

Cabot, Richard C., *What Men Live By,* Houghton Mifflin Co., Boston and New York, 1914.

Cadman, S. Parkes, *Adventure for Happiness,* The Macmillan Co., New York, 1935.

Carnegie, Dale, *How To Win Friends and Influence People,* Simon and Schuster, New York, 1937.

Chandler, Arthur, *Christian Religious Experience,* Longmans, Green and Co., London, New York, 1929.

Clark, Elmer T., *The Psychology of Religious Awakening,* The Macmillan Co., New York, 1929.

Condé, Bertha, *What's Life All About?* Charles Scribner's Sons, New York, 1931.

Day, Albert Edward, *Jesus and Human Personality,* The Abingdon Press, New York, Cincinnati, Chicago, 1934.

Galloway, George, *The Principles of Religious Development,* Macmillan and Co., Ltd., London, 1909.

Garlick, Phyllis, L., *The Wholeness of Man,* Second Edition, The Highway Press, London, 1943.

Harkness, Georgia, *Religious Living,* The Edward W. Hazen Foundation, Inc., Distributed by Association Press, New York, 1937.

Hepner, Harry Walker, *It's Nice to Know People Like You,* D. Appleton-Century Co., New York, 1939.

Holman, Charles T., *Getting Down to Cases,* The Macmillan Co., New York, 1942.

Kunkel, Fritz, *In Search of Maturity,* Charles Scribner's Sons, New York, 1944.

Kunkel, Fritz, *Let's Be Normal,* Ives, Washburn, New York, 1929.

Kunkel, Fritz, *What It Means To Grow Up,* Charles Scribner's Sons, New York and London, 1936.

Lewis, C. S., *Christian Behaviour,* The Macmillan Co., New York, 1944.

Lichliter, H., *The Healing of Souls,* The Abingdon Press, New York, 1931.

May, Rollo, *The Springs of Creative Living,* Abingdon-Cokesbury, New York, Nashville, 1940.

McKenzie, John G., *Modern Psychology and the Achievement of Christian Personality,* Second Edition, The National Sunday School Union, London, ...

McKenzie, John G., *Personal Problems of Conduct and Religion,* The Macmillan Co., New York, 1932.

McKenzie, John G., *Psychology, Psychotherapy, and Evangelism,* The Macmillan Co., New York, 1940.

Norborg, Sv. *Varieties of Christian Experience,* Augsburg Publishing House, Minneapolis, Minnesota, 1937.

Peale, Norman Vincent, *You Can Win,* The Abingdon Press, New York, 1938.

Peale, Norman Vincent, *The Art of Living*, Eighth Printing, The Abingdon Press, New York, 1940.

Rice, William Francis, *The Psychology of the Christian Life*, Blessing Book Store, Inc., Chicago, 1937.

Richmond, Winifred V., *Making the Most of Your Personality*, Farrar & Rinehart, Inc., New York, 1942.

Stolz, Karl R., *The Psychology of Religious Living*, Cokesbury Press, Nashville, 1937.

Stolz, Karl R., *Tricks our Minds Play on Us*, Cokesbury Press, Nashville, 1939.

Strecker, Edward A., and Appel, Kenneth E., *Discovering Ourselves*, The Macmillan Co., New York, 1932.

Tansley, Arthur George, *The New Psychology and Its Relation to Life*, Dodd, Mead and Co., New York, 1929.

Warner, H. E., *The Psychology of the Christian Life*, Fleming H. Revell & Co., New York, 1910.

Weatherford, W. D., *Personal Elements in Religious Life*, Methodist Publishing House, Nashville, 1916.

Weaver, E. W., *Building a Career*, Association Press, New York, 1922.

Werner, Hazen G., *And We Are Whole Again*, Abingdon-Cokesbury, New York, Nashville, 1945.

Werner, Hazen G., *Real Living Takes Time*, Methodist Publishing Co., Nashville, 1948.

Wicks, Robert Russell, *The Reason for Living*, Charles Scribner's Sons, New York, 1935.

Wieman, Henry Nelson, *Religious Experience and Scientific Method*, The Macmillan Co., New York, 1926.

Worchester, Elwood, *Making Life Better*, Charles Scribner's Sons, New York, London, 1933.

C. Sickness — Health

Bailey, Harriet, *Nursing Mental Diseases*, The Macmillan Co., New York, 1926.

Bannister, H., *Psychology and Health*, The Macmillan Co., New York, 1936.

Brown, Charles Reynolds, *Faith and Health*, Thomas Y. Crowell Co., New York, 1924.

Brown, William, *Psychological Methods of Healing*, University of London Press Ltd., London, 1938.

Cabot, Richard C. and Dicks, Russell L., *The Art of Ministering to the Sick*, The Macmillan Co., 1937.

Cobb, W. F., *Spiritual Healing*, G. Bell and Sons, Ltd., London, 1914.

Cutten, George Barton, *Three Thousand Years of Mental Healing*, Charles Scribner's Sons, New York, 1911.

Dicks, Russell L., *Meditations for the Sick*, Willett, Clark & Co., Chicago, New York, 1937.

Dicks, Russell L., *Who Is My Patient*, The Macmillan Co., New York, 1941.

Dicks, Russell L., *And Ye Visited Me*, Harper & Brothers, New York and London, 1939.

Dougall, Lily, *The Christian Doctrine of Health*, The Macmillan Co., New York, 1923.

Dresser, Horatio W., *A Physician to the Soul*, G. P. Putnam's Sons, New York, London, 1908.

Fitzgerald, David Bruce, *The Law of Christian Healing*, Fleming H. Revell Co., New York, 1908.

Gehman, Henry E., *Practical Health Talks*, The Stratford Co., Boston, 1926.

Hiltner, Seward, *Religion and Health*, The Macmillan Co., New York, 1943.

Huckel, Oliver, *The Habit of Health, How to Gain and Keep It*, Thomas Y. Crowell Co., New York, 1909.

Liotta, Matthew A., *The Connection Between Religion and Medicine*, J. J. Little and Ives Co., New York, 1935.

MacDonald, Robert, *Mind, Religion and Health*, Funk and Wagnalls Co., New York, 1908.

Northridge, W. L., *Health for Mind and Spirit*, The Abingdon Press, New York, 1938.

Rhodes, Geoffrey, Editor, *Medicine and the Church*, Kegan, Trench, Trubner & Co., Ltd., London, 1910.

Seabury, David, *How Jesus Heals Our Minds Today*, Little, Brown & Co., Boston, 1940.

Sheatsley, J., *The Lord Thy Healer*, Lutheran Book Concern, Columbus, Ohio, 1948.

Smith, T. Waddelow, *The Mind in Health and Disease*, Balliere, Tindall and Cox, London, 1925.

Stieglitz, Edward J., *The Second Forty Years*, J. B. Lippincott Co., Philadelphia, New York, 1946.

Stolz, Karl R., *Making the Most of the Rest of Life*, Abingdon-Cokesbury Press, New York, Nashville, 1941.

Walsh, James J., *Religion and Health*, Little, Brown & Co., Boston, 1920.

Walsh, William T., *Scientific Spiritual Healing*, D. Appleton and Co., New York, 1926.

Weaver, Edward E., *Mind and Health, with an Examination of Some Systems of Divine Healing*, The Macmillan Co., New York, 1913.

Wise, Carroll A., *Religion in Illness and Health*, Harper & Brothers, New York, London, 1942.

Worchester, Elwood and McComb, Samuel, *The Christian Religion as a Healing Power*, Moffat, Yard & Co., New York, 1909.

Zweig, Stefan, *Mental Healers, Franz Anton Mesmer, Mary Baker Eddy, Sigmund Freud*, Translated by Edan and Ceda Paul, The Viking Press, New York, 1932.

D. Sex and Family Life

Bowman, Warren D., *Counseling With Couples for Marriage*, Brethren Publishing House, Elgin, 1948.

Cabot, Richard C., *Christianity and Sex*, The Macmillan Co., New York, 1938.

Dexter, E. W. A. and Dexter, R. C., *The Minister and Family Troubles*, Richard R. Smith, Inc., New York, 1931.

Goldstein, Sidney E., *Marriage and Family Counseling*, McGraw-Hill Book Co., Inc., New York, 1945.

Gray, A. Herbert, *About People*, Charles Scribner's Sons, New York, 1934.

Groves, Ernest R., *Christianity and the Family*, The Macmillan Co., New York, 1942.

Lawes, Frank A., *The Sanctity of Sex*, Good News Publishers, Chicago, 1948.

Marr, H. C., *Psychoses of the War, Including Neurasthenia and Shell Shock*, Henry Frowde, Oxford University Press, Hodder and Stoughton, London, 1919.

Piper, Otto A., *The Christian Interpretation of Sex*, Charles Scribner's Sons, New York, 1941.

Reik, Theodor, *Psychology of Sex Relations*, Farrar & Rinehart, Inc., New York, 1945.

Reynell, W. R., *Sexual Neurosis*, Longmans, Green, London, New York, 1931.

Stern, Edith M., (with the collaboration of Samuel W. Hamilton), *Mental Illness a Guide for the Family*, The Commonwealth Fund, New York, 1942.

Terman, L. M. and Miles, Catherine Cox, *Sex and Personality*, Houghton, Mifflin, New York, and Boston, 1936.

Waterink, J., *Puberteit*, N. V. Gebr., Zomer en Keunings, Mij., Wageningen, 1948.

Weatherhead, Leslie D., *The Mastery of Sex Through Psychology and Religion*, The Macmillan Co., New York, 1940.

E. Effects of War

Burkhart, Roy A., *The Church and the Returning Service Man*, Harper and Brothers Publishers, New York, London, 1925.

Eder, M. D., *War-shock. The Psycho-Neurosis in War Psychology and Treatment*, P. Blakiston's Son & Co., Philadelphia, 1917.

Gillespie, R. D., *Psychological Effects on Citizen and Soldier*, W. W. Norton & Co., Inc., New York, 1942.

Holman, Charles T., *Personal Problems of Men in the Armed Forces*, Federal Council of Churches of Christ in America, New York, 1944.

Humensky, J. J., *Chaplain Service in a Mental Hospital*, The Catholic University of America, Washington, 1937.

Millet, J. A. P., *The Church and Returning Service Personel*, Third Printing, *Counseling to Meet the Needs*, Federal Council of Churches of Christ in America, New York, 1945.

Mott, Fred W., *War Neuroses and Shell Shock*, Henry Frowde, Oxford University Press, Hodder & Stoughton, London, 1919.

Pratt, George K., *Soldier to Civilian*, Second Printing, McGraw-Hill Book Co., Inc., New York, 1944.

Rees, John Rawlings, *The Shaping of Psychiatry by War*, W. W. Norton & Co., Inc., New York, 1945.

Smith, G. Elliot and Pear, T. H., *Shell Shock and Its Lessons*, Second Edition, Longmans, Green and Co., London, 1917.

Wood, Leland Foster, *Pastoral Counseling in Family Relationships*, The Commission on Marriage and the Home of the Federal Council of the Churches of Christ in America, New York.

Millet, J. A. P., *The Church and Returning Service Personnel*, Third Printing, *Counseling*

F. Physical, Mental, and Spiritual Hygiene

Bassett, Clara, *Mental Hygiene in the Community*, The Macmillan Co., New York, 1934.

Bruce, H. Addington, *Scientific Mental Healing*, Little, Brown, and Co., Boston, 1911.

Campbell, Charles Macfie, *A Present Day Conception of Mental Disorders*, Harvard University Press, Cambridge, 1924.

Campbell, Charles Macfie, *Towards Mental Health*, Harvard University Press, Cambridge, 1933.

Campbell, John D., *Everyday Psychiatry*, J. B. Lippincott Co., Philadelphia, 1945.

Carroll, Robert S., *The Mastery of Nervousness*, The Macmillan Co., New York, 1917.

Chappell, Matthew N., *In the Name of Common Sense*, The Macmillan Co., New York, 1938.

Cloustin, T. S., *The Hygiene of the Mind*, Fourth Edition, E. P. Dulton & Co., New York.

Cotton, Ethel, *Keeping Mentally Alive*, G. P. Putnam's Sons, New York, London, 1931.

Deutsch, Albert, *The Mentally Ill in America*, Doubleday, Doran & Co., New York, 1938.

Dresser, Horatio W., *Health and the Inner Life*, G. P. Putnam's Sons, New York, London. 1907.

Elliot, Harrison Sacket and Elliot, Grace Loucks, *Solving Personal Problems*, Henry Holt and Co., New York, 1936.

Evans, W. F., *Mental Medicine: A Theoretical and Practical Treatise*, H. H. Carter, Boston, 1881.

Evans, W. F., *Esoteric Christian and Mental Therapeutics*, H. H. Carter & Karrick, Boston, 1886.

Evans, W. F., *Soul and Body: or the Spiritual Science of Health and Disease*, Colby & Rich, Boston, 1876.

Evans, W. F., *The Divine Law of Cure*, H. H. Carter & Co., Boston, 1885.

Evans, W. G., *The Mental-Cure*, Colby & Rich, Boston, 1875.

Fallows, Samuel, *Health and Happiness, or Religious Therapeutics and Right Living*, A. C. McClurg & Co., Chicago, 1909.

Fink, David, *Release From Nervous Tension*, Simon and Schuster, New York, 1943.

Fisher, Irving and Fish, Eugene Lyman, *How To Live*, Funk and Wagnalls Co., New York, London, 1919.

Fletcher, Peter, *Mastering 'Nerves,'* Rich & Cowan, Ltd., London, 1937.

Fosdick, Harry Emerson, *On Being a Real Person*, Harper and Brothers, 1943.

Groves, Catherine, *Get More Out of Life*, Association Press, New York, 1941.

Hamilton, Edward John, *Mental Science*, Robert Carter & Brothers, New York, 1886.

Hill, H. W., *The New Hygiene*, The Macmillan Co., New York, 1925.

Howard, Frank E., and Patry, Frederick L., *Mental Health, Its Principles and Practice with Emphasis on the Treatment of Mental Deviations*, Harper & Brothers, New York, 1935.

Janet, Pierre, *Psychological Healing, A Historical and Clinical Study*, Translated from the French by Eden and Cedar Paul, Two volumes, George Allen & Unwin Ltd., London, 1925.

King, D. Macdougall, *Nerves and Personal Power*, Fleming H. Revell Co., New York, 1922.

Klein, D. B., *Mental Hygiene, The Psychology of Personal Adjustment*, Henry Holt and Co., New York, 1944.

Mac Leod, A. B., *Mental Hygiene as Taught by Jesus*, The Macmillan Co., New York, 1925.

Moore, Don Thomas Verner. *Personal Mental Hygiene*, Grune & Stratton, New York, 1944.

Oliver, John Rathbone, *Psychiatry and Mental Health*, Charles Scribner's Sons, New York, London, 1936.

Phaup, Minnie Rob, *Recent Relations of Mental Hygiene and Religion*, Doctorate Thesis, University of Chicago, 1930.

Preston, George H., *The Substance of Mental Health*, Farrar & Rinehart, Inc., New York, 1943.

Querido, Arie, *Home Care of the Mental Patient*, Oxford University Press, Humphrey Milford, London, 1936.

Randall, J. Herman, *Mind and Body*, H. M. Caldwell Co., New York, Boston, 1909.

Randall, John Herman, *The Mastery of Life*, Robert M. McBride & Co., New York, 1931.

Ray, Marie Beynon, *Doctors of the Mind*, Little, Brown & Co., Boston, 1946.

Ray, Marie Beynon, *How to Conquer Your Handicaps*, The Bobbs-Merrill Co., Indianapolis, New York, 1948.

Rucknick, Christian A., *The Mental Life*, Longmans, Green & Co., New York, 1928.

Sheen, Fulton J., *Peace of Soul*, McGraw-Hill Book Co., Inc., New York, Toronto, 1949.

Sidis, Coris, *Nervous Ills, Their Cause and Cure*, Richard G. Badger, The Gorham Press, Boston, 1922.

Simpson, Jerome Henry, *Pastoral Care of Nervous People*, Morehouse-Gorham Co., New York, 1945.

Smith, James H., *Technique for Living, Essential Books*, New York, 1944.

Valentine, Cyril H., *The Treatment of Moral and Emotional Difficulties*, Student Christian Movement Press Ltd., London, 1937.

Walsh, William S., *The Inferiority Feeling*, E. P. Dutton & Co., Inc., New York, 1928.

White, William A., *The Principles of Mental Hygiene*, The Macmillan Co., New York, 1919.

Williams, Frankwood E., and others, Addresses by, *Social Aspects of Mental Hygiene*, Yale University Press, New Haven, 1925.

Woodworth, Robert Sessions, *Psychology, a Study of Mental Health*, Henry Holt and Co., New York, 1921.

G. Counseling

Adamson, Elizabeth Ingram, *So You're Going to a Psychiatrist*, Thomas Y. Crowell, New York, 1936.

Anderson, Standley E., *Every Pastor a Counselor*, Van Kampen Press, Wheaton, 1949.

Belton, George Francis, *A Manual for Confessors*, New and Revised Edition, A. R. Mowbray & Co., Ltd., London and Oxford, Morehouse Publishing Co., Milwaukee, 1931.

Bingham, Walver van Dyke, and Moore, Bruce Victor, *How to Interview*, Harper & Brothers, New York, 1934.

Bonnell, John Southerland, *Psychology for Pastor and People*, Harper & Brothers, New York and London, 1948.

Deschweinitz, Karl, *The Art of Helping People out of Trouble*, Houghton Mifflin Co., Boston, New York; The Riverside Press, Cambridge, 1924.

Dicks, Russell, *Pastoral Work and Personal Counseling*, The Macmillan Co., New York, 1944.

Dicks, Russell L., *Pastoral Work and Personal Counseling*, The Macmillan Co., New York, 1945.

Dresser, Horatio W., *Knowing and Helping People*, The Beacon Press, Inc., Boston, 1933.

Ernst, Karl J., *The Art of Pastoral Counseling*, Zondervan Publishing House, Grand Rapids, 1941.

Garrett, Annette, *Interviewing*, Family Welfare Assoc. of America, New York, 1942.

Hiltner, Seward, *Pastoral Counseling*, Abingdon-Cokesbury Press, New York, Nashville, 1949.

May, Rollo, *The Ministry of Counseling*, Federal Council of Churches of Christ in America, New York, 1944.

May, Rollo, *The Art of Counseling*, Cokesbury, Nashville, 1939.

Oldfield, R. C., *The Psychology of the Interview*, Methuen & Co., Ltd., London, 1940.

Rogers, Carl E., *A Counseling Viewpoint*, Commission of Religion and Health-Federal Counsel of Churches of Christ in America, New York, 1945.

Rogers, Carl J., *Counseling and Psychotherapy*, Houghton Mifflin Co., New York, 1942.

Schindler, Carl J., *The Pastor as Personal Counselor*, Muhlenberg Press, Philadelphia, 1942.

Smith, D., *Christian Counsel*, Hodder and Stoughton, New York, London.

Wright, Milton, *The Art of Conversation*, Garden City Publishing Co., Inc., New York, 1941.

Young, Pauline V., *The Art and Science of Interviewing, A Sociological Analysis*, McGraw-Hill Book Co., New York, London, 1935.

V. Articles

Achelis, E. C., "Pastoral Theology", *The New Schaff-Herzog Encylopedia of Religious Knowledge*, Baker Book House, Grand Rapids, 1950, Vol. VIII, pp. 373-377.

Bauslin, "The Model Pastor," *The Lutheran Quarterly*, Vol. 36, New Series, July, 1906, pp. 382-403.

Boisen, Anton, "Theological Education Via the Clinic," *Religious Education*, Vol. 25, 1930, pp. 235-239.

Boisen, Anton T., "Concerning the Relationship Between Religious Experience and Mental Disorder," *Mental Hygiene*, Vol. 7, 1923, Quarterly Magazine of the National Com. for Mental Hygiene, Inc., New York, p. 302.

Bone, H., "Personality Reconstruction," *Christianity and Mental Hygiene*, 1938, Committee on Religion and Health, Federal Council of the Churches of Christ in America, p. 53.

Bower, "The Organization of Religious Experience," *The Journal of Religion*, Vol. III. 1923, pp. 34-50.

Brooks, Philip, "The Minister and His People," *The Harvard Theological Review*, Vol. I, Number 2, April, 1908, Macmillan Co., New York, pp. 223-239.

Conn, J. C. M., "The Menace of New Psychology," *The Evangelical Quarterly*, April, 1939, London, pp. 118-148.

Cronback, Abraham, "Psychoanalysis and Religion," *The Journal of Religion*, Vol. 2, November, 1922, pp. 588-599.

Day, Frank E., "Pastoral Visiting and Pulpit Strength," *The Methodist Review*, Vol. LXXXIV, No. 6, No. 458, November, December, 1902, Eaton and Mains, New York, pp. 877-882.

Dobbins, G. S., "Theological Education in a Changing Social Order," *The Review and Expositor*, Vol. XXXII, April, 1935, No. 2, pp. 180-196.

Dobbins, G. S., "Facing Pastoral Problems," *The Review and Expositor*, Vol. XXXIII, April, 1936, No. 2, pp. 188-195.

Dobbins, Gaines S., "Facing Pastoral Problems," *The Review and Expositor*, Vol. 24, January, 1937, No. 1, pp. 60-71.

Dobbins, Gaines S., "Facing Pastoral Problems, The Problem of Pastoral Visiting," *The Review and Expositor*, Vol. XXXIV, April, 1937, No. 2, pp. 218-225.

Dunsmore, Marion Hiller, assisted by Crebe, L. M. and Pearman, E. O., "The Relation of the New Psychology to Religion," *The Methodist Review*, Vol. 106, May, 1923, The Methodist Book Concern, New York, pp. 415-425.

Fahs, R. Z., "Suggestions for Pastoral Visiting," *Methodist Review*, Vol. XC, No. 4, Whole Number 492, July-August, 1908, Eaton & Mains, New York, pp. 531-537.

Fisher, D. W., "The New Psychology," *Presbyterian and Review*, Vol. II, 1891, pp. 607-623.

Geikie, Cunningham, "The Preacher in Daily Life," *The Homiletic Review*, Vol. XXXVI, Nov., 1898, No. 5., pp. 387-394.

Gillies, Andrew, "Nerves and Religion," *The Methodist Review*, Sept. 1924, Vol. 107, The Methodist Book Co., New York, pp. 765, 772.

Hastings, Thomas S., "The Parish and the Minister." *The Schaff-Herzog Encyclopedia of Religious Knowledge*, Baker Book House, Grand Rapids, 1950, Vol. VIII, pp. 377-379.

Heisler, C. W., "The Pastor Among His People," *Lutheran Quarterly*, Vol. 24, New Series, 1894, pp. 481-499.

Hewitt, C. E., "The Personal Work of the Pastor," *Baptist Quarterly Review*, Vol. 12-13, October 1890, pp. 407-417.

Hiltner, Seward J., "The Psyche and Modern Theology," *Christendom*, Vol. VI, Spring, 1941, No. 2, pp. 234-245.

Hiltner, Seward J., "What Kind of Hate?" *Christendom*, Vol. VIII, Autumn, 1943, No. 4, pp. 484-494.

Hiltner, Seward J., and Fortson, John L., "Pastoral Counseling in Wartime," *The Expositor*, May 1942, Vol. XLIV, No. 5, pp. 221, 254, 255.

Hiltner, S.; Rice, O. R.; and York, W. H., Ed. Committee, "Conference on Christianity and Mental Hygiene," Federal Council of Churches of Christ in America, Inc., New York, 1938.

Hewitt, C. E., "The Personal Work of the Pastor," *Baptist Quarterly Review*, Vol. 12-13, Oct. 1890-91, pp. 407-417.

Holman, Charles T., "When the Clergyman and the Psychiatrist Meet," *Journal of Religion*, Vol. XVI, October, 1936, No. 4, The University of Chicago Press, Chicago, pp. 432-444.

Jones, Rufus, M., "Psychology and the Spiritual Life," *The Journal of Religion*, Sept., 1921, Vol. I, No. 5, pp. 449-461.

Kelly, F. Joseph, "Importance of the Pastoral Office," *The Ecclesiastical Review*, Vol. LXXIX, No. 3, Sept. 1928, pp. 237-242.

Kelley, William V., "Psychology for the Pastor," *The Methodist Review*, Vol. V. Jan., 1898, pp. 115-119.

Leuba, James H., "A Study in the Psychology of Religious Phenomena," *American Journal of Psychology*, Vol. VII, No. 3, 1896, pp. 309-385.

Lapsley, Robert A., "Pastoral Theology," *The Presbyterian Quarterly*, Vol. III, April, 1889, Anson D. F. Randolph & Co., New York, pp. 233-242.

Love, John, Jr., "Ministerial Blues," *Baptist Quarterly Review*, Vol. 14, April, 1892, pp. 150-176.

Mackay, John A., "The Adequacy of the Church Today," *"Christendom,"* Vol. VI, Autumn, No. 4, 1941, pp. 483, 494.

Marshall, Henry Rutgers, "Psychotherapeutics and Religion," *Hibbert Journal*, Vol. 7, 1908-1909, pp. 295-313.

McNeill, John T., "Historical Types of Method in the Cure of Souls," *The Crozer Quarterly*, July, 1934, Vol. XI, No. 3, pp. 323-334.

Miller, E. "The Pastor for the Times," *Lutheran Quarterly*, Vol. 23, New Series, 1893, Article II, pp. 173-194.

Miller, Robert Henry, "Pastor, Care for Your Homes," *The Expositor and Homiletic Review*, Jan. 1936, F. M. Barton Co., New York, pp. 9-11.

Murray, I. G., "The Pastor Getting Started and Getting On," *The Review and Expositor*, Vol. XXXII, April, 1935, No. 2, pp. 197-203.

Newcomb, T., "Christianity and Mental Hygiene," *Conference Report*, 1939, p. 199.

Oliver, John Rathbone, "Psychiatry and the Confessional," *Scribner's Magazine*, July, 1930, pp. 60-66.

Parker, H. W., "Pastoral Visitation," *The Homiletic Review*, New Series, Vol. XXI, Oct., 1899, p. 569.

Peabody, A. P., "The Importance of Personal Character in the Ministry." *The Homiletic Review*, Vol. XXV, March, 1893, pp. 195-202.

Rogers, Carl Ransom, "Therapy in Guidance Clinics," *Journal of Abnormal Social Psychology*, American Psychological Association, Inc., Chicago, pp. 289-299.

Starbuck, Edwin D., "Some Aspects of Religious Growth," *American Journal of Psychology*, Vol. IX, No. 1, 1897, pp. 70-129.

Stolz, Karl Ruf, "The Church and Psychoanalysis," *Methodist Review*, Vol. III, March, 1928, pp. 176-185.

Stratton, George Malcolm, "Where Has Psychology Left Religion," *Journal of Religion*, Vol. III, Jan., 1923, University of Chicago Press, Chicago, pp. 51-63.

Van Norman, Emery E., "Cooperation between Clergyman, Psychiatrist and Social Worker," *Religious Education*, 24, 1929, pp. 624-630.

Warner, Horace E., "The Pastor Among Men," *The Homiletical Review*, New Series, Vol. XXXIV, July 1897, pp. 87-92.

Weigle, E. D., "The Ministry and Current Social Problems," *Lutheran Quarterly*, Vol. 24, New Series, Oct., 1894, pp. 467-480.

Williams, Daniel D., "Contemporary Theology and Mental Health," *Christendom*, Vol. VI, Autumn, 1941, No. 4, pp. 505-516.

Wilm, E. C., "The New Psychology and Personality," *Methodist Review*, Nov., 1908, pp. 939-948.

Wyckoff, Albert Clark, "The Psychologist Among The Theologians," *The Bible Magazine*, Feb., 1915, pp. 150-158.

INDEX

INDEX

I. Bible Reference Index

Genesis 1:26 183
Genesis 3:17 137
Genesis 8:21 137
II Samuel 12:1-15 .... 200, 201
I Kings 17:18, 19 196
Job 2:3 113
Job 13:15 90
Psalm 23 77
Psalm 25:7 137
Psalm 27 77
Psalm 27:8 122
Psalm 42 77
Psalm 42:1 122
Psalm 42:5 197
Psalm 46:1 77
Psalm 46:10 197
Psalm 50:10, 12 198
Psalm 51:5, 10 137
Psalm 62:1, 2 197
Psalm 63:1 122
Psalm 73:17 90
Psalm 91 77
Psalm 103 77
Psalm 103:3 114
Psalm 110:9 137
Psalm 116:12-14 122
Psalm 121 77
Psalm 139:23, 24 198
Proverbs 11:14 260
Proverbs 15:22 260
Isaiah 1:1-9 137
Isaiah 1:3 197
Isaiah 6:1-13 90
Isaiah 6:5 198
Isaiah 26:3 77
Isaiah 41:10 77
Isaiah 43:1-28 90
Isaiah 53:6 135
Isaiah 55:11 174
Jeremiah 1:1-19 90

Jeremiah 8:6 106
Jeremiah 31:31-34 93
Jeremiah 50:6 135
Matthew 3 196
Matthew 5:48 133
Matthew 6:24-34 91
Matthew 6:33 118
Matthew 9:36 187
Matthew 10:5-11 202
Matthew 10:6 135
Matthew 10:11-42 202
Matthew 26:36-46 113
Matthew 26:58 201
Matthew 28:18-20 203
Matthew 28:19, 20 187
Luke 2:52 122
Luke 9:60 187
Luke 13:3 106
Luke 15:7 106
Luke 19:10 135
Luke 22:20 196
John 1:23 201
John 1:26 201
John 1:29 201
John 3:1-16 196
John 3:16 77
John 6:35 .... 136, 161
John 9:3 113
John 11:25, 26 136
John 14 77
John 14:4-14 198
John 14:6 112
John 16:8 137
John 21:15 203
Acts 1:7, 8 203
Acts 2:4 196
Acts 2:14-21 106
Acts 4:12 .... 135, 197
Acts 6:3 196
Acts 9:1-9 99
Acts 10:44 .... 106, 196
Acts 15:28 196

Acts 16:14, 15:30-33 106
Acts 18:1-7 106
Acts 19:2 196
Acts 20:28 ....26, 117, 196
Romans 3 200
Romans 3:11-18 137
Romans 4:20 198
Romans 5 200
Romans 5:9 196
Romans 5:20 137
Romans 7 .... 137, 138, 198
Romans 8 .... 77, 138, 198
Romans 8:1 135
I Corinthians 1:21 187
I Corinthians 2:7-16 197
I Corinthians 5:17 133
I Corinthians 6:19, 20 188
I Corinthians 11:25 196
I Corinthians 13 138
I Corinthians 15 138
I Corinthians 15:58 .... 117, 198
II Corinthians 10:5 196
II Corinthians 12:7 113
II Corinthians 12:9 77
II Corinthians 12:10 198
II Corinthians 13:11 133
Ephesians 1:4, 5, 7 133
Ephesians 1:7 196
Ephesians 4 138

Ephesians 5 138
Ephesians 5:1, 2 198
Ephesians 6:17 174
Philippians 3 .... 138, 196
Philippians 3:12-21 117
Philippians 3:13-14 198
Philippians 4 .... 138, 196
Philippians 4:4-8 117
Colossians 1:14 196
Colossians 3 .... 138, 196
Colossians 3:1 117
II Thessalonians 2:13 135
I Timothy 1: 15 198
II Timothy 1:12 198
II Timothy 2:1 144
II Timothy 2:3 144
II Timothy 3:17 117
II Timothy 4:1-5 204
II Timothy 4:2 .... 144, 187
II Timothy 4:5 144
Titus 3:5 196
Hebrews 1:14 135
Hebrews 12:2 90
I Peter 1:19 196
I Peter 2:5 133
I Peter 5:7 77
II Peter 1:21 196
I John 3:2 198

II. Author and Subject Matter Index

Adam's Sin 136, 137
Adams, H.
    Know human nature and minds of people 53
    Many mental cases need attention 60, 61
    Seminary training needed 144
Adler, A.
    Life is only a coöperation 88
    Soul is only a psychic force 101
    Stark humanistic conception of God 88
Affliction-Lessons learned 72-76
Agar, F. A. Practical aspects of pastoral work 51
Allnatt, F. J. B. Pastor must have active spiritual life 50
Ambassadors, Spiritual commission for
    According to Paul 209
    Christ is the answer 207-208
    God's word needed to serve 207
    Goulooze, W. God's sovereignty does not limit man's duty 207
    Halliday, W. F. World needs a physician 208
    Mc Kenzie, J. G. Spiritual conversion is not a reshuffling of conscious and sub-
        conscious motives 208
    Pentecostal power for a great purpose 209
    The King's Business 208
Ames, E. S.
    Conversion is a sudden change 97, 98
    Emotional experience of conversion 97, 98
Anderson, J. B.
    Divine means only a human consciousness of it 88
    Human conception of God 88
Anderson, S. Christian viewpoint in counseling 159
Atomic energy. Influence on life 19, 20
Attitude of afflicted people, Questionnaire report 113-115
Baker, A. E. God is a symbol of psychic energy 88
Balmforth, H., Dewar, L., Hudson, C. E., Sara, E. S.
    Experience makes better competence for minister 53
    Individual treatment of people 56
Barbour, C. E.
    Academic psychology cannot help us 90
    Man was made to be like God 103, 104
    No antagonism between psychological determinism and freedom of the will 93, 94
Barrett, A. Biblical basis of interpretation 33
Bassett, C.
    Conferences by ministers help people 82
    Homes are shattered because of serious problems 82
    Minister can call aid of Christ to help 92
    Minister in position to really help people 166

Bauslin, D. Pastoral capacity for leadership 49
Bavinck, H. Christian view in defining God 86
Bavinck, J. H. Soul, the wonder-work of God 103
Baxter, R.
    Cherished the great commission 204, 205
    Counseling, Importance of 32
    Individuals, Special attention of 30
    Practical godliness 26
    Live the pastoral life 26,27
Beck, J. New Testament basis of pastoral theology 38
Bedell, G. T.
    Discover mental state of patient 41, 42
    Draw out parishioner's mind 47
    Know human nature 47
    Know peculiarities of the case 44
Beebe, J. A. Cordial coöperation of minister with doctor 178
Behaviour in our times 81, 82
Bell, G. K. A. Expressing the gospel in changing conditions 59
Berkhof, L. Definition of sanctification 120
Bernard, T. A. We may not isolate the spiritual 48
Bible
    Bible truth is important, according to G. Stevens 85
    Christian living described in the Bible 125
    Comfort. Our sole comfort from the Bible 33
    Individuals, Bible selections for 95, 96
    Individual needs according to Bible texts 31
    Individual work based on the Bible 54
    Individual cases in relation to the Bible 33
    Pastors must know how to use the Bible 173, 174
    Personality conceptions from the Bible 138
    Personality. Complete conception in the Bible 134
    Psychologists not interested in use of Bible 173
    Selection of Bible passages from questionnaire 77
    Soul conception must be Biblical 101, 102, 103
Biblical application
    Barrett, A. Used the Biblical basis 33
    Bridges, C. Importance of individual cases in relation to the Bible 33
    Everts, W. W. Selections of Scripture for individuals......................... 33
    Smith, J. The Bible is our sole comfort 33
    Thompson, H. Recommended Bible texts for individuals 33
Biblical basis of pastoral theology, according to P. D. Kidder 37
Biological interpretation of conversion 97-100
Biological, psychological, spiritual interpretation of conversion 103-107
Blackwood, A. W. Individual attention 57
Blaikie, W. G. Effective preaching 38
Blanton, S. and Peal, N. V. Coöperation between minister and doctor 184
Boisen, A. T.
    Pastor must know people intensively 153
    Pastor must speak with authority on sex questions 128
    Physical illness is a big problem for the pastor 108, 109
    Religious worker has advantages for cooperation 179

Bonar, A. A.
    Entire chapters of the Bible for pastoral work 45
    Individual needs are important 42
    Seven classifications of individuals 42
Bone, H. Psychiatrist is a specialist, not just for every minister 189
Bonnell, J. S.
    Complete counseling program for pastor 158
    Minister must have a unique approach 192
    Minister must know sex problems 128
    Use of the Bible in working with people 173
Booth, A. Govern personal temper 27
Brackenbury, H. B. Medicine is a social service and the doctor must coöperate 183
Bridges, C.
    Classifications of pastoral duties with individuals 31
    Experience the main teacher 28
    Importance of individual cases in relation to Bible 33
    Skill gained by experience more than a training 144
Brooks, P. Pastor must have human relationships 52
Bruce, W. S.
    Types change 154
    We may not condemn people as wholly irreligious 151
Burnett, Bishop. Consider the sick, the troubled in mind 31
Cabot, R. All ministers should have sickness experience 199
Cabot, R. C. and Dicks, R. L. Bible is important in working with the sick 173
Calkins, R. Christ's method of Scripture usage 172
Calling, Pastoral. No substitute, according to W. C. Martin 61
Carle, C. Freud did not overemphasize sex 126
Case Study
    Classification of case study 42, 43
    Examples of case study 42
    Individual case study 41, 42
Chambers, O. Special case study 56
Christ Jesus
    All of life must be brought under Christ's power 179
    Author and finisher of our faith 90
    Be Christlike in dealing with social problems. E. D. Weigle 57, 58
    Bread of life 136
    Commissioned men as ambassadors 195,196
    Counseled by Jesus 43
    Gives integrated living 133
    Gives the real mind cure according to W. A. Sadler 197
    His great commission 196, 197
    Individual method used by Christ 41, 42
    Method of using Scripture by Christ 172, 173
    Ministers are born-again by power of Christ 196
    Ministers must know God through Christ 195-198
    Obedience to Christ, by G. Herbert 27
    Recognize Christ, by R. H. Hollington 89
    Regeneration only through Christ, according to E. L. House 92
    Secret of life is in Christ, according to B. Conde 196
    The answer for everything is in Christ 207, 208
    Turn to Christ for spiritual development 134, 135

Christian life
Difference between efficient living according to psychologists and right living 137, 138
Jesus Christ gives integrated life 148
Minister must live a clean moral life himself 148
Christian living 119-138
Berkhof, L. Definition of sanctification 120
Biblical conception of holiness 121
Christian religion the source and substance of complete Christian living 135, 136
Cunningham, W. Apostolic days were not completely rozy 120
Day, F. E. Development of spiritual life 120
Elliott, H. S. and Elliott, G. L. Original nature of man neither good or bad 122
Halliday, W. F. Popular conception of holiness inadequate 121
Jefferson, C. E. Sheep need to be fed-likewise people 120
Link, H. C. Bible authentic textbook on personality 122
Littlejohn, A. N. An equilibrium of life 120
Mackenzie, J. G. Psychology interested only in instinct and emotion 119
Martin, E. D. Keep alive spirit of progress 121
Morgan, G. C. Pastor will perfect the saints 121
Newcomb, T. Personality develops through striving 121
Psychology not interested in Christian living 119
Sex in Christian living 125-131
Stolz, K. R. Religion as a rallying center 121
Weatherhead, L. D. A universal craving exists for God 122
Christianity
Able to alter the whole course of personality 133
A supernatural way of life, by C. E. Hudson 92
Does not make all morbid souls 112
Power of Christianity to solve problems, according to F. Kunkel 23
Religion of personality in Christianity 131, 132
Church
Institutional church was ignored by W. James 91
The church hesitant to accept responsibility for mental hygiene 23
The church lives by the great commission of Christ 205
Therapeutic value of the church, according to K. R. Stolz 23
Coe, G. A.
Disagreement among the writers of psychology 18
Only a hint of infinite God 87
Psychological training needed in seminaries 144, 145
Relation between psychology and pastoral theology is not desired 91, 92
Commission
Ambassadors for Christ 209
Baxter, R. Cherished the commission 204, 205
Challenge of the early disciples 202, 203
Church history reveals an accepted commission 204
Church lives by this great commission of Christ 205
Commissioned of God 202
Goulooze, W. God's sovereignty encourages our service 207
Grand pastoral leaders felt this commission 204
Halliday, W. F. The world needs the great physician 208
"I am a Stranger here," a hymn about our commission 208
McKenzie, J. G. A cherished commission brings a genuine conversion message .. 208
Minister must know his commission 202-209

Opportunities challenge our commission 207
Our spiritual commission is important 207
Paul challenged Timothy with a commission 204
Paul practiced the missionary challenge 204
Preparation of apostles 202, 203
Program of missions outlined 203
The great commission 203
Used in constitution of the church 205
Use present techniques for this commission 206, 207
We have lost this great commission 206
Community, Know your community 60
Conde, B. Jesus Christ gives integrated living 133
Conference
  A Protestant conference 161-167
  Bassett, C. Endorses the help of conference opportunity 166
  Help of a secretary for a conference 166
  Home calling of the minister 164
  Importance of the name 163, 164
  Inviting people to come 167
  Necessity of a conference time 162, 163
  No intitutionalized Protestant conference 163
  Northridge, W. L. Quoting Jung's questionnaire of people seeking help of
    minister, priest, or physician 163
  Place of Protestant minister in relation to the Roman Catholic priest ... 162
  Place of Roman Catholic Confessional 161-162
  Regulation of time 164
  Room setting of conference 164, 165
  Saving of time and effort by pastor 166
  Spiritual periodic check-up 165
  Stolz, K. R. Protestantism and confession 163
  Watson, J. People need a time of open heart discussion 162
Conference period, necessary according to T. J. Tidwell 61
Confessional, Place of Roman Catholic 161, 162
Conklin, E. S. Soul is seldom recognized by psychologists 102
Conscience. Advise people on matters of conscience, by A. Gerard 32
Conveniences influence our nervous tension crisis 20, 21
Conversation
  Adapted to circumstances, by S. Miller 44
  Friendly conversation, by T. L. Cuyler 47
  Rules for religious conversation, by W. Meade 32
  Vitalized conversation, by I. S. Spencer 44
Conversion 97-107
  Biological interpretation of conversion 97-100
  Ames, E. S. Emotional experience 98
  Cutten, G. B. We deal with conversion incompletely 99-100
  Dewar, L. We must see conversion as a whole 100
  Hollingworth, H. L. Conversion data variable 100
  Howley, J. Unification of psychic life 98
  James, W. Conversion different from Lutheran experience of justification 98
  Need complete understanding of conversion 100
  Norborg, S. Conversion is not a narrow frame of uniformity 99
  Waterhouse, E. S. Conversion is a change of direction 99

Biological, pschological, Spiritual view of conversion 103-107
    Barbour, C. E. Man is made like God 103-104
    Biblical basis of conversion 106-107
    Difference in people's experience of conversion 104
    Norborg, S. Conversion more than merely relaxing 106
    Norborg, S. Conversion a total experience 104-106
    Spiritual conversion necessary 105
    Woodworth. R. S. Psychology does not like the 'tang' of the word soul 105
Conversion, not a reshuffling of the conscious and subconscious motives 208

Counseling pastoral
  Application period of history 60-61
    Adams, H. There are many mental cases 61
    Martin, W. C. No substitute for pastoral calling 61
    Pattison, T. H. Adaptability required 60
    Tidwell, T. J. A conference period is important 61
    Watson, J. Protestants are behind Roman Catholics 60

  Beginnings of pastoral counseling 32
    Baxter, R. Method of counseling 32
    Everts, W. Minister must be known as counselor 33
    Gerard, A. Counseling the *hope-so* Christians 32
    Meade, W. Rules for religious conversation 32

  Development period of counseling 43, 44
    Counseling opportunities 43, 44
      Geikie, C. Jesus followed counseling method 43
      Hall, C. C. Confidential fellowship is enriching 43
      Love, J. Jr. Opportunity means duty 44
      Watson, J. Open door of greater service 43

    Counseling suggestions 44
      Bedell, G. T. Know peculiarities of each case 44
      Kidder, P. D. Clear discernment necessary 44
      Miller, S. Adapt conversation to circumstance 44
      Spencer, I. S. Vitalized conversation 44
      Tilden, W. P. The art of listening 44

  Systematic Counseling 156-176
    Anderson, S. Christian viewpoint in counseling 159
    Benefits of psychology 157-158
    Bonnell, J. S. Complete technique for counseling 158
    Dicks, R. L. Counseling for the average pastor 158
    Hiltner, S. Recorded accounts of interviews 158-159
    Martin, W. C. Basic techniques of counseling are as old as Christianity 157
    May, R. Underlying principles of counseling 157
    Protestant conference 161-167
    Systematic family visitation 167
    Systematic use of the Bible 172-173

Crisis
  Crisis in applied psychology 17, 18
  Crisis of our times 81-83
  Nervous tension crisis 20, 21
    Influenced by modern conveniences 20, 21
    Many physical breakdown experiences in people 21
    Waterhouse, E. S., quoted on "headline mentality." 21

Pastoral psychology for the crisis 21-25
  Christian psychology needed in our crisis 21
  Dobbins, G. S. Minister must study psychology 22
  Fallows, S. Opportunity of clergyman is here 21
  Halliday, W. F. Days of psychological unrest here 21
  Halliday, W. F. World needs the spiritual physician 22
  Holman, C. T. Cure of souls is urgent 22
  Kemp, C. F. Noble work of many pastors in crisis 24
  Kunkel, F. Christianity the key for our crisis 23
  Ligon, E. M. Psychology can help study in our crisis 22
  Ministry. Utilize our opportunities today 23
  Rogers, C. F. Entire conception of pastoral theology must be raised 22
  Stolz, K. R. Minister must reach persons as well as crowds 23
  Trueblood, E. The race with catastrophy is on 24
Psychological crisis 17
  Martin, E. D. Psychological thinking revolutionary 17
  Waterhouse, E. S. Exaggerations in psychology 17
Social crisis 18-20
  Atomic era brought social changes 19-20
  Cattell, R. B. Our days culturally are momentous 20
  Crowd psychology influencial in social crisis 19
  Dobbins, G. S. Ours is a revolutionary time 22
  Kraines, S. H., and Thetford, E. S. Manage your mind 20
  Sorokin, P. A. We live between two epochs 18
  Sudden changes in pastorate due to social crisis 21
  Trueblood, E. Interpretation of social impact of the atomic bomb era 19
  Trueblood, E. Quoted A. Schweitzer on the collapse of our civilization 19, 20
  Waterhouse, E. S., Our age is different socially 19
  World War II added to social crisis of our time 19
Crosby, H. Pastor must have enthusiastic love for Christ 36
Cults
  Seek to find an answer for suffering 113
  Seek to minister to one phase of life 117
Cunningham, W. Apostolic days were not altogether rozy 120
Cutten, G. B.
  Conversion must be studied, but incompletely 99, 100
  Seminary traning is needed 144, 145
  Religion is man's highest reach 85
Cuyler, T. L.
  Friendly conversations important 47
  Visit inside and outside of the fold 40
Dawson, G. Pastor, physician and nurse ought to have psychotherapeutic knowledge 179
Day, F. E. Development of spiritual life 120
Deathbed visiting 40
De Jong, P. Y. Importance of visitation 167, 168
Demarest, D. D. Harmonious spirit of the pastor 36
Dewar, L. Conversion must be seen as a whole 100
Dewar, L. and Hudson, C. E. Psychology has limitations on Christian living 124
Dicks R. L.
  Counseling for the average pastor 158
  Pastor must go to people 169
  Suffering brings maturity of soul 199

Divorce. The importance of the question today 129
Dobbins, G. S.
    Counseling is to help people 161
    Discover human, that is, religious need 54
    Ours is a changing world 59
    Personal examination by the pastor of himself 51
Doctor and minister 177-194
    Beebe, J. A. Cordial coöperation needed 178
    Blanton, S., and Peale, N. V. Coöperation demonstrated 184
    Boisen, A. T. Religious worker has advantages for coöperation 179
    Brackenbury, H. B. Medicine is a social service and doctor must coöperate 183
    Dawson, G. Pastor, physician and nurse ought to have some psychotherapeutic
        knowledge 179
    Doctors have been trained in secular schools and are often foreign to religion 182
    Doctors, particularly non-Christian doctors, are slow to welcome work of minister 181
    Douglas, L. C. Do not meddle with the work of the doctor 178
    Duty of the doctor to coöperate with the minister 181, 182
    Gerberding, G. H. Coöperate with the doctor 178
    Gladden, W. Obey orders of the doctor 178
    Ikin, A. G. Need closer coöperation between doctor and the minister 180
    Jacoby, G. W. Goals should be same for doctor and minister 180
    Jung, C. G. Clergyman stands before a vast horizon of service 180
    Liotta, M. A. Doctors should be interested in the supernatural 182
    Luke, the beloved physician of the Bible 182
    Oliver, J. R. Doctors welcome understanding ministers 183
    Pastoral theology demands close coöperation 181, 182
    Physicians are on equal basis with pastors 183, 184
    Rhodes, G. Each should esteem the other 181
    Sadler, W. A. The pychiatrist must be more than a master mechanic 183
    Total life must be brought under the power of Christ 179-180
    Wells, J. D. Doctor must know the minister in order to allow him visits 173
    Willcox, G. B. Doctors are often irreligious and usually not sympathetic with pas-
        tors 177
    Worcester, E. and Mc Comb, S. Demonstrated coöperation 184
    Vinet, A Pastor ought to learn from physician about the patient 177
Doctor should be invited to lecture on sex to young people 130
Douglas, L. C. Do not meddle with the work of the doctor 178
Dunsmore, M. H. Christianity a religion of personality 132
Dykes, J. O. General calling on individuals necessary 54
Edwards, R. H. Person mindedness 56, 57
Elijah knew God 196
Elliott, H. S. and Elliott, G. L. Original nature of man neither good or bad 122
Ellis, W. Soul no longer a welcome idea 102
Environment. Personality development related to social environment, by C. T. Holman 132
Erdman, C. R.
    Classification of individual needs 151
    Ten classifications of individuals 55
Everts, W. W. Bible texts for individual needs 31, 33
Experience and common sense method 28, 29
    Bridges, C. Experience is the main teacher 28
    Gerard, A. Prepare for private duties 29
    Herbert, G. Reply on experience 29

Experience. Personal experience of the pastor. 35
Experience. Reply on experience, by F. Kunkel 145
Experience. Skill gained by experience more than by training, according to C. Bridges 144
Fahs, R. Z.
    Know the home 52
    Times have changed everything 58
Fairbairn, P. Comprehensive analysis of pastoral theology 38
Faith healing, stressed by the cults 117
Fallows, S. Minister has a grand opportunity today 23, 185
Family
    Attitude of family toward visiting 40
    Family problems, discussed by C. Bassett 82
    Family problems not always revealed unless home visitation is made 169
Fears. Complexity of modern fears, by P. Bradley 82
Feeling. Profound respect for feeling by W. James 123
Fisher, D. W. Soul is not just a psychic expression 102
Freinfels, R. M. Soul interest is reviving 102, 103
Freud, influence on the teaching on sex 124, 125
Fritz, J. H. C. Classification of cases 55, 56
Garvie, A. E. Find out people's interests 52
Geikie, C. Jesus followed counseling opportunity 43
Gerard, A.
    Advise people on matters of conscience 32
    Discover particular situations 31
    Prepare for private duties 28, 29
Gerberding, G. H.
    Individual case study based on the Bible 54
    Ministers should coöperate with doctors 173
Gladden, W.
    Adapt work of church to conditions 58
    Know life from people themselves 52
    Know real agents of special field 46
    Obey orders from the physician 178
God
    Imperfect conception of God 86-90
        Adler, A. Believed in stark humanism 88
        Baker, A. E. God a symbol of psychic energy 88
        Coe, G. A. Only a hint of the infinite in his writings 87
        Hollington, R. D. Recognized God and Christ 89
        Hughes, T. H. God and Christ proclaimed 90
        James, W. Ours is an empiricist criterion 87
        King, I. Idea of God built up 88, 89
        Leuba, J. H. Gods only a subjective existence 88
        McKenzie, J. G. God the source of all energy 89
        Moore, D. T. V. God a supreme intelligence 88
        Pratt, J. B. Lacked view of supernatural 87
        Weatherford, W. D. God dwells within us 89
    Minister must know God through Christ 195-198
        Biblical conception of sin important 197
        Conde, B. Importance of Holy Spirit in idea of God 196

Elijah knew God 196
John the Baptist knew God 196
Know the Holy Spirit to understand God 196
Know the plan of salvation which God gives 197
Paul knew God 196
Sadler, W. S. Christ is the real mind cure 197
Godliness. R. Baxter on practical godliness 26, 27
God's sovereignty, encourages our services, by W. Goulooze 207
Gospel
    Full gospel, not a gospel of psychotherapy 117
    Pastoral psychology not to be divorced from gospel 23
    Relevant gospel for all of life, by G. Harkness 134
Goulooze, W.
    Bible passages and their use in *Victory over Suffering*, and *Manual of Ministers, Elders and Deacons* 174, 175
    God's sovereignty and man's duty 207
Granger, F. Religious feeling is not uniform 152
Green, P. Methods differ with people 31
Group study 154, 155
    Bruce, W. S. Types change in people 154
    Norborg, S. Three groups in congregation 154
    Oliver, J. R. Classification of Psychoses 154
    Oliver, J. R. Minister must know types and groups 155
    Schindler, C. J. Cannot escape grouping people in congregations .. 155
Groves, E. R. The minister must know himself 141
Gunsaulus, F. W.
    Honor to be in the ministry 50
    Spiritual life comes near people 52
Hall, C. C.
    Confidential fellowship enriches 43
    Copy the work of a physician 41
Hall, G. S. Recognized the gap between pastoral theology and psychology .. 91
Halliday, W. F.
    Minister must know himself before God 141
    Our present peculiar psychological unrest 82
    Popular conception of holiness inadequate 121
    The world needs the great physician 208
    Understand the home 168, 169
Harkness, G.
    Christian gospel relevant for all of life 134
    Family disturbances are many 110, 111
    People are different, variant molds 152
Harmon, N. B. Jr.
    Coolness and composure necessary for minister 50
    Manifest presence of mind 192
Harrington, M. Understand mental tensions 112
Heisler, C. W.
    Be a man of heart and love 37
    Old fashioned pastoral visit necessary 39
Hepner, H. W. Self examination does not come merely by reading of books .. 142
Herbert, G.
    Obedience to Christ 27
    Prepare for systematic visits 29

Rely on experience 28
Hewitt, A. W. Place of the rural pastor 51
Hewitt, C. E. Emphasis on experience 144
Hiltner, S.
  Accounts recorded of interviews 158, 159
  Counseling is to help people 160
  Importance of religion to health 135
  Physical and mental illness always related 116
  Suffering strain brings emotional response to surface 113, 114
  Total number of church related hospitals 109
  Understand emotion of patient 193, 194
Hollington, R. D. Recognize Christ and God 89
Hollingworth, H. L. Data of biological sciences more variable than those of mechanics
  and physics 100
Hollingworth, H. L. and Poffenberger, A. T. Disagreement between psychologists is
  marked 18
Holman, C. T.
  Importance of counseling opportunities 160
  Importance of visiting in the home 163
  Man's sin in Adam 136, 137
  Personality development related to social environment 132, 133
  Religion the most powerful aid for making adjustments 134
  Seminaries must "overhaul" training 145
  Urgency of the cure by the minister 22
Holy Spirit
  In conversion 105
  Ministers must be led by the Holy Spirit 196
  Pastors must possess the Spirit 36
  Practical knowledge comes through the Spirit of God, according to E. Pond...... 150
  Room must be left for the Holy Spirit in religion, according to H. Warner 85
Home
  Importance of calling on the home, by C. T. Holman 168
  Know the home, according to R. Z. Fahs 52
  Understand the home, by W. F. Halliday 168, 169
Hoppin, J. M.
  Choice Bible passages are important 45
  Friendly manner of the pastor 36
  Make special preparation for sick visitation 40, 41
  Spiritual insight comes from above 150
  Three classifications of people 43
  Well-rounded service of pastor 37, 38
Horton, W. M. Coöperation possible between pastoral theology and psychology 93
Hospitals. Total number of hospitals, church related and soldiers hospitals 109
House, E. L. Regeneration throughout Christ 92
How, W. W.
  General and specific visiting 40
  Know careful approach 47
Howley, J. Conversion is unification of psychic life 98
Hudson, C. E. Christianity is a supernatural way of life 92
Hughes, T. H.
  Christ must be proclaimed 90
  Three basic needs in life 95

Human nature
- Knowledge of human nature 52-54
  - Adams, H. Know human nature and the minds of people 53
  - Balmforth, H. Dewar, L., Hudson, E. E., Sara, E. S. Experience makes better competence 53
  - Brooks, P. Have human relationship 52
  - Dobbins, G. S. Discover human religious need 54
  - Fahs, R. Z. Know the home 52
  - Garvie, A. E. Find out people's interests 52
  - Gladden, W. Know life from people themselves 52
  - Gunsaulus, F. W. Spiritual life comes near people 52
  - Joseph, O. L. Know actualities of life 53
  - Mc Kinney, A. H. Jesus knew people 23
  - Rogers, C. F. Two classes of ministers in relation to human interests 52, 53
- Psychological understanding of human nature 47, 48
  - Bedell, G. T. Minister must know make-up of individual 47
  - Littlejohn, A. N. Know sinfulness of sin in individual 47
  - Miller, E. Know human nature of your own people 47
  - Weidner, R. F. Know all the relations of human life 47

Hygiene, Mental, physical, and spiritual hygiene 115-118
- Bible emphasis in Christian living for hygiene 117
- Cults seek to minister to hygiene life 117
- Hiltner, S. People seldom sick—only mentally 116
- Mental, spiritual, and physical hygiene a total unity 117, 118
- Pastor, the key of total living 115
- Pastoral duty is to teach spiritual hygiene to the healthy, according to G. B. Cutten 115
- Preston, G. H. Man the chief threat to mental health 115
- Sadler, W. A. Aid of religious influences to help people 116
- Sadler, W. A. Christ is the real mind cure for all 116
- Spiritual hygiene must be taught and lived 117

Hymn selections reported in questionnaire 76

Ikin, A. G. Need closer coöperation between minister and doctor 180

Illness. The reason for illness 112-113

Illness. Mental illness must be faced 110-112
- Average family problems 111
- Duty of the minister to the mentally ill 111, 112
- Harkness, G. Family life a fertile place for psychic disturbances 110
- Harrington, M. Understand mental tensions 112
- Ministers should realize our mental illness situation 110
- Murray, J. A. C. Multiplied mental disorders today 111
- Norborg, S. Christianity does not make morbid souls 112

Individual
- Individual case study, applicatory period of history 54-57
  - Balmforth, H. Dewar, L., Hudson, C. E., Sara, E. S. Individual treatment is necessary 56
  - Blackwood, A. W. Individual attention 57
  - Chambers, O. Special case study 56
  - Dykes, J. O. General calling made individual 54
  - Edwards, R. H. Person-mindedness 56, 57
  - Erdmans C. R. Ten classifications of individuals 55

Gerberding, G. H. Individual study based on Bible 54
Gladden, W. Know the times and circumstances 55
Jefferson, C. W. Medicine gives us the clue for individual work 54
Kemp, J. W. Reach person where he is 55
Fritz, J. H. C. Classifications of cases 55, 56
Pym, T. W. See people's moral difficulties in light of their past history 55
Quale, W. A. Importance of individual work 54
Individual case study, beginnings period of history 30, 31
Baxter, R. Special attention paid to some people 30
Bridges, C. Classifications for pastoral duties of individual cases 31
Burnett, Bishop. Consider the sick, the troubled in mind and the dissenters 31
Everts, W. W. Bible texts for individual needs 31
Gerard, A. Discover particular situations 31
Green, P. Methods differ with people 31
Individual case study, period of development in history 41-43
Classifications of individuals 42, 43
Bonar, A. Seven classifications of individuals 42
Hoppin, J. M. Three classifications of individuals 43
Plummer, W. A. Seven classifications of individuals 42
Van Oosterzee, J. J. External and internal states 42
Vinet, A. External and internal states 42

Examples of case study 42
Bonar, A. Individual needs 42
Spencer, I. S. Case records and treatment 42
Wells, J. D. Distinguish various cases of a sick and dying 42
Importance of case study 41, 42
Bedell, G. T. Discover mental state of patient 41
Hall, C. C. Copy the work of the physician 41
Latham, H. Jesus used individual method 41
Waynne, F. R. Keep flock before you as individuals 42
Individual life situation 151-153
Boisen, A. T. Intensive study of particular cases 153
Granger, F. Religious feeling is not uniform 152
Harkness, G. Life not expressed in uniform way 152
Know individual where he is 151-153
Oliver, J. R. Know past life of individual 153
Seabury, D., we are not simple creatures 153
Individual. Psychological understanding of individual 47, 48
Bedell, G. T. Draw out the parishioner's mind 47
Bernard, T. A. Cannot isolate the spiritual 148
Cuyler, T. L. Friendly conversations of the pastor 47
How, W. W. Difficulty in knowing state of the soul 47
Jacoby, G. W. Goals of minister and doctor should be the same 180
James, J. A. Sincere and earnest ministry is important 27, 28
James, W.
Conversation other than Lutheran interpretation of justification 98
Definitions are not needed 84, 85
Ignored the institutional church 91
No thought of defining soul 100, 101
Ours is an empiricist criterion 86, 87
Profound respect for feeling 123

Jefferson, C. E.
    Sheep need to be fed, likewise spiritual sheep 120
    Medicine gives us the clue for individual work 54
John the Baptist
    A fine example 201
    He had the right spirit 201
    Knew God 201
Jones, W. L. No need for definitions of religion 85, 86
Joseph, O. L. Know actualities of life 53
Josey, C. C. Development in conceptions of religion 85
Jung, C. G.
    Clergyman stands before a vast horizon of service 189
    Soul conception lacking 101
    When people find religion they find life 136
Kemp, C. K. Person of pastor is important 143
Kempt, J. W. Reach the person where he is 55
Kidder, P. D.
    Have clear discernment of the individual 44
    Strong Biblical basis necessary 37
King, I. Idea of God is built up 88, 89
Kunkel, F.
    Christianity the power to solve our problems 23
    Ministers rely on experience 145
    Psychology needs religion and religion needs psychology 93
    Religious experience not understood by psychologists 124
Latham, H. Jesus used individual method 41
Leach, W. H. Few ministers should try to be psychiatrists. 189
Leadership. Cultivate capacity for leadership, by D. Bauslin 49
Leiffer, H. M. Pastor must have religious faith and experience 142
Lessons learned by people from sickness and suffering 72-76
Leuba, J. H. God only a subjective existence 88
Life situations
    Know life situations-emphasis in pastoral theology 150, 151
      Bruce, W. S. We may not condemn people as wholly irreligious 151
      Erdman, C. R. Classification of individual needs 151
      Hoppin, J. M. Spiritual insight comes from above 150
      Mc Kinney, A. H. Find real condition of mind and heart of individuals 151
      Pond, E. Practical knowledge is also under the Spirit of God 150
    Life situations. Importance of knowing. See index under Individual life situa-
      tions 252, 253
Listening. The art of listening, recommended by W. P. Tilden 44
Littlejohn, A. N.
    Christian living means equilibrium in life 120
    Know sinfulness of sin 47
Love, J. Jr.
    Opportunity of counseling means duty 44
    Possessing the Holy Spirit 36
Lyman, A. J., The pastor in human relations 59
Lynch, F. Epicurean pagan teaching is rampant today 58
Mackenzie, J. G. Psychology interested only in instinct and emotion 119

Man
 Manners, personal manners of the pastor 35, 36
 Salvation necessary 93, 94
 Total depravity of 93
Martin, E. D.
 Changes came because of psychology 17
 Keep alive progress and liberalism 121
Martin, W. C.
 Basic techniques of counseling are as old as Christianity...................... 157
 No substitute for pastoral calling 61
Mason—Detailed rules for visiting 30
May, R. Underlying principles of counseling 157
Mc Kenzie, J. G.
 Bible complete description of personality development 134
 Cherished spiritual commission will bring a real conversion message 208
 Spiritual conversion not a re-shuffling of the conscious and sub-conscious motives .. 208
Mc Kinney, A. H.
 Find real condition of mind and heart in situations 151
 Jesus knew people 53
Meade, W.
 Be a shepherd of souls 27
 Rules for religious conversation 32
Medicine gives us the clue of operation 54
Mental cases. Many mental cases today, suggested by H. Adams 61
Mental, physical and spiritual hygiene. See index under Hygiene ....
Mentality. Headline mentality—Waterhouse claimed this to be our trouble 21
Methods. Differ with different people 31
Miller, E. Know the climate of the soul 47
Miller, S.
 Adapt conversation to circumstance 44
 Dignity and conduct of minister are important 35, 36
 Know practical books and pious men 144
 Official systematic visiting 39
Minister
 Advantages of minister as counselor 160, 161
 Dobbins, G. S. Bring individual to Christ 161
 Hiltner, S. Counseling is to help people 160
 Holman, C. T. Important opportunities for minister 160
 Overstreet, H. A. We fail to use simple techniques 160
 Pastor is the key person 160
 Schindler, C. J. Success only as people are brought to Christ 161
 Ministerial conversation 193, 194
 Cabot, R. C. and Dicks, R. L. Talk to people where they are 193
 Conversation must be directed, like a physician's 193
 Conversation must be guarded 193
 Failure to get patient's point of view 193
 Hiltner, S. Understand emotion of patient 194
 Lack of preparation for conversation 193
 Spirit of indifference by ministers 194
 Minister and doctor 177-194
 See index for detailed topical and author index of this subject 248

Minister and doctor. Minister in coöperation with doctor 184-194
   Fallows, S. Minister has grand opportunity 185
   Minister can speak to subject on Sunday in church and privately 186
   Minister should know his wares 187
   Minister should welcome advice of doctor 186
   Ministerial attitude in coöperation with doctor 185
   Minister's main duty is salvation of souls 186
   Valintine, C. H. Religion is the only cure 186
   Wise, C. A. Habits of minister with people must be checked 186
Minister. The minister himself 141-144
   Groves, E. R. Know yourself to be successful 141
   Halliday, W. F. Minister must know himself before God 141
   Hepner, H. W. Self examination does not come by merely reading books 142
   Hiltner, S. Missed consecration of pastor in writings 143
   Hughes, T. H. Consecration necessary to help others 142
   Kemp, C. F. Person of pastor is important 143
   Leiffer, H. M. Pastor must have deep religious faith 142
   Pastor's personal appearances will reflect his spiritual life 142
   Paul gave advice for young minister, Timothy 144
   Rogers, C. R. Lacked consecration for service in writings 143
   Schindler, C. J. Pastor as counselor must have spiritual emphasis and life 143
Minister, must know himself 202
   Bible shows our wickedness, even though we serve in the profession of the
      ministry 201
   Cabot, R. C. All ministers should be sick at sometime in their life 199
   Dicks, R. L. Suffering brings maturity of soul 199
   High standards must be achieved 201
   Importance of suffering toward understanding 199, 200
   John the Baptist had the right spirit 201
   Ministers must know genuine Christian living 200
   Ministers must know they are sinners 198
   Murray, J. A. C. Ministers are often maladjusted 200
   Murray, J. A. C. We must be like John the Baptist 201
   Paul was a "chief" sinner 198
   Self examination necessary like the Psalmist 198
Minister must know his commission 202-209
   See index under Commission 244, 245
Minister must know God through Christ 195-198
   See index under God 249, 250
Minister must not be a psychiatrist 189-191
   Bone, H. A psychiatrist is a scientific specialist, not to be applied to just every
      minister 189
   Bonnell, J. S. Minister can practice "pastoral psychiatry" 190
   Leach, W. H. Few ministers should try to be psychiatrists 189
   Ministers have the key to today's problems 191
   Ministers need scientific-spiritual point of view 190
   Minister should know symptoms 190
   Mulder, J. D. The field of psychiatry is large, intended only for specialists 190
   Northridge, W. L. Know characteristic symptoms 191
Ministerial training 147-149
   Associated with psychiatrist in field work—good training 148, 149
   Clinical training by psychiatrist 148, 149

Middle class people are in need of advice and help 147
Minister must live a clean moral life himself 148
Training is needed for ministers 147
Ready books of reference needed in pastor's study 148
Moore, D. T. V. God is a supreme intelligence 88
Morgan, G. C. Pastor will help perfect the saints 121
Mulder, J. D. Field of psychiatry is large, intended only for specialists 190
Murray, J. A. C.
    Mental illness, increased in modern life 111
    Ministers are often maladjusted 200
Murphy, T.
    Attitude and atmosphere of family toward visiting 40
    Pastoral Theology shows activity of pastor 38
    Visit to get acquainted 39
Nervous tension crisis 20, 21
    See index of detailed material 246
Newcomb, T. Personality develops from striving 121
New Testament, the basis for pastoral theology, according to J. Beck 38
Norborg, S.
    Christianity does not make all morbid souls 112
    Contended for difference between religious and Christian experience 92
    Conversion more than merely relaxing 106
    Conversion is a total experience 104
    Conversion is not a narrow unrealistic form of uniformity 99
    Critique on lack of definitions among psychologists 86
    Three groups in a congregation 154
Northridge, W. L.
    Complete souls cure throughout fellowship with God 135
    Minister must know characteristic symptoms of trouble 191
    Quotation of Jung's questionnaire about people seeking help of minister, priest
    or physician 163
Obstacles in the way of coördination between pastoral theology and psychology 84-90
    Imperfect conception of God 86-90
    Imperfect definitions of religion 84-86
    See index, under *God* 249, 250
    See index, under Religion 261, 262
Oliver, J. R.
    Classification of Psychoses 153
    Doctors should welcome understanding ministers 183
    Know past life of cases 153
    Minister must know types and groups of people 155
Overstreet, H. A. We fail to simplify techniques of counseling 160
Pastor
    Person of the pastor, from application period of history 49-52
    Agar, F. A. Practical aspects of work 51
    Allnatt, F. J. B. Active spiritual living 50
    Bauslin, D. Capacity for leadership 49
    Dobbins, G. S. Personal examination 51
    Gunsaulus, F. W. Honor in the ministry 50
    Harmon, N. B. Jr. Imperturbality 50
    Hewitt, A. W. Rural pastoral interests 51

Luccock, H. W. Danger of minimum spiritual life 51
Pym, T. W. Pastor must be a specialist 50
Sheepshanks, J. Pastor's personal life 49
Person of the pastor, from developmental period of history 35-37
Personal devotion of the pastor 36, 37
  Crosby, H. Love for Christ 36
  Demarest, D. D. Harmonious character 36
  Heisler, C. W. A man of heart and feeling 37
  Hoppin, J. M. Attractive and friendly person 36
  Love, J., Jr. Possess the Holy Spirit 36
  Taylor, W. M. Sympathy should be real 36
Personal experiences of pastor 35
  Davis, P. S. Personal experiences 35
  How, W. W. Personal holiness 35
  Smith, H. W. Study experience 35
  Spooner, E. Personal experiences of the pastor 35
Personal manners of the pastor 35, 36
  Miller, S. Dignity of the minister 35, 36
  Peabody, A. P. Build personal character 36
  Shedd, W. G. T. Religious, intellectual and social character of the pastor 36
Person of the pastor, from history of beginnings 26-28
  Baxter, R. On practical godliness 26
  Booth, A. Government of personal temper 27
  James, J. A. Sincerity and earnestness needed 27, 28
  Meade, W. Shepherd of souls 27
  Pond, E. Piety and strong faith needed 27
  Smith, J. Manner of life of pastor 27
  The Pastor's Manual, a caution for pastoral life 27
Pastor, person of. See index on Minister, the minister himself, and the minister
  must know himself 255, 256
Pastor. Counseling
  See complete index details under *Counseling, pastoral* 246
  See index for *Conversation, a Protestant Conference* 245
  See complete index for *Minister, advantages of ministers as counselor* 246
  See index for *Scripture, systematic use of Scripture* 262
  See index for detailed material under *Crisis. Pastoral psychology of the Crisis*
  .... 246, 247
Pastoral Psychology for the crisis 21-24
  See index for detailed material under *Crisis. Pastoral psychology for the Crises*
  .... 246, 247
Pastoral Theology
  Coördination of pastoral theology and psychology for pastoral psychology 92-96
  Barbour, C. L. No antagonism between them in reality 94
  Horton, W. M. Coöperation possible 93
  Hughes, T. H. Three basic needs in life 95
  Kunkel, F. Psychology needs theology and theology needs psychology 93
  Kunkel, F. The greatest psychologist was Christ 95
  Swisher, W. S. Church must get in touch with the world to do work correctly .. 94
  Wise, C. A. Clinical experience good for pastors 94
  Pastoral theology needs psychology 83, 84
  Adams, H. We need knowledge of Jesus to serve the mind 83
  Pastors must see this need 83

Rogers, C. F. The entire level of efficiency must be raised 84
Pastoral Theology. Organized pastoral theology 37-39
    Beck, J. New Testament basis 38
    Blaikie, W. G. Needed for effective preaching 38
    Cannon, J. W. Complete, systematized 37
    Fairbairn, P. Complete analysis 38
    Hoppin, J. M. Well-rounnded service of pastor 37, 38
    Kidder, P. D. Biblical basis 37
    Murphy, T. Activity of the pastor 38
    Shedd, W. G. T.. Combined with homiletics 38
    Wayland, F. Material in form of letters 37
    Van Oosterzee, J. J. Historical, systematic 38
    Vinet, A. Material, moral and spiritual 38

Pastoral Theology. Separation of pastoral theology and psychology 91, 92
    Bassett, C. Minister can do much to the situation 92
    Coe, G. A. No relation desired 91
    Hall, G. S. Recognized the gap 91
    House, E. L. Regeneration through Christ 92
    Hudson, C. E. Christianity is a supernatural way of life 92
    James, W. Ingnored the institutional church 91
    Norborg, S. Contended for difference between religious and Christian experience 92

Pattison, T. H. Adaptability is required 60
Paul
    Captivated by Christ 196
    Challenged Timothy with the great commission 204
    Chief of sinners 198
    Gave advice on the ministry to Timothy 144
    His spiritual conversion 99
    Practiced the missionary challenge 204
    Secret of suffering 113

Person. Person mindedness, according to R. H. Edwards 56, 57

Personal bearing of the minister 191, 192
    Bonnell, J. S. Difference in approach, just like doctors 192
    Cultivation of personal bearing 191-192
    Harmon, N. B. Have coolness and presence of mind 192
    Spirit of personal appearance 191

Personal devotion of the pastor 36, 37
    See index for detailed material under *Pastor, person of* 258

Personal manners of the pastor 35, 36
    See index for detailed material under *Pastor, person of* 257-258

Personality
    Bible, the authentic textbook on personality 122
    Develops from striving, according to T. Newcomb 121
    Development (personality development) 131-138
    Biblical conceptions of personality development 138
    Christian religion, source and substance of complete Christian living 135, 136
    Christianity able to alter whole course of personality 133
    Conde, B. Christ gives integrated living 133
    Dunsmore, M. H. Christianity a religion of personality 132
    Harkness, G. Christian gospel relevant for all of life 134
    Hiltner, S. Importance of religion to health 135

Holman, C. T. Man's sin in Adam 137
Holman, C. T. Religion the most powerful aid for making adjustments 136, 137
Jesus Christ is the bread of life 136
Jung, C. G. When people find religion they find life 136
McKenzie, J. G. The Bible has complete description for personality develop-
ment ....,........... 134
Northridge, W. L. Complete soul cure through fellowship with God 135
Psychologists do not envision complete Christian living in personality develop-
ment 131
Pym, T. W. Difference between efficient living and right living, as described
by the psychologists 137
Richmond, W. V. Psychology helps us understand some of the riddles of life .. 133
Sadler, W. A. Turn to Jesus Christ for development of personality 135
Stevens, S. N. Therapeutic value of religion 135
Stolz, K. R. Know the last four laps of life 134
Wise, C. A. Denies importance of religion in personality development 133
Piety, Necessity of, by E. Pond 27
Pitkin, W. B. Mental illness a world epidemic 111
Plummer, W. A. Seven classifications of individuals 42
Poem selections reported in questionnaires on sickness and suffering 76, 77
Pond, E.
Eight classes of people 31
Have good judgment 28
Know the sheep spiritually 29
Necessity of piety 27
Visiting brings contact 29
Pragmatic, in Christian living 123-125
Christian living described in the Bible in true sense 125
Dewar, L., and Hudson, C. E. Psychology has limitations on Christian living 124
James, W. Profound respect for feeling 123
Kunkel, F. Religious experience not understood by psychologists 124
Selbie, W. B. Pragmatism really explains religion away 123
Waterhouse, E. S. Feeling cannot describe religion 124
Pratt, J. B
No place for the soul 100
Not bothered with definitions 84
Preaching. Preaching complex among ministers 187-189
Avoid preaching complex 188
Experience in preaching 187
Feeling in preaching 187, 188
Preach to individuals 189
Preaching commanded by Christ 187
Preaching is important for the minister 187
Soul consideration in preaching 188
Preston, G. H. Man is his own threat to hygiene 115
Psychology
Applied psychology
Emergence of applied psychology 17, 18
Psychology is in every field now 18
Psychological understanding of community 46, 47

Geikie, G. Study business conditions 46
Greer, D. H. Parishes must be worked differently 46
Gladden, W. Know real events of special field 46
Warner, H. W. Study business conditions 46
Weigel, E. D. Pastorates change 46, 47
Wilcox, G. B. Pastoral duties are modified 47
Psychological crisis. See index under *Crisis* 246, 247
Psychological understanding of human nature 47
Bedell, G. T. Know human nature 47
Littlejohn, A. N. Know sinfulness of sin 47
Miller, E. Know the climate of the soul 47
Weidner, R. F. Know the relations of life 47
Psychological understanding of the individual 47, 48
Bedell, G. T. Drawn out parishionier's mind 47
Bernard, T. A. Cannot isolate the spiritual 48
Cuyler, T. L. Friendly conversations 47
How, W. W. Know careful approach 47
Psychology. Disagreement among writers 18
Coe, G. A. Disagreement pronounced 18
Hollingworth, H. L. and Poffenberger, A. T. Disagreement must be noted 18
Much disagreement today 18
Psychology. Its glamour 17
Pym, T. W.
Difference between efficient living and right living according to the psychologists 137
Moral pathology needed in seminary training 145
Pastor must be a specialist 50
See people's moral difficulties over against past history 55
Qualifications of the pastor 141-149
The minister himself. See index under *Minister* 256
Questionnaire on sickness, suffering and sorrow
Final questionnaire 66, 69
First questionnaire 65, 66
People who received the questionnaire 69, 70
Recommendation of other people through the questionnaires 77, 78
Religion
As a rallying center, according to K. R. Stolz 121
Clash between religion and science due to war 19
Imperfect definitions of religion 84-86
Bavinck, H. Christian view of definitions 86
Bavinck, J. H. Biblical psychology 86
Bungling of definitions 86
Cutten, G. B. Religion is man's highest reach 85
James, W. Definition not needed 84
Jones, W. L. No need of definition 85, 86
Josey, C. C. Development in conceptions of religion 85
Norborg, S. Critique on lack of definitions 86
Pratt, J. B. Not bothered with definitions 84
Steven, G. Biblical truth important 85
Thouless, R. H. A felt practical relationship 85
Warner, H. Room for the Holy Spirit 85
Waterink, J. Biblical psychology 86
Wise, C. A. Attempt to discover a way of life 85

Importance of religion to health, according to S. Hiltner 135
Religion the most powerful aid in making adjustments 134
Religion the only cure, by C. H. Calintine 186
Therapeutic value of religion, according to G. Stevens 135
When people find religion they find life, by C. G. Jung 136
Religious faith, necessary for pastors, according to H. M. Leiffer 142
Richmond, W. V. Psychology helps understand some riddles of life 133
Rogers, C. F.
  Demonstrate patient investigation 59
  Pastoral theology must be lifted to a higher plane 84
  Psychology of sex is important 127
  Rogers, C. R. Hypothesis for counseling 157
  Two classes of ministers in human interests 52
Sadler, W. A.
  Christ gives the real mind cure 197
  Religious influences help 116
  The psychiatrist must be more than a master mechanic 183
  Turn to Jesus for development of life 135
  Turn to Christ, for only Christ satisfies 206
Salvation
  Minister's main duty in preaching and serving 186
  Necessary for man's welfare 93
Sanctification
  Berkhof's definition of sanctification 120
  Necessary 120
  Popular conception of holiness inadequate, by W. F. Halliday 121
Schindler, C. J.
  Cannot escape grouping people in congregations 155
  Counseling only successful when people are brought to Christ 161
  Pastor as counselor must have spiritual emphasis 143
Science, clash between science and religion came to a head due to the war 20
Scripture
  Applied Scripture 45
    Bonar, A. A. Entire chapters of the Bible used 45
    Hoppin, J. M. Chosen Bible passages 45
    Taylor, W. M. Search the Bible for passages to use 45
    Thomas, W. H. G. Experience is the best teacher 45
    Ware, J. F. Selections of Scripture for all needs 45
  Systematic use of Scripture 172-176
    Bonnell, J. S. Use of Bible with people 173
    Cabot, R. C. and Dicks, R. L. Indicated Bible is important with sick 173
    Calkins, R. Discussed Christ's methods of Bible usage 172
    Fewer ministers are using the Bible with the sick 173, 174
    Goulooze, W. Set of Bible passages printed in *Manual for Ministers, Elders
      and Deacons* 174, 175
    Goulooze, W. Use of Scripture in book, *Victory over Suffering* 175-176
    Jesus used this method 172
    Link, H. C. Used Bible passages 173
    Pastor must know people to use Bible well 174
    Psychology writers not interested in use of Scripture 173

Seabury, D. People have different titanic forces 153

Selbie, W. B. Pragmatism really explains religion away 123

Seminary training 144-147

    Adams, H. Courses needed for special training 144

    Bedell, G. T. Depend on experience mostly 144

    Bridges, C. Skill gained by experience more than by training 144

    Coe, G. A. Psychological training necessary 145

    Cutten, G. B. Need for training 145

    Hewitt, C. E. Emphasis on experience 144

    Holman, C. T. Seminaries must "overhaul" training 145

    Improvement in seminary training by means of trained psychiatrists added to staff 146

    Internship of student with understanding pastor 146, 147

    Kunkel, F. Ministers rely on experience 145

    Miller, S. Know practical books and pious men 144

    Pym, T. W. Moral pathology training needed 145

    Students spending some time in mental hospitals 146

    Weatherhead, L. H. Quoting Mackenzie on need for training 145

    Wise, C. A. Average seminary not training candidates properly 146

Sex in Christian living 125-131

    Boisen, A. T. Pastor must speak with authority on sex questions 128

    Bonnell, J. S. Minister must know sex problems 128

    Carle, B. Indicated Freud was not over-sexed 126

    Climacteric in men and women recognized 129

    Dexter, E. W. A. and Dexter, R. C. Minister plays important part in family life of

        people 128

    Freud, S. Disregarded religion 126

    Freud, S. Teaching influenced sex 125, 126

    Link, H. C. Too much attention has been given to sex 127

    Minister is not a sex specialist 128

    Minister's relation to sex 127, 128

    Minister must keep young people informed 130

    Minister should invite lecturing physician to church 130

    Modern divorce question important 129

    Sex obsession 19

    Sidis, C. Freud's ideas were barbaric 126

    Stieglitz, E. J. Freud has overstimulated sex question 131

    Stieglitz, E. J. Interprets "Sex and Age" 129

    Stolz, K. R. Making the most of the rest of life 129

    Weatherhead, L. D. A classic writer on sex 129-130

Shedd, W. G. T.

    Character of clergyman 36

    Professional visiting important 39

Sheepshanks, J. Pastor's personal life 49

Shoemaker, S. M. Two hundred diseases recognized by science 112

Sick. Consider the sick, the troubled in mind and dissenters, according to Bishop

    Burnett 31

Sickbed. Sickbed visiting important 40

Sickness, suffering, and sorrow reported in questionnaires 71, 72

Sin

Know sinfulness of sin, by A. N. Littlejohn 47
Man's original nature neither good nor bad, according to H. S. Elliott and G. L.
Elliot 122
Ministers must know their lost condition 197
Paul, a chief of sinners 198
Suffering not always due to personal sin—cases of Job and man born blind 113
We must know we are sinners 198

Smith, J.

The Bible is our sole comfort 33
Life of the pastor described 27

Social Crisis 18-20

Sociological approach 57-60

Bell, G. K. A. Manner of expressing gospel changes with changing conditions 59
Dobbins, G. S. Ours is a changing world 59
Fahs, R. Z. Times have changed everything 58
Gladden, W. Adapt work of church to conditions 58
Lyman, A. J. Pastor in human relations 58, 59
Lynch, F. Epicurean pagan teaching is rampant 58
Rogers, C. F. Patient investigation necessary 59
Tidwell, J. B. Know the community 61
Weigle, E. D. Be Christlike in dealing with social problems 57, 58

Soul. Interpretation of soul 100-103

Adler, A. Soul only a psychic force 101
Bavinck, J. H. Soul, the wonder work of God 103
Biblical conception of soul necessary 101-102
Conklin, E. S. Soul seldom recognized by psychologists 102
Dunsmore, M. H. Soul discussion important 102
Ellis, E. Soul no longer a welcome word to many 102
Fisher, D. W. Soul not just a psychic expression 102
Freienfels, R. M. Soul interest reviving 102, 103
James, W. Lack of definition of soul 100
Jung, C. G. No soul 101
Pratt, J. B. No place for soul 100
Steven, G. Soul means a spiritual end 101
Waterink, J. Biblical conception of soul 103

Spencer, I. S.

Case records and treatment of individual 42
Vitalized conversation 44

Spiritual life

Cannot isolate the spiritual from the physical 48
Know the spiritual life of the sheep, according to E. Pond 29
Necessary, according to F. J. B. Allnatt 50
Pastor's personal appearance reflects his spiritual life 142
Turn to Jesus Christ for spiritual development, by W. A. Sadler 135
Victory in pastoral counseling means spiritual life 143

Steven, G.

Biblical truth is important for religion 85
Soul means a spiritual end 101

Stevens, S. N. Religion has a therapeutic value 135

Stieglitz, E. J.
    Freud has overemphasized the sex question 131
    Reference to sex and age 129

Stolz, K. R.
    Know the last four laps of life 134
    Making the most of the rest of life 129
    Ministers are not adequately prepared for their work 23
    Protestantism and confession 163, 164
    Religion is a rallying center 121

Strickland, F. L. Child and animal are alike 101

Students
    Internship with understanding pastors 146, 147
    Spending time in hospitals for Seminary training supplement 146

Suffering
    Attitude of afflicted people 113-115
        Hiltner, S. Suffering strain brings emotional response to the surface 114
        Optomistic view of suffering 114
        Pessimistic view of suffering 113, 114
    Importance of suffering, from questionnaire reports 108-110
        Boisen, A. T. Physical illness a big problem for the pastor 109
        Hiltner, S. Total number of church related hospitals 109
        Problem to be faced by pastor 109, 110
        Soldier hospitals 109
        Wise, C. A. Tremendous loses due to illness 109
    Mental illnesses 110-112
        Harkness, G. Family disturbances are many 111
        Harrington, M. Understand mental tensions 112
        Norborg, S. Christianity does not make all morbid souls 112
        Multiplied, problems due to time of living 111
        Murray, J. A. C. Mental illness increased in our day 111
    Mental, physical and spiritual hygiene 115-118
        Biblical, spiritual hygiene is important 117
        Cults make use of mental processes 117
        Cults seek to minister to one phase of life 117
        Cutten, G. B. Minister must teach spiritual hygiene 115
        Hiltner, S. Physical and mental illness always related 116
        No gospel of psychotherapy, but full gospel 117
        Preston, G. H. Man is his own threat to hygiene 115
        Sadler, W. A. Religious influences help 116
    The reason for illness 112, 113
        Modern cults seek to give the answer 113
        Paul's secret of suffering 113
        Shoemaker, S. M. Two hundred diseases recognized by science 112
        Suffering, not due to personal sin of Job, or man born blind, recorded in the
        Bible 113

Suffering. Research on suffering through questionnaires 65-70

Swisher, W. S. Church must get in touch with world for work 94

Sympathy. Real sympathy necessary 36

War. Influence of war is still with us 20

Ware, J. F. W.
    Selections of Scripture for all needs 45
    Visit with selections of Scripture well in hand 40
Warner, H. E. Study business conditions 46
Waterhouse, E. S.
    Changes of education, industry and post war problems 19
    Conversion is a change of direction 99
    Feeling cannot describe religion 124
    Headline mentality 21
    Pastor's personal appearances will reflect spiritual life 142
Waterink, J.
    Biblical conception of the soul 103
    Biblical psychology 86
Watson, J.
    Open door of counseling is a great service opportunity 43
    People need a time of open heart discussion 162
    Protestants are behind Roman Catholics 60
Wayland, F. Material written in form of pastoral letters 37
Waynne, R. F.
    Keep flock before you as individuals 42
    Make special study of each sick patient 41
Weatherford, W. D. God dwells within us 89
Weatherhead, L. D.
    Classic work on sex 129, 130
    Universal craving in man for God 122
Weidner, R. F. Know the relations of life 47
Weigle, E. D.
    Be Christlike in dealing with social problems 58
    Clergyman's activity embraces all relations of human life 47
Wells, J. D.
    Distinguish various cases of the sick and dying 42
    Doctor must know the minister to allow him visits 178
    Sickbed and deathbed visiting 40
Willcox, G. B.
    Ministers are sometimes too sombre and careless 177
    Pastoral duties are modified 47
Wilm, E. C. Repudiation of soul is an old position 102
Wise, C. A.
    Attempt to discover a way of life 85
    Average seminary not training sufficiently 146
    Clinical experience valuable for pastors 94
    Denies importance of religion in personality development 133
    Habits of ministers with people ought to be checked 186
    Tremendous losses due to illness 109
Woodworth, R. S. Psychology does not like tang of word "soul" 105
Worcester, E. and Mc Comb, S. Coöperation between doctor and minister important .. 184
World moral organization. Need of, according to E. Trueblood 19
World War. Influence of World War II 20
Young People. Keep them informed 130